PHILOSOPHICAL EXPLORATIONS
A Series Edited by George Kimball Plochmann

Bertrand Russell's Dialogue with His Contemporaries

ELIZABETH RAMSDEN EAMES

Foreword by
GEORGE KIMBALL PLOCHMANN

SOUTHERN ILLINOIS UNIVERSITY PRESS

CARBONDALE AND EDWARDSVILLE

Excerpts from William James's *The Meaning of Truth,* edited by Fredrick B. Burkhardt, Fredson, Bowers, and Ignas K. Skrupskelis (Cambridge: Harvard University Press, 1975) reprinted by permission of the publisher. Copyright © 1975 by The President and Fellows of Harvard College.

Excerpts from *The Philosophy of Bertrand Russell,* vol. 5, Library of Living Philosophers, edited by Paul Arthur Schilpp (Evanston and Chicago: Northwestern University, 1944) reprinted by permission.

Excerpts from the Ottoline Morrell correspondence and Bertrand Russell's manuscript no. 220.011250 on Truth reprinted by permission of the Bertrand Russell Archives, McMaster University.

Excerpts from the Bertrand Russell correspondence reprinted by permission of the Harry Ransom Humanities Research Center, the University of Texas at Austin.

Excerpts from the unpublished letters of G. E. Moore reprinted by permission of Timothy Moore.

Excerpts from the unpublished letters of Alfred North Whitehead reprinted by permission of Harriet E. Whitehead.

92 91 90 89   4 3 2 1

Library of Congress Cataloging-in-Publication Data

Eames, Elizabeth Ramsden.
  Bertrand Russell's dialogue with his contemporaries / Elizabeth Ramsden Eames; foreword by George Kimball Plochmann.
      p.   cm. — (Philosophical explorations)
  Bibliography: p.
  Includes index.
  I. Russell, Bertrand, 1872–1970. II. Title. III. Series.
B1649.R94E19 1989
192 — dc 19   88-31125
ISBN 0-8093-1516-5   CIP

for Morris
my partner in dialogue

Contents

Foreword
George Kimball Plochmann   *ix*

Preface   *xiii*

Russell and His Contemporaries: Dates of Interchanges   *xvii*

1. Introduction   1

2. Russell and the Idealists   7
2.1. Russell as Idealist and Critic of Idealism   7
2.2. Russell and Joachim   12
2.3. Russell and Bradley   19
2.4. Summation of Issues   30

3. Russell and Moore   33
3.1. Russell and Moore: Joint History   34
3.2. Ethics, Cause, and Free Will   46
3.3. Knowledge and the Real   51
3.4. On Skepticism   57
3.5. Summation of Issues   58

4. Russell, Frege, and Meinong Before 1905   60
4.1. Current Issues   61
4.2. Historical Context   64
4.3. Russell and Frege to 1905   68
4.4. Russell and Meinong to 1905   78

5. Russell, Frege, and Meinong: 1905 and After   87
5.1. "On Denoting"   87
5.2. Russell's Criticisms and Assumptions   92
5.3. Russell and Frege after 1905   94
5.4. Russell and Meinong after 1905   95

6. Russell and Whitehead   99
6.1. The Friendship of Russell and Whitehead   99
6.2. Collaboration on *Principia Mathematica*   105
6.3. The End of the Collaboration   118
6.4. Whitehead's Divergent Views   121
6.5. Matter, Space, and Time: Two Views   128
6.6. Russell and Whitehead as Analytic Philosophers   134

7. Russell and Wittgenstein   136
7.1. Russell in 1911   136
7.2. The Encounter with Wittgenstein   139
7.3. *Theory of Knowledge: The 1913 Manuscript*   143
7.4. Wittgenstein's Criticisms and New Ideas   153
7.5. Wittgenstein's Influence: The First Wave   159
7.6. Wittgenstein's Influence: The Second Wave   162
7.7. Divergence   167

8. Russell and the Pragmatists   170
8.1. Russell and Schiller   171
8.2. Russell and James   186
8.3. Russell and Dewey   204

9. The Legacy of the Dialogue   215
9.1. Russell's Methods of Argument   216
9.2. Writing on Russell   219
9.3. Philosophy after Russell   221
9.4. The Future of Analysis   227

Notes   233

Bibliography   262

Index of Names   279

Index of Subjects   283

Foreword
George Kimball Plochmann

Tʜɪꜱ ʙᴏᴏᴋ, ᴀꜱ ᴀ rapid glance over any page will demonstrate, is the product of extremely painstaking research: the careful examination of mountains of available materials, published or not, that pertain to the interchanges conducted in three languages over several decades by one of the leading philosophic controversialists of this century. Bertrand Russell's exchanges with his elders in philosophy, with his contemporaries, and with one of his outstanding pupils are brought to life in a judicious exposition meticulously documented and then judged with insight, sympathy, and yet impartiality.

Tracking down lines of private communication and public debate, lines somewhat tangled in the case of Russell and his correspondents, is a task not often undertaken on this level. Dr. Eames has conducted a serious philosophical exploration, rather than a lighter biographical excursion. One will search her pages in vain for sidelights on the evidently enthralling Lady Ottoline Morrell or any of her predecessors and successors in Russell's affections, or on the choleric Dr. Albert Barnes, or on the fatuous lawsuit brought against the philosopher by Mrs. Jean Kay. Instead, this book attends to the business of hard thinking about several of the most eminent and influential minds in the Western world during this century's first half.

Historically speaking, the nine men in their correspondence of (in Whitehead's case) their collaboration with Russell reflected and also set much of the tone, content, and methods dominating Anglo-American and German philosophy of those decades. Many of the issues arising at this time can be signaled by pairs of contraries such as the following:

absolute-relative	whole-part
intellect-sense	sense-nonsense
subject-object	true-false
necessary-probable	simple-compound

term-proposition	consistent-inconsistent
symbol-thing	process-result
thought-language	theoretical-practical
primitive-derived	mathematics-logic
pure-applied	psychology-logic

These pairs (given here in no particular order) do not belong uniquely to the period when Russell was carrying on what seems to ordinary mortals a Gargantuan correspondence. One finds many such pairs fully displayed and explored in the writings of the ancient Greeks, the thirteenth-century scholastics, the founders of modern science four hundred years later, and the iconoclasts of the eighteenth century. To argue, however, that all of them together were prominently dealt with in those earlier periods would require much ingenuity and a bit of special pleading. Descartes, for example, thought his mathematical method could be infallible in regard to the order and quantity of all bodily substances, but it would be well-nigh impossible to show that, like Frege and Russell (and of course Whitehead), he sought to found mathematics upon a logic still more fundamental. Indeed, Descartes, Bacon, Pascal, Spinoza, Locke, and Leibniz, several of them distinguished mathematicians, scarcely mention logic at all, with the exception of Leibniz, who had an especially strong influence upon Russell in the early years. The Absolute meant much to Bradley, and Plato had absolutes of his own, but these were of small consequence to a host of philosophers beginning with Aristotle. Many of the pairs occupied St. Thomas throughout his adult life, though the pair *primitive-derived* did not.

Now it cannot be said that Russell confronted all of these dual topics at any one time, but eventually he did have to deal with them, some of them very thoroughly and many times over, as dictated in part by the concerns of his correspondents. In some degree his solutions to the problems raised in connection with these terms had to be adjusted to the persuasions and capacities of the persons with whom he was talking, corresponding, or debating in print. It is a nice point, to be settled in the individual cases, whether accommodation of this sort runs the danger of turning into a chameleon dialectic. But Russell had his own specific reasons for agreeing, just as much as for disagreeing, with his discussants.

Although Lord Russell was a writer with a very clear literary style, one containing few impediments to his being thoroughly understood by either fellow philosophers or the general public (I except some of his more technical papers and the immense and immensely difficult *Principia Mathematica,* of which he was coauthor), his work has been unusually hard to grasp in its entirety by both classes of his readers. For although he was a man of strong convictions, he was also one of great sensitivity to questions raised, if not always doctrines enunciated, by others, and, first to last, he sniffed out the winds of philosophic wars and responded almost immediately, embodying as he did the first three requirements laid down by Plato for the philosopher: that he be keen in perception, quick in pursuit, and strong in battle. Yet one is also reminded of a remark made by Jan Sibelius when asked to compare himself with Richard Strauss. The Finn with the overwhelming brows said in his halting English, "Strauss very up-to-date, very contemporary, very much *now*. Sibelius for all time."

It would be wholly unfair to suggest that Russell was but a man attuned to his own epoch, yet it is certainly true—and Dr. Eames demonstrates this beyond doubt or cavil—that Russell's principal doctrines reflected, although very rarely through simple borrowing, this literary contracts with other thinkers. A tennis player, no matter how expert, is partly dependent upon the decisions and adroitness of his opponent, and Russell, who invariably entered into a new correspondence with plenty of views of his own, just as regularly progressed through it feeling obliged to make alterations, slight or sweeping, that betrayed an impact whether of his antagonist or his ally. At the same time, Russell labored to convince or even instruct when he felt it necessary. In that respect, at least, he *was* contemporary, very much *now*.

On the other hand, tendentious or concordant letter-writing did not cause most of the other parties to these exchanges to alter *their* stands. One doubts that William James or John Dewey became less pragmatic, even in their secret thoughts, for all their contacts, epistolary or personal, with Russell, or that F. H. Bradley and H. H. Joachim moved any closer to a realist position. There are possible exceptions. G. E. Moore developed much of his own realism along with Russell; A. N. Whitehead labored for almost a decade with Russell on their collaborative three volumes of *Principia,* which one recent expert referred to as the "holy book" of modern logic; and Ludwig Wittgenstein, whose extraordinary logico-philosophic treatise lays down many strange answers to riddles unasked and which often seems designed to try to topple the Whitehead-Russell book from its high place—Wittgenstein, for all his snarled relations with Russell, learned much from him in the years of his apprenticeship; and then there was Gottlob Frege, who conceded that Russell had indeed discovered a paradox that raised serious objections to the logistic theory of classes. But by and large, his correspondents appeared to leave a greater impress upon Russell than he did upon them. For this reason, if for no other, the question of the unity of Russell's thought (to which Dr. Eames alludes many times) is of course a most difficult one.

Did Russell have a method capable of absorbing the thought of others without occasioning an inevitable overhaul of his own? Kant managed to incorporate the judgments he found in other men by making exceedingly fine-cut distinctions: Newton, Leibniz, Berkeley, Wolff, Baumgarten all found a home in the critical philosophy, being accorded small but not uncomfortable apartments. *Everyone* found a home in Hegel's dialectic, but for a different reason; he had evolved an all-embracing method which by its essence had to make room in some thesis or its opposite or in a compound of the two for all his predecessors. History both inspired and confirmed Hegel's own philosophy, furnishing content and even the form by which it could be expressed. Neither the particular slicing method of Kant nor the enveloping method of Hegel was practiced by Russell, at least not throughout his whole career, and the upshot was that his chief responses often consisted of repetitions or verbal reformulations of what he had said and published previously, or of what might be called ad hoc reactions to the opinions of Bradley, Alexius Meinong, Dewey, and the rest. This may account for the apparent doctrinal and methodological shifts in what sometimes appears to have been an episodic career, shifts later denied or affirmed, praised or attacked, by persons with historical interests. Continuities and discontinuities can be discerned, since what began as answers to letters frequently found a way into the many books by which the philosopher became one of the best-known of twentieth-century thinkers. This fame may have been augmented by the notoriety of Russell's amatory life, his pacifism, his winning of a Nobel Prize for Literature, his contractual disagreements in the United States, and his second stint in a British jail, this time for his stand against nuclear weapons. Even so, his reputation rests on solid ground.

Dr. Eames pays close attention to the finished volumes of Russell as well as to his more piecemeal letters and reviews, and expounds with much clarifying detail what have appeared to be or have really been major shifts in his system of ideas. It is a topic as fascinating as it is important, and her study is valuable for the history of a significant strand in the thought and culture of our time.

Preface

T HIS BOOK IS THE result of research interests that I have pursued over many years. My doctoral dissertation was a study of the epistemological issues raised in the published exchanges between John Dewey and Bertrand Russell. In tracing the history of their interactions, I was impressed with its resemblance to an extended personal conversation or argument on philosophical themes. This forty-year sequence of comments, criticisms, responses, and amended criticisms resembles an ongoing Platonic dialogue. Since then, I found such interaction between philosophers a useful framework for interpreting their philosophies and have come to use the term *dialogue* in this extended sense to mean published or unpublished work and correspondence, short or long, in which philosophers exchange and reciprocally criticize their ideas. I thus use *dialogue* to include interchanges which may extend over many years and include intervening periods of silence, and have come to see such dialogues as constituting the growth of a philosopher's thought. It seems to me that philosophers of the past, who are not present in current exchanges in journals or in person, tend to be seen only in terms of their major works, and thus both an important dimension of the growth and development of their ideas and an illuminating perspective on their mature work are missed. It is also true that puzzling remarks and what appear to be digressions in the arguments of some authors make sense when one realizes that the author is responding to a contemporary critic without specific acknowledgment of the exchange that has taken place between them.

As I came to explore in more detail the work of Bertrand Russell in terms of the development of his ideas, I arrived at conclusions concerning some themes in his work at variance with the prevailing interpretation. When my "The Consistency of Russell's Realism" elicited Russell's approval ("You interpret my philosophy better than most"), I was encouraged to continue the work of interpreting his philosophy. In 1964 I had the opportunity of visiting

Lord Russell at his home in London, and of hearing his responses to questions that had arisen in my study of his thought. These inquiries led, in 1969, to the publication of *Bertrand Russell's Theory of Knowledge,* a book in which Russell himself expressed taking pleasure.

In the course of the research for this 1969 book I was able to visit the newly acquired collection of Bertrand Russell papers at McMaster University. Kenneth Blackwell, the newly appointed archivist, was engaged in ordering and cataloging stacks of material which had recently arrived from England in a number of large trunks. He showed me a puzzling prize among the papers — a segment of a hitherto unknown book manuscript in Russell's hand on the topic of theory of knowledge. After studying the manuscript, I proposed that the missing first 142 pages might have become the six *Monist* articles of 1914 and 1915. Subsequent detective work by Blackwell and me confirmed this surmise. The research received the essential support of the Harry Ransom Humanities Research Center of the University of Texas, at Austin which allowed access to the letters of Bertrand Russell to Ottoline Morrell and later provided copies of these letters to the Bertrand Russell Archives. The Bancroft Library of the University of California at Berkeley provided Victor Lenzen's paper with Russell's comments and the notes and conversation of Professor Lenzen himself; the library and archives of Harvard University made available records and T. S. Eliot's notes and papers from the courses Russell taught at Harvard in 1914; and the Special Collections of Southern Illinois University's Morris Library provided letters and records in the Open Court Publishing Company's papers that threw light on the articles. The Bertrand Russell Archives at McMaster University are the most important resource for such scholarship, and the ever-growing collection of correspondence and other material taxes the powers of selection of any scholar who uses them.

In 1976 I received permission from McMaster University and the Bertrand Russell estate to edit the unpublished manuscript on theory of knowledge. With the assistance of an editing grant from the National Endowment for the Humanities and the help of Jo Ann Boydston and Donald Cook of the Center for Scholarly Editions, this work was completed and received the Center's seal of an approved text. Later this work became part of the project entitled *The Collected Papers of Bertrand Russell* and was published as Volume 7 of the papers: *Theory of Knowledge: The 1913 Manuscript* (London: George Allen & Unwin, 1984).

During the entire period of research for both works, I found more and more material of value to my continuing study of Russell through his interactions with his contemporaries. This research was supported by a grant from the

American Philosophical Society and with research grants from Southern Illinois University, for all of which I am grateful.

The present work is thus a culmination of extended and varied research interests. The full body of material explored in the course of this work would far exceed the limits of one volume. Perhaps one day volumes of Russell's letters, hitherto unpublished papers, and reading notes will all be edited and published. In this work I have selected only certain of his interlocutors, correspondents, and critics. My intent is to show the issues that emerged in Russell's exchanges, both published and unpublished, with certain other philosophers, and to interpret the resulting reciprocal influences and reactions. In some cases the published comments and unpublished letters were only parts of extended personal conversations. These conversational parts of Russell's interactions with Moore, Whitehead, and Wittgenstein in particular are tantalizingly glimpsed through letters. Nevertheless the considerable written material available provides the basis for further scholarship and more complete understanding, an aim which this book is intended to further.

In acknowledging the contribution of others to this work, I must record my appreciation of Bertrand Russell himself, not only for his conversation and correspondence with me, but also for the openness with which he allowed his papers to be made accessible to all. This was a gift to history of a kind other philosophers, such as Wittgenstein and Whitehead, have regretably denied us. I must also record my appreciation of the late Countess Russell for receiving me into her home, in 1964 and again in 1977. On the later occasion she was generous in allowing and aiding my search for material in Russell's library. This encouragement was graciously offered and thankfully accepted.

I must also acknowledge my debt to the students in the seminars on the philosophy of Bertrand Russell and on analytic philosophy, which it has been my privilege to teach for many years. The shared attempt to unravel the crosscurrents of influence and reaction, the fascination of reading the evaluations of one another by twentieth-century philosophers, and the perennial pleasure of reading the letters in which their controversies took shape became part of the interpretative framework within which this work is set. It was essential to have the help of the knowledgeable people in the Bertrand Russell Archives, including Carl Spadoni, Diane Kerss, and, especially, my colleague and friend Kenneth Blackwell, with whom I have explored many a vein of Russell lore—I hope to our mutual benefit. In addition to the research institutions previously acknowledged, the library of the University of California at Los Angeles gave me access to Russell's letters to F. C. S. Schiller, and the British Museum provided rare Meinong material. Other colleagues who have made significant contributions to this work include John A. Broyer and Lewis E. Hahn, for valuable critical comments and corrections of the manuscript; Jo Ann Boydston and Alan M. Cohn, for suggestions on sources of information; Janet Ferrell Smith, from whom I learned much about the Meinong-Russell interactions; Victor Lowe, for valuable suggestions on the relation of Russell and Whitehead; and Carol Keane, for assistance with the material on F. H. Bradley. A particular debt must be acknowledged to the editor of this series, Professor George Kimball Plochmann, for his advice and encouragement. Among those who assisted in typing various parts of the manuscript are Pam Haughawaut, Cathy Hamer, and Ruth Cook. Finally, it is only through my lifelong philosophical interchanges with Morris Eames that I have come to appreciate how vital such dialogue is to philosophical vision and criticism.

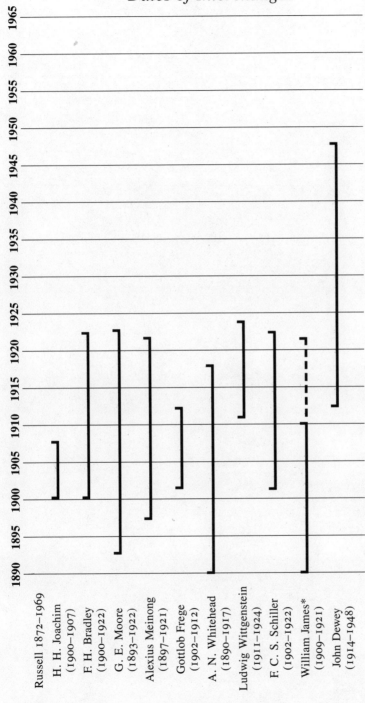

Russell and His Contemporaries:
Dates of Interchanges

Russell 1872–1969

H. H. Joachim
(1900–1907)

F. H. Bradley
(1900–1922)

G. E. Moore
(1893–1922)

Alexius Meinong
(1897–1921)

Gottlob Frege
(1902–1912)

A. N. Whitehead
(1890–1917)

Ludwig Wittgenstein
(1911–1924)

F. C. S. Schiller
(1902–1922)

William James*
(1909–1921)

John Dewey
(1914–1948)

*James died in 1909, but Russell continued to discuss his philosophy.

*Bertrand Russell's Dialogue
with His Contemporaries*

I

Introduction

THE CENTURY THAT BEGAN with the birth of Bertrand Russell in 1872 may be seen as a divide in human intellectual history, and this is evident in Russell's own philosophy. On the one hand, the Western scientific revolution of three centuries created a climactic change in way of life and outlook throughout the world, satisfying old needs and creating new ones, shifting traditional values, and generating new problems. This extension of the technique of science affected the ancient discipline of philosophy, giving it a new technical competence and divorcing it, at least for a time, from its traditional theological and ethical concerns. In this respect, Russell was a pioneer of new "scientific" methods of analysis in philosophy. On the other hand, Russell belonged still to the older century, where the philosopher was a man of the world to whom no interest was alien, no information irrelevant, no problem "nonsensical." In this tradition a philosopher may see his abstractions as bearing practical fruit, at least indirectly, in the solution of human problems, and he is optimistic about the use of intelligence in solving those problems. From this viewpoint, a comprehensive, systematic philosophical synthesis is seen to be extremely difficult and demanding, involving interrelations of history, the sciences, and mathematical logic; yet this goal is intelligible and worth striving for. In this sense, Russell's philosophy bridges the gap between the old, represented by the idealism dominant in Europe in the late nineteenth century, and the new, represented by analytic philosophy of the late twentieth century.

As a transition between the old and the new, Russell's philosophy was rooted in the British empiricist tradition of David Hume and John Stuart Mill, and his study of the history of Western philosophy led him to give especial value to the method of Descartes and the perspectives of Leibniz. At Cambridge he was converted to idealism, and, although he later rejected it, the vision of the whole did not cease to be significant to him.

As a pioneer of analysis, Russell was among the first to set forth the ideal of a precise and definite method for philosophizing, deliberately modeled on that of science. The new technique was that of mathematical logic, and its use entailed a tentative, methodical, detailed working out of the ancient problems of space, time, matter, and cause.[1] For Russell it was part of the attitude of a scientist to be open to any insight, whether from mathematics, physics, history, or psychology, and to the contributions of current books and professional articles and the conversations of friends. Along with this sensitivity to the ideas of others went an open-mindedness toward change, a willingness to modify and correct his own earlier views. Russell has remarked that philosophy should be like science, cooperative, progressive, and tentative; and not like theology, consistent, monolithic, and dogmatic. His ability to change and his unusual responsiveness to others earned him a reputation for inconsistency[2] and, unfortunately, encouraged a neglect of the direction and outcome of his changes.

Not only was Russell unusually open to the influence of others but also he exerted an important influence on his contemporaries. His colleagues among professional philosophers, such as G. E. Moore and A. N. Whitehead, were directly affected by his presence and work. Through the medium of his many books and articles, and, in some cases, through his lectures, a large number of students, such as Ludwig Wittgenstein and Norbert Wiener, were stimulated with new ideas and new problems. Russell's impact has been important in all contemporary analytic schools of philosophy, and this impact has been both positive and negative. For some Russell was a model who provided a dream and the tools to achieve it; for others Russell has been a challenge, opposition to be overcome. Rudolf Carnap is an example of the first kind of impact; J. O. Urmson of the second.[3] To a wider public, Russell's deep concern for the problems that confront humanity today has made him the exemplar of an intellectual and a philosopher.

It is too early to see just how far Russell's influence will extend in space and time, or to predict the degree to which the philosophy of the twenty-first century will be Russellian or anti-Russellian. However, in tracing Russell's interactions with his contemporaries, we can see those who influenced him positively and those who served as a stimulus to his rebellion, those for whom he provided guidance and those who revolted against him. In this story of Russell's relations with his contemporaries there is a century of philosophy from nineteenth-century idealism to contemporary linguistic analysis. It is the history of lively interchange, criticism and rebuttal, polemics, textual analysis, and the changing temper of philosophical debate.

Several writers have commented on Russell's unusual habit of acknowledging the contributions of others to his own thought and of documenting the
changes in his own position.[4] Recently, several writers have challenged
Russell's interpretation of other philosophers.[5] But Russell's use of the
material of others can be put in a different context from that of punctilious
etiquette or careless scholarship. When one tracks down many of the articles
he wrote (as distinguished from his larger and more systematic works), one
finds that he spent much time in writing book reviews, critical essays, replies
to criticism—bits of polemic that have received little attention. In addition,
one can see that, in almost every major work, he presents his own ideas
against the background of those with whom he agrees and those to whom he
gives credit for his own insights (as in his tribute to Whitehead in *Our
Knowledge of the External World*)[6] and against the background of points of
view to which his own is offered as an alternative (as in his references to
Meinong and Frege in "On Denoting").[7] When another philosopher (even
someone little known) writes an article criticizing some point in Russell's
philosophy, the latter often will write a long rejoinder, joining issue on the
debated point (as to Miss E. E. C. Jones in "Knowledge by Acquaintance and
Knowledge by Description").[8] On other occasions, Russell has ignored
critical comment, not troubling to answer it.

All this points to the particular way Russell approaches other philosophers. Russell does not approach them, whether living or dead, as a
meticulous scholar whose question is "What exactly did X say?" or "What
exactly did X mean?" Rather, he approaches them as a scientist might
approach the work of other scientists, asking "What ideas can I get from this
writer?" or "What are the hints, or clues, or suggestions that I can turn to my
own use?" As for comment on his own work, Russell is no more concerned to
go back and defend some earlier writing of his than a scientist would be to
defend an old hypothesis, once inquiry had moved beyond it. But if the
comment concerns a problem of current interest or debate, it is worthwhile to
reply and reopen the issue to debate, perhaps even to acknowledge that the
critic has a point and after that revise the earlier view. The work of others,
then, is for Russell a resource for current philosophizing; he asks what
contributions can they make, what dangers and dead ends can they warn us
of, what hints can they provide?

The attitude Russell takes toward other philosophers is indicated by the
preface to his *Critical Exposition of the Philosophy of Leibniz,* where he
distinguishes two approaches to the study of a thinker of the past: the
historical approach, seeking to describe such matters as the growth of the

philosopher's thought and the influences that played upon him; and, second, the philosophical approach, trying to understand and evaluate a philosopher's system as truth, this may legitimately include the "pruning away" of those opinions seemingly "inconsistent with his main doctrines."9 It is the latter task to which Russell addressed himself, and which can be seen as the model of his attitude to other philosophers, living and dead.

Russell's work received attention early in his life, at least from the 1890s onward; he was part of a group of scholars at Cambridge who would later become the leading figures in Anglo-American philosophy in our century. During his years there as student, fellow, and lecturer, until about 1914, Russell was in active debate with these colleagues and with others in Britain such as F. H. Bradley and F. C. S. Schiller, and abroad, with such men as Alexius Meinong and Louis Couturat. They read and reviewed each other's work; they corresponded and discussed. Russell also carried on discussions with the pragmatists and new realists in the United States, for whom his work was an important stimulus. A new generation of philosophers grew up, nurtured on Russell's work and developing it in new kinds of analysis, such as logical empiricism and analytic pragmatism. His work has thus been a major part of the twentieth century, and few philosophers have been untouched by it.

In any study of the twentieth century and of Russell's participation in its philosophical movements, we have ready to hand a major resource in the Bertrand Russell Archives at McMaster University. At the same time that the holdings of the Russell collection have been made available for study, various other research institutions have also been used to supply biographical, bibliographical, and editing projects with the required material. For instance, critical editions of John Dewey and William James have also used such material, as have studies such as those of I. Grattan-Guinness in his *Dear Russell-Dear Jourdain,* Ronald Clark in his biography of Russell, the edition of Wittgenstein's *Letters to Russell, Keynes and Moore,* to mention only a few. By such means, for the first time, a full sweep of knowledge of our own century and its philosophers is becoming available. Important among these scholarly works will be the Collected Papers of Bertrand Russell, with its critically edited unpublished and inaccessible writings; the total correspondence may eventually be part of this work, but the volume of this material is so great, and the complexities of editing it so formidable, that we can expect that it will be some time before this is accomplished.10 However, the correspondence in the Bertrand Russell Archives shows one how much light is shed on Russell's own intellectual development and on his relations with other thinkers through the informal letters he wrote to or about his philosophical colleagues. When this is added to a study of the lesser-known reviews and polemical literature published during his lifetime, but is now little studied, a picture of the interactions between Russell and other thinkers emerges, interesting in itself and illuminating the twists and turns by which Russell's own thought and twentieth-century philosophy have taken form. The unusual length of his active life (1872–1969) and the unusual breadth of his reading, interests, and acquaintance make this a large part of the history of our own epoch.

It is partly owing to Russell's own conception of philosophy as being, like science, a matter of the increment of precise, piecemeal, and partial studies, that contemporary philosophers tend to be brought up within the confines of a "school" and to study attentively only the work of philosophers in that tradition. This current educational practice also reflects the enormous expansion in the number of books and articles published, a number that prohibits any one individual keeping up with a wide range of work (as Russell himself did). Anglo-Americans have been, in the present generation, rather more limited to our own language than were European scholars of the past, and certainly more than was Russell. The narrowness and chauvinism thus produced have made it difficult for us to see the philosophical world in any rounded way, or to obtain a perspective on our own traditions and our own time which is not seriously foreshortened and biased. The new scholarly publications should help this situation, as should the numerous translations now becoming available. Yet many recent writers still complain of this lack of perspective, and it seems evident that both the Anglo-American analytic tradition itself, and the *oeuvre* of Bertrand Russell in particular, have suffered because of this lack of context.

Because of the wealth of material available, a choice had to be made of the philosophers who were to be presented in this study. The selection was based on three criteria: those philosophers with whom Russell's relations were significant for philosophy as a whole; those who were themselves philosophers of stature and represented influential points of view; and those with whom Russell had extensive interactions. Even so some interesting and important figures had to be excluded, such as George Santayana, Louis Couturat, and A. J. Ayer. But it seems that the most important interactions were centered around idealists (F. H. Bradley and H. H. Joachim), G. E. Moore, A. N. Whitehead, G. Frege and A. Meinong (grouped together because of the common problems involved), Wittgenstein, and the pragmatists (F. C. S. Schiller, William James, and John Dewey). The various dialogues with the philosophers centered around certain recurring problems, hence these are the focus of attention in the following chapters. These topics include: the nature of relations; pluralism versus monism; the relation of the subject and object in knowledge; the analysis of experience; the definition of truth; the analysis of belief; the nature and status of logical "objects" and "truths"; theory of meaning. These have been in the forefront of philosophical discussion in our time, and Russell's dialogue with his contemporaries promises to illumine them.

2

Russell and the Idealists

2.1 Russell as Idealist and Critic of Idealism

RUSSELL HAS GIVEN SEVERAL different accounts of his life at Cambridge, his relations with his teachers and fellow-students, and of his intellectual development from an initial attachment to the philosophy of John Stuart Mill, through a conversion to idealism in his senior year under the influence of John Ellis McTaggart and his other teachers, to the eventual revolt when he adopted realism, following the lead of G. E. Moore. But in spite of his narratives and a similar one by Moore,[1] and in spite of the availability of Russell's published work of the period 1896–1911, it is easy to underestimate the importance of idealism for his development and the amount of attention he paid to idealist philosophy. Aside from one article on Russell's polemics[2] little interest has been shown in the *Mind* articles that contain the published exchange, and the voluminous correspondence of the Bertrand Russell Archives has not yet been widely reviewed. In his study Carl Spadoni shows that Russell was influenced by idealism (neo-Hegelianism is Spadoni's term) for a long time following the point in the late '90s when Russell reported himself and Moore to have escaped from that "hot-house". His research is based on a thorough study of the correspondence of the period, especially the letters written to his wife, Alys Russell. There is no doubt that Russell's ideas took shape over a period of time and that he retained portions of his earlier views even after the rebellion against idealism. However, it is also true that an important break was made from the earlier Kantian and Hegelian periods with Moore's famous paper on judgment; it was negatively the rejection of the position that the object of the knowing relation is internal to that relation, and positively it was the adoption of a kind of Platonic conceptual realism which may be seen in *The Principles of Mathematics*. In my study the focus will be on what was written and published between

Russell and his idealist adversaries; thus the points on which they diverge and the time at which these differences were expressed should be clear.[3]

An additional factor obscuring the issues is that our contemporary view tends to regard nineteenth-century British idealism as a shadowy, not very formidable target of the new realists, an impression very different from the actual situation at the turn of the century, when idealism was philosophical orthodoxy and opposition to it a cause for controversy. One can argue that Russell's concern with traditional epistemological and metaphysical issues, his bringing of all technical logical questions back to their fundamental philosophical implications, his rejection of the otherwise congenial work of the logical positivists, all stem from his conceiving of issues in the categories he learned from idealism. In any event, the conversations and written exchanges with contemporary idealists formed an important concern of the fifteen years from his senior year in college to 1911. It should be noted that Russell engaged in discussions and debates with many contemporary idealists: He mentions James Ward and Ellis McTaggart as his idealist teachers at Cambridge, the latter being responsible for his conversion to idealism in the first place. Bernard Bosanquet was also a contemporary idealist with whom Russell was acquainted and whose book he reviewed. I have selected for detailed discussion two idealists with whom Russell carried on a long dialogue through letters, published articles, and reviews; these are F. H. Bradley, the best-known of British idealists, and Harold H. Joachim, much less well-known but a persistent correspondent of Russell's.

Although Russell obtained his degree in mathematics, and most of his early published writing was in that field, he was far from satisfied with the science as it was regarded at Cambridge. When his degree requirements were completed he abandoned for a time his mathematical studies and turned with delight to philosophy, embracing it and adopting idealism as his own. He dreamed of a synthesis in which his wide-ranging interests in history, politics, economics, ethics, science, and mathematics could all be included. His fellowship dissertation, an attempt to work out a Kantian philosophy of mathematics, was published in 1896 as *An Essay on the Foundations of Geometry.* For the following two years he studied physics and attempted an Hegelian analysis of mathematics and science; this Hegelian period was represented by an 1899 article "On the Relations of Number and Quantity." In the same year Moore's paper on judgment,[4] containing the first major rejection of idealism in the form of a refutation of the Kantian view of concepts, was published, and Russell tells us he followed Moore into pluralism and realism the following year. Russell's first published rejection of idealism occurred in the book on Leibniz in which he criticized the theory of internal relations.[5] The Leibniz book appeared in 1900, and the following year Russell published a series of articles on relations and order expressing a new realism and employing the logical method he had learned from G. Peano. The *Principles of Mathematics* of 1903 gave a full treatment of the same themes and was an important and influential book. As will become evident, the new realism was epistemological in challenging the internality of the object of knowledge, metaphysical in opposing a monistic worldview, and Platonic in holding to the independent reality of concepts.[6]

The Principles of Mathematics included several important criticisms of idealist logic, and stimulated a response from Bradley. In the same year Moore published his celebrated "Refutation of Idealism"; Moore and Russell were now regarded as young iconoclasts attacking the orthodox and well-thought-out doctrines which a generation of scholars had erected on the foundations of German idealism; the two men were seen as the proponents of a new and extravagant realism. From 1903 to the beginning of World War I, Russell's work included his and Whitehead's *Principia Mathematica,* numerous articles on topics in mathematical logic, reviews (notably the series which introduced the works of Meinong to English-speaking readers), polemical writings presenting his attack on, and alternative to, idealism, and the *Problems of Philosophy,* which represented the realist position he held in 1911.[7] What was the alternative to this now-suspect idealism?

In the controversy with idealism there were three central issues on which Russell represents himself and Moore to be opposed to the basic tenets of idealism. One of these points, most often referred to as a basic issue by Russell, is that of the analysis of relations; for Russell, the idealists err, as does Leibniz, in believing that the relations between terms are somehow grounded in the nature of the terms related. This means that the relation has a kind of necessity—the terms being what they are, the relation cannot be other than it is. It also means that the relation has a kind of internal bond, a unity that prevents any sundering of one term from another, or of the relation from the terms, by any work of analysis. With all of these statements Russell is in disagreement.[8]

The second major point on which Russell expresses his disagreement refers to idealist logic. One of its major weaknesses is the acceptance of the subject-predicate analysis of propositions. Leibniz becomes involved in the difficulties of internal relations in part because he does not challenge this traditional logical analysis, and modern logicians such as Bradley become involved in the same problems. Bradley, in a letter prompted by his reading of Russell's book on Leibniz, protested this characterization of his analysis of propositions, and Russell apologized, acknowledging that he had relied on

Bradley's earlier *Logic* and had disregarded *Appearance and Reality*. Later, in 1905, Russell attributed to Bradley the insight that universal affirmative propositions were concealed hypotheticals. Russell's view of the failures of subject-predicate analysis in the hands of idealist logicians remained unchanged, however, as we shall see.[9] If all propositions, including relational propositions, are made to fit the subject-predicate mold, then the relation and its second term are joined as predicate by a copula to the first or subject term.[10] Logically, this has the consequence of making nonsense of common-sense inferences of conversion, and of the syllogisms which depend on the symmetry or transitivity of relations. From *Peter is the brother of John* it ought to be possible to infer that *John is the brother of Peter.* From *The lamp is to the right of the book* and *The book is to the right of the pen,* it ought to be possible to infer that *The lamp is to the right of the pen.* But neither inference is compatible with the subject-predicate analysis of traditional logic, according to Russell.

In two extended passages in *The Principles of Mathematics* Russell again criticizes the traditional views of philosophers concerning relations.[11] In one of these passages he takes the case of an asymmetrical relation. symbolized as *aRb,* and shows the two ways in which philosophers committed to the subject-predicate logical form have striven to analyze the relation. The monadistic approach, proposed by Leibniz and Hermann Lotze, would treat the proposition as equivalent to two different propositions, one asserting the relation as adjectival of *a,* the other as adjectival of *b.* But the subject-predicate form restricts the connection of the adjective with the subject to identity or diversity, and neither of these is asymmetrical. If *a* and *b* are related by *a*'s being larger than *b,* then if the relation is divided into two, as *a is larger than b* and *b is smaller than a,* there will be no connection between these last two propositions. In order for any logical relation to be established between them, some further proposition would have to be devised to state the equivalence of the two propositions, and this would lead to an infinite regress. On the other hand, if the original proposition, *a is larger than b,* is formulated in terms of a single relation such as "differing in size," as in *a differs in size from b,* which would allow the inference that *b differs in size from a,* the difficulty is that there is no indication of whether *a* is larger than *b* or *b* is larger than *a.* In any case, according to Russell's argument, the monadic analysis of relational propositions fails.

The other analysis attempted by philosophers Russell terms "monistic," and this he attributes to Spinoza and Bradley, who treat the proposition *aRb* as a whole; the proposition asserts nothing about *a* or *b,* but only about a whole composed of *a* and *b* and R. Thus if *a* is said to be *larger than b,* this might be translated as a statement that there is diversity of magnitude between *a* and *b*. But again, there is nothing in such a statement of a whole to indicate the direction of "sense" of the relation in the case of asymmetrical relations. Russell points out the particular difficulties attaching to the relation of whole to part, for if the relation with its terms is considered as a whole, then either term, or the relation itself, must be considered as a part of the whole. In that case, the statement of that part includes an asymmetrical relation, and is itself the statement of the whole. Thus if *a is larger than b* is thought of as a whole, and if there is an attempt to formulate one term of that whole, say, *a,* it can only be stated as *a-as-part-of-whole-which-is-'a is larger than b';* and this is both asymmetrical (and thus is no solution to the problem) and includes a restatement of the whole itself and hence fails to be an analysis. A regress of wholes is implied in a monistic analysis of relations, just as a regress of parts is required in the monadistic analysis of relations.

Russell argues that some different analysis of relations as external, and some different form of symbolizing relations, such as the one he proposes, are necessary if a satisfactory analysis of number, quantity, order, space, time, and motion is to be worked out.[12]

The metaphysical consequence of the subject-predicate analysis may be damaging also, if the subject is identified with the "real" or "substance," and the predicate with qualities or properties that inhere in, or belong to, the real or substance. Russell gives Bradley credit for pointing out the contradiction involved in the diversity between predicate and subject in such cases. Unless one limits oneself to saying *The existent exists* or *the real is real,* there must always be a contradiction between predicate and subject. This leads the idealist to say that the contradiction is overcome by the widening of the scope of the subject; thus, to say that *the pen is red* has a limited truth but is also a contradiction in that the pen and the color are only partial realities within a larger reality in which many different entities and many different colors and noncolors are equally real. In its limitation and partiality each specific judgment is false; this is seen in the diversity of subject and predicate. The idealist is driven metaphysically to seek a wider and wider reality, and a wider and wider truth. For Russell each inquiry and each proposition should be treated as an entity in itself; we may know partial truths, which are yet quite true. We may understand parts of the universe without taking their relation to the universe as a whole into account. The two assumptions, that there is one reality, and that reality is all of one kind, are equally unwelcome; Russell describes himself as a radical pluralist, and links his pluralism to the taking of terms and relations as external and separable from one another.[13]

A third failing of idealist logic and its analysis of knowledge is its tendency to be psychological and mentalistic. Since the one kind of reality it espouses is of the nature of mind, it is natural that idealist logicians such as Bradley and Lotze should analyze concepts, mathematical terms, relations, and predicates in terms of mental entities or operations, and proceed from an analysis of the logic of propositions to an analysis of thought and the thinking process, which for those men they represented. Moore's "The Nature of Judgment" was aimed at this mentalistic analysis of judgment and opposed it with an analysis of concepts as objective. Russell tried in a similar way to treat the proposition as objective and its terms as real, that is, as having a logical status rather than a psychological one.[14]

A fourth major point in the criticism of idealism concerns the analysis of the knowing relation of subject and object. For the idealist, the object of knowledge is taken as being within the knowing process, or the object of experience is taken as a part of experience. For Russell, and for Moore, it is essential to view the object of knowledge as apart from, independent of, the knowing relation. When we know something, then that something is what it is regardless of whether it is known or not, and this independence of the object must be reflected in our definition of truth—itself an example of an external relation; knowledge is itself an external relation and the known object may have any kind of reality, either similar to, or different from, that of the subject.

> On fundamental questions of philosophy, my position, in all its chief features, is derived from Mr. G. E. Moore. I have accepted from him the non-existential nature of propositions (except such as happen to assert existence) and their independence of any knowing mind; also the pluralism which regards the world, both that of existents and that of entities, as composed of an infinite number of mutually independent entities, with relations which are ultimate, and not reducible to adjectives of their terms or of the whole which these compose.[15]

It is the insistence on the externality of the object known to the knowing relation that leads to some of the extravagances of early realism with Moore and Russell. Whether the object be a color, a commonsense object, a scientific object, a universal, or a mathematical entity, it is declared to be what it is independent of our knowledge of it, and this leads to a kind of Platonic realism with respect to universals, numbers, and so forth.[16]

2.2 *Russell and Joachim*

The controversies with individual idealists in which Russell was engaged during this period involved two persons, Harold Joachim and F. H. Bradley.

Joachim was an old acquaintance, a neighbor of the family, who had given Russell a list of books of philosophy to read before Russell went to Cambridge. He was some years Russell's senior, a don at Merton College, Oxford, and the author of three books, one on logic, one on ethics, and one called *The Nature of Truth*. The two men carried on a correspondence from 1900 to 1907, but it was as a response to Joachim's book on truth that the published part of the dispute arose.

Earlier, Joachim had complained to Russell of Moore's misinterpretation of Kant, of Russell's "caricature" of Hegel, of Russell's misstatement of Bradley's concept of the subject of a proposition, and wrote that Moore's "Refutation of Idealism" was a "confusion from one end to the other." He found Russell and Moore's treatment of the "sensible world" incomprehensible and objected to their "Platonism."[17]

In 1906 Joachim wrote *The Nature of Truth,* in which he proposed to deal with all the extant theories of truth and to end by defending his own. The first chapter consists of a criticism of what he calls "the traditional correspondence theory of truth," in which truth consists in the correspondence of a judgment with what is real; the second chapter is a criticism of the view that truth is an independent entity, the view he attributes to Russell and to Moore, while the third defends his own theory. In the preface he tells how he sent a draft of the second chapter to Russell for his comments and criticisms and thanks Russell for his careful, detailed comments. In spite of Russell's criticisms, however, he justifies publishing the attack on Moore and Russell without change, since he believes that things they have said could certainly be interpreted in the way he has interpreted them, in spite of the fact that Russell objected to Joachim's presentation of his view.

Following publication of *The Nature of Truth,* Russell wrote a sharp critical review in *Mind* to which Joachim took exception, although in a letter he gave Russell permission to go ahead and print it. Moore also published a comment on the book, to which Joachim replied. Russell subsequently published a more friendly and less technical review in *The Independent Review,* and a longer, more philosophical article in *Proceedings of the Aristotelian Society*[18] in which he generalized his criticism of Joachim to an attack on the idealist theory of truth and offered a realist alternative to it. This was later reprinted under the title "The Monistic Theory of Truth" in Russell's *Philosophical Essays.*[19] Although it is true that publishing an attack on an opponent's position over his objections is not entirely justifiable, it may be pointed out in Joachim's defense that, in the years between Russell's first attack on idealism and 1907, there had been a considerable change in Russell's position, particularly in regard to truth. In any case, the issues between the two thinkers bear examination.

One of Joachim's major criticisms centers around the Russell-Moore analysis of sensation. He understands their position to be that in sensation there is direct contact with the Real, but that in this contact the nature of the Real is unaffected by its presence to a sentient consciousness, so that what is apprehended in sensation has in its own nature exactly the characteristics which the sensing individual apprehends it to have. Joachim finds this position almost incomprehensible, and he points out that no argument or evidence is presented; there is only a flat statement. In addition, he finds that certain obvious difficulties with this position are not dealt with. For instance, if the object in sensation corresponds to some structure in the sensing subject, what is this latter structure? Is it a mental configuration of ideas, or is there no mental schema corresponding to that of the independent object? If the latter, then what does correspond to the form of the object, and where is it located? Is not the realist position of Moore and Russell involved in all the familiar difficulties of the correspondence notion? How is it possible in any case to find any evidence that experiencing makes no difference to a fact?

Difficulties with the definition of truth are even more severe, for Joachim interprets Moore and Russell to be arguing that there are true propositions and false ones and that is all that can be said about them; they are intuitively apprehended as being true or false with no further proof. Joachim, outraged at this dogmatism, contrasts the assertions of the theory he is attacking with the insights of the common man:

> Greenness is, for the theory, an ultimate entity in the nature of things, which has its being absolutely in itself. How, under these circumstances, greenness can yet sometimes so far depart from its sacred aloofness as to be apprehended (sensated or conceived); and how, when this takes place, the sensating or conceiving subject is assured that its immaculate *perseitas* is still preserved—these are questions to which apparently the only answer is the dogmatic reiteration of the supposed fact: "It is so; and if you cannot see it, you are wanting in philosophical insight". But the plain man, as well as the philosopher, has his 'insight'. He will tell you that greenness is to him a name for a complex fact, the factors of which essentially and reciprocally determine one another. And he will say that if you choose to select one factor out of the complex, and to call it 'greenness', there need be no dispute about the term; but, as thus isolated, your greenness is an abstraction, which emphatically, in itself and as such, is not *there* nor *anywhere*. If you appeal to your doctrine of a 'unique relation', and urge that greenness *both* 'is there' in itself and *also* is (at times or always) in relation to sentient or conceptual consciousness, he will ask you how you reconcile this 'both' and 'also'.

He will question in what sense it is *the same* greenness, which is *both* in itself and *also* in relation to something else. And, if you deny that there is here anything to reconcile, he will appeal to *his* 'insight'. Who shall say that *his* is the insight of a lying prophet, whilst *yours* bears the divine stamp of truth?[20]

Joachim finds difficulty with the treatment of identity in Moore and Russell (a familiar theme in Joachim's letters to Russell as well). For instance, if the realist speaks of the greenness of the paper and the greenness of the leaf as being the same, or identical, there seems no more warrant for this assumption that for one that if I have a penny in my pocket and you have a penny in yours, the penny is numerically and identically the same penny. For Joachim identity always means that things apparently diverse are yet parts of one unity, and this seems inapplicable to the view he is criticizing.[21]

Joachim finds that there are certain philosophical assumptions in which the idealist and the Moore-Russell realist are fundamentally opposed. In stating these in terms of monism versus pluralism, and of the defense of internal as opposed to the defense of external relations, he is undoubtedly correct. The problem for the monist, he says, is to introduce diversity into the unity of the one; the problem for the pluralist is to introduce unity into the fundamentally atomistic, separate, simple units. He reasons that the difficulties faced by the monist are easier to solve than those faced by the pluralist and that, in fact, Russell and Moore's "solutions" are merely names for the problems. The recommended method of analyzing complexes into simples produces ultimately irreducible units, each separate and simple and "in itself." How could a collection of such simples form any kind of unity? The answer is: by virtue of an "external relation"; for Joachim this is the name of an insoluble problem. One such relation is the relation of knowledge in which the known object and the knowing subject are each independent, or externally related. How can an independent object yet be known to be independent? The answer given is by means of "immediate apprehension"; for Joachim this is the name of another insoluble problem. How can simple, eternal, and self-identical units enter into many and different and changing complex unities? The answer is by being related into points and moments; for Joachim, again, this is the name for another insoluble problem.[22]

The continuation of the debate in *Mind* proved inconclusive. Russell responded to Joachim's plain man argument with predictable pithiness:

Mr. Joachim alleges that the plain man is on his side. I have been tempted to ask some plain man what he thought greenness was, but have been restrained by the fear of being thought insane. Mr. Joachim, however, seems to have been bolder. Considering the difficulty of finding a really plain man nowadays, I presume he asked his scout, who apparently replied: "Well, sir, greenness is to me the name of a complex fact, the factors of which essentially and reciprocally determine one another. And if you, sir, choose to select one factor out of the complex, and to call it greenness, I will not dispute about the term, for I know my place, sir; but as thus isolated, your greenness is an abstraction, which emphatically, in itself and as such, is not *there* or *anywhere*." At least, this is what I gather from the opinion of the plain man reported on p. 42. "Who shall say," he concludes, "that *his* is the insight of a lying prophet, while *yours* bears the divine stamp of truth?" The answer to this question would require a whole treatise; for the present, therefore, I will confine myself to Mr. Joachim's contention that *mine* is the insight of the lying prophet while *his* bears the divine stamp of truth.

Joachim, in a letter, acknowledged this response to be deserved.[23]

But on more substantive issues Russell expresses something close to despair concerning the possibility that any way of settling the issues between them can be worked out. Joachim's remarks, Russell says, amount to the conception, *If A is independent of B, then A cannot be related to B;* that if a whole be made up of parts, then it is no genuine whole; that external relations are not relations. These are the very points that the theory he is questioning asserts. Russell concludes that the only kind of argument which is likely to produce any progress in philosophy in a situation in which two views are fundamentally opposed is one of the form of a *reductio ad absurdum*. Had Mr. Joachim taken his opponent's assumptions and positions and worked out their implications in such a way as to show that they had false, inconsistent, or unwelcome consequences, he might have effectively criticized them. As it was he merely asserted that their position was to him inconceivable or unimaginable and made the assumption that it was therefore false.[24]

Moore joined the discussion with a more sanguine approach, proposing to show Joachim that if he would render precise exactly in what sense an object may or may not be regarded as "independent" of one's knowledge of it, grounds for settling or at least clarifying the dispute might be arrived at. But the hope proved futile, as in his responses Joachim qualified the meanings of Moore's alternatives in such a way as to reintroduce the philosophical points at issue.[25]

A more comprehensive treatment of the distinctions between the idealist theory of truth and that of Russell is given in the latter's article first published under the title "On the Nature of Truth" in the *Proceedings of the Aristotelian Society* (1906–7), later published in *Philosophical Essays* as "The Monistic Theory of Truth."[26] In this paper Russell uses Joachim as a representative of the idealist theory of truth and deals with many of the points brought up in the previous controversy. Russell's main objections to the idealist view are these: first, the monistic theory of truth holds that there is but one truth which is one and whole; thus every partial or particular truth is not quite true by virtue of its one-sidedness. If this is applied to the statement of this theory, then the statement itself is not quite true, for it has a contradictory aspect, since if the statement that truth is one and is whole is not true, then it is not one and whole, or, at least, the statement is lacking in completeness in some way. Since the idealist must claim that this is the case, any statement of the monistic theory may be false, since it may follow from the false rather than from the true part of the theory.

Second, when idealist principles are applied to the relation of the whole to its parts, difficulties are encountered. For Joachim, for instance, a whole is not truly a whole for which there are distinguishable parts, thus a whole in this philosophy does not properly have parts, hence is no whole. Since the idea of a whole as a complex composed of simples is not acceptable, for idealism a whole must be a complex composed of complexes, and, as a consequence, there is no longer any basis to distinguish which is the complex that is the whole, and which is the complex that is the part.

Third, as far as theory of error is concerned, the idealist theory meets additional serious problems. Since truth consists in the recognition of the partial, and hence false, nature of every specific judgment, there is no good basis for distinguishing the specific judgments which common sense discriminates as true or false. If the proposition *Bishop Stubbs was hanged for murder* is false in the sense that the gentleman in question died peacefully in his bed, then either it is judged to be false according to some other, nonidealist sense, or it is as false as any other partial truth—for instance, *Bishop Stubbs died in his bed*.

Fourth, it is customary for idealists to try to escape this last consequence of their theory by maintaining that coherence means the coherence of all means of knowing, including "experience" as a source of knowledge. Thus, the statement that the bishop was hanged for murder is false in the sense that it does not fit in with the whole of experience, which includes the facts that the realist also claims make the proposition false. But Russell denies that this means of escape is open to the idealist; if "experience" is the basis for the rejection of a false proposition, it is experience in the sense of specific experiences such as the observation of the dying prelate in his bed, not experience in the sense of a "whole experience," for experience as a whole includes experiences of nonfactual images as well as of truths.

In the remainder of the essay Russell attacks what he takes to be the basic assumption of idealism, the internality of relations. He attempts to show that the unsatisfactory aspects of the idealist theory of truth follow from this theory of relations and that the reasons given for the acceptance of the theory are not as cogent as they appear. Joachim's statement of the nature of truth involves truth as a whole embracing everything in the universe, so that no partial truth is quite true because it does not include the whole of truth. In the same way, the theory of internal relations, grounding the relation between terms in the nature of terms that are related, is forced to pass from the partial nature of the original related terms to a more complete reality of which these terms are only parts, and finally, each separate complex can be understood fully only in the context of the whole of reality. When the consequences of the regress of truths and the regress of relations are drawn, Russell argues that it appears that there are no diversities, no relations, no truths, but one reality, one whole, and one truth. He ascribes this consequence to the arguments in Bradley's *Appearance and Reality* as well as to Joachim's view of truth. Russell diagnoses two reasons for the favor in which idealists hold the axiom of internal relations: one is the principle of sufficient reason; the other is the consideration that if any pair of terms were related otherwise than they are in fact related, they would be different from what they are. He argues that these are really one consideration, for the principle of sufficient reason seems to mean that for anything to be what it is, or to be related to another thing as it is related, it must have some rational principle of explanation embodied in it. For Leibniz, for instance, an analytic truth such as $2 + 2 = 4$ has the necessity of the principle of identity, but a factual truth, such as that the sun is shining today, must *also* have a sufficient explanation why it is so and not otherwise. This demand for a kind of rational necessity seems to be involved also when it is argued that if two terms were related in a different way, then they would be different terms. For, logically, from the falsity of any given proposition, anything will follow, and if the terms were other than they are, it follows that they would be numerically diverse from what they are, but it does not follow that they would have different natures, unless one has made a prior assumption of the internality of relations.

Against these considerations Russell sees no reason to abandon the pluralism that takes each thing to be what it is in itself, or the theory of external relations that takes the terms of the relations to be separate from the relations, the relations assumed to occur as they do occur without any presupposed rational principle involved in them. The implications of this position are also that there may be partial truths that are yet quite true, and that one piece of knowledge need not be false because of its isolation from other knowledge.

2.3 Russell and Bradley

Russell had an extensive correspondence and a published controversy with another contemporary British idealist, F. H. Bradley. Bradley was a far more substantial philosopher than Joachim, and the most respected of all contemporary philosophers at the time when he and Russell were carrying on their exchange. Russell tells us that he was an undergraduate when Bradley's *Appearance and Reality* was published, and was told by McTaggart that the book "says everything that can be said on the subject of metaphysics." This was in 1893, and Russell had already studied Bradley's *Principles of Logic* of 1883. When, five years later, in 1898, Russell became a critic of idealism, it was natural that Bradley should be a target of his criticisms. In *The Philosophy of Leibniz* in 1900, Russell pointed out the consequences to Leibniz's metaphysics of the subject-predicate mode of analysis of propositions, how this led him to a certain notion of substance, and to the doctrine of internal relations. He then went on to say that this was of importance in contemporary philosophy in the logic of idealism; he mentioned Bradley, referring to a passage in his *Logic*.[27] This reference brought a response from Bradley, and their correspondence continued until 1922.[28] Since Russell was neither an intimate friend of the great idealist, as he was of Moore and Whitehead, nor even an old acquaintance, as with Joachim, their letters were formal and largely confined to philosophical issues. There is a kind of quaint charm in the tone of the correspondence: Russell is deferential and Bradley gracious in ways that suggest mutual respect and seriousness of philosophical purpose, as well as politeness. When Bradley refers to Russell or addresses him directly he speaks of his "great promise," apologizes for his own inability in mathematical logic, and, on the occasion of Russell's attempting to be elected to Parliament, urges him not to give up philosophy, a field in which his gifts are very great.[29] For his part, Russell writes "I hope you will allow me to say that I have always learned a great deal from your philosophy, and, although I now disagree with it, it has been very helpful to me."[30] Russell often expresses gratitude for Bradley's criticisms, and not infrequently backs down before their onslaught. The tone of the correspondence, Russell's respect and Bradley's condescension, the fact that Bradley often apologizes for a delay in writing owing to ill health, and his frequent wish that he were younger so that he could study mathematical logic, might lead one to suspect that Bradley was near retirement when the correspondence began in the year 1900. But in fact there was only a sixteen-year difference in their ages. Bradley's work was done at a very early age: he was twenty when he wrote *Ethical Studies,* twenty-seven when he published his *Logic,* and thirty-seven when *Appearance and Reality* said "the last word" on metaphysics. Although he was forty-four and Russell twenty-eight when their correspondence began, Bradley was already a well-established figure in philosophy.

In addition to the correspondence between Bradley and Russell, there is a considerable volume of published controversy: Russell referred to Bradley in *The Philosophy of Leibniz,* and, in a similar context of relational logic, in *The Principles of Mathematics;* he also included Bradley in his criticism of the idealist theory in "The Monistic Theory of Truth." Bradley dealt with these criticisms of his work by Russell and with some points in *The Principles of Mathematics* in "On Appearance, Error, and Contradiction" in the 1910 volume of *Mind.* To this counter criticism Russell replied in an article in *Mind* of the same year, "Some Explanations in Reply to Mr. Bradley." Again Bradley responded in *Mind,* the following year, in "Reply to Mr. Russell's Explanations."[31]

The first criticism that Russell makes of Bradley concerns his acceptance of the subject-predicate mode of analysis. This mode, as we have seen, Russell regards as prejudicial to the important class of relational propositions, and as leading to a monistic metaphysics, particularly if coupled with the notion of substance. He cites Bradley's work as a contemporary example of this kind of error. In particular, Russell notes that in this analysis all propositions ascribe a predicate to reality as the ultimate subject. In such an interpretation of the world, the subject of the proposition tends to represent all of reality so that every relation, every attribute, is, in the end, predicated of this reality. Every distinction and every partial truth is swallowed up in this total reality. This is a familiar theme in Russell's criticism of idealism and is repeated in "The Monistic Theory of Truth." On this occasion, however, when Bradley writes to Russell challenging this interpretation of his philosophy, Russell replies that the passage was not intended as a conclusive disproof of Bradley's position, but was intended only as a means of opening the discussion, and that Russell has not traced the ideas through *Appearance and Reality.*

In *The Principles of Mathematics* there are some ten references to Bradley, the chief of which are again attacks on idealist logic. Russell objects to the notion that predicates, as adjectives, are, or refer to, attributes of subjects that are substances, and that the latter are in some metaphysical sense more real than their attributes.

It is interesting and not unimportant to examine very briefly the connection of the above doctrine of adjectives with certain traditional views on the nature of propositions. It is customary to regard all propositions as having a subject and a predicate, *i.e.* as having an immediate *this,* and a general concept attached to it by way of description. This is, of course, an account of the theory in question which will strike its adherents as extremely crude; but it will serve for a general indication of the view to be discussed. This doctrine develops by internal logical necessity, into the theory of Mr. Bradley's Logic, that all words stand for ideas having what he calls *meaning,* and that in every judgment there is something, the true subject of the judgment, which is not an idea and does not have meaning. To have meaning, it seems to me, is a notion confusedly compounded of logical and psychological elements. *Words* all have meaning, in the simple sense that they are symbols which stand for something other than themselves. But a proposition, unless it happens to be linguistic, does not itself contain words: it contains the entities indicated by the words. Thus meaning, in the sense in which words have meaning, is irrelevant to logic. But such concepts as a *man* have meaning in another sense: They are, so to speak, symbolic in their own logical nature, because they have the property which I call *denoting.* That is to say, when *a man* occurs in a proposition (e.g. "I met a man in the street"), the proposition is not about the concept *a man,* but about something quite different, some actual biped denoted by the concept. Thus concepts of this kind have meaning in a non-psychological sense. And in this sense, when we say "this is a man," we are making a proposition in which a concept is in some sense attached to what is not a concept. But when meaning is thus understood the entity indicated by *John* does not have meaning, as Mr. Bradley contends; and even among concepts, it is only those that denote that have meaning. The confusion is largely due, I believe, to the notion that *words* occur in propositions, which in turn is due to the notion that propositions are essentially mental and are to be identified with cognitions.[32]

This passage shows how far Russell has come from idealist logic at this time and how divergent are his views from those of Bradley; the rejection of the linguistic or psychological status of propositions in favor of some view of a proposition as an entity, the restriction of meaning to denoting, the Platonism with respect to the reality of concepts and universals, all express a realism as far removed from the view of idealist logic as it is possible to be. It is to this period, probably, that Russell refers when he speaks of his sense of liberation in abandoning idealism as a stuffy hothouse, adding, "When I rejected this axiom [of internal relations], I began to believe everything the Hegelians disbelieved."[33] At this period, the mentalistic and psychological aspects of idealist theory of meaning and logic were rejected. It is hardly surprising that Bradley, in his response, indicated that there were some points in which the alternative theory of meaning Russell offered was not itself completely clear.

We have seen that the chief criticism of idealism offered by Russell in *The Principles of Mathematics* concerns the subject-predicate analysis of propositions, especially as it touches the failure to deal adequately with relations. The alternatives offered by Russell here were a doctrine of external relations, and a formulation of relational propositions that allowed the symmetry, asymmetry, transitivity, reflexivity of relations to be taken account of in the form of the argument. Bradley's monistic view of relations fails particularly in coping with asymmetrical relations in general and the relation of whole to part in particular, according to Russell's criticism. Although much of Russell's *The Principles of Mathematics* is formidable for one who confessed himself illiterate in mathematics, Bradley went through the book with some thoroughness and wrote a long and detailed letter about it to Russell. This letter, dated February 4, 1904, has as a chief theme (a theme also present in the article in *Mind* in which Bradley refers to the book and its criticisms of his own philosophy) Russell's introduction of technical terms without regard to the philosophical issues involved in this usage. Bradley raises questions about the meaning of terms either unfamiliar to him or which seem to be at odds with traditional usage: *disjunction, implication, assertion, negation, class, zero.* Clearly, Bradley has put his finger on concepts of central importance to Russell's mathematical logic, or, indeed, to almost any logic.34

Bradley questions the strangeness of the meaning of *implication,* a relation holding when the antecedent is true and the consequent true, and this is defined to mean that in any proposition in which the antecedent is true and the consequent false, the implication is false, but in all other cases it is true. It is clear to Bradley, and Russell admits, that this is not the usual meaning of term *implication,* but Russell says this meaning is central to his logical method, and it has to have a name. In formulating this definition Russell claims it as a right to construct technical terminology where needed, and dismisses Bradley's question as stemming from his failure to recognize the technical vocabulary as distinct from the ordinary usage of terms.35 But, Bradley argues, even granting that *implication* and *disjunction* function in a special way in Russell's theory, there are still philosophical problems connected with them. For instance, if, as you say, a proposition consists of entities rather than meanings, what kinds of entities are disjunctions and implications? Is there not something conceptual or mental in a disjunction or an implication, a relation of meanings rather than of entities? Russell confesses that there is a difficulty; it may be that there are factual disjunctions or factual implications, but in any case in *The Principles of Mathematics* he did not propose to solve related philosophical problems. A subsequent volume was intended to deal with these problems.[36] (This subsequent volume became instead *Principia Mathematica*.)

A similar point is raised by Bradley concerning Russell's concept of *assertion*. Bradley believes that the concept of asserting involves meaning rather than fact; it refers to one's belief in a proposition. But although Russell again says he has given the term a technical meaning, he agrees that the issue is not completely clear. Bradley regards the use of *negation* as requiring some kind of metaphysical or philosophical justification or interpretation, and criticizes Russell's using the concept without such a justification. Here again the denial of a proposition, like its assertion, may well involve an element of meaning. The possibility and status of a negative referent for a negative term also demand treatment. Here Bradley touches on a point which was to cause Russell difficulty for years; in the period of logical atomism he tentatively adopted the existence of "negative facts," while in a later period he came closer to Bradley's position and contended that a negative proposition represents something like a disappointed expectation.[37]

Bradley also points out that unresolved philosophical problems attach to Russell's concept of *zero*. Later, in 1910, Russell came to admit this, that when he wrote *The Principles of Mathematics* he had not thought through the issues involved, and that he would no longer maintain the same position with respect to *zero*.[38]

A major difficulty for Bradley in the understanding of *The Principles of Mathematics* was Russell's use of the principle of identity. For Bradley, identity involves some diversity between the things that are said to be identical. Although the evening star appears in the evening sky and the morning star in the morning sky, yet they are the same star; although 2 plus 2 appears to be different from 4, yet they are equal; although the tall, dark-skinned man in the turban appears to be a different person from the well-known detective, yet the turbaned Indian is really the same detective in disguise. In all cases of the use of identity there is an apparent diversity or difference which is denied, or overcome, by the revelation that the difference is not real. If this is the case with identity, then how can Russell speak of the identity of a thing with itself, of a class with its members? In the case of relations, how can Russell speak of the relation involving diversity? Yet for Russell reflexivity, the relation of *a* to *a,* is tied in with the meaning of identity, indeed, with its very definition. For Bradley this is conceptually impossible. Joachim had the same difficulty with Russell's concept of identity.[39]

This problem, and that of the relation of a thing to itself, are bound up with two other points at issue between the idealists and Russell. The issue of internal and external relations is bound up with the status of identity in the following way: let us suppose that an idealist, looking at the relation of marriage between a husband and a wife, sees it as an internal relation. The idealist would then say the marriage has a kind of wholeness or unity, and that the term of the relation is what it is by virtue of that relation. A husband could not be called a husband, apart from his relation of marriage to his wife. In fact the marriage, as a relation, is a certain being or nature of the wife, as wife, and of the husband, as husband. Now it makes sense to describe such a relation as symmetrical and as intransitive; but what sense would it make to describe it as irreflexive? The question *Can a husband be a husband to himself?* is nonsensical and demonstrates the impossibility of understanding a relation by its analysis, that is, by treating it as external.

The same considerations apply if we think of a whole or a unity and of its parts. For the idealist a whole is, by definition, something which cannot be broken into parts without distortion or destruction. It is only by abstraction that we can speak of a part as a constituent of a whole. But for Russell a whole *is* its parts; the only unity involved is the order provided by the external relation by virtue of which the parts are parts of this whole. It is possible, then, for a complex to be analyzed into its constituents without distortion. On the issue Russell and the idealists seem always to be in unresolvable conflict.

If there is one concept in *The Principles of Mathematics* controversial from any point of view, it is that of *class*. In the first place, Russell, by employing Peano's method and notation, had worked out definitions of numbers and built up an apparatus capable of formulating relational propositions such as are required for both logic and mathematics. It was a major step toward the logicizing of mathematics, but it required the assumption of the existence of classes, numbers, and predicates. Although at this stage of Platonic realism Russell welcomed these entities as part of the real world, yet, in the interest of the building up of a logical scheme with as few assumptions as possible, they were less welcome. Unfortunately, in the course of this work Russell came upon a contradiction that proved impossible for him to resolve or remove, within the limits of the system he had developed. This was the famous contradiction of classes of classes not members of themselves. In distinguishing between those classes that are members of themselves (such as the class of all classes, or such as not-men), and those classes that are *not* members of themselves (such as the class of tables), Russell asks of the class of classes which are not members of themselves, *Is it a member of itself?* The answer to the question seems to involve a contradiction, for if we assume that the class of classes which are not members of themselves *is* a member of itself, it must be a class which is not a member of itself, and if we assume that the class of classes which are not members of themselves *is not* a member of itself, then it is a member of itself. In the book Russell describes the variants of this contradiction, such as that of the greatest cardinal number and the liar paradox, but he is unable to give more than a few hints on how it may be possible to resolve them by some theory of types.[40]

Bradley's comments on the treatment of the concept of class in *The Principles of Mathematics* are directed toward the difficulties he believes a radical pluralist must face in introducing a concept of class into his system. For in order to have a class there must be something that collects the class together as a class, and where, in Russell's view of the world, could such a bond be found? Bradley sees nothing in the members of the class capable of collecting them, because each individual is radically separate from all other individuals. Nor is there anything outside the individuals capable of binding its members together into a class. Bradley's question is not "How does Russell deal with the problem of the contradiction which he discovered?" but rather "How does he even *have* a class without a contradiction in his own logical and metaphysical principles?" For Bradley, Russell's kind of radical pluralism would exclude the possibility of wholes and classes entirely. But even if it be granted that Russell can have a concept of class, the meaning of a class which is a member of itself is as baffling as that of a term of a relation which is related to itself. That such a contradictory concept leads to a further contradiction could hardly be surprising, and for all his courtesy, Bradley cannot refrain from remarking that it is difficult for him to understand how a philosopher could present an entire systematic philosophy of mathematics, admitting in his presentation that there is an unresolvable difficulty, and yet not be led to question whether there might not be something wrong with the basic premises of the system.[41]

In response to Bradley's criticism, Russell in 1910 freely admits that the concept of class of the *Principles* was full of difficulties, but in the meantime the source of the problems that Bradley encountered has been revealed. Russell has discovered a technique by which the philosophy of mathematics can be constructed, numbers and all, without recourse to classes, by treating such concepts as incomplete symbols. (Russell refers to his *Mind* article of 1905 "On Denoting" and to the forthcoming *Principia Mathematica*.) If the new method of constructing classes be accepted, the contradiction of classes which are not members of themselves can be dealt with, Russell believes, by a theory of types, which has been worked out symbolically and refined in the interim between 1903 and 1910.[42]

I have mentioned that one of the differences between the view of relations as internal held by idealists and the view of relations as external held by Russell is the kind of *ground* of the relation assumed in either case. Bradley criticizes Russell's view of relations in much the same way as does Joachim, by asking "Where in your system is there cause for the relations' holding where they do hold? Why are the unities and complexes as they are?" Russell's answer is that there need be no reason or ultimate cause; the relations are where they are; the unities exist where they do exist. But this is not a satisfactory answer for the idealist, for it seems to him that philosophy is bound to produce grounds or reasons for things being as they are. In reply, Russell says to Bradley, you are really asking for a principle of sufficient reason, some kind of metaphysical necessity holding between the terms of the relations. For Russell this is an inadmissible demand on the part of philosophy, but for Bradley, although he admits that in his own theory he has not worked this out completely, he feels that philosophy is committed to seeking rational explanations for things being as they are, and that Russell's view cannot do this, since it regards relations as sheer juxtapositions and unities as unexplained occurrences. This is one point at which the discussion of necessity and possibility enters the debate between Russell and the idealists; there are others as well.[43]

Another issue emerges from the discussion with respect to what is to be excluded from philosophy or is inadmissible on logical grounds in a philosophical system. In his early criticism of Bradley, Russell pointed out that Bradley himself had written that his own subject-predicate logic, and his own assumption about reality, had the consequence of making every proposition which predicated some attribute of some subject contradictory. Since for the idealist Reality and Truth are one and whole, any specific proposition attributing specific attributes to specific subjects is contradictory by virtue of omitting or ignoring all the rest of reality and all remaining attributes. This is evident in the divergence between subject and predicate, a divergence to be overcome in the context of the whole of Reality on pain of an ultimate schism in the Real. Russell implies that such a contradictory consequence might well lead to the rejection of the assumptions on which it is based. But for Bradley this kind of contradiction, which he admits, does not lead to the rejection of the system in which it occurs as logically contradictory. He regards such a contradiction as inevitable in any partial judgment; it leads him only to caution that any particular judgment is true within limits, the limits of recognizing its own one-sidedness.[44]

On the other hand, for Bradley as for Joachim, there is a kind of logical impossibility in Russell's premises which ought to lead to their rejection. Joachim cannot understand how a relation can be analyzable and yet form a unity—it is logically impossible. Bradley cannot understand how one can speak of a term as being related to itself, or of something as being identical with itself—it is logically impossible. He establishes this logical impossibility by a kind of thought experiment; he presents to himself in imagination the question "What would it mean for something to be identical with itself?" He cannot succeed in conceptually presenting to himself such an idea, hence it is logically impossible. But for Russell this is merely a case of psychological limitations, and there is no reason to limit the logically possible to what one's imagination is capable of presenting to oneself.[45] Although Russell does not draw this implication, it might be thought that here a basic idealist premise is involved, namely, "The real is rational and the rational is real."

The concept of necessity is present in the issue between Russell and the idealists in another way. Bradley's criticism seemed to require in response some inclusion of the concepts of possibility and necessity in the logical scheme which Russell was presenting. But Russell's response was that he had no need of the concepts of possibility and necessity in his logic; he could get along without any modal concepts. The kind of logical scheme he had in mind could set up ways of manipulating symbols that would be sufficient for dealing with mathematical concepts, and, he claimed, would be applicable to other forms of argument as well without introducing any such basic concepts as are expressed by "may" and "must." Russell says that when one speaks of a proposition as being "necessarily true" or "possibly true" or "necessarily false," these alternatives can be translated adequately in terms of *all, some,* or *none.* (The logical formulations of propositional functions will be discussed in detail in chapter 4.) For Russell this translation of necessity and possibility preserves all the required meanings without introducing any metaphysical concept of necessity such as idealists seem to require.[46]

So opposed were Russell and Bradley on these points regarding the ultimacy of wholes and relations, the need for rational principles of explanation, and the criterion of logical possibility, that it became apparent there was a limit to what they could argue about. Russell maintained that one way of evaluating a philosophical system is in terms of its closeness to common sense and to scientific knowledge, and, on that basis, his kind of pluralistic realism was superior. Bradley responded that it is first necessary for you to prove that your view *is* closer to common sense and to science, since his own idealism was forged with the intent of being faithful to just these values.[47]

When a criticism is leveled against an idealist theory of truth, account must be taken not only of Joachim's presentation but also of Bradley's, for the latter has his own version of such a theory, but it is not Hegelian. The sense in which Bradley holds that every specific truth is not quite true is the sense in which, however complete may be one's knowledge of the world, it is always subject to revision in the future. The only complete truth would be a final truth, not subject to revision in the future, all the truth that could ever come out, a view of the whole of reality. Hence any truth accessible to us here and now is provisional and incomplete and must incorporate a recognition of its own incompleteness in itself. A totally coherent truth, in a logical sense, would be totally inclusive. But no extant systems of belief are so complete and hence, if they claim to be true, they contradict themselves. Thus, to claim that 2 *plus* 2 *equals* 4 is unconditionally true involves a contradiction, not in the sense that 2 *plus* 2 *does not equal* 4, but in the sense that this is not the whole of truth and may be revised as mathematical knowledge, and knowledge of the whole of reality, becomes complete.[48]

Hence, to Russell's charge that the statement of the coherence theory of truth must be false by its own criterion, Bradley replies that the statement of the coherence theory is incomplete, and, in that sense, contradictory. This does not mean that it is to be rejected but that, like all partial truth, it must be understood as open to revision.

In response to Russell's criticism that the coherence theory provides no way of distinguishing between one coherent body of belief and another contrary but equally coherent body, Bradley, like Joachim, points out that Russell is assuming coherence to mean logical consistency, while for them it means completeness and comprehensiveness. If one were to point out that there may be two kinds of geometry — Euclidean and non-Euclidean — each perfectly coherent internally, Bradley answers that truth is incoherent if it includes two mutually incompatible systems; we must seek for some means of having one geometry include the other, or of having both included in some still more comprehensive geometric system. Bradley's meaning of *coherence* thus not only includes the goal of completeness but also demands that new experiences and new aspects of knowledge be incorporated within the extant body of truth. Hence this theory of truth is not, as Russell implied, nonempirical; new specific experiences add to the body of available knowledge which is to be made coherent, and one can reject a logically consistent set of beliefs in terms of its not according with experience.[49]

Bradley charges that Russell has left many aspects of his own theory of truth unsettled and undefined, so that no meaningful comparison can be made of the worth of their two different theories of truth. There is some validity to this charge, since, as we shall see, different versions of the new realist theory of truth had appeared. The view that propositions are, of themselves, true or false, as roses are white or red, is clearly expressed in the discussion of Meinong in 1904. This view is attributed to Russell by Joachim in 1906, but Russell's response may be read as disowning it, at least in part.[50]

At any rate, it was not until 1907 that Russell put forward a relational view which made the truth of a belief dependent on its agreement with fact, rather than derivative from the ultimate truth of a proposition. In "On the Nature of Truth and Falsehood," however, Russell does set out in some detail the theory he himself defends in order to show, as he believes, its superiority in accounting for those matters with which the idealist theory had failed to deal satisfactorily.[51]

At the beginning of this essay, Russell formulates his own method of analysis. Our problem is to tell what we mean by truth, and we approach it by referring to a certain vague concept which we feel is fundamental but about which we are not clear. We then detach the concept from the "mass of irrelevancies" with which it is involved, and put before the mind the abstract opposition upon which our distinction of truth and falsehood depends. In doing this we try to resolve the complex and confused into the simple and clear; we try to make the resulting analysis square with the confused belief with which we began, and yet also be intrinsically clear and evident.

One important idea contained in our common but confused notion of truth is that there are two poles to the truth of a belief; there is the psychological or judgmental pole (a belief is not there to be true or false unless someone entertains it), and an external or factual pole (what makes the belief true or false is some fact outside of the belief). The problem is; What is the relation between the belief and the fact? Russell considers as a basic premise that there are three different ways in which an object may be before the mind: the thing perceived may be related to the perceiver by the act of perceiving; the thing imagined may be before the mind as an object, but in a different relation; in judgment there is yet another, different way in which the object of a belief is related to the believer. This relation between what is judged and the judgment of it may be conceived in two ways, the first of which is attributed to Meinong, the second of which is Russell's own. In Meinong's way, the believer is related to a single fact—for example, that Charles I died on the scaffold. But here the difficulty is to account for error, since, if the believer judges that Charles I died in his bed, there is no such fact to correspond to this false belief. But if the difference between true and false beliefs is that the former have objects while the latter do not, then the difference would be "intrinsic" rather than dependent on external fact.

If the first (Meinong's) way is rejected, Russell suggests the alternative view that belief is a relation of the believer to the terms and relations of the belief—that is, of me and Charles I and death and a scaffold. In this case, error consists not in the absence of objects, since Charles I and death and his bed are all existent objects, but in the difference between the relation of one of the terms to the other and the relation attributed by the belief. The relation of belief to its object, then, is a multiple one; a true judgment is one in which the components of the multiple relation of the fact are related in just the way that the components of the relation are stated in the judgment to be related. There is thus a congruence between the relation of John and Mary and love in reality with the terms *John* and *Mary* and *love* in Richard's judgment, as in "Richard believes that John loves Mary." If John *does* love Mary in fact, then Richard's belief is true and the judgment correct.

There is also an important distinction between the relation of mind to the object in perception, and the relation of the mind to the object in belief, or judgment. In perception there is a two-term relation, that of acquaintance, between the object perceived and the perception of it; it is thus not subject to error. If Othello saw the white handkerchief on the floor, he simply did see it. But judgment is a multiple relation involving the internal relations of the components of the judgment. If Othello judged that Desdemona loved Cassio, he was wrong if in fact she did not love Cassio. Joachim was mistaken in reading the difficulties of the realist correspondence theory into the view of perception held by Russell. But it seems that Bradley was correct in finding unresolved difficulties in this theory of truth, and Russell later made important emendations in it. At least Russell's two essays "The Monistic Theory of Truth" and "On the Nature of Truth and Falsehood" draw a clear contrast between his own view and that of idealism.

2.4 Summation of Issues

If we try to assess the significance of the controversy between the idealists and Russell, we notice at once the correctness of the diagnosis that what divides them is the issue of internal versus external relations. The positions of Bradley and Joachim—that a whole or unity which can be analyzed into components is no unity, that there must be some rational necessity in terms being related as they are, that a relation which is reflexive is a contradiction in terms, and that a specific truth must confess its one-sidedness—are all linked to the view that relations are not just juxtapositions of terms otherwise independent of one another but are grounded in the nature of the terms related and ultimately in the whole of reality of which the relation is part.

For such basic issues as the nature of relations, the nature of wholes, or the possibility of analysis, it is difficult to find grounds on which they can be decided, or any kind of evidence that can be adduced to support one or the other claim. In the last article of the discussion, Bradley, although he allows for the possibility of further exchange, leaves the basic issue much as he found it. He is still in doubt regarding an external relation:

> The terms are to contribute nothing, and so much I understand. But I
> still do not know whether Mr. Russell takes the relations apart from any
> terms to be thinkable. To be consistent he should, in my opinion, hold
> this view, but I cannot say that he does so. If all that is meant is that this
> or that term contributes no more than any other term, clearly, from so
> much, absolute externality and pluralism do not follow. On the other
> hand, a relation apart from terms is to me unmeaning or self-destruc-
> tive, and is an idea produced by an indefensible abstraction.[52]

Joachim expressed doubt whether he could ever come to an agreement on
basic issues with Russell and, in a letter, claims only that "at least we agree
on criticizing that rubbish of pragmatism."[53] Russell, in his reply to Bradley,
had said "The chief hope of philosophical progress seems to lie in the
endeavour to discover clearly the exact points of difference between divergent views. For example, it appears self-evident to Mr. Bradley that a relation
implies diverse terms, whereas to me this appears by no means self-evident.
Such a state of things is eminently unsatisfactory, and seems to lead to a
deadlock."[54] He goes on, however, to suggest using a kind of inductive
argument, testing philosophical premises against their consequences to
common sense and science. This, however, would clearly not have settled
matters. Once the clarification of differences had been accomplished, little
more could be done, and the controversy ceased.

Although it is true that the controversy was discontinued rather than
settled, we should not overlook the basic areas of agreement that made it
profitable for the discussions to continue for a quarter of a century and placed
Russell in the historical continuity of the British philosophical tradition.

In the first place, Russell and Joachim and Bradley shared a certain view of
what philosophy is. This was not a specifically idealist view but a traditional
one. According to this view, philosophy must be able to describe the world as
it exists in terms more comprehensive and systematic than any other forms of
knowledge can provide. Whether the relations characteristic of nature be
internal or external, they are the way nature is; nature has relations of one
kind or another; and the descriptions of both philosophies cannot each be
totally correct. Hence there is a point to citing examples and arguing from
observed "facts." Philosophy must likewise be able to describe the way in
which knowing takes place: the place of perception, concepts, universals,
and so on in knowledge, and the criteria of truth and falsity. If their
arguments seem to us to be partially within the domain of psychology, there
was no sharp division between philosophy and psychology in those days.
Both Russell and Joachim analyze the relation between the perceived blue

and what, if anything, is blue, and both adduce arguments from the way memory functions as distinct perception. A theory of truth incorporating criteria for distinguishing true from false judgments is a major concern of both philosophies.

Furthermore, as far as Russell and the idealists are concerned; the methods as well as the scope of philosophy have much in common. Experience, commonsense knowledge, and scientific knowledge are important reference points for both. What experience shows, what the plain man believes, and what science tells us are important; any argument showing that a theory is in conflict with one of these is agreed to constitute a kind of disconfirmation of the philosophy. Any evidence that a philosophy is preeminently compatible with these is to be regarded as a form of confirmation. In this sense, British idealism is still linked with the empiricist tradition, and as for Russell, his roots are in Hume and Mill. A connection with British thought in the period following World War II can also be discerned, especially with respect to the empiricism of common sense.

Another kind of methodology acceptable both to idealists and to Russell is what the latter calls the *reductio ad absurdum* method. This, too, is traditional, and both parties to the dispute use it. Bradley uses this form of argument in criticizing the concept of class in Russell's *Principles of Mathematics,* alleging that the unwelcome consequence of an admitted and unresolved contradiction renders the definition of class worthy of rejection. Russell, in a similar way, argues that the theory of truth of idealism makes the commonsense criteria of the true and the false meaningless, and thus requires the rejection of "the monistic theory of truth."

These common convictions regarding the purposes and methods of philosophy, learned by Russell from his idealist teachers and shared with them as part of the common tradition of philosophy, he never deserted. They form the basis of the recent claim that Russell belongs on the other side of the twentieth-century "revolution in philosophy."[55] But if in some respects he continued in the older tradition of philosophy, his realist revolt and his use and defense of the method of analysis remained distinctively nonidealist and made him a pioneer. While both of these tendencies in his thought were relatively constant—the first linking him with idealism, the second with Moore—other aspects of his philosophy (for instance, his definition of truth) underwent considerable change under the impact of other men, such as Alexius Meinong, William James, and Ludwig Wittgenstein. These influences upon Russell and his reciprocal influence will be the subject of future chapters. The earliest, most powerful, and most intimate of such interactions was with G. E. Moore.

3
Russell and Moore

Bertrand Russell and G. E. Moore: There can scarcely be two figures in philosophy of whom so much is known concerning their characters, habits, and the impressions they made on others. Both are close enough to our own time for many people to be able to report from memory their conversations, eccentricities, and the devotion they inspired in their admirers. It would be difficult to find a more striking contrast between two personalities. Russell in retrospect appears flamboyant, always involved in controversy, vigorous, immensely productive, and, beyond his work as a philosopher, deeply involved in causes such as disarmament, votes for women, marriage reform, freedom for political prisoners, and world peace. Moore, on the other hand, seems very scholarly, indeed pedantic, conservative, almost puritanical; never involved in controversy, he was universally respected for his philosophical gifts, yet published much less work than Russell. Moore confessed, in his autobiographical contribution to Paul A. Schilpp's Library of Living Philosophers volume on his work, that he was fundamentally unwilling to work unless forced into it by commitments to take part in symposia for which he had to prepare a paper. Yet he is known for the meticulousness of his scholarship and the disinterested honesty of his philosophical inquiry. Most of Moore's life was spent in the academic quiet of Cambridge, teaching the same courses and living with the same wife, in blameless anonymity. Russell's life spanned continents and involved him in countless lawsuits, two jail sentences, four marriages, and innumerable contributions to politics, science, mathematics, philosophy, history, and literature, earning him worldwide notoriety and fame. At the same time, both men were analytic philosophers who shaped our present mode of thought and were important influences on each other.

The close intellectual relations between Russell and Moore have been well known for a long time. In many of the prefaces to Russell's books, from *The*

Philosophy of Leibniz to *The Problems of Philosophy,* generous credit is given to the ideas of Moore.[1] In addition, many footnotes in Russell's early books and articles refer us to Moore's work.[2] Since 1942, when the *Philosophy of G. E. Moore* was published in The Library of Living Philosophers, we have had an explicit account of the friendship and collaboration of Moore and Russell, a friendship also recounted in Russell's autobiographical essay in *The Philosophy of Bertrand Russell,* and later in his three-volume autobiography.[3] But a full understanding of the influence of Moore upon Russell and of Russell upon Moore must depend on a study of their work, and this has not been addressed directly (although much can be learned from A. J. Ayer's analysis in *Russell and Moore: The Analytic Heritage*).[4] In an essay in *The Philosophy of G. E. Moore,* Susan L. Stebbing tells us that she had proposed such a study and had made notes on the work of Moore and Russell preparatory to a paper for the Schilpp Library volume on the subject. The notes, however, were lost in the bombing of London; she herself became ill; and the work was never completed.[5] In undertaking a brief study of the subject, we must do without Stebbing's long association with both philosophers, but we have the advantage of the letters from the Bertrand Russell Archives, a correspondence apparently incomplete, since it consists mostly of Russell's letters to Moore, but extending from 1896 to 1958, when Mrs. Moore wrote to Russell expressing her appreciation of his obituary for Moore. Two approaches are to be taken: first, a history of their association as reconstructed from the available letters, accounts, and published materials; second, pursuing a suggestion of Stebbing's, a comparison of the ideas in the work of the two men in the historical order in which they were written. The outcome of such a comparison may illumine the development of the thought of each.

3.1 Russell and Moore: Joint History

The long association of the two philosophers can be divided into five historical periods, according to the closeness of their contact and the extent of their interactions. The first such period, from 1893 to the middle of 1900, is that of their greatest intimacy, friendship, and reciprocal influence. Russell had come to Trinity College, Cambridge, as a disciple of John Stuart Mill, and as we have seen, had found himself surrounded by teachers who were idealists. But he was doing his major work in mathematics, and it was not until his senior year that he completed his student work in that field and turned his full attention to philosophy. Moore had come to Trinity with a strong classical background and had accepted Lucretius as his philosophical prophet. Under the influence of Ellis McTaggart, G. F. Stout, and James

Ward, both Moore and Russell became idealists for a time. Russell remembers Moore's passionate defense of materialism, and Moore tells us it must have been his arguments against McTaggart that impressed Russell, who in turn, remembers Moore as an undergraduate:

> In my third year, however, I met G. E. Moore, who was then a freshman, and for some years he fulfilled my ideal of genius. He was in those days beautiful and slim, with a look almost of inspiration, and with an intellect as deeply passionate as Spinoza's. He had a kind of exquisite purity. . . . Moore, like me, was influenced by McTaggart, and was for a short time a Hegelian. But he emerged more quickly than I did, and it was largely his conversation that led me to abandon both Kant and Hegel. In spite of his being two years younger than me, he greatly influenced my philosophical outlook.[6]

Moore protested that Russell's acknowledgments of Moore's influence had led some to think that he was the senior and the teacher of Russell, but, as a matter of fact, it was the other way around: he had always been a student of Russell's and closely studied his work, more than that of any other philosopher, and his status as student rather than as teacher was attested to by the fact that he had attended many of Russell's lectures, while Russell had attended only one of his.[7] Moore's disclaimer seems somewhat disingenuous for a philosopher known for his candor, since we find few encomiums and many criticisms of Russell in Moore's work, in contrast to the frequent admiration expressed by the other man. It is true, however, that Moore's later papers contain many references to Russell's work, while Russell's acknowledgments to Moore are all in his earlier writings. Paul Levy, in *G. E. Moore and the Cambridge Apostles,* traces in some detail the progress of their friendship during their early years. His hypothesis of hostility on the part of Moore and jealousy on the part of Russell, which he bases on reminiscences and on letters not yet publicly accessible, seems on the whole not to fit their continued association and especially their philosophical collaboration. It is to the latter, in any case, that our attention is directed.[8] Whatever one may conclude about which of them was the teacher and which the learner, in that collaboration it appears that Moore did lead the revolt against idealism. As we have seen, his paper "On the Nature of Judgment" was the first published criticism of the idealist treatment of the object of knowledge.

During this early period of their association, they were first fellow students during Russell's third and fourth years and Moore's first and second years as undergraduates. Russell married in 1894, and after he and his wife, Alys, had spent some time in Germany studying German Democratic Socialism, he wrote his fellowship dissertation on an idealist philosophy of mathematics. He was elected to a fellowship in 1895, and in 1896 he published a book on German Democratic Socialism and a series of articles on geometry from a Hegelian point of view.[9] Moore meanwhile had passed his Tripos and had begun work on his fellowship dissertation on Kantian ethics. Moore's dissertation failed to win a fellowship, and we find Russell writing to solace him with an account of the political causes of this failure.[10] Moore then wrote a second dissertation on Kant's view of reason, winning his fellowship in 1898. Russell's dissertation *An Essay on the Foundations of Geometry,* which attempted to base geometry on a Kantian view of space, was published in 1897 and widely praised, although by the time it was in print he had already passed from a Kantian to a Hegelian basis for philosophy of mathematics and was seeking a ground for a new synthesis in physics. The following year, 1898, Russell began the practice of spending part of each year in Cambridge, and thus was in closer contact with Moore. That year he started work on Leibniz, preparatory to his teaching McTaggart's course while he was away. That study, and his conversations with Moore, initiated his shift away from idealism. The letters of that year refer to Moore's analysis of concepts, to his dissertation, and to Russell's labors on *Principles of Mathematics.*[11] It was also the year of Moore's first lectures on ethics and of his publication of the article entitled "Freedom."[12] In this article Moore analyzes Kant's account of freedom and finds it to contain inconsistencies in its treatment of the will as both uncaused and the basis of moral freedom. Moore argues that natural causal connections must exist between the will of the agent and what he does, for otherwise freedom will have no ground. Such a causal connection does not mean that his will is determined by factors outside himself, since he is causing his own action. The conception of freedom developed here as a critique of Kant appears later as part of Moore's own ethical theory.

In the year 1899 both young men began important projects: Moore published a paper, "The Nature of Judgment," intended as a criticism of, and alternative to, Kantian idealism in its view of judgment and of concepts.[13] This article was regarded by Russell as the first clear statement of the new realist position that he and Moore were beginning to oppose to idealism. It begins as a criticism of Bradley's theory of judgment. Quoting Bradley's statement that truth and falsehood depend upon our relation to reality, and that ideas are symbols of something beyond themselves, he shows that Bradley slips over to the position that the idea, or meaning, is part of the content of our mind. Moore, on the contrary, holds that the idea used in judgment is not a part of the content of our mind, and that truth and falsity are not dependent on the relation of ideas to reality. This seems confusing, since one would expect the idealist to deny that truth and falsehood depend on reality, the realist to affirm it. The realism put forth in this article, however, is a Platonic realism in which both the subject and the predicate of a judgment stand for concepts that are constituents of a proposition.

"When, therefore, I say 'This rose is red,' I am not attributing part of the content of my idea to the rose, nor yet attributing parts of the content of my ideas of rose and red together to some third subject. What I am asserting is a specific connexion of certain concepts forming the total concept 'rose' with the concepts 'this' and 'now' and 'red'; and the judgment is true if such a connexion is existent."[14] He goes on to argue that a proposition is a synthesis of concepts, each of which is immutable, and hence that the proposition is a complex of concepts. Truth belongs to the complex rather than to the simple and depends upon whether the relation which holds the synthesis together is an existent or not. Moore goes on to compare his view with that of Kant; Moore substitutes concepts for Kant's sensations and gives an analysis of necessity different from Kant's, one in which the empirical judgment is one constituted by concepts involved with time. These judgments, corresponding to Kant's a priori judgments, are constituted by concepts unaffected by time. Both kinds of judgments are marked by necessity, a necessity depending neither upon the mind nor upon the world outside the judgment but rather upon the concepts themselves; all are necessarily false or necessarily true. In his article entitled "Necessity" (1900), Moore defines a necessary proposition as one having logical priority in its being implied by a large number of propositions. This is quoted with approval by Russell in his article "Is Position in Time and Space Absolute or Relative?" (1901).[15]

Moore also published in 1899 a critical review, from a realist point of view, of Russell's book on geometry.[16] Moore finds that Russell's treatment of geometry, insofar as it is argued on a philosophical ground, is full of contradictions and exhibits weaknesses akin to those afflicting the philosophy of Kant, on which Russell's treatment of geometry is based. Not unlike Kant, Russell argues that the test of the a priori is whether experience would be impossible if a certain axiom were denied, and, although he states that this is not a psychological test, in fact it turns out that the only thing it can be is psychological. Referring to Russell's use of the possibility of experience, Moore says that he "seems actually to use this conception in such a way as to incur both the objections which can be urged against Kant's distinction between *a priori* and empirical, namely, (1) that the distinction is not absolute, (2) that the *a priori* is confused with the object of psychological experience."[17] The review is devastating not only in Moore's detailed account of the book's weaknesses and contradictions but also in his overall rejection of its fundamental point of view. By the time the review was published, Russell himself agreed with most of Moore's criticisms.[18] He had gone on to try to find a Hegelian basis for philosophy of mathematics, and, finally, to seek a foundation in the kind of conceptual realism which Moore had advocated in his essay on judgment. This realism, as it appears in Moore's articles on necessity, freedom, judgment, and identity (the last appeared in 1901),[19] has the form of a conceptual realism where each term in the proposition is an entity and related to every other term by logical necessity. The anti-idealist themes of these articles are directed at Kant (as with the criticism of freedom and of judgment) and against contemporary idealists such as Bradley (as in the criticism of the idealist concept of identity as consisting in identity in difference, in contrast to Moore's view that identity may be either numerical or of qualities, and that for the former it makes sense to speak of self-identity). Russell voiced the same anti-idealist and realist themes in *The Principles of Mathematics,* and attributed the philosophical ideas expressed in the book to Moore. His realism in this volume is a term-realism in which not only concept terms but class terms, individual terms, and fictitious terms are entities, as are the propositions in which they occur. The opposition to idealism takes the form of an attack on the doctrine of internal relations.[20] The theme of relations is the most distinctive both mathematically and philosophically in the book. (It was written by the end of 1900, but Russell did not publish it until 1903, because of the unsolved contradiction of classes not members of themselves.)

In 1899 Russell first reviewed Alexius Meinong's work, the work of a philosopher whose realism was to be influential for Russell and, for a time, very close to the position that Moore and Russell had been developing in the analysis of knowledge. By the middle of 1900 the outlines of the new realism, now publicly identified as that of Moore and Russell, had taken shape; it was based on an analysis of knowledge in which the object of knowledge is said to have a reality and existence independent of knowing, consciousness, or experience. This realism also is tied to a radical pluralism that rejects the monism of mind and mind-processes in favor of the reality of different kinds, body and mind, concept and percept, universal and particular, logic and science. For Russell, one of the reasons for rejecting idealism is its unsatisfactory philosophy of mathematics, but for Moore the analysis of knowledge is a more vital issue. Their "exuberant" form of realism had not yet revealed all its difficulties; it was a program rather than a fully worked-out set of doctrines. As the various issues of the new realism emerged, and as Moore and Russell labored on their particular projects, the differences in their points of view became more marked. But, as the century began, they were in close contact, and Moore was helping Russell read proofs for the Leibniz book, assisting him with his greater knowledge of Latin to check footnotes and appendixes, and remarking in a letter that perhaps Russell attributed greater logical consistency to Leibniz than that author had actually possessed. This help is reflected in the letters and acknowledged by Russell in the preface to the book.[21] It is interesting that, in his article "Identity" of 1901, Moore refers to Russell's work on Leibniz and points out that Leibniz's treatment of the law of sufficient reason and the principle of the identity of indiscernibles involves him in admitting the distinction between conceptual and numerical identity, a point, says Moore, that Russell had overlooked.[22]

Russell meanwhile reported in letters to Moore that he read a paper on time at Oxford, where those he met struck him as "grossly ignorant." Russell attended the International Philosophical Congress in Paris; he wrote to Moore, who had not attended, an enthusiastic report on the congress[23] and promised him a paper on the word *any*. Russell's attendance at this congress marked the beginning of a new phase in his intellectual life; he looked back upon it as a most important event that introduced him to the work in mathematical logic being done by Giuseppe Peano and his pupils and set him to working on the logic of relations, which was to consume the rest of the year, and, with its consequent problems, the next ten years. One of the effects of this new interest was that Moore and Russell began to diverge in their professional interests; Moore tells us that Russell had urged him to learn mathematics, but he did not, and so could not follow the new work Russell was doing. Alfred North Whitehead became Russell's closest collaborator. Moore, for his part, published a paper on necessity that year and continued the work he had already begun in 1898, a book on ethics.

The second period of Moore's and Russell's association was one of fewer interactions in person, and in letters as well, as appears from the extant correspondence. It lasted from the end of 1900 until about 1908–10. It was during this period that Russell spent all day for eight months of every year at the enormous labors that resulted first in the *The Principles of Mathematics* and then (with Whitehead) in *Principia Mathematica*. It was the most sustained and intense period of intellectual effort of his life and, for most of the time, was intensely frustrating, as he strained to solve what had appeared first as a trivial contradiction. At the same time the even tenor of his personal life was shattered, first by the experience of "mystic illumination" when he became sensitive to the sufferings of humankind, by his ardent desire for children, and, subsequently, by the end of his love for his wife, Alys.

Although there was a divergence of interests and associations between Moore and Russell during this period, it was by no means a break in communication. Early in the period, from 1901 to 1903, Moore was still in Cambridge on his fellowship, and letters testify to Russell's concern with the problem of the fellowship being renewed, and with other means for Moore's support. He urged Moore to hurry the book (presumably the appearance of *Principia Ethica* would make the renewal of the fellowship more likely); he also responded with great seriousness to Moore's question as to whether he ought to try for a professorship at University College which would entail heavy teaching duties or try to live and work on his small inheritance.[24] (Moore took the latter path, thus falling in with Russell's suggestion.) From 1903 to 1908, Moore lived in Edinburgh; *Principia Ethica* was published in 1903 and drew warm praise. Russell wrote enthusiastically to Moore and published a favorable review of it;[25] he challenged only some of what he considered to be the overly conservative aspects of its practical implications. In this period Moore wrote several of the papers later included in *Philosophical Studies* (1922), including "The Refutation of Idealism" and "The Nature and Reality of Objects of Perception."[26] The correspondence continued with talk of a cooperative volume on "practical ethics" of Moore, Russell, and some of their friends, and of plans for a reading party.[27] Russell recommended Meinong to Moore with the comment that the Austrian's position was very close to Moore's. On several occasions, Russell wrote of what he had heard of Moore; he said he had heard that Moore had found some arguments in favor of idealism, but this was denied with great gravity; Russell also wrote that he had heard that Moore believed that he was able to solve Russell's contradiction, but Russell advised that this is impossible without using mathematical logic, because any nonlogical solution would involve self-contradiction. Moore wrote in praise of "On Denoting," saying that he began reading it in disagreement with Russell and ended by agreeing with him.[28] Moore announced his intention to apply the technique of the analysis of incomplete symbols to the definition of good.

Moore mentioned in a letter to Russell of 1905 that he had finally completed his review of Russell's book for the *"Archiv."* No such review was published so far as we know, and we do not know what *"Archiv"* is referred to, but there is among Moore's papers an unpublished review of *The Principles of Mathematics,* and it is likely that this is the review in question.[29] Further corroboration is the reference in the review to Russell's recently published "On Denoting," which Moore mentions as being superior in its discussion of *all, any, a,* and *the* to that of the book. This review is of some interest, for it is by no means uncritical of Russell's philosophical assumptions, and it also attempts some detailed criticism of the more mathematical and logical aspects of the book.[30]

Moore begins by criticizing Russell's claim to have shown that mathematics can be deduced from purely logical principles, protesting that Russell has not shown that there can be only one analysis of number deducible from such principles and suggesting that there might be more than one such concept. Thus the initial claim would not hold. Moore also sees a gap between the deduction of mathematics and the application of its concepts to the real world; such a system, for instance, might be deduced but still not be applicable to counting. The argument of the book comes down, Moore says, to an incompatibility between Russell's definition of pure mathematics and his two basic propositions regarding its logical definability and deducibility.

Moore's review further criticizes Russell's use of *implication* at some length, accusing him of internal inconsistency for using principles of deduction other than implication as it had been defined by Russell. Moore also claims that the definition of *material implication* has absurd consequences. He himself proposes that *implication* is "a simple concept which is not equivalent to any complex except complexes in the analysis of which it is itself involved." Moore goes on to criticize the treatment of *continuity* and of *infinity* in Russell's book, pointing out that there are meanings of these terms other than those that Russell discusses. Moore's apparent assumption is that in offering definitions, axioms, and postulates of a logical and mathematical system, Russell ought to be able to arrive at definitions of concepts corresponding not only with the needs of the mathematical system but those of common sense as well. In reviewing this book, as in his review of Russell's work on geometry, Moore disclaims any mathematical knowledge; perhaps he had come to feel that his philosophical criticisms could not be disentangled from the mathematical system within which Russell's philosophical assumptions were developed. At any rate, the realism of Russell's book was not challenged, and there is apparent agreement between the two on the kind of Platonic term-realism expressed in the book.

Russell wrote a paper entitled "The Elements of Ethics," and in a letter to Moore he says of it, "It's only yours boiled down."[31] Russell's expressed desire to meet and "hear your current views" was perhaps satisfied, because Moore returned to London to lecture in 1908. No letters survive of the period from the end of 1907 to 1921.

Although the period 1907 to 1921 was one of diminished interaction, there were certain themes in common in the philosophies of Russell and Moore that continued throughout this time: the opposition to idealism expressed in the controversy with Joachim, discussion of sense-data, attention to problems of ethics, interest in free will and determinism, parallel criticisms of pragmatism, and concern with the problem of the relation of the object of knowledge to the knowledge of it. This last problem, especially in connection with perception, was the subject of detailed analysis by Moore in both "The Refutation of Idealism" (1903) and "The Nature and Reality of Objects of Perception."

In the first of these articles, which achieved considerable fame and was widely believed to have given the *coup de grace* to idealism, Moore attacks the Berkeleyan *esse est percipi* argument. Having shown that some version of this argument appears in many idealist proofs that the object of knowledge is somehow within our knowing or experiencing, Moore demonstrates that there is no reason to make such an assumption. Rather, he proposes that when we see the blue of the flower, that sensation of blue is as much in the flower as in our eyes (or mind). The theme of the object of knowledge as having a reality beyond the psychological reality of its presence in consciousness became a central theme of realism and marked a new phase of Moore's thought in which the concept-realism of "On the Nature of Judgment" became the realism of sensation and common sense. In the second article, "The Nature and Reality of Objects of Perception" (1905–6), Moore begins to face some of the puzzles of this realism of sensation; this article asks whether I have reason to believe in the existence of other persons who have experiences like my own. Moore argues that, whatever they say, philosophers have acted on this assumption. He goes on to try to disentangle the strands of the argument that might be put forward for solipsism, and, in the end, he comes to believe that the issue rests on whether the things that we observe, and especially those he calls sense-contents, do exist and are real. As against both Thomas Reid and Berkeley, Moore thinks there are no conclusive reasons for doubting this, but the article calls for renewed inquiry.

In the period 1908 to 1914 this problem of the analysis of perception was of major concern to both Russell and Moore. It was a prominent theme in the lectures that Moore gave in London in 1910, and it is these lectures that Russell briefly acknowledges in the preface to *The Problems of Philosophy* of 1912.[32] The material on which Moore's lectures were based was not published until 1953, in *Some Main Problems of Philosophy,* where in the preface Moore tells us that chapters 1 through 10 are the lectures to which Russell referred.[33] It is here that Moore presents the analysis of perception in terms of sense-data; the problem of the relation of those data to inferences about the nature of the object perceived; a dualistic interpretation of subject and object, mind and matter, and universal and particular; and a position of realism that asserts the independent reality of logical truths and concepts. These Moore-Russell themes—emphasizing the distinction between knowledge by acquaintance and knowledge by description, the term *sense-data* for the objects of sensory awareness, and the problem of inference from one to another—first appeared in print in "Knowledge by Acquaintance and Knowledge by Description," a paper read by Russell before the Aristotelian Society and published in their *Proceedings* for 1910–11.[34] (As a matter of historical interest this seems to be the first published use of the famous, or infamous, term *sense-data* in the Moore-Russell discussions; however, if Moore's first ten chapters of *Some Main Problems of Philosophy* are a verbatim version of his 1910 lectures, he may have used the term first—since the first ten lectures were given before Christmas 1910, while Russell's lecture to the Aristotelian Society was delivered March 6, 1911. At any rate, we can specify the time and place of their joint concern for the problems of perception from which the term emerged.)

In 1910 Russell accepted an invitation to return to Cambridge as a lecturer, and the following year Moore also returned there. Moore remained there for the rest of his academic life, with the exception of an excursion to the United States in the 1940s. Russell remained based in Cambridge except for a sojourn at Harvard University from March to June of 1914. But the advent of the war in August 1914 took him away from the academic world and his philosophical interests and eventually, by action of the college, separated him from Trinity College. Prior to Russell's trip to the American Cambridge, however, he and Moore were in contact both in person and in philosophical interests. In 1912 each wrote a small and influential volume for the *Home University Library:* Russell's *The Problems of Philosophy* and Moore's *Ethics*.[35] These two books might well be taken as a joint manifesto of a kind of innocent realism that scarcely survived their publication. A whole generation of philosophy students was introduced to the problems of ethics through Moore's book (or through his *Principia Ethica*), and to the problems of theory of knowledge through *The Problems of Philosophy*. But the rather deceptively simple statements of the latter book were immediately subject to difficulties, revisions, and emendations by Russell. In fact the philosophical publications of Russell between this book of 1912 and "The Philosophy of Logical Atomism" of 1919 show the development of problems inherent in the book—the status of sense-data, the nature and validity of inferences from sense-data to commonsense beliefs and scientific knowledge, the analysis of belief, and difficulties concerning knowledge of the past, of the self, of logical truths, and of universals. As for Moore, almost all his subsequent writing in philosophy centered on epistemological questions generated by the analysis of subject, object, sense-data, and commonsense knowledge. Although they were concerned with the same range of problems, however, the techniques adopted for solving them, and the conclusions reached, were strikingly different. As for *Ethics,* neither Moore nor Russell did important subsequent work along the lines laid down in that book. Russell renounced ethical realism under the impact of Santayana's criticisms, while Moore turned his attention almost entirely to epistemology, with the exception of two articles reprinted in *Philosophical Studies* (1922) and his discussion of criticisms in his Library of Living Philosophers volume of 1942. Nevertheless, his distinction between questions of the definition of good and questions of what one ought to do and his discussion of the "naturalistic fallacy" and free will remained important themes in subsequent work on ethics.

The year 1911 was marked by the appearance of Ludwig Wittgenstein on the Cambridge scene. He came as a student of Russell's new logic, but Russell soon recognized that he was a source of important new logical insights. For a time, then, during 1912 and 1913, Moore, Russell, and Wittgenstein all were in Cambridge, while Whitehead was in contact with them from London. The impact of Wittgenstein was much the strongest and most immediate on Russell, as we shall see in a subsequent chapter. Moore was impressed by Wittgenstein's ability also, and one of the versions of the "Notes on Logic" was written by Moore from Wittgenstein's explanations while they were on holiday in Norway.[36] But Moore tells us that it was only after the war, when Wittgenstein returned to Cambridge, that he became a close student of Wittgenstein's ideas and was influenced by them. For Russell, as we shall see in chapter 7, the entire influence, or most of it, seems to have been before the war.

Another contemporary viewpoint influential on Russell in this period was that of William James's "neutral monism," a concept against which Russell struggled from 1913 until 1919. Again Moore seems not to have been vitally affected by this doctrine, although he did criticize it.[38] In Moore's criticism of James's *Pragmatism,* the focus is on the definition of truth, and the strategy is to ask exactly what James is claiming truth to be. In characteristic fashion Moore contends that had James argued that verification has a good deal to do with truth, instead of arguing that it *is* truth; had he argued that *some* truths are useful, instead of arguing that *all* truths are useful; had he argued that *some* truths are made true, instead of arguing that *all* truths are made true, Moore would have agreed with him. Moore then adduces examples of what seem to him and to common sense to be exceptions to James's universalized claims: truths that cannot be verified, nonutilitarian truths, and timeless truths. In effect the criticisms are similar to Russell's but are expressed in more carefully qualified form.

We may set the end of the second period of collaboration with Moore at the beginning of 1914, when Russell left for America to give the lectures

published as *Our Knowledge of the External World.*[39] Intellectually, he was
applying his own logical techniques of the method of construction to a range
of problems springing from, or connected with, the epistemological concerns that he shared with Moore, on the model of Whitehead's application of
these to points in space and moments in time. Although Moore studied this
and responded to it, the response was not that of a collaborator but of
someone with a different point of view.

Moore's discussion of epistemological matters can be seen in two articles
of this period, "The Status of Sense-Data" (1913–14) and "Some Judgments
of Perception" (1917–18).[40] In the first of these articles he defines *sense-data*
as distinguished from the event of sensation, uses the term *sensibles* to
include the objects of imagination and memory as well as of sensation and to
include objects which may be the data of sensation (their becoming sensations depends upon our nervous system). He thus gives a realist meaning to
sense-data, but also expands his previous treatment in the direction of a
subject-act-content-object analysis. He turns his attention, in the latter part
of this article and in the second one, to the relation between what is "directly
seen" and the "object seen." The first is the sense-datum—a colored patch,
say; the second is the object—the inkwell or the coin. What is the relation
between these two? Moore wrestles with this question, giving serious consideration, falling short of commitment, first to a Lockean, and then to a Russellian
answer (the "Mill-Russell" view, as Moore interprets *Our Knowledge of the
External World*). In his response to critics in the Schilpp volume he is still not
clear on this issue.[41] In general he moved closer to maintaining that commonsense objects exist, as other persons exist, just as we believe them to, whether a
philosophically cogent argument can be developed for this view or not. In his
volume of essays, *Philosophical Studies,* published in 1922, he included two
critiques of idealism along lines also found in Russell. "The Conception of
Reality" deals with the consequences that would flow from Bradley's doubts of
the reality of time, if such doubts were serious ones; a characteristic Moorean
tactic against other philosophers is to trace the absurdities to which the
philosopher would be committed were his generalizations to be brought down to
the details of his own life. "External and Internal Relations" is a meticulous
criticism of the doctrine of the universality of internal relations as Moore shows
it to be implied in the work of idealist philosophers.[42] This makes for an
interesting comparison with the similar criticism offered by Russell in "The
Monistic Theory of Truth," part of his "On the Nature of Truth" (1906). The
theme is the same, but the way in which the details of the view are stated and
brought home to their proponents is once again more careful and qualified with
Moore, more slashing and witty with Russell.

I consider the period from 1914 to 1922 one of the divergence of Moore and Russell so far as their intellectual development is concerned. It seems that their friendship also became less warm, as the result of different interests and ways of life. It might have appeared that, when Russell accepted a lectureship at Trinity in 1910, he was entering a period of tranquility and academic respectability. He was nearing forty; his great collaborative work on *Principia Mathematica* was over and would assure him recognition as a major figure; his marriage had settled down to a friendly nonintimacy; and his politically exciting campaign on behalf of the suffragette movement had yielded to a little quiet campaigning for other candidates. Moore, too, as he returned to Trinity, could look forward to a tranquil career of academic achievement. It turned out that way for Moore, but Russell's personal and political life both were stormy. His final separation from Alys, his affair with Lady Ottoline Morrell, his return from American adventures to an England on the brink of war, and his continuing efforts to end the war—all this removed him from his academic retreat and took him along very different paths from those of Cambridge. He and Moore could hardly have lived two more different lives; Moore taught, married, had children, and apparently did not embroil himself at all in controversy, although he supported Russell when the latter was removed from his fellowship, and when he was tried and sent to jail. They would never again be in close personal contact, nor would their philosophical paths again run parallel.

The distance that these two philosophers had moved from one another is evident in the reviews that each gave of the other's work: Moore reviewed Russell's *The Analysis of Mind* in 1921; Russell reviewed Moore's *Philosophical Studies* in 1922.[43] The marked divergence of their points of view justifies calling this the end of the relation between them. All that needs to be added is some consideration of the later criticisms that Moore offered of Russell. Their personal contacts were few; there were letters concerning the evaluation of Wittgenstein's work and concerning the possibility of Russell's teaching at Cambridge, which are reproduced in Russell's *Autobiography*, and, after World War II, there was an exchange of letters concerning an invitation to take part in disarmament meetings.

3.2 Ethics, Cause, and Free Will

One of the areas of philosophy in which it is quite clear that Moore was the leader and Russell the follower (although he later broke away from Moore's position) is ethics. Ever since his doctoral dissertation on Kant, Moore had been concerned with the problems of ethics and, in particular, the effort to work out a theory avoiding the faults of both utilitarianism and Kantian ethics. This is clear in the syllabus of the course that he offered in 1898,[44] and it is equally clear in *Principia Ethica*. A major contribution of the book is the sharp distinction between ethics and morals: The first is the consideration of the nature of good, the second that of how one ought to act in order to achieve the good. These are separate questions, but, for Moore, both are within the scope of philosophy. The means of achieving good are extrinsic values and can be argued, reasoned, and inferred about; judgments in this area rest on the relating of means to ends. The normal outcome of this part of ethical inquiry is the setting up of rules or maxims of the kind that are usually taken as a guide to conduct. But in the matter of the good, the situation is quite different; for the good has the kind of ultimacy in ethics that sense-data have in epistemology; one cannot infer concerning what the good is, or deduce its nature from something else; it is just there. One can only apprehend or grasp or recognize the good. For Moore, this is where previous ethical systems have gone wrong; utilitarianism tried to define the good in terms of some more ultimate and observable quality, pleasure; idealism tried to define the good in terms of some more ultimate ideal not yet realized. But for Moore, to define the good is to try to analyze it in terms of something more simple and ultimate; the good itself is the simple at which analysis must stop. In addition to this error, utilitarianism had erred in defining good in terms of an observable quality; but good is a simple quality which is as recognizable as red is, but unlike red, is not observable. This is the source of the so-called naturalistic fallacy in ethics, the attempt to define the good, which is indefinable, in terms of an ultimate quality which is observable. But if Moore claims that good is not a natural quality and is indefinable and that one can apprehend it, he is not saying that it is a supernatural quality, that it is ineffable, or that it can be intuited in some sense in which the intuition cannot be in error or be open to challenge. Good is indefinable in the sense that no further analysis of the judgment *x is good* can be made, and it is intuited only in the sense that it is immediately apprehended, but this does not imply that such apprehension is error-free.

The best way to describe Moore's position in *Principia Ethica* is to say that he is a realist with respect to ethics. For him, the apprehension of a certain situation as "good" involves the assumption that the "good" exists apart from the apprehension; in the same way the apprehension of the rose as "red" involves the assumption that the quality "red" exists apart from the awareness of it; and in the same way the concept "equality" exists apart from the consciousness of the concept. In this sense, Moore's position in ethics is anti-idealist, antisubjective, and antipsychological. There were difficulties with Moore's position because the apprehension of a situation as good meant treating the total situation as a kind of complex unity in which the agent, the act, the circumstances and the consequences were all involved. To combine the simplicity of good as the end point of an analysis with good as a quality belonging to a complex produced philosophical difficulties that became more apparent as time went on. But in *Principia Ethica* the position was one of an ethical realism apparently compatible with the general realist position that Moore and Russell were adopting, and philosophically more sound than the alternative idealism and utilitarianism.

Russell, then, followed Moore in taking the position of ethical realism, as is evident in "The Elements of Ethics," and, indeed, Russell freely admits that it is Moore's position. This essay was published in 1910 in *Philosophical Essays*. How did it come about, then, that in 1917 he remarks, referring to "A Free Man's Worship" in the preface to *Mysticism and Logic*, "I feel less convinced than I did then of the objectivity of good and evil"?45 Subsequently, he adopted the position that made ethics almost a part of psychology, relating the good to what is desired, hence, making it relative rather than absolute, subjective rather than objective. Russell reports that his change with respect to the objectivity of the good came about as the result of Santayana's criticisms. Santayana wrote a long review of *Philosophical Essays* in the *Journal of Philosophy* and also wrote a criticism of Moore's and Russell's position in *Winds of Doctrine*.46 In general, his attack was directed against the kind of naive realism that they adopted; to say that the grass is really green or that benevolence is really good cannot be taken to mean that the green is substantively in the grass, or the good substantively in the benevolence, any more than to say the liquor is intoxicating is to say that it is "dead drunk in the bottle." This is to suggest the replacement of a *causal* realism for the original naive variety.

Russell was already moving in the direction of modifying his original realism, with its Platonic view of concepts and numbers and its naive treatment of sense qualities. He had seen how numbers and other concepts can be replaced by linguistic techniques which do not involve the assumption of the existence of numbers as entities—that is, classes become propositional functions. He accepted the view of science that the perception of a color quality is the end of a causal sequence that begins with light rays and a retina. Some different analysis of "good" must also be found.

In changing his position in ethics so abruptly, however, Russell was not really departing from all the assumptions that he had shared with Moore; the later "noncognitive" position in ethics adopted by Russell has much in common with the earlier Moore position. The noncognitive position holds that to call something *good* is to say that I approve it and wish you would too; to say something is *evil* is to say that I disapprove it and wish you would too. Other judgments asserting other value qualities are concealed statements of approval, or else are statements of means to ends that are approved. This distinction is the same as that between ethics and morals, between statements of intrinsic and statements of extrinsic value. If the unanalyzability and reality of the good is replaced with the treatment of *good* as a word signifying approval, then we see the position of the later Russell to be closely analogous to the one he had shared earlier with Moore. Statements of extrinsic value, of instrumental goods, are merely statements of means to ends, and hence can be analyzed in the same way as can any other causal statements. They are not specifically ethical, although they are cognitive. Most of the propositions constituting part of traditional ethics are of this kind. It either is or is not a well-founded causal judgment that "what a web we weave when once we practice to deceive." However, to say "lying is morally wrong" is not a judgment which can be evaluated cognitively; it means only "I disapprove of lying."

The parallel between the ethical realism of the *Principia Ethica* and the ethical noncognitivism of the reply to criticisms in the volume on Russell's philosophy of The Library of Living Philosophers is thus very marked. This is further confirmed by Moore himself, wavering on the issue of the independent reality of good, and admitting, in reply to criticisms of the Library of Living Philosophers volume devoted to his philosophy, that perhaps Charles Stevenson is right and *good* can be analyzed as a statement of approval.[47] It is clear that if the basic distinction of intrinsic and extrinsic goods is accepted, there is a tendency for ethical statements to be absorbed into statements of means to ends on the one hand, and statements of approval or disapproval on the other.

There is a philosophical problem connected with the subject-matter of ethics, on which the position of G. E. Moore has commanded considerable attention, generating a controversy that continues into the present. This is the problem of formulating the sense of freedom of the will which is required for moral responsibility and would yet be compatible with the kind of causal determinism that we may assume to hold throughout nature. The *locus classicus* of the discussion is the final section of the 1912 *Ethics,* where Moore argues that, in order for moral responsibility to be asserted, what is required is that the individual "could have done otherwise" than what, in fact, he did do. In an extended analysis, Moore takes the "doing otherwise" to mean: if the individual had chosen to do otherwise, he would have done so. He then argues that this entails a perfectly ordinary meaning of "could" similar to the one involved in saying that the boat could have done twenty knots, although, in fact, it went much slower. In other words, the range of possible speeds, like the range of possible actions, does not mean that there is any breach of causal law involved, since what did happen had causes, just as some other outcome would have had causes. Hence there is a compatibility of free will (in the sense required for ethics) with causal determinism (in the sense in which we ordinarily use causal concepts). Whatever the merits of this position, it is interesting that its initiation goes back to Moore's early essay on freedom, in which he opposes the Kantian conception of freedom with a naturalistic position in which to act "freely" is said to be analogous to the wheel in a watch moving "freely." There is implicit in this position an understanding of nature as marked by causes that are not of the "compelling" kind of rigid determinism, and of man, like nature, as marked by regularities and continuities of behavior.

A similar view of freedom is characteristic of Russell's famous analysis of cause in relation to the "free will problem." In the chapter "On the Notion of Cause, with Application to the Free-Will Problem," in *Our Knowledge of the External World*, as in the essay of 1912, Russell argues that philosophers have misunderstood the meaning of cause for science and attributed compulsion and other features to it that are inappropriate.[48] The result of this misunderstanding is to suppose that if causality applies in human behavior, then we are subject to some external coercion; Russell argues instead that human behavior is subject to some regularities, which would make it predictable if more were known of desires and attitudes, but which do not, in any meaningful sense, eliminate moral responsibility, since our own desires and motives are the causes of our actions, and this is the very condition required for morality. For Russell, this is part of a criticism of the philosophical concept of cause; for Moore, it is part of a defense of the concept. Yet the consequences of their arguments are similar, and, although it goes beyond the evidence to speculate on these positions as being the result of collaboration, or of the influence of one upon the other, it is worth noting that in 1897 Russell was writing to Moore to the effect that, in Moore's essay "Freedom," the latter was mistaken in arguing against the predictability of human behavior. In a subsequent letter, Russell appears to have been convinced by Moore's position on predictability. At least we can see evidence of philosophical interchange on the issue.[49]

In contrast, a hint of conflict on the conception of cause can be seen in the criticisms that Russell offered of the "traditional" view of cause in his essay of 1912, "On the Notion of Cause," read before the Aristotelian Society and later reprinted in *Mysticism and Logic*. In order to comprehend what philosophers understand by cause, Russell consulted Baldwin's *Dictionary of Philosophy and Psychology* for the meaning of the term. The definitions in question were written by Moore in 1900 when he contributed a number of entries to that dictionary. In the course of showing the untenability and mutual incompatibility of the definitions, Russell also destroys the meaning of *necessary* which would lead one to include it in a definition of cause. "Causality (1) The necessary connection of events in the time-series. . . ." Russell, in this essay, gives his definition of *necessary* as applying only to propositional functions in cases where they are true for any value of the variable in contrast to the application of *necessary* to events (an application Moore had been willing to make, as we saw). He goes on, later in the essay, to reinterpret the first definition according to his own treatment of necessity. First, however, he rejects the second Baldwin formulation, which defines cause as "whatever may be included in the thought or perception of a process as taking place in consequence of another process. This is rejected as psychological (a judgment which one would expect Moore to share). The third definition defines *cause* and *effect* in terms of the contiguity of events in a time series; and Russell finds difficulties with the concepts of event and of time-series which make this definition insufficient. Russell continues by discussing other aspects of traditional philosophical meanings given to *cause,* and concludes by offering a very severely curtailed concept, that of a differential equation, that is, observed regularity expressed in mathematical terms, which in science replaces the old causal laws and involves none of the difficult metaphysical problems that have clung to older philosophical concepts. The contrast between the commonsense and traditional philosophical concepts of cause enshrined in Moore's definitions and the scientific, nonmetaphysical concept of cause espoused by Russell is characteristic of the increasing divergence in the work of the two philosophers.[50]

3.3 Knowledge and the Real

Issues in theory of knowledge were at the center of the joint revolt of Russell and Moore against idealism, and to those issues both of them turned after the completion of their work in logic and ethics respectively. The initial revolt, as we have seen, concerned the assertion of what idealism had denied, that the object known exists independently of the knowing relation, and is what it is, regardless of how, or by whom, or whether it is known at all. This realism with respect to the object of knowledge seemed to have first embraced a naive or direct realism with respect to sense qualities, a Platonic realism with respect to concepts and universals, and an ethical realism with respect to the good. Naive realism with respect to sense qualities can be seen in Moore's "The Refutation of Idealism" and is remembered by Russell as their early position. Moore later judged the argument of the essay unsound and raised the question "Just what is the relation between the sense quality and the object?" But the first analysis to which this relation was subjected seems to have been one close to that of Meinong, first stated by Russell but adopted by Moore: the relation of awareness, or acquaintance, or apprehension holds between the subject doing the sensing and the object sensed. It is what Russell calls a subject-act-content analysis in which one sees red—the one is the subject, the seeing is the act, and the red is the content. The relation of awareness or acquaintance is a direct two-term relation in which, at least initially, no distortion or interpretation of the object intervenes. Idealism had argued that the "object" necessarily shares the mind-reality of the subject, but Moore and Russell insisted on the separate reality of the object, hence, on a pluralism in which the object may be material or physical at the same time that the subject is, as perceiver, mental. The result of this was a kind of mind-body dualism that Russell explicitly rejected about 1919 in favor of neutral monism, but that Moore apparently retained, although in his 1952 publication of the lectures of 1910–11, he notes that he no longer holds that sensation is knowledge or that acquaintance is a two-term relation, as had been held in the early lectures, and as Russell claimed in *Problems of Philosophy*.

When the object is thought of not as a sense-quality but as an object such as a table, complications arise because what is given in the relation of acquaintance is not a whole table, but only a datum in some way connected with the table. Russell attempted to solve the problem by making the distinction between knowledge by acquaintance and knowledge by description, and by explaining that our knowledge of objects is built up of inferences from sense qualities given in acquaintance from which we construct the picture of the object. Hence from square, brown, smooth, hard, and so forth we construct the table. Since Russell was primarily concerned with validating judgments, he proposed that his theory of descriptions be used as a technique for translating propositions purportedly about tables into a set of propositions about brown patches. Moore identified this view as "the Mill-Russell theory that objects are built up out of congeries of sense-data," and, using *Our Knowledge of the External World,* he defended it against some mistaken criticisms, yet hesitated himself to accept it. According to Moore, there are three possible views of the relation of the sense-data to the object: first, that they are identical; second, that the object causes the sense-data; and third, the Mill-Russell view. About each alternative he had reservations: he leaned toward the identity of datum and object but noted that, at most, the sense-data are partial and the object is whole, so the identity must hold between sense-data and part of the *surface* of the object. He rejected the causal view because of too many difficulties with the concept of cause; he defended, yet did not adopt, the Mill-Russell theory. (It seems likely that Russell's view was closer to a combination of the causal and the constructional concept of the object, since he distinguished between what was there, molecules grouped so that light waves bounced off, hit the retina, and so forth, and what were the minimum assumptions required to build a logical structure from the data of sense to the statements of science and common sense.)

The three answers to the question "What is the relation between the sense-datum and the object?" involved many difficulties for both Moore and Russell. For instance, when Macbeth "saw" the dagger before him, what did he see? If seeing ordinarily implies that the object seen exists, what about this case? What kind of object is involved in awareness of the self? When one is aware of a complex object, is it *given* as complex? If so, are the components of the complex also given at the same time, or sometimes analyzed out? Is the speckled hen just indeterminately speckled or does it have a specific number of speckles which must be determined by subsequent counting? Can a sense-datum ever be mistaken? Is a sense-datum always of a present moment, or can there be a sense-datum of a past moment? If there cannot be, how is knowledge of the past, or awareness of the continuity of experience, to be explained? Such questions troubled both Moore and Russell, but it seems that after Russell's *Our Knowledge of the External World,* their answers were worked out without collaboration and with little agreement, although each studied the work of the other.

Another issue of realism of concern to both Moore and Russell involved considerable modification of the position of each and finally ended with a divergence of opinion between them: that of realism with respect to universals. We saw that Moore's early essays set forth a Platonic realism in which concepts exist independently of mind, and this was accepted by Russell. In *The Principles of Mathematics* this extreme realism was set forth with credit to Moore; every term has a referent, an entity of some kind. Numbers are real, relations are real, qualities are real, predicates are real, even propositions exist as entities outside of any judging mind.

The first modification of this Platonic realism came when Russell devised a means of avoiding the assumption that numbers subsist as real entities by working out a way of considering them as classes of classes. When classes themselves were seem to be replaceable by propositional functions, and the latter were thought of merely as logical expressions, it was no longer necessary to introduce classes of any kind as entities. Although Russell pointed out that this did not mean that numbers or other classes do not exist, it did make them superfluous in a logical system. In *Problems of Philosophy* Russell still spoke of the awareness of logical truths, but they, along with all analytic propositions, were finally rendered tautologies in Russell's mind by Wittgenstein's analysis. In other words, the scope of the universals or concepts was continually decreasing in Russell's thought, although he still maintained a dualism of universals and particulars as late as 1911. He later moved more in the direction of a modified nominalism. Moore underwent a similar change in his view of universals, although he appears to have shifted more slowly and retained a dualistic approach.

The change in the treatment of value qualities and of sense qualities seems to indicate a less restrained realism with respect to universals. That Russell was to some extent the leader in this change can only be suspected on the grounds that he was the one whose interest in the special techniques of the logistic method took him in this direction.

In treating propositions as entities in themselves Russell and Moore seem to have shared an extreme position with respect to the status of propositions: that they are neither mental nor linguistic nor logical entities but are complexes composed of the constituents of the propositions. This was suggested by Moore's essay on judgment, quoted by Russell, incorporated into *Principles of Mathematics,* and endorsed in Russell's review articles on Meinong. It was even said that true and false propositions differ as do white and red roses.

Moore, in Baldwin's dictionary (1902), offered the following in the course of a definition of *truth:* "If the proposition is to denote, not a belief or a form of words, but an *object* of belief, it seems plain that a truth differs in no respect from the reality to which it was supposed merely to correspond, e.g. the truth that I exist differs in no respect from the corresponding reality — my existence." The definition explicitly rejects a correspondence view, and, accordingly, the editor adds a traditional definition of truth as correspondence. Moore's discussion continues:

> So far, indeed, from truth being defined with reference to reality, reality can only be defined by reference to truth: for truth denotes exactly that property of the complex formed by two entities and their relation, in virtue of which, if the entity predicated be existence, we call the complex real — the property, namely, expressed by saying that the relation in question does truly or really hold between the entities.[51]

In 1910, however, Russell rejected this "exuberant realism," which he had earlier shared, and proposed that beliefs are true or false, and, derivatively, propositions which express beliefs are so, the truth status depending on the fact to which the belief refers.

In his lectures of 1910–11, Moore also made a considerable change in his definition of truth and acknowledged that the view he had formerly held required emendation. He no longer maintained that all sentences refer to propositions which are true or false and which exist. The sentence expresses a proposition (or meaning), and this refers to a fact, if it is true. The proposition does not have being on its own, nor does it have intrinsic truth or falsity. It is possible, he argues, to think and talk of beliefs about things that have no being. If a person believes that Moore is not in London when in fact he is, that belief, that Moore is not in London, is not the name for something.[52]

This shift in Moore's views on the nature of the proposition and the definition of truth was parallel to Russell's, except that Russell was still troubled about what a false belief may be said to refer to, and hence, as we shall see, he developed the "multiple-relation" theory of truth in order to provide such a reference. Moore does not address this issue, but it appears that he shared with Russell some modifications of the original conception of propositions and of truth. As we shall see, Russell's relational theory as developed in "The Monistic Theory of Truth" met with criticism on the part of Wittgenstein, and the eventual result of the latter's infuence was a considerable modification of the opinions that Russell had shared with Moore. Moore himself studied the work of Wittgenstein, but he evinced less of a response to the challenge of his criticisms.

The themes of theory of knowledge seem to show that as time went on the divergence of the two points of view was linked to Russell's greater emphasis on using the techniques of logical analysis. Although Moore was not a mathematician, he retained his interest in Russell's mathematical work; his response to Russell's "On Denoting" was enthusiastic, but he did not imitate it, and when he studied *Our Knowledge of the External World,* he recognized but did not adopt its method, although it might be thought that the method could offer an escape from some of his problems. His response to Wittgenstein seems to have been similar. At the same time, we see a growing insistence on commonsense knowledge. The distance between the position of the two men is apparent in the reviews that each wrote of the other's work in the early 1920s.

Moore wrote a review (1921) of Russell's *The Analysis of Mind* in which he evaluated the scope of the book as the attempt to apply to this subject the kind of analysis Russell had earlier applied to the objective world in *Our Knowledge of the External World.* Moore is skeptical of Russell's having removed the act and the subject from the analysis of experience; he wonders

if he has considered all arguments in their favor. But Moore acknowledges
that failing to find these in experience is a reason to abandon them. He is
puzzled by and critical of Russell's new treatment of universals. Instead of a
dualism of universal and particular in which a universal relation binds
particulars, Russell's new view makes such relations particulars binding
particulars.

In response to this review Russell wrote to its author to say that his own
way of treating universals in his account of the meaning of general words was
in response to Wittgenstein's interpretation of the theory of types, to the
effect that universals could not be related to particulars. Wittgenstein had
persuaded him, he said, that the apparent difficulties of this position were
not "insuperable."[53] It seemed that Russell had moved away from the ideas
that he and Moore had shared, and that Moore was not aware of how he had
changed his views or why. Neither Russell's book nor his letter offers a clear
explanation.

The following year Russell reviewed Moore's *Philosophical Studies,*
praising the care and thoroughness of his analysis and pointing out that his
concern is to "uphold common sense" in the face of great difficulties in doing
so; he praises Moore's cautious acknowledgment of all the problems in
passing from what is immediately given in sense to the physical object, such
as the inkstand, from which the analysis starts. In a critical conclusion to the
article, Russell reprimands Moore for not taking sufficient account of
physics. "Physics represents the best that can be done for common sense by
careful observation and reasoning, it represents, therefore, what a common
sense philosopher ought to try to vindicate as against sceptics and idealists."
Moore, of course, does not use physics in his analysis of commonsense
knowledge and hence earns Russell's comment: "Mr. Moore's method tends
to become somewhat verbal and dry for lack of material which science could
supply and for the same reason his valuable gift of precision tends to become
unduly linguistic." Of course, it is the linguistic and commonsense themes in
Moore that have been most appreciated by current philosophers, but, for
Russell, common experience and common language cannot prevail over
science.[54]

It is interesting that in their original revolt against idealism both men were
asserting common sense in the face of a philosophy which, as they thought,
sacrificed common sense to theoretical consistency and metaphysical assumptions. But the role played by common sense turned out to be significantly different in their own philosophies. For Moore, there may be a
philosophical problem involved if I hold up my hand in front of my face and I
ask what connection there is between the visual sense-datum of the hand and

the physical object. But no philosophical argument can persuade him that there is not a hand there. It is incontrovertibly true that there just *is* a hand there; nothing can be more certain than that. For Russell, however, the problem of the connection between the sense-datum of a hand and the actual hand is to be solved by the application of logical techniques of restatement and by an analysis of the causal process by which light is reflected from the object, reaches the retina, and so forth. If his logical techniques and his scientific knowledge require him to maintain a position which appears noncommonsensical, then he is prepared to do that. (After all, it does not seem to common sense that the hand is a large cluster of molecules in motion.)

In his volume *Philosophical Papers,* published in 1959, the year following his death, G. E. Moore had collected a number of his essays written between 1923 and 1944. These, as we have seen, lie beyond the period in which he and Russell had much significant personal contact. Yet two of the papers in the collection are directed at Russell's ideas, and several other papers make references to his work. "Russell's Theory of Descriptions," originally published as a contribution to the Library of Living Philosophers volume on Russell, is a detailed, meticulous analysis of one of Russell's statements of this classic theory. Moore concludes that in spite of various inaccuracies and ambiguities in the presentation, it does successfully analyze a large class of propositions employing certain kinds of phrases and justifies F. P. Ramsey's praise of it as a "paradigm" of philosophical analysis. In his response to Moore in the reply at the end of the volume, Russell acknowledges that his ordinary language was ambiguous and sloppy (a reason to prefer the symbolism of logic), and that there are occasions on which "the" is used when it does not fit his pattern of definite descriptions. He does not address all of Moore's objections, such as the one to "material implication" or the confusion of "sentence" and "proposition," both of which have been said to infect his logical as well as his commonsense language.[55]

3.4 On Skepticism

Moore's references to Russell in other essays in *Philosophical Papers* include his objection to the latter's account of "existence" in the context of a propositional function rather than of a proposition. He holds, against Russell, that statements of existence are significant in the context of the relation of sense-data to a thing. In his account of Wittgenstein's lectures in 1930–33, Moore several times refers to Russell in correcting what he believes to be Wittgenstein's misinterpretation of what Russell had argued.[56]

Most of the comments made concerning Russell in this volume reflect a close study of his texts and a need on Moore's part to "answer Russell" where their views diverge. This especially is true of Moore's discussion of skepticism.

The sense in which the philosophy of common sense is critical of Russell is clear in an essay of Moore's of the 1940s, "Four Forms of Scepticism," included in *Philosophical Papers*.[57] Using passages from *The Analysis of Matter* and *An Outline of Philosophy,* in which Russell raises questions critical of commonsense assumptions, he classifies four kinds of skepticism set forth by Russell: with regard to one's knowledge of one's self; with regard to knowledge derived from one's own memory; with regard to the existence of other people like oneself; and, finally, with regard to the existence of external objects. Moore finds Russell's arguments inadequate to support a complete skepticism and concludes that Russell's doubts rest upon four assumptions: that the things doubted are not known immediately; that they do not follow logically from anything known immediately; that, if the first two assumptions are true, then the supposed knowledge is based on an analogical or inductive argument; and, lastly, that anything so based cannot be certain. Moore concludes:

> What I can't help asking myself is this: Is it, in fact, as certain that all these four assumptions are true, as that I *do* know that this is a pencil and that you are conscious? I cannot help answering: It seems to me *more* certain that I *do* know that this is a pencil and that you are conscious, than that any single one of these four assumptions is true, let alone all four. That is to say, though, as I have said, I agree with Russell that (1), (2), (3) *are* true; yet of no one even of these three do I feel *as* certain as that I do know for certain that this is a pencil. Nay more; I do not think it is *rational* to be as certain of any one of these four propositions, as of the proposition that I do know that this is a pencil. And how on earth is it to be decided which of the two things it is *rational* to be most certain of?[58]

3.5 Summation of Issues

The passage on skepticism reflects a good deal that is common in the two philosophers as well as a vital point of difference. Both were empiricists and realists; both practiced a method of meticulous analysis. In these respects they appreciated each other and tried to improve each other; Moore, in two articles, an early one on internal and external relations and a 1940 article on Russell's theory of descriptions, attempted to qualify and correct Russell's accounts. But for Russell logic was the proper vehicle of precise analysis and science, both physics and psychology, and linguistic dissection were tools of philosophical inquiry, while for Moore the patient description of what could and could not be found in experience and of what could be inferred from it, or said of it, had to take commonsense beliefs as a touchstone.

In his contribution to a memorial symposium on G. E. Moore published in *The Listener,* Russell praised his lifelong passionate pursuit of truth, his candor and simplicity, and attributed to him the accomplishment of turning British philosophy back to the kind of analysis at which it had excelled before the advent of idealism. His criticism of Moore's philosophy is that it had sought literary precision, but was ignorant of and oblivious to what science had to offer.[59] This seems a just appraisal: Moore excelled in saying precisely in ordinary language what he wished to say, and in clarifying philosophical questions in terms of various specific statements in ordinary language to which they might be equivalent. This has been a very influential technique in philosophy since his time, although he himself did not regard philosophy as being about language but about the world. For Russell, not common sense alone, but common sense enlightened by science provides the data for philosophy; for him ordinary language is but a substitute for the only precise formulation of philosophical questions, that of logic. Thus Russell was often imprecise both in expressing his own thoughts in ordinary language and in representing the views of others in such language. But he succeeded in using ordinary language to stimulate philosophers to seek the scientific construction of philosophy through precise symbols and the use of science, a search that has also left its mark on the philosophy of this century.

In these respects we shall see the contrast in Russell's philosophizing between the influence of Moore and that of logicians such as Frege and Whitehead.

4

Russell, Frege, and Meinong Before 1905

O NE HUNDRED YEARS AFTER Gottlob Frege and Alexius Meinong began their work and more than seventy-five years after Bertrand Russell published his famous essay "On Denoting" (1905), in which he favorably contrasted his own theory of descriptions with their theories, the issues involved are still the subject of frequent and lively debates in professional journals. The vitality of the contemporary discussion shows the extent to which the arguments raised at the turn of the century have remained relevant to current philosophical interests. The multiple conflicting interpretations of each philosopher and of the meaning and merits of their cross-criticisms indicate that no final assessment of their positions is yet possible.

One aspect of the discussion has tended to be less emphasized, however, and that is the full range of the exchanges between Russell and Frege and between Russell and Meinong. Now that more of the historical material is accessible, it is possible to arrive at a more balanced view of the issues in the context of the position each man held.[1] When some of the mysteries and misunderstandings are thus cleared away, the place of the philosophical interactions between Russell and Meinong and between Russell and Frege in the development of Russell's thought during those years becomes clearer. It is also possible to have a better view of the emergence of the themes of analytic philosophy, themes still of importance in the late decades of the twentieth century, although the passage of time has led us to see them somewhat differently.

The organization of this chapter and the next will be as follows: the introduction will review current issues to which the work of the three philosophers has been found relevant and will place Russell's interactions with Meinong and Frege in the context of his ideas at the turn of the century; the second section will deal with the interactions between Russell and Frege prior to 1905 (Russell's "On Denoting"); the third section will deal with interactions between Russell and Meinong during the same period. In chapter 5 a first section will discuss "On Denoting" in terms of Russell's criticisms of his two correspondents; a second section will describe later interactions between Russell and each of them. The interactions of both Meinong and Frege with Russell were quite different from those between Russell and other philosophers such as G. E. Moore, A. N. Whitehead, and Ludwig Wittgenstein, with whom Russell had close, intimate, and continued contact; they were also different from his interactions with Bradley or the pragmatists, where it was not so much a matter of close friendship as of long familiarity with their work, ideas, and traditions. Evidently Meinong and Russell never met; their interactions took place in published books, articles, and reviews, and in a correspondence on the issues discussed in the publications.[2] In the case of Frege, too, there seems to have been no meeting, but in addition to the well-known appendixes in which each man discussed the work of the other and the essay "On Denoting," their exchanges took place in a substantial correspondence.[3] The exchanges with Meinong can be dated between 1897, with the publication of the first work of Meinong reviewed by Russell, and 1921, the date of the publication of *The Analysis of Mind,* the last work in which Russell undertook a serious discussion of Meinong. Russell's interchanges with Frege began with Russell's letter of 1902 and continued until 1912, although for the most part they took place in the first two years of this period.

4.1 Current Issues

One of the chief contexts in which Russell's interpretations and arguments concerning Frege and Meinong have become current is that of the theory of reference. As questions of meaning have dominated discussion in Anglo-American philosophy in the twentieth century, the problem of how words and sentences refer and the problem of what assumptions are made in one's analysis of language have been of particular importance. When these topics are discussed, for instance, by Leonard Linsky in his *Referring* (1967),[4] it is obligatory to include Russell, Meinong, and Frege and their criticisms, cross-criticisms, and alternative views as a background. Frege's famous distinction between sense and reference, Meinong's position regarding objects of reference, and Russell's theory of descriptions in its semantic aspect are all part of the necessary background for the current discussion of how words and sentences "mean," to what they "refer," how meanings and references are related, and what kind of analysis can be given when a lack of reference or a denial of meaning is involved. Critics have taken positions as widely varied as these: that Russell's inability to distinguish between *use* and *mention* made his criticism of Frege otiose;[5] that his intransigent bivalence with respect to propositions obscured the common sense of Meinong's position with respect to fictitious and impossible objects;[6] that Russell exposed an important weakness in Frege's view of *sense;*[7] and that Russell made clear the bizarre consequences of Meinong's "'Fido'-Fido" theory of reference, although unfortunately without noticing the dangers of his own adherence to a less extreme version of that same theory of meaning.[8] Although the intervening years between 1905 and the 1980's have seen many important clarifications and systematizations of semantics, agreement is not within sight, and the arguments of Frege, Meinong, and Russell are still relevant.

A second and related philosophical problem may be termed that of "ontology." What reals, existents, entities, or beings are we committed to by our logic, our theory of meaning, or our theory of knowledge? This has become a lively issue among writers following in both the Russellian and the logical empiricist traditions. Some have basically seen the problem as one determined by the consequences of a formal system; this group includes Rudolf Carnap, W. V. Quine, and Nelson Goodman.[9] Others have found the epistemological and linguistic aspects of philosophical analysis to raise questions in terms of a view of reality—whether, that is, reality consists of events, entities, or quality instantiations; this group would include Gustav Bergmann and Reinhardt Grossman.[10] Whether the philosopher is drawing out the implications of "to be is to be the value of a variable" or working out the way an action sentence can be construed in terms of event-descriptions,[11] the common ancestor of these philosophical concerns seems to lie in the issues of what has being, subsists, exists, is an object, or must be denied the status represented by this terminology. These issues are important ones among the three philosophers under discussion, although their origin is much further back in time.

A third area of current philosophical concern which touches issues going back at least to our protagonists is that of a choice between a two-valued extensional logic, such as the work of both Frege and Russell embodied, and an alternative logic, which might be one of several kinds: intensional, modal, multivalued (or "deviant" as this may be pejoratively termed). Meinong's work may be considered suitable for a logic which takes account of "possible," "impossible," and "necessary" as classifications of propositions and objects. The discussion of "possible world semantics" connects the choice of a logical system with the analysis of reference just mentioned. In a recent volume on Meinong, Jaako Hintikka and Karel Lambert raise such questions.[12] Recent work by Terence Parsons and R. and V. Routley refers to the writing of Meinong as a precedent for the kind of analysis of possible and impossible objects in which they are interested.[13] It has been pointed out that an implicit assumption of Russell's prevented his seeing any validity in Meinong's "non-existent existences" and in his protesting that they led to violations of the laws of noncontradiction and excluded middle. This assumption was that all propositions must be within the scope of a two-valued and extensional logic.[14] It was an issue not only between Meinong and Russell in the old days but also between Strawson and Russell in more recent times.[15]

A different kind of current inquiry seeks to describe and evaluate both major and minor philosophers of the past and to trace their influence on the development of the ideas which are part of our heritage. The untangling of historical strands of thought has become important to the current interpretations of the work of Frege and Meinong. Should we look at Frege as influenced by Kantianism and thus, although he was opposed to the psychologizing of logic, an objective idealist by virtue of conceding a status of a priori truth to logical laws?[16] Should we trace the origins of his thought to Bernard Bolzano or to his contact with Edmund Husserl[17] or to both? How close is Meinong's connection with Franz Brentano, and is his realism closely parallel to Husserl's phenomenology?[18] Current historical studies raise questions of the background, the influence, and the allegiance of these philosophers; the fact that the studies sometimes result in widely different interpretations and heated debates reflects the current importance of the ideas. The conducting of such historico-philosophic studies marks a maturity of method that can ask not only what method means to us today, but also what it means to the philosopher in question, and what this history contributes to our understanding.

This historical retrospective on the philosophers of our recent past has returned attention to a major and recently ignored issue in twentieth-century philosophy—that revolving around epistemological realism. The relation between the knowing subject and the object known; the degree to which maintaining the object of knowledge to be real commits one to a direct (naive) or representative realism; the kind or kinds of objects that must be categorized in such a realist epistemology—all these matters are being looked at again in a perspective different from the one dominating philosophical discussion between 1910 and 1940. The interest in such problems is partly intellectual and historical, reconstructing our own philosophical history, and partly a temperamental revulsion against an overly technical or overly linguistic approach, in the interests of what might be called "a refined common sense."[19]

4.2 Historical Context

In order to understand the puzzling aspects of the attitude Russell took and
the criticisms that he made of both Meinong and Frege during the period
prior to 1905, it is necessary to put ourselves back into the position which he
held and the problems with which he dealt from 1899 through 1904. As we
have seen in the preceding chapter, during the 1890s, with G. E. Moore
leading the way, Russell emerged from idealism. But this emergence was into
a strange position: the rejection of Kantianism centered on insisting that
what one knows or judges about has its reality and is what it is regardless of
its relation to the knower. Hence a judgment must be analyzed into a subject
about which something is judged (and this subject, whatever it is, has its
being independent of the maker of the judgment) and a predicate that is
related by the judgment to the subject. The predicate, too, has its own reality,
as a concept that is what it is regardless of its being related in a judgment to
the subject. Russell expresses this position in the statement from the
beginning of *The Principles of Mathematics:*

> Whatever may be an object of thought, or may occur in any true or
> false proposition, or can be counted as *one,* I call a *term.* This, then, is
> the widest word in the philosophical vocabulary. I shall use it as
> synonymous with the words unit, individual, and entity. The first two
> emphasize the fact that every term is *one,* while the third is derived from
> the fact that every term has being, *i.e. is* in some sense. A man, a
> moment, a number, a class, a relation, a chimaera, or anything else that
> can be mentioned, is sure to be a term; and to deny that such and such a
> thing is a term must always be false. [20]

Russell goes on to quote G. E. Moore "On the Nature of Judgment," and
following him distinguishes two kinds of terms: things and concepts. He
connects the first with an expanded sense of proper name, and the second
with predicate or relation. In many propositions, such as that expressed by
The table is brown, the subject term is an individual existent physical object
and the predicate is a concept—brownness. The former would be said to
exist, the latter to *subsist.* This Platonic translation of Kant formed the
philosophical foundation of the logical and mathematical inquiry that was the
chief concern of *The Principles of Mathematics;* the dualism of sub-
ject/object, physical/mental, existent/subsistent created a set of problems
for Russell in both the technical and philosophical aspects of the work.
Russell was fully aware of the problems, and they form the background
against which, at this time, he studied the work of Meinong and Frege.

Just as the word *term* is not used as a name for an entity but for an entity
itself (as explained in the quotation above), a related unfamiliar meaning is

given to the word *proposition* by Russell. It stands for what is neither a linquistic nor a mental entity; it is expressed by a sentence, but Russell seems to regard the linguistic form of the sentence as a kind of transparent medium transmitting the proposition and its constituents by means of words. One is accustomed to thinking of the proposition as asserting some relation among its terms, and of the terms as referring to whatever they are terms for. But for Russell, at this time, the *terms* are the entities, and the proposition consists in the complex of those terms. If one utters the sentence *Brown is ill,* for instance, the proposition consists of Brown, the man whose name is spelled B - r - o - w - n, and the concept of being ill. This extreme realism allows Russell, on the one hand, the advantage of escape from the psychologizing of logic that robs logic and mathematics of their proper objectivity, and endows the propositions of logic and mathematics with their own status, independent of what experience or thought might provide. On the other hand, the very status of terms as entities and the reality of propositions created both philosophical and technical problems. It is immediately obvious, to take some examples, that the status of a false proposition, or of a negative existential proposition, or of a proposition in which fictitious entities occur, will pose difficulties for Russell's position. We shall find as well that there are many kinds of terms and sentences that seem not to fit his analysis: when one refers to *a man,* as in *I met a man,* which man is not indicated; how then can such a phrase refer to a specific man who would be the constituent of the proposition? Furthermore, the construction of definitions of number in the hands of Peano and of Frege requires a distinction between the class and the individual which is or is not a member of the class, and, in the case of the null class and the unit class, this seems essential. But how can this be compatible with a theory that considers a class a collection of individual entities?[21] These were some of the problems that came to the surface in the exchanges that Russell had with Meinong and with Frege.

Russell had been led to write *The Principles of Mathematics* by the intersection of two influences suggesting solutions to a long-term problem of his, that of providing an adequate philosophical basis for mathematics. The philosophical impetus came from Moore, as Russell tells us in the preface to the first edition, with the realism that promised an objective and non-psychologistic framework of philosophy. Russell had already tried both Kantian and Hegelian idealism without success; he was not attracted by the formalist view that cut away all objective foundations by regarding mathematics as symbols and the rules for symbols. Nor did the intuitionism that saw the foundation of mathematics in the manipulation of number and form derived from experience appear adequate to Russell. In fact, during this period Russell was opposed to empiricism in philosophy in general, as well as in philosophy of mathematics.[22]

In all the accounts given of his work in mathematical logic, Russell has recorded his debt to contemporary mathematicians such as Georg Cantor and Richard Dedekind and to pioneers such as George Boole, but he dates his attempts at founding mathematics on logic and thus the second influence on *The Principles of Mathematics* from his attendance at an international congress of mathematics in Paris during the summer of 1900. There he met Giuseppe Peano and his colleagues, heard their papers, and was impressed by their precision and the simplicity of their symbolism. He studied their work and, during the next six months, mastered Peano's symbolism and its use, then went on to work out his own contribution to the logic of relations. This "intellectual honeymoon" ended in his encounter with the contradiction of classes that are not members of themselves. As was pointed out earlier, Russell was to spend the next decade trying to solve the contradiction and the other problems that he and Whitehead encountered in working out the system of *Principia Mathematica*.[23]

The Principles of Mathematics bears witness on almost every page to the impress of Peano; generous attributions and footnotes to Peano's work, his articles, and the *Formulaire de Mathématique* abound. But there are also indications of dissatisfaction with Peano and acknowledgments that had Russell known of Frege's work he would have incurred an even larger debt to Frege than to Peano.[24] Russell offers, as an instance of Peano's contributions to his thinking, first and foremost the idea of reducing mathematics to logic by developing a system in which the primitive, undefined notions are nonmathematical (the logical ideas of implication, disjunction, and negation) and in which the way was shown to derive the deductive system of mathematics from these undefined logical primitives. The symbolism developed by Peano was particularly helpful, in contrast to what Russell regarded as the overly arithmetical attempts of Boole to derive logic from mathematics, and in contrast to the abstruseness of Frege's symbolism. Peano's primitive propositions, expressed in the new symbolism, made possible the rigorous derivation of number and a number system (although Russell saw room for improvement in this derivation). Russell credits Peano with the invention of the propositional calculus and the class calculus, the twin foundations upon which Russell himself built the calculus of relations. (Before *The Principles of Mathematics* was published, Russell discovered that Frege had anticipated his own work and that of Peano, hence the attribution had to be changed.) He also credits Peano with the adaptation to logic of the mathematical notions of functions and variables (again Frege had anticipated this), and with the distinction between real and apparent variables (now called unbound and bound variables). The variables also led Peano to distinguish propositions from propositional functions, the latter containing terms such as *x*, which serve as place-markers, similar to such words as *something* and *someone*. These propositional functions become propositions when the variable is replaced by a determinate term. The proposition then can be judged true or false. (This idea was also present in Frege's work, as we shall see.) If we say *x is mortal*, this is a propositional function in which *x* stands for any value that may be placed there. If we replace the *x* with *Bertrand Russell*, the propositional function becomes the proposition *Bertrand Russell is mortal* and can be said to be true. If we replace the *x* with *Mount Everest*, the proposition which results, *Mount Everest is mortal*, is false. In this case the variable is unbound and is called a real variable; if the proposition were *for any x, if x is human, x is mortal* the variable is said to be bound by the quantifier (the symbol that tells us it holds for any *x*, expressed in the Peano-Russell symbolism as (*x*)), and can be said to be true for any value of *x*. In similar fashion, symbols may express the meanings that in ordinary English are expressed with *some, all*, or *none*. For instance, if we say *Some Greeks are philosophers*, the symbolism of Peano showed how this could be expressed by saying that there is at least one value of the variable *x* for which it is true that Greeks are philosophers.

In spite of Russell's indebtedness to Peano, there are several points on which he is critical of him. Russell finds that Peano did not need all the primitive propositions of his system, but could derive some of them from others. For Russell, the minimal number of primitive propositions was a desideratum, although he did not overtly express the methodological rule of Ockham's razor, which later he was to stress. In general, he found a lack of rigor in the selection of the minimum of indefinables and in the derivations from primitive notions. For instance, in the definition of the number system there is no indication for the system necessarily to be the one we have beginning with 0 and proceeding with 1, 2, 3 . . . ; any system, such as 100, 101, 102 . . . , within which the numbers bore appropriate relations to one another would satisfy his definitions. Russell found this defective. He suggested that instead of the three kinds of definition offered by Peano, only one kind is needed, nominal definitions — that is, definitions of names rather than of things. On the subject of classes, Russell had many problems with Peano's treatment, which, although adequate for the needs of the deductive system, lacked, in Russell's view, a philosophical basis. These misgivings concerning classes were entertained by Russell against Frege's treatment of classes as well, and will be discussed presently.

At any rate, whatever their logical or philosophical shortcomings, the contributions of Peano had provided the technical impetus for Russell's work in mathematical logic. Before he completed the writing of his book, however, two major discoveries put that project in a totally different light: one was his recognition of the aforementioned contradiction of classes that are not members of themselves, the other was his reading and understanding of the importance of the publications of Frege.[25]

4.3 Russell and Frege to 1905

Russell reported that, although he had possessed a copy of Frege's *Begriffschrift* for some years, he did not master the symbolism or work through Frege's system until he made an intensive study of the first volume of *Grundgesetze der Arithmetik* (The Basic Laws of Arithmetic) during 1902. According to Russell's letter to Frege dated June 6 of that year, he had known of the latter book for six months and was currently studying it. In this letter he also asks for reprints of Frege's other work. When Russell wrote this letter to Frege, *The Principles of Mathematics* was already complete, so he made acknowledgment to Frege in the appendix. Russell's purpose in writing the letter was to apprise Frege that he had discovered a contradiction regarding the class that is not a member of itself. Frege's letter in response (dated June 22, 1902) acknowledged the serious repercussions of the contradiction on his system, especially on his Axiom V, and reported that, as his own second volume of the *Grundgesetze* had already gone to press, he would discuss the effect of the contradiction in an appendix to that work.[26]

The exchange of views in the respective appendixes and in their correspondence reflects Russell's and Frege's different philosophical and logical standpoints not only with respect to the contradiction, but on a number of other issues, and provides a background against which Russell's brief and disputed criticism of Frege's view of reference in his essay "On Denoting" can be better understood.

In appendix A to *The Principles of Mathematics,* Russell gives an overview of Frege's general philosophic position and the points in his logicist program in which Russell sees room for differences or for problems of interpretation. For the most part the expository portion is a straightforward account of Frege's essays "Sinn und Bedeutung" (Sense and Reference), "Begriff und Gegenstand" (Concept and Object), and the first volume of *Grundgesetze der Arithmetik.* There are points, indeed, where Russell has difficulty understanding Frege and in placing his writing into the context of Russell's own framework of ideas. Where Russell is clear (or believes that he is) on points developed by Frege that bear on the logicist program—for instance, on the interpretation of classes—Russell tends to change his mind under Frege's influence, renouncing some of his own arguments in the body of the book. So, if Frege finds the contradiction presented by Russell to be a serious problem for his own work, Russell, for his part, was willing to make important emendations of his own positions, on the strength of Frege's arguments. There are, however, a number of points on which no decision was reached and Russell seemed to be vacillating between a position already arrived at and new ideas presented by Frege. This is true, for instance, in the case of the proposed solutions to the contradiction, on which Russell's final word in appendix A is that some solution similar to Frege's will probably be found to be satisfactory, but in appendix B, a different solution based on a tentative early sketch of the theory of types is put forward.[27]

The first point discussed by Russell in his presentation of Frege's ideas in appendix A of *The Principles of Mathematics* is the distinction of *Sinn* and *Bedeutung;* today this is usually translated by *sense* and *reference,* but Russell used *meaning* and *indication* as the usual equivalents of the German words. According to Frege, writes Russell, terms and predicates, propositions and assumptions, all have this dual aspect of meaning. When a word is used as a subject term, it may be said to *express* its meaning, or sense (which might be said to be what we understand to be the meaning of the word apart from a specific context). At the same time, in a given context, it also refers, or indicates, or designates, some object for which it stands, as a name stands for the individual for whom it is a name. When a word is used as a predicate term it has both a sense and a referent; in this case the sense is what we might call the intension; the referent is what we might call the concept designated. If one says *This sugar lump is a cube,* the phrase *this sugar lump* refers to the object in question, while *is a cube* refers to the concept designated. So far, Russell is inclined to agree with Frege's distinction and to find that it might be used to solve some problems that he has run into with what he calls "denoting concepts." For Russell, a problem has arisen because, given his own referential view of the connection between subject phrases and the terms for which they are names, and that between predicate phrases and the concepts for which they are names, it is difficult to apply that analysis to such phrases as *a man* in *John met a man,* since the phrase names neither a specific determinate man, nor the concept *man* as in *John is a man.* He holds that such phrases refer to "denoting concepts." In such a proposition, the concept expressed in *a man* denotes some man, the one John met, and the person is not himself a constituent of the proposition but is only referred to by the "denoting concept" expressed in *a man.* The denoting concept is the not himself a constituent of the proposition but is only referred to by the "denoting concept" expressed in *a man*. The denoting concept is the constituent of the proposition in that case. Remembering that, for Russell, the proposition is not a verbal entity but a complex in which the entities designated by the words of the corresponding sentence are themselves constituents, we can see how Frege's conception of *Sinn* and *Bedeutung* might fit with Russell's view, although Frege himself did not share the view of the proposition held by Russell.[28]

Russell also sees advantages to the distinction of sense and reference in the case of statements of identity; as explained by Frege, a statement of identity might be seen simply as asserting the identity of one name with another, in which case the *referent* of one name is equated with the *referent* of another name, as *"Hesperus* means *Lucifer."* Or the identity-statement might reveal the identity of the *sense* of two phrases, as "The morning star is the same as the evening star." The distinction thus shows why statements of identity are often not trivial but informative; replacing one name with another does not change the truth-value of the proposition, but identifying a name with a phrase expressing the sense of a word might be informative—that is, it might have a different sense but the same truth-value. Russell thinks this analysis might apply to phrases beginning with *the,* namely, *the so-and-so,* and recommends it to Meinong for cases in which the phrase might lack a referent, such as *the golden mountain.*[29]

But Russell raises a number of problems with this analysis, which appear in the correspondence, the appendix, and later in "On Denoting." With respect to proper names, Russell does not see how a proper name could have a sense which would be a meaning other than as a name for its referent. It seems to him obvious that the name-referent relation exhausts any meaning that a name-symbol could have; this also means that Frege's analysis would be of no help in dispelling the difficulty of what a fictitious name, such as *Pegasus,* stands for.[30]

Russell also expresses puzzlement over what Frege means by saying that a proposition has both sense and meaning, and that the sense was the *Gedanke* and the referent the truth-value of the proposition. In the first place, he is troubled about what he perceives to be the psychologistic nature of the *Gedanke*—what could this be other than what one happens to think about when one entertains the proposition?[31] It seems obvious, Frege responds, that when one speaks of the meaning of a proposition it must be some objective thought-object: When one asserts the proposition *Mont Blanc is 4000 meters high,* surely the mountain with its snowfields could not itself be a constituent of the proposition?[32] But for Russell that is what he means by a proposition. This difference comes out clearly in the correspondence, and it appears that it could not be resolved. Further, Russell asks, how could Frege say that a proposition refers to the True if it is true, to the False if it is false? That would mean that all true propositions have the same reference, and all false ones the same as well. That is what it did mean, but Frege tries to show the necessity of his position; although the meanings of the proposition, that is, their senses, are different, yet since each true proposition could substitute for every other true proposition without change of truth-value, one must think of them as identical in this way. And what else is there for propositions to refer to?[33]

Another puzzle related to the sense-reference distinction has to do with Frege's treatment of meanings in indirect contexts. One of the advantages of his analysis, Frege points out, is that he is able to distinguish the meanings involved in direct contexts, such as *The earth revolves around the sun,* and in indirect contexts, such as *Copernicus believed that the earth revolves around the sun.* In the first case the sense of the proposition is expressed, that is, the thought having to do with the earth's revolving around the sun; in the second case, the thought of the earth's revolving around the sun is designated rather than expressed. As the name *Copernicus* refers to a man, the phrase *that the earth revolves around the sun* refers to the thought. It is possible for propositions to have sense and not reference; Frege says this is the case with legend and poetry. But where we are concerned with truth, this meaning (reference) is the True or the False. For Russell, a different concept of a proposition, and a bias in favor of meaning on the model of naming, makes it difficult to understand or accept Frege's view, in spite of some logical advantages which it seemed to offer. For Frege, on the other hand, Russell is unclear on what he means by a proposition; Russell's use is that of the mathematician, his own use that of the logician. The differences concerning the nature of a proposition—whether we think of it, with Frege, in terms of the sentence as a linguistic expression of a thought that refers to either the True or the False, or, with Russell, as a complex of constituents which are the referents of the names in the linguistic form of the sentence—these differences are important for their supporting arguments. For Frege, Russell often neglects to distinguish between the sign and the thing signified, confusing what is talked about or referred to with the thought and the expression of the thought. For Russell, Frege's theory of meaning is often unduly linguistic and psychological and has its arbitrary aspects.[34]

The use of the mathematical notion of function and accompanying variable is a device used by Peano and Russell, but in Frege this concept has a wider application and a special interpretation.[35] The mathematical model is used by him to explain what is meant by *function, argument, variable,* and *value:* if one considers the following mathematical expressions, $2^2 + 2$, $3^2 + 3$, and $4^2 + 4$, it is apparent that there is something that does not vary in the expressions, and something that does vary. Let the stable part be represented as it appears and the varying part be represented by empty parentheses, then the expressions appear as $(\ )^2 + (\ )$, and this representation is common to all three expressions. We may then refer to the stable part of each of these expressions as its *function;* the various numbers may be called *arguments* of the function, that is, *2, 3,* and *4.* In mathematics (and in mathematical logic) it is customary to represent the empty spaces enclosed in brackets by a small letter from the end of the alphabet, and this is called a *variable,* so that the expression in question would be written $x^2 + x$. We may also speak of the *value* of the function; in the examples given the values would be *6, 12,* and *20,* respectively. It is possible also to have functions with more than one argument-place, as in $x^2 + y$, in which case the x place would take one argument, the y place another. There is no restriction on the number of variables possible in a mathematical expression. Frege took this notion of function, argument, value, and variable and applied it in a general way and in all contexts, not merely in mathematical ones. Hence, in analyzing any phrase, it is possible to use these terms; for example, *George V, King of England* can be analyzed as the function *king,* the argument *of England,* and the value *George V.* We could think of *king* as a function which might be satisfied by any number of arguments. *Cain is the brother of Abel* can be looked on as the function of *brother of* a relation holding between two arguments *Cain* and *Abel.* This might be represented in a number of ways, *Cain is the brother of X, Y is the brother of Abel,* or *Y is the brother of X.*

In passing from phrases to propositions there are several important points to be noticed: Frege points out that the subject-predicate analysis of propositions can be replaced by a function-argument analysis in which the traditional subject becomes the argument and the traditional predicate becomes the function. We must see the roles of these two parts of the proposition very differently he says: the argument refers to something that is the subject concerning which the proposition makes a statement; it is thus an object referred to and can be thought of as standing alone and able to be thought of, or referred to, outside of the proposition; the function, however, cannot stand alone, as its open parts, signified by the variable, reveal it to be incomplete or "unsaturated" *(ungesättigt).* In fact it is because of the open or unsaturated aspect of the function that the proposition can form a unity necessary to its making some statement. What the function refers to is a concept, and the argument completing the function is essentially the statement of an object falling under a concept. Hence when we say *Socrates is human,* we are saying that the object *Socrates* falls under the concept *human.* The concept may be predicative, as in the case of *human,* or relational, as in the case of *Cain is the brother of Abel.* The examples given are of objects falling under first-level concepts, but it is also possible for there to be first-level concepts falling under second-level concepts, as when we speak of *humanity* as falling under the concept *mortality.* On *any* level there may be one or more than one variable. In treating nonmathematical functions, we may speak of the value of the function as its truth or falsity for a given argument or range of arguments. This allows Frege to equate the extension of a function with what Peano calls a *class* or Russell calls both *class-concept* and *class.* Thus, the extension of a class, which Russell thought of as being made up of individual objects taken collectively, is picked out by the function for which the individuals can be arguments for the value *true.* This enables one to speak of a null class as a function for which *no* argument yields the value *true,* the unit class as one for which only one argument yields that value.

The terminology of *Gegenstand* (object), which is the referent of the subject-term of the proposition and thought of as an argument for a function, and of *Begriff* (the concept), the referent of the predicate term of the proposition, thought of as the function, had obvious attractions for Russell. It fit in with the realism of *The Principles of Mathematics,* which had already identified the subject phrase as referring to an object with being, and the predicate phrase as referring to a concept that subsisted. Important differences emerged, however, in the way in which Frege and Russell employed the distinction of *Gegenstand* and *Begriff* and in the limitations put upon the function-argument form.[36] Frege insisted that it was never possible for a concept to take the subject place in a proposition; his reasons were, first, that the unsaturated or incomplete nature of the function means that it cannot be an object (for self-subsistence is the defining character of an object), and, second, that when a concept appears in the subject-place, as in the example *'Humanity' falls under the concept of mortality,* there is a difference of level; we are speaking of a first-level concept falling under a second-level concept, and this must not be confused with an object falling under a first-level concept. Frege avoids this by placing the concept, word, or phrase in inverted commas (what would be called semiotic quotation marks today) to indicate that it is the *name* of the concept, rather than the concept itself, which is the subject of the proposition, and thus the object referred to. Hence *Humanity falls under the concept of mortality* protects us against the violation of the level-distinction and the temptation to think of the concept as an object. Russell, in *The Principles of Mathematics,* had realized that there were restrictions on the possibility of placing the concept name in the subject position, but he had found that it is sometimes possible, and hence he did not accept Frege's restriction. He was especially opposed to the device of placing the concept-name in inverted commas, because he thought that a merely linguistic reality was then referred to—that is, the name of the concept rather than the concept itself, and this was unacceptable according to the argument of the appendix of *The Principles of Mathematics*.[37] Moreover, in his logical scheme, he used concept symbols by themselves without variables or arguments, and to this practice Frege strongly objected. Thus in the correspondence a serious difference in the interpretation of functions emerges; the unsaturatedness of concepts for Frege makes it impossible to use them according to Russell's practice, while for Russell Frege's restrictions did not make sense.[38] These issues were also connected with the discussion of classes, which will be treated presently. It is interesting that, in correspondence with Philip Jourdain concerning *Principia Mathematica,* Frege in 1912 is still objecting to Russell's free use of functions in the argument of that work. For recent interpreters of Frege, the use of inverted commas in expressing functions as subjects of propositions has been a problem and has led to adding to the roster of entities required by Frege's system "function-correlates"; these are whatever is referred to by the function expression enclosed in inverted commas.[39] The issue is revived again by Russell in "On Denoting," as we shall see.

It seems that another difficulty of interpretation arose over Russell's tendency to construe Frege's assertion-sign (⊢) in such a way as to equate the difference between Frege's proposition accompanied with an assertion-sign with his own *proposition* and with Meinong's judgment, and Frege's proposition *not* accompanied by an assertion-sign with his own *unasserted proposition* and Meinong's *Annahme.* This interpretation would have been pleasing and corroborative for Russell, as it fits his idea that there is some entity which is the identity of the proposition, whether this is doubted, believed, desired, or denied. (As we shall see, this creates a number of problems for Russell as well.) Frege, however, disowns Russell's interpretation, remarking that to say *Socrates is human* is to assert that Socrates is human; and that he, Frege, is not interested in the psychological accompaniments of the proposition but only in its logical status. This produces another difficulty for Russell in making sense of Frege's treatment of the proposition, while for Frege it is another way in which Russell is on the wrong track in dealing with propositions as logical entities.[40]

No topic discussed in *The Principles of Mathematics* presented more difficulties for Russell than that of classes. Not only was this the area in which the troublesome and recalcitrant contradiction emerged (to be discussed later), but also the nature of the class, the relation of the class to its members, and the relation of a class to a class of classes, the apparently various ways in which classes figured as subjects and predicates in propositions, and the assumptions needed concerning classes in order to construct arithmetic — all placed constraints on Russell and posed problems for him. In terms of the realism claimed for his position, the implicit desire for minimal ontological assumptions, and the requirements of arithmetic, an extensional view of classes seemed to be required. Thus, if a class of humans could be seen as a collection of John, Mary . . . , this would satisfy one requirement, to have as constituents of propositions existent entities, the individuals here grouped under a common name. But this way of treating classes involved difficulties with infinite classes, null classes, and unit classes. It also posed problems for finite but indeterminate classes. Both Peano and Frege found it important to separate the class from the individual member of the class. Russell, in the body of his book, disputes this. What would be the reality of a class apart from its members? Although he and Peano and Frege agree in defining numbers in terms of classes of classes, Russell is not prepared to take the class as separate from its members, even in the perplexing cases of the unit class and null class.[41] Accordingly, Russell tries to escape the difficulty by distinguishing the class-concept from the class. The former can be treated intensionally and has its status as a concept, whereas the class it defines has an infinite number of members or a finite number of members, one member, or no members. But members are terms, and are to be distinguished on the one hand from numerals symbolizing them and on the other hand from concepts. Also Russell finds a difficulty with the extensional treatment of classes when he tries to analyze how collections enter as units, as individuals, taken as one and one, or as individuals taken as one of many. Russell is not satisfied with his own treatment of classes under this analysis.[42]

In the appendix in which he discusses Frege's treatment of classes, he finds that, although Frege has admitted a distinction between the class and its members, Frege's methods treat the concept of the class in a way that fits in with the needs of arithmetic. For Frege a function defines a class; whatever things can be the arguments for a given function constitute such a class. Thus, instead of thinking of humans as the collection of John, Mary . . . , Frege's way of expressing this is to say that the class of humans is constituted by whatever can be put in the place of the variable for the function *human*. After long discussion, Russell tentatively accepts Frege's view, although he is not completely satisfied with it. Frege's conception gives a basis for distinguishing the class from its members; for a unit class the *Begriff* in question specifies the class, but what falls under it is not the function itself but the argument. As Russell says, neither he nor Frege has found a way to work out a solution to the contradiction of classes that are not members of themselves, so all views of classes must be regarded as defective until this is done.[43]

With respect to the contradiction, both Russell and Frege found it destructive. The logicist program required the resolution of the antinomy, or preferably a way of avoiding the contradiction altogether that would be rationally defensible, not arbitrary, and logically compatible with the deductive system. In their respective appendixes each suggested a possible solution without eliminating the other's counterproposal. The suggestions were later developed into more completely worked-out solutions—Russell's and Whitehead's in *Principia Mathematica,* Frege's at the hands of later logicians building upon his work, at least according to some interpretations.[44] The rudimentary ideas of Frege and Russell at this early stage can be compared fruitfully.

The contradiction emerged when Russell began thinking about classes of classes. Suppose we divide all classes into two groups—those that are members of themselves (such as classes of classes) and those not members of themselves (such as teaspoons). Of the later class we may ask the question, "Is the class of things *not* members of themselves a member of itself?" The answer is a contradiction, for if the class of things not members of themselves is not a member of itself then it is not a class of things not members of themselves. On the other hand, if the class of things not members of themselves *is* a member of itself, then it does not belong to the class of things not members of themselves. Russell finds no easy answer to this puzzle and connects it with other contradictions, such as that of the greatest cardinal number, and the classical puzzle of Epimenides the Cretan who said "All Cretans are liars." (If he was lying, not all Cretans are liars, but if he was telling the truth, he was not lying and thus contradicted the original statement.) In all, these contradictions Russell sees a common theme of reflexiveness which seems to be connected with the contradiction—that is, the statement that led to the contradiction is taken to apply to itself. Accordingly, Russell thinks the solution to the contradiction might lie in some restriction placed on the scope of the proposition in question to allow it to apply only to classes of a lower level of abstractness. Epimenides' statement applies to the statements made by Cretans, but to speak of their statements, his own about theirs is included in the things referred to by his statement. Thus, what seems to be required is that the statement about classes be on the level of classes of classes, so that the statements or classes referred to be always of a level lower than that of what is said about them. In appendix B of *The Principles of Mathematics* there is no formal elaboration of this suggested solution, and the suggestion has, as Russell says, an ad hoc air. Yet it seems that such a solution has some reasonable connection with an explanation of the way in which the contradiction arises.45

Frege's suggestion is somewhat different. In the appendix to his own work he evaluates the contradiction as arising from an unnoticed assumption in his Axiom V. This says, roughly, that (a) if whatever falls under one concept also falls under another, then the two concepts are equal in extension, and that (b) two concepts are equal in extension if and only if whatever falls under one falls under the other. After eliminating other solutions in terms of limitations on the law of excluded middle, or in terms of a classification of proper and improper objects to the former of which alone the law applies,46 Frege turns to a detailed discussion of Axiom V. He finds that one part of Axiom V (a) holds, but (b) does not hold. Hence if Axiom V were to be reformulated and the deductions worked out in detail, the system might be saved. Finally, Frege suggests the necessary restriction on the equation of equality of extensions and value-ranges of concepts might be achieved by some such statement: "If two functions are equal in their range of values then they have equal values for any argument that is not the value range of one of the functions."47 This reformulation has the effect of prohibiting the reflexivity of reference from which, as Russell had argued, the contradiction arose. Neither Russell nor Frege seems to feel entirely sure that the hypotheses could be worked out, but confident that something of the kind could save the situation and prevent the emergence of the contradiction.

The correspondence of the period shows both Russell and Frege experimenting with different solutions to the problem presented by the contradiction. Frege did not pursue any further discussion of it following the appendix of the *Grundgesetze, II* (1903). Russell, for his part, writes of two different possible solutions, including the so-called no-class theory, but both he and Frege find them unsatisfactory. In the end, it is a version of Russell's suggestion in appendix B, the theory of types, which in one form or another supplies such an answer as *Principia Mathematica* provides.

It was left for later logicians to explore alternatives. There have been disputes over whether Frege's suggestion was or was not tenable; Russell thought Frege turned to geometry as a possible foundation for mathematical logic because of his failure to solve the contradiction. Peter Geach holds that Frege's suggestion was a good one, preferable to Russell's and used later by other logicians. This is disputed by W. V. Quine, who is the later logician in question.48 Robert Sternfeld holds that Frege's system was not even vulnerable to the contradiction in spite of what both Russell and Frege held to be the case. The conflicting interpretations reflect the entire recent debate over the work of Frege and Russell at the turn of the century.[49]

4.4 Russell and Meinong to 1905

During the period that Russell was working out the philosophical ideas and logical techniques that took form in *The Principles of Mathematics* and are expressed in the publications and correspondence of the period between the late 1890s and 1905, he was interested in and influenced by the work of Alexius Meinong, whose research and background were strikingly different from Russell's. Meinong was much influenced by his teacher Franz Brentano and by the concept of "intentional inexistence" which the latter had employed. Meinong was interested primarily in a combination of psychology and philosophy. He came to philosophy through a criticism of Kant and had studied Hume and published two detailed analyses of him. In Graz he set up the first experimental psychological laboratory in his native Austria and strove to weave together what could be found about human perception and knowledge through psychological studies with a philosophical approach centering on epistemological questions. He adopted a realist standpoint for the analysis of both knowledge and valuation. The first work of Meinong's to come to Russell's attention was *Über die Bedeutung des Weberschen Gesetzes* (On the Meaning of Weber's Laws), published in 1896 and reviewed by Russell in *Mind* (April 1899). Weber's laws concern the measurements of stimuli and sensations and state that "the increase of the stimulus necessary to produce an increase of the sensation bears a constant ratio to the total stimulus."[50] Meinong's work dealt with the mathematical treatment of sensations. Russell praised the thoroughness of its empirical method, but he did not recognize in it any emerging strands of realism. Meinong, writing to J. S. Mackenzie to acknowledge the latter's intervention in having Russell review the work, indicated that he felt Russell's treatment accurate and hoped that he would respond to his new work, in which he tried to take account of Russell's criticisms. Russell subsequently received copies of *"Über Gegenstände höhere Ordnung und deren Verhältnis zur inneren Wahrnehmung"* (On Objects of Higher Order and Their Relation to Inner Perception), *"Abstrahieren und Vergleichen"* (Abstractions and Comparisons), and, in 1902, Meinong's book *Über Annahmen* (On Assumptions). Russell made a close study of these works, as the reading notes in the Bertrand Russell Archives make evident, and he found the realism of Meinong in some ways compatible with his own. Both believed that every intellectual activity aimed at some object, and took as their aim to uncover the nature of the activity and the characteristics of the objects concerned. The difference, however, was that Meinong's approach was psychological and epistemological, and Russell's, at this period, primarily logical. Russell's study of Meinong is reflected in the series of articles in *Mind* for 1904, "Meinong's Theory of Complexes and Assumptions."[51]

Meinong's study of objects of "higher order" dealt with objects derived from other objects and, in particular, with complexes founded on lower-order objects. Lower-order objects would be those such as are presented in sensation — simple, direct, and concrete; from these could be built complexes, including comparisons, abstractions, and class-concepts, and universals. All presentations and higher-order ideas had objects as well as contents. For Meinong, the first level of representation was the direct presentation of an object by way of content perceived by the subject through an act. Sensation would be an example; the act of seeing provides the subject with the idea of the blue tubular quality of a seen flower (the content), and this content is directed toward the object itself, which would exist and be what it is whether it was seen or not — that is, the flower itself. On the second level, an act of judging or of entertaining a judgment has as its content *that such and such is the case,* and this in turn is directed toward an object. This object Meinong calls an *Objektiv,* and it is a complex in which the constituents are the objects of a lower order.

Another topic which proved to be of crucial importance in the evaluation of Meinong's thought, both by Russell and by other critics, was the issue of the being attributed to the *Objekta* and *Objektive.* In the first place, Meinong was committed to the position that all intellectual processes and attitudes were directed toward, or referred to, some object. This was an attitude very similar to that expressed by Russell at the beginning of *The Principles of Mathematics.* But for Meinong this did not mean that all *Objekta* or *Objektive* have the same kind of status with respect to being. Some objects directly presented to us are existent objects: the flower we see, the sound we hear, and so forth. Other objects of presentation are not existent but are subsistent: the number 2, for instance. Generally these two classes are mutually exclusive: In an *Objektiv,* however, both kinds of objects may be present; the *Objektiv* itself may be said to subsist. Thus far, the categories of being are similar to Russell's; in *The Principles of Mathematics* he too had existing objects, or terms, such as the table, and subsisting predicates or concepts, such as brown. Meinong also distinguished between the *Objektiv* which attributes existence and that which attributes the "being so" of something. Hence *that X is* would be an example of an *Annahme* of the first kind; *that X is so-and-so* an example of the second kind. He referred to the first kind as *Sein,* the second as *Sosein*. Thus it is possible to speak of the being-so of a complex, that certain characteristics are associated, and this may be done whether the objects in the complex are existent, subsistent, or neither. In some cases, the assertion of the characteristics of a complex may not rest on experiential evidence and may have little to support its claimed factuality; in others it may be supported by convincing evidence—in either case *that X is so and so* has an *Objektiv*. There are also cases where the being-so is demanded by logic: for instance, *that the angles of a triangle make 180°,* or *that $2^2 = 4$*—such assertions are necessary. There are also cases where the being-so has to do with fictitious or impossible objects. Hence we know that the golden mountain is golden and that the round square is round, even though no existent or subsistent entities are there to be referred to by the *Objektiv*. Hence objects may be existent, subsistent, or neither.[52] Meinong attributes that status of *Quasisein* to impossible or fictitious objects; later he calls such an object *Aussersein*—beyond being and nonbeing.[53]

In the three articles in *Mind* of 1904, "Meinong's Theory of Complexes and Assumptions," Russell attempts to do three things: first, to report to an English audience the philosophical content of the two articles of Meinong, "Gegenstände höherer Orderer," and "Abstrahieren und Vergleichen," and of his 1902 book *Über Annahmen*. In accordance with this goal, many passages in the three articles review Meinong's statements, carefully tied to page and chapter, and are comparable to the details of the reading notes on these works that Russell made. The second goal is to interpret and criticize Meinong's theory of knowledge in the light of Russell's own opinions on the topics discussed. The third goal is to clarify some of the problems in the theory of knowledge addressed by Meinong and to come to a satisfactory solution for them. Since Meinong's views were not expressed with complete clarity and included some concepts, such as *Quasisein,* that were later amended, and some distinctions, such as that of content and object, that were not clearly delineated (as Meinong later confessed), it is not surprising that Russell is baffled by some passages and must correct his reading of Meinong by referring to the latter's subsequent work.[54] In addition, Russell, as we have seen, is committed to an extreme realism of terms and propositions during this period and reads Meinong against this background. Most significant of all, Russell's preoccupation with certain pressing problems of his own—concerning the nature of truth and the status of objects involved in fictions, negative existential judgments, and errors—provides the dominant theme of these articles, revealing Russell's search for a solution.

With respect to Meinong's discussion of the level of presentation in terms of subject, act, content, object, Russell sees an obstacle in the relation of object to content. He agrees that in presentation, its content, which he takes to be psychical, does not have the properties of the object, nor does the act share in the properties of the content. So the act of presentation is not itself blue while the content is, and the content is not extended, while the object is. Hence, the distinctions of act, content, and object are unobjectionable in themselves. But Russell feels that for Meinong so intimately connected are the act, content, and object, that the psychical nature that undeniably belongs to the act is shared by content and object. Russell seemed to require a dualism of presentation and object which would divide them off sharply from one another—the object is what it is and is unaffected by its relation to a subject, or to the act of presentation, or to the content of the presentation. It is not clear in the discussion whether Russell is calling for a direct two-term relation with no distinction of content and object, or whether he is calling for a representative realism in which the content represents, or is caused by, an object entirely external to the presentation of it. It *is* clear, however, that presentation for him is to be interpreted more broadly than on Meinong's theory, for he returns again and again to ask why Meinong did not hold that the *Objektiv* is presented. For Russell, apparently, presentation can be a kind of relation between anything known and the subject, so long as this relation is direct. And he seems to think a number of kinds of objects can be presented in this way, including propositions.[55]

Russell realizes that for Meinong the intervention of the level of judgment, especially with the *Annahmen,* is necessary in order that some objects of higher order can arise, for the simples of presentation must be unified into a complex with the aid of the cognitive relation of judgment or assumption. Russell is favorably impressed by Meinong's analysis of a complex and spends considerable space in the articles reporting this. He agrees that *a* and *b* and R together make up the complex *aRb,* and that the complex is not just the addition of R to the terms *a* and *b* but that R occurs in such a way, and in such a binding relation, as to create a unity. With Meinong's analysis of relations and abstractions by such means Russell is inclined to be in agreement. He, too, is interested in complexes and in the relation of a complex to the simples constituting it.

Concerning Meinong's attempt to analyze the different ways in which simples are composed into complexes, Russell challenges some relations of the *Inferiora* to the *Superiora;* both the comparison that arranges qualities or magnitudes into greater or less, and the combination that adds the color to the shape, or one unit to another, are satisfactory, but when Meinong attempts to use a dependence of logical priority, Russell criticizes the one-way inference by which one can say that a complex implies its simples, but not vice versa.

He also finds that when Meinong contrasts two kinds of relations within a complex, founded and unfounded, and classifies the former as ideal and as involving necessary relations, while the latter are said to be real and to involve existential and hence contingent relations, he makes some assumptions about necessity with which Russell must disagree.[56]

In the cases of differentiating various attitudes to the complex, Russell fully agrees with Meinong's important distinction between judgment and assumption, which he likens to Frege's treatment of assertion. Meinong finds a variety of cognitive attitudes (and valuational attitudes as well) that can be taken to what might be expressed as *that so and so*. One may entertain, or consider, or imagine, or guess, or hypothesize *that so and so,* and these attitudes involve the terms and relations of the complex. But this is a different thing from affirming or denying *that so and so*. Meinong points out the large variety of situations in which such assumptions occur prior to, or without any commitment of, belief or disbelief. When one does assert or deny such assumptions, then judgment has entered in, and it is possible to speak of truth and falsity, but so long as no judgment of affirmation or denial is made, no distinction of truth or falsity is relevant. In all cases on the level of judgment, whether of assumption or of affirmation, there is an *Objektiv* involved — what corresponds to the objects of the level of presentation and is the relation or combination of those presented objects.[57] This *Objektiv* Russell likens to his and G. E. Moore's proposition, which, it will be recognized, is a complex constituted of objects and concepts, existent and subsistent, respectively. For Russell, however, it is not correct to say that the assertion or assumption designates something beyond itself — as he says, Meinong's *Objektiv* is like his proposition with the "yes" or "no" left out. The *Objektiv* could be said to be *the fact that so and so*. Russell holds that Meinong's *Objektiv* has a merely immanent status as an object, although it is not clear why he believes this, since he equated Meinong's assumptions with his own propositions, which *have* transcendent reality.[58] The difference seems to be that Meinong's analysis refers to the psychological and cognitive aspects of judgment (as opposed to what Russell regards as proper — that is, for judgments to be presentations). In other words, it seems that in criticizing Meinong for not including judgments and assumptions as presentations, Russell means that in Meinong's formulation, the act of judging or assuming makes its objects part of that psychical process, while bare presentation would allow the object to be other than, and separate from, the act and content of presentation. Russell confesses that he is not sure he understands what Meinong means by "presentation," and as we shall see, it seems that a basic difference between their two ways of looking at the relation between the object and the cognitive process is involved.

The recurrent issue in Russell's critique of Meinong concerning the relation of object (or *Objekt*) to the act-content parts of the relation between subject and object seems to be that between immanence and transcendence, a pair of alternatives that Russell sets up as a basis for the classification of kinds of theories of knowledge.[59] In general, what he means by *immanence* is that the object of knowledge (whether presentation, belief, assumption, or whatever) is considered as within, or dependent upon, the subject and the subject's psychical processes. On the other hand, *transcendence* means that the object has a status independent of, outside of, the subject and is not itself "psychical" (unless the object is itself "mental"). For Russell, there seem not to be degrees of immanence—the criteria of the categories are: first, what process is in question (an object may be transcendent for presentation, immanent for judgment), and, second, whether the judgment or awareness involved is veridical or nonveridical. On this pair of rather strange dichotomies Meinong's position is said to be that the object of presentation is transcendent when the presentation is of something that exists, otherwise it is immanent; whereas for the level of judgment, the object is immanent, whether the judgment is true or false. The reasons for this classification by Russell of Meinong are not entirely clear. With respect to presentation, Russell remarks that so far as he can see, if an object has subsistence or quasi-being, it is the same as if it does not exist. This argument seems to depend on Meinong's position that in objects of a higher order, and in the apprehension of all complexes, assumptions enter in, and, if assumptions enter in at all, this deprives any putative objects of their independent status (so far as Russell is concerned). Thus although Russell is prepared to welcome the distinction between judgment and *Annahmen,* and although he finds the *Objektiv* to correspond to his own and Moore's proposition, at the same time the epistemological distinctions of presentation and judgment and the dependence of the *Objektiv* on constituents into which judgment enters contaminate Meinong's epistemology with the immanence of idealism.

There are two other themes of Russell's interpretation and critique of Meinong related to this surprising indictment that he is insufficiently realistic. One theme is Meinong's treatment of necessity. As we have seen, Meinong distinguishes two kinds of relations in discussing objects of higher order: one was ideal, known logically, and necessary; the other real, known empirically, and contingent. In treating such a relation as necessary, Meinong confronts Russell's denial of necessity as having any status beyond one involving the assignment of truth values. Russell says that it appears that if any relation seems to be unaffected by a context in time, Meinong regards the relation as itself a necessary one. For Russell the correct interpretation is to say that when the relation is expressed in a sentence, that sentence will remain true whatever variables of time are placed within it. To say of a certain judgment that it is always true means that one is actually referring to a propositional function containing a variable and asserting that whatever values replace the variable to make a proposition, that proposition will be true. This position, of course, is Russell's customary logical formulation of "possible," "impossible," or "necessary," where modality is restated to make such statements amenable to an extensional analysis.

Meinong makes a similar error in dealing with "necessary propositions" when he unwittingly uses propositional functions rather than propositions as examples.[60] These logical points of difference have considerable philosophical importance, as it turns out, for possible or impossible objects (on Russell's interpretation of modality) cannot escape the disjunction between being or nonbeing, or the scope of the laws of logic. This difference between the views of Meinong and Russell is already evident in 1904; in later exchanges it becomes even more decisive, as we shall see.

A third and related area of discussion reveals the accumulated opposition of Russell to Meinong's thought, and, at the same time, reveals even more strikingly the problems faced by Russell in formulating his own realism. One question is: What is the relation between a negative proposition and the denial of a proposition? Logic requires that the two be equivalent in truth value, but if an affirmative proposition be constituted by the object and the concept of existence, is a negative proposition to be constituted by the object and the concept of nonexistence? Or could we say that the judgment of denial attaches to the being of a complex, the affirmation to the nonbeing of a complex? Again, it seems that when a proposition is asserted, all we have is the proposition itself, but when a proposition is denied we have another level—for the proposition then has the being of the negation of the being. These can scarcely be equivalent in form, although the meaning may be the same. But when we introduce the distinction of assertion and judgment, as with Frege, Meinong, and Russell, the denial of an assumption seems to be equivalent to the denial of an assertion, as denial is the opposite of assertion. How can the inferences permitted by a two-valued logic be consistent with a class of sentences which are not asserted? It seems that it makes sense to construct a hypothetical argument bound by the rules of logic, which is customary in mathematics; yet, in the context of contrasting the denial of an assumption with the denial of an assertion, contradictions seem to threaten.[61]

A problem Russell poses for Meinong at the end of his articles seems to be a vital one for his own philosophy as well. As we saw in a preceding chapter, F. H. Bradley had remarked that with all the difficulties that Russell found in the idealist theory of truth, neither he nor Moore had proposed one of their own, let alone one that would be clearly superior to those they criticized. The difficulty with a theory of truth is clearly evident in the passages in question. With respect to truth and falsity, Russell says that there are two possibilities. The first is that knowledge is the affirmation of true complexes, and error the affirmation of false complexes; in that case, both true and false complexes (or *Objektive,* or propositions) have being. The second is that judgment has no *Objektiv* except when there is a true proposition, so true and false apply to judgments but not to propositions, and the object is the fact to which the true judgment corresponds. This is not an easy choice; Meinong, says Russell, has chosen the latter in holding the object of the presentation to be immanent when false, transcendent when true; the *Objektiv* to be always immanent. This amounts to the second alternative and the espousal of a correspondence theory of truth. Russell is critical of this theory of truth, partially because it denies the being of false propositions, and he cannot see how a proposition without being can be meaningful. The matter of the relation of judging itself, in contrast to the particularized relation which a true or false judgment asserts, is also involved, but the general conclusion that Russell reaches is that, since there are attitudes and attributions, some contradictory to others, that can be made from a single unasserted proposition, such as *my going to town yesterday,* this proposition itself must have transcendent reality, whether it is said that my going to town was dangerous, advisable, that I did go, or would have gone, or did not go. Hence false propositions are transcendent. Russell goes on to discuss the relation between true and false, affirmative and negative, belief and disbelief. He concludes that there must be true negative propositions but leaves open the question whether disbelief is distinct from belief in the negation. He also leaves unsettled whether the assertion of a proposition is different from the assertion that a proposition is true.[62]

Russell concludes the discussion of truth with his famous remark, "There is no problem at all in truth and falsehood; that some propositions are true and some false, just as some roses are red and some white; that belief is a certain attitude towards propositions, which we call knowledge when they are true, error when they are false."[63] Despite that confident statement, Russell has two areas of dissatisfaction with his own treatment of truth and falsity. One is that it does not seem to account for our preference for truth over falsity (but this seems not a logical objection). The second source of uneasiness is the feeling that true propositions express facts while false ones do not. But what do we mean by fact? Is the occurrence or presence of something a fact, its nonoccurrence or absence not a fact? Russell thinks not; both affirmative and negative existential propositions report facts if they are true, even on a correspndence view. Yet, as he says, "it is hard to regard A's existence, when true, as a *fact* in quite the same sense in which A's non-existence would be a fact if it *were* true."[64] Russell thinks this must be due to a prejudice in favor of what can be perceived and has no logical foundation. We are left with an unanalyzable difference between true and false, and an unexplained, perhaps ethical, preference for the former over the latter.[65]

After the publication of the three articles in *Mind*, Meinong writes directly to Russell, responding to his letter and the articles, complimenting Russell on his understanding of his work, and finding close similarities in their thought. He thanks Russell for sending him *The Principles of Mathematics* and for the reference to Frege, both of which have been unknown to the Graz school. He sends Russell the first of the series of articles on *Gegen-standstheorie*, of which three have already been published; the other two will be sent by their authors. Meinong invites Russell's response to the new work.

Russell duly received the full contents of the collection of the work of the Graz school published under the title *Untersuchungen zur Gegen-standstheorie und Psychologie*. Russell studied the text closely and apparently had some correspondence concerning it with E. Mally and R. Ameseder, who were among the contributors. He published a review of the volume in *Mind*, in the same issue that carried his own landmark "On Denoting."[66] The new work from Graz showed the development of a theory of objects as a special discipline which crosses the lines of traditional fields, is wider than metaphysics (which takes account only of real objects), and includes mathematics. Russell found the position to have moved further away from psychologism toward a greater realism and seemed to approve both of the theory of objects itself and the realism expressed.

The chief questions that Russell poses in his review and in letters have to do with two related topics: impossible objects in terms of possibility and necessity, and the categories of existence, subsistence, and a third kind of being. Both of these topics Russell now views in terms of an alternative mode of explication which he has just developed. For this reason, Russell's evaluation of the categories of objects developed by the Graz school to solve the problems of an object realism capable of dealing with meaningful statements referring to nonexistent or contradictory objects proceed from a standpoint quite different from that of the 1904 articles or of his early letters.

5
Russell, Frege, and Meinong: 1905 and After

5.1 "On Denoting"

IN 1905 RUSSELL SENT a short paper entitled "On Denoting" to *Mind*. The editor, G. F. Stout, responded that the paper was "preposterous," but, on Russell's assurance that it was a very important paper, he published it.[1] It has turned out that the judgments of both editor and author have been concurred in by later commentators. As the first presentation of the theory of descriptions, it broke new ground; as the basis of a continued controversy with respect to some portions of the argument, it has presented difficulties of understanding. The theory of descriptions itself has not been a source of ambiguity since it was presented formally in *Principia Mathematica* and informally in several subsequent writings of Russell (although its merits have been hotly debated). The difficulties have centered on the arguments Russell presented against the views of Frege and Meinong that he considered alternatives to the theory of descriptions. These arguments have been analyzed, reconstructed, judged to rest on misunderstandings of Frege and Meinong, to be just to Frege and Meinong, evaluated as hopelessly flawed, or defended.[2] Against the background of Russell's views during this period and the exchanges between Russell and Frege, and Russell and Meinong, we will briefly review the argument of the essay.[3]

"On Denoting" begins with a statement of the problem which Russell describes as that of seeing what kind of propositions denote, and of seeing for those which do not appear to denote, how their meaning is derived. The problem of denoting, then, is the same problem as that of what kind of object must be assumed to be, to exist, or to subsist when a term occurs in a proposition that appears to be about that term. Russell begins by defining a denoting phrase, attempting to work this out in terms of its form. It is a phrase referring to *the such and such*, or *a so and so, something*, or *everything*. After citing a number of examples, Russell distinguishes the denoting phrase from what the phrase refers to, and phrases occurring in direct contexts from those occurring in indirect contexts—for example, *Scott is the author of Waverley* from *George IV knew that Scott was the author of Waverley*. Russell then introduces the notion of a propositional function, showing how sentences containing *all* and *some* can be formulated as propositional functions without their subject terms necessitating the existence of what their terms refer to. To say *X is human* commits one to no assertion about the existence or nonexistence of humans, as there may be no argument which can replace the *X*. But if the propositional function *X is human* is made into a proposition by substituting *Socrates* for *X*, then the name commits one to an existent for which it is a name, and the proposition is true or false, according as the name does or does not have an appropriate referent. Russell also points out in the beginning of the essay that the problem to which he is addressing himself has important implications; he is making an epistemological distinction between knowledge by acquaintance and knowledge by description, a distinction that turned out to be of crucial importance philosophically. What is directly presented and therefore that with which we have acquaintance, is what would be denoted, and the problem consists in analyzing situations in which the denoting phrase occurs in the sentence, although no presentation of an object of acquaintance corresponds to it.

The next section of the essay is the one around which controversy and strongly differing interpretations have arisen. Russell here contrasts the new theory he is advocating with solutions to the problem put forward by Meinong and Frege. The references are brief and the argument obscure. Russell's earlier views and his earlier critiques of Meinong and Frege turn out to be relevant to this argument. Russell attributes to Meinong the doctrine that any grammatically correct denoting phrase stands for an object, and says that this involves Meinong in apparent contradictions in the case of fictitious or self-contradictory terms such as *the golden mountain* or *the round square*. How is Meinong to deal with *The existent King of France exists* or *The round square is round?* If the sentences are denied, a contradiction results.

With respect to Frege, Russell has more to say, since this was a view which he had himself accepted earlier. He repeats the distinction worked out by Frege between *Sinn* and *Bedeutung* and uses the example of *the centre of mass of the solar system at the beginning of the twentieth century* as an example of a phrase of which the sense (*Sinn*), or meaning, is complex and has constituents, but of which the denotation (*Bedeutung*) is simple. The advantage of Frege's analysis is that it makes sense to assert identity because one may be connecting meaning (*Sinn*) with denotation (*Bedeutung*). But the difficulty is that in some cases there seems to be only meaning and no denotation. One would expect that a Fregean analysis of the following two propositions would be parallel, but they are not: *The king of England is bald* and *The king of France is bald* (in 1905). The first sentence can refer *the king of England* to its denotation, the man himself; the second cannot do the same for *the king of France,* which has no denotation. If this situation requires us to look for the meaning (sense) in the second case, whereas we looked for the denotation in the first, it should provide some logical reason for doing so in terms of the form of the proposition.

Russell sets up alternatives for the solution to this problem: either provide some denotation for such denoting expressions for which there is no denotation, or abandon the option that denotation is what is involved in propositions containing denoting phrases. Meinong takes the first alternative by providing objects for every presentation and every assumption, whether they concern existents, subsistents, or neither. Frege, Russell says, also takes the first, identifying such phrases as denoting the null class, and such propositions as denoting the False. Meinong's view involves him in breaches of the law of noncontradiction, which does not hold for nonexistent or impossible objects. Frege's analysis provides an "artificial" solution committing him to assert that all false propositions and vacuous denotations have the same denotation.

Russell, for his part, adopts the second possibility, that denotation is not concerned in the analysis of propositions containing these problematic phrases. (It may be noted here that Russell had formerly criticized Meinong for being insufficiently realistic, and, in *The Principles of Mathematics,* had adopted a term-realism with the exception of the discussion of denoting concepts. Here, however, he represents himself as having held Frege's view, apparently referring to his partial adoption of the distinction between *Sinn* and *Bedeutung*.) The criticism of Meinong is clear, and the same as that contained in letters and the 1905 review. The criticisms thus far made of Frege are two: no reasons dependent on logical form illumine the contrasting analyses of two propositions of the form *the such-and-such . . .* in which one subject has a denotation, and the other does not (for example, the *king of England* and *the king of France*), and second, Frege is forced to supply an artificial denotation, in the False or the null class. The first criticism may be judged to have a point; the second attributes to Frege a motive for adopting his view of the denotation of a proposition quite other than what his own argument claims.

Russell's argument proceeds to present three puzzles that provide a test for an adequate theory of denoting phrases. These puzzles are similar to the problems raised in the conclusion of Russell's Meinong articles of 1904, but here the solutions provided are sharply different. The three puzzles are: first, if a name and a descriptive phrase mean the same, then one could be substituted for the other without loss or change of meaning. This, however, does not seem to be the case, as when, in Russell's example, George IV wanted to know if Scott were the author of *Waverley,* not if Scott were Scott. Second, an apparent breach in the law of excluded middle occurs in propositions in which the subject term is not an existent or subsistent entity. Hence, it is neither true nor false that *The king of France is bald.* Third, it is always contradictory to deny the being of anything, since this denies the being of the nonsubsistent subject term, or affirms the nonbeing of the subject (the problem referred to by W. V. Quine as "Plato's beard").[4]

The next section of the argument is one upon which the greatest difficulties of interpretation have centered. It must be confessed that the argument is unclear, but whether this is owing to some carelessness in formulation and can be corrected, as Herbert Hochberg argues, or is hopelessly flawed by a carelessness of use and mention, as John R. Searle argues,[5] some insight into assumptions made by Russell may be gleaned and the basis for this third criticism of Frege elicited.

Russell begins by outlining the very distinction between use and mention that he appears to violate in the argument, but he does this by distinguishing a denoting phrase in its customary meaning or primary occurrence, and its use when the phrase itself is in question, or its secondary occurrence. The difference is between *The first line of Gray's Elegy is a proposition* and *'The first line of Gray's Elegy' is not a proposition.* If we assume, as Russell does, that the meaning of a phrase is what it denotes, as *Scott* means Scott (the name *means* the man), we find this will not work for the example. In the first proposition the denotation of the first six words is *The curfew tolls the knell of parting day,* but if we insert that in the first proposition, the denotation of the sentence becomes the tolling of the knell, and this is said to be a proposition. In the second proposition, where the words are enclosed in inverted commas, the denotation is the same six words but without the inverted commas. In neither case is the analysis of meaning (sense) what was required. Hence, the argument has the form of a *reductio ad absurdum* and leads to the conclusion that some other analysis is required for denoting phrases. Here, it should be noted, Russell is making two assumptions: that the basic meaning of words or phrases is their direct denotation, and that the proposition has as its constituents the denoted entities themselves. Neither assumption is shared by Frege; on the other hand, what Frege does mean by *Sinn* is far from clear, and Russell's argument would seem to underline that point. Both the assumptions and the question are revealed in the footnote: "In this theory [Frege's] we shall say the denoting phrase *expresses* a meaning; and we shall say that both of the phrase and of the meaning that they *denote* a denotation. In the other theory, which I advocate, there is no *meaning,* and only sometimes a denotation."[6]

Russell, in passages of complicated argument, shows examples of the failure of Frege's theory (as he interprets it) by showing that when we try to distinguish the meaning from the denotation of a denoting phrase, we either fail to preserve the distinction or else we fail to find any logical relation between meaning and denotation. For if we ask for the meaning of a denoting phrase, we either get its denotation (which is thus not distinguishable from its meaning), or we find the meaning in the denoting phrase enclosed in inverted commas (which is not what is wanted either). For the meaning of this last phrase (the denoting phrase in the inverted commas) is just its denotation, and that is the original phrase itself (and that is not what is wanted either). Russell concludes:

> The difficulty in speaking of the meaning of a denoting complex may be stated thus: The moment we put the complex in a proposition, the proposition is about the denotation; and if we make a proposition in which the subject is 'the meaning of C', then the subject is the meaning (if any) of the denotation, which was not intended. This leads us to say that, when we distinguish meaning and denotation, we must be dealing with the meaning: the meaning has a denotation and is a complex, and there is not something other than the meaning, which can be called the complex, and be said to *have* both meaning and denotation. The right phrase, on the view in question, is that some meanings have denotations.[7]

Hence, Russell finds no solution to the puzzle of the relation of meaning and denotation, and this shows that there is something wrong with Frege's analysis. Thus, then, is the third criticism of Frege's theory.

Turning to his own alternative theory, Russell first addresses the point that the meaning of denoting phrases, unlike that of the usual words in sentences which refer to terms in propositions, must be interpreted only in the context of the entire sentence in which each occurs. Russell provides a rephrasing of the sentence in which the denoting phrase occurs that is equivalent in meaning but in which the original denoting phrase itself disappears; the truth values are maintained, and the new sentence has only words that denote in the usual way. Thus, if the denoting phrase causing the problem is *the author of Waverley,* the sentence in which it occurs is translated from *Scott is the author of Waverley* to *One and only one entity wrote Waverley and Scott was identical with that one.* (Russell is here using an informal statement of the rephrasing.)

The puzzles that Russell had proposed as tests of his theory can now be solved. The name and the denoting phrase are not equivalent in meaning and cannot be substituted for one another; and it is clear what George IV wanted to know: whether one and only one person wrote *Waverley* and if that person was Scott. The second puzzle of sentences appearing to be about nonexistent entities is also resolved by this new translation; for the sentence *The king of France is bald* becomes the sentence *There is an entity which is now king of France, and this entity is bald*. Since the first part of the sentence is false, the entire conjunction is false, but this falsity does not commit us to a hairy and nonexistent king of France. The third problem of committing ourselves to the being of entities of which the being is denied in a given proposition can be resolved as well, since on translation the first part of the conjunction can be denied without the entire conjunction becoming meaningless. Thus talking about a *golden mountain* is now possible, since it can be asserted that a golden mountain is golden, and on analysis this means that there is an entity such that it is a mountain and is golden, and similarly with the round square and all other fictitious or, as Meinong called them, "impossible objects."

Russell concludes the essay by pointing out that the new way of dealing with denoting phrases is useful in mathematical contexts in showing that a contextual definition of the meaning of a mathematical expression can be given. He also asserts that sense is now provided for statements of identity, as we can understand why denoting phrases would require connection with names and might not be obvious or tautological in the sense in which two names would be. Finally, Russell refers to the epistemological significance of the distinction between knowledge by acquaintance, in which we are directly aware of the entity answering to the word or phrase, and knowledge by description, in which we must reinterpret the word or phrase in order to replace it with words having direct denotation. This division of kinds of knowledge had wide-ranging consequences in Russell's theories, as also did the method of construction that was the technical aspect of the theory of descriptions.

5.2 Russell's Criticisms and Assumptions

In retrospect, putting Russell's "On Denoting" in the context of what he had previously written about meaning, and his previous responses to Meinong and Frege, it seems that the criticisms of them offered in this essay rest on assumptions that Russell made and that were not shared by the philosophers he criticized. Thus—it has been pointed out—Russell assumed that all meaningful statements must be subject to a uniform analysis of meaning and truth. Probably neither Meinong nor Frege agreed, and certainly some modern critics such as P. F. Strawson do not. Meinong held that it is only for statements asserting existence or subsistence that the laws of logic apply, but not to statements concerning fictitious or impossible objects; hence he claimed that his theory was not subject to Russell's criticism. Frege did not respond directly to this criticism, but, in correspondence with Russell over the question of the True and the False as denotations of propositions, he argued that in the realm of poetry, fiction, or fantasy, no questions of truth or falsity are involved. It is only with science that we are concerned with truth, and by implication, this is the only realm in which logic and theory of meaning analyses need apply.[8]

On another point, Russell assumed that the fundamental tenet of any theory of meaning had to be the relation of naming between a word and what the word stood for, and this was the chief reason for rejecting Frege's analysis, and for finding his own to be an important advance. It is doubtful if either Meinong or Frege shared this assumption. Meinong was accustomed to speak in this way, but the direction of presentation and judgment toward objects was not necessarily to be conceived on the model of an act of naming; in fact, intentionality, as derived from Brentano, seems to preclude this. As for Frege, of course, he was responsible for the distinction between what are now called "sense" and "reference," and the latter does seem to be patterned after the relation of a name to what it names. Yet it is clear that there may be sense without denotation, as in the cases of fictitious objects, and, on the other hand, even proper names have sense as well as reference. Both positions are explicitly rejected by Russell. (And it is fair to say that Frege did not explain clearly what the "sense" of a proper name might be.) In any case, this assumption of Russell's clearly underlies the rejection of the other theories that he considers.

A third assumption clearly made by Russell but not shared by Meinong or Frege is that the proposition itself is constituted by the referents of the words of the sentence expressing it. For both Frege and Meinong there is no difficulty over a level of meaning between the verbal expression, the sentence, and the object-complex which corresponds to it. This intermediate level is the proposition—its presence makes possible an escape from the most drastic of Russell's imputed consequences, the creation of realms of Meinongian beings and nonbeings, and the lack of any realm of meanings apart from objects, concepts, and the True and the False in Frege.

When one reviews "On Denoting" in the context of the interactions between Meinong and Russell and between Frege and Russell, another aspect of its meaning presents itself. Although Russell is concerned to differentiate his new view from its competitors, one is struck more by what has been absorbed from those competitors than by what is rejected. First, the very distinction of knowledge by acquaintance and knowledge by description is strikingly similar to the two-level analysis of presentation and judgment in Meinong earlier criticized by Russell. Not only the two levels, but also Meinong's notion of the founding of objectives on the higher level on the objects presented on the lower level is similar to the relation between the referents of acquaintance and the meaning of descriptive phrases reduced to those referents by Russell's analysis. Second, when we consider Frege's influence, although there is still a strong realist tone in Russell's treatment of the proposition, the analysis of propositional functions, the ways of defining classes (which Russell shared with Frege, and learned from him) were bringing him closer to a more linguistic view of the proposition. This is clear in the movement from the "denoting concept" of *The Principles of Mathematics* to the "denoting phrase" of "On Denoting." It is evident also in the way in which the very doctrine that he criticized in Frege, that of the *Sinn* and *Bedeutung* distinction, was one he adopted himself, although the *Sinn* turned out to be reducible to *Bedeutung,* at least in part. When one speaks of meaning in the way in which this is done in "On Denoting," the proposition itself as a complex of entities is already in danger. The lapses of the distinction between use and mention, and the failure to be clear about the occasions when he is speaking of the sign and when of the thing signified, for which Frege had already admonished him,[9] are signs of a vacillation in the view of the proposition which was to become even more marked in the ensuing years.

5.3 *Russell and Frege after 1905*

Although the last letter from Frege to Russell is dated 1912, essentially their correspondence on philosophical issues ceased in 1904. Apparently Frege did not respond directly to Russell's remarks in "On Denoting." One of the most interesting sidelights on Frege's thinking of this period is derived from his correspondence with P. E. B. Jourdain.[10] Jourdain, a student and friend of Russell's, attempted a systematic history of mathematical logic, writing descriptions of the contributions of living mathematical logicians, giving his subjects the opportunity to correct those accounts, and intending all of them for publication. In the case of Frege we have that account as corrected by Frege, and we also have their correspondence. In this exchange, Jourdain asks Frege "Whether, in view of what seems to be a fact, namely, that Russell has shown that propositions can be analyzed into a form which only one assumes that a name has a 'Bedeutung', etc., not a 'Sinn', you would hold that 'Sinn' was merely a psychological property of a name."[11] Frege replies in the negative, citing the fact that when we interpret the meaning of a proposition we do so by interpreting the meaning of the words; hence when we say *Etna is in Sicily,* we must have the meaning of the name *Etna* in mind, as the mountain itself with its lava fields is not a constituent of the proposition. As against Jourdain's supposition that the sense may be something subjective, Frege cites a case of two explorers mapping a country from two different perspectives and each giving a different name to a mountain that they later discover to be the same mountain. Here the mountain and the map are objective and the discovery that *Ateb is Alpha* is a scientific and objective discovery, not a psychological, subjective one. It seems, then, that Frege's interpretation of meaning is unchanged by the theory of descriptions.

After Frege had received a copy of *Principia Mathematica,* Jourdain asked his opinion of it. Frege's reply was critical. He found it almost impossible to read because of the authors' failure to distinguish the sign from what was signified. He also disapproved of treating the symbols for functions as if they could stand alone. Frege's objections to the expression *variable* apply to its use in *Principia Mathematica,* and he points out that it is not clear whether it is "supposed to be a sign or the content of a sign."[12]

It is hinted in the record of their correspondence that, in a letter now lost, Jourdain may have discussed Frege's means of overcoming the contradiction of classes that are not members of themselves, a means that had been suggested in Frege's appendix to the second volume of the *Grundgesetze.*[13] Russell, for his part, henceforth treated Frege as part of the history of mathematical logic and regarded Frege's later work on the foundations of geometry as a tacit admission of the failure of his logicist program of founding arithmetic on logic due to the destructive effects of the contradiction. This seems not to have been correct. In commenting on Jourdain's account, Frege gives no indication of having abandoned his logicist program or of having shifted its connection from arithmetic to geometry, as suggested by Russell.[14]

5.4 Russell and Meinong after 1905

So far as Meinong was concerned, Russell published reviews of the work of the Graz school in 1905, 1906, and 1907. In both the correspondence and the reviews, several issues were raised again; Russell found Meinong's defense of his views against Russell's charge of contradictions inadequate. To say that an existent golden mountain does not exist is contradictory, and no real distinction between "existing" and "exists" can be allowed. Nor is Russell able to accept the claim that some kinds of propositions having to do with impossible objects can be exempt from the laws of logic. He is also critical of Meinong's treatment of non-Euclidean geometry, holding that both Euclidean and non-Euclidean geometries are simply the consequences of following out the implications of different hypotheses and that neither makes statements about whether parallel lines meet or do not meet, or whether there are or are not straight lines. The geometric characteristics of physical space must be investigated empirically. The letters include passages in which both philosophers express a large measure of agreement concerning the theory of objects and the status of mathematics as part of such a theory, but on their basic disagreements there is no progress, and Russell is convinced that his analysis in "On Denoting" gives a way of avoiding what, to him, are the unacceptable contradictions of Meinong's theory.

Russell returned to the work of Meinong and gave serious consideration to its epistemology in later studies. In 1913 Russell wrote a book on theory of knowledge which was not completed and not published (except for the early chapters printed in *The Monist* for 1914–15). This work was aborted, apparently due to Wittgenstein's criticism, but the part that was written, and the seminar taught on the topic of theory of knowledge at Harvard in 1914, drew heavily on Meinong's work.[15]

In developing his concept of acquaintance in the early chapters of this 1913 manuscript, Russell analyzes acquaintance into a relation between a subject, an act, and an object expressed by the formula $S-A-O$ which is later changed, in order to take care of self-consciousness, to $S'-P-[(\exists S).(S-A-O)]$. The only difference between Meinong and Russell seems to be that Meinong interposes between act and object the content of the presentation. Russell gives a long analysis of the claim for "content" and a response to it. Meinong argues that the difference between one presentation and another can be found neither in the act (the difference between awareness of green and awareness of yellow, for instance) nor in the object, hence those differences must be differences of content. Russell argues that not only does he not find any element in his experience corresponding to content, but he finds no necessity for assuming it, since the difference between one presentation and another can be sufficiently accounted for by differences in the act (sensation versus imagination) or in the object (yellow versus green). Essentially, Russell seems to assume that, in the direct two-term relation of acquaintance, the quality attributed to sensation is there and is what it is. What was held by Meinong to be a difference between object and quality (table versus brown) is held by Russell to be due to interpretation or inference to the object, on the basis of sensed qualities.[16]

Russell again turns to Meinong's writings when discussing the nature of the proposition. In this same 1913 manuscript, the nature of the proposition is a crucial topic and is referred to again and again. Having considered and rejected the ideas that the proposition is a linguistic entity, that it is the meaning of a sentence, and that it is the common meaning of a set of sentences, Russell introduces Meinong's concept, which, he says, is similar to his own in some respects. Meinong speaks of two aspects of belief, or conviction, as opposed to affirmation or negation; he regards the first as the mark of a belief, the second as the mark of an assumption. Russell invokes the theory of descriptions to explain his present agreement with Meinong in accepting a two-level analysis of presentation and judgment (which he had formerly rejected), and in rejecting the identification of his proposition with Meinong's *objektiv* (which he had formerly accepted). Russell holds (in 1913) that the proposition, not the belief, is true or false, but, as the proposition is itself an incomplete symbol, it must have a context in which its truth or falsity can be determined. There is no intrinsic mark by which this can be determined. Whatever the proposition is, it is *not* the associated belief or judgment, nor the object referred to by a belief. It seems that Russell realized in the course of his analysis that there was less disagreement between himself and Meinong than he first had thought.[17]

Russell refers to Meinong's views on two other topics: the definition of truth and the nature of self-evidence. With respect to truth, Russell seems to begin by assuming that Meinong holds that the objects of belief are themselves true or false. But in the end it is the earlier Russell who proves to be the best representative of this view which he is now rejecting.[18] With respect to self-evidence, Meinong's views are quoted, approved, but said to be insufficiently analyzed.[19] It would seem that the changes in Russell's opinions between 1905 and 1913 have brought him closer to Meinong in his analysis of acquaintance, his theory of the relation of understanding to acquaintance, and his theory of the proposition, as well as his notions of truth and self-evidence. At any rate, he seems to regard Meinong as a philosopher whose theory of knowledge is worthy of serious consideration.

By the time that Russell wrote *The Analysis of Mind,* in 1921, he still regarded Meinong as an important figure in epistemology, but his own views had again shifted, this time in a direction more opposed to Meinong's. There are scattered references to Meinong in the discussions of memory and self-evidence, but the chief references are critical. Russell states—and rejects— two aspects of Meinong's treatment of acquaintance as an introduction to his own confession of the adoption of neutral monism. One aspect of Meinong's theory of experience to which Russell had not referred previously was the intentionality of the concept of presentation (which Russell said Meinong had taken over from Franz Brentano). This view—that presentation involves an act, a content, and an object toward which the act is directed—is now totally rejected. No content can be empirically discovered in experience and neither can an act. Under the influence of William James, the subject-object dualism of the description of experience which Meinong (and formerly Russell) had adopted is now rejected. Experience consists of events or particulars to be classified as objective or subjective according to whether the laws of physics or psychology are relevant to their understanding. The influence of J. B. Watson's behaviorism and of James and his fellow realists has supplanted the former analysis of acquaintance, destroying not only the Meinongian analysis of presentation, but, as the text of the book makes clear, the entire dual structure of acquaintance and description.[20]

In later references to Meinong, especially in the retrospective accounts of his own philosophical development written after World War II, Russell carelessly refers to Meinong as a multiplier of entities that were rendered unnecessary by Russell's theory of descriptions. These later references offer whatever justification there may be for considering Russell's treatment of Meinong a "travesty."[21]

Russell changed a great deal in the years between 1897 and 1920 encompassing the interchanges between himself and Frege and himself and Meinong. His logic found its program, its contradictions, its posited solutions, and its fuller statement. At the same time, new ideas and new problems arose in his epistemology. *The Problems of Philosophy* (1912) might be considered a flash of clarity before the darkness of new difficulties engulfed Russell's theory of knowledge. To the scaffolding of the logic and theory of knowledge of the period, Meinong and Frege made important contributions, more perhaps than Russell himself realized. The difficulties were due to implications that emerged from his thought under newer influences, especially those of Wittgenstein and the pragmatists, influences to be discussed in later chapters.

6
Russell and Whitehead

O F ALL THE INTELLECTUAL figures with whom Russell had prolonged and important interactions, none was at the same time so close a collaborator and friend and so commanding a figure in twentieth-century philosophy as Alfred North Whitehead. Yet relatively little attention has been paid to this collaboration. This may be accounted for by the familiarity of the character-ization of their friendship and cooperation by Russell in "My Intellectual Development" in the Library of Living Philosophers volume devoted to his philosophy, and later, in *My Philosophical Development* and in his *Auto-biography*. Whitehead's own brief references to their friendship and collab-oration in the Library of Living Philosophers volume on his philosophy raised no difficulties and presented no discrepancies.[1] Yet because of their friendship and because of their philosophical influences on each other, there is much that is of interest and of value in understanding their respective points of view.

6.1 The Friendship of Russell and Whitehead

Russell came to Cambridge as an entering student in 1890; his mathematical entrance papers had been evaluated by Whitehead, who was then a fellow of Trinity College and eleven years senior to Russell. Although Whitehead's interests in mathematics and in philosophy were similar to Russell's and although both were members of the Apostles (the secret Cambridge discus-sion group), their differences in age and status meant that their relationship was one of teacher to student. In their respective accounts of their under-graduate days, the persons who were named as influential at that time of their lives were quite different. But in 1895, when Russell was elected a fellow of the college, a new phase of their relationship took shape. By then both were married, and both were interested in mathematics, its relation to physics, and theories of space and time. During the late 1890s Whitehead wrote and published what was intended to be the first volume of his *Universal Algebra*,[2] and this work was parallel to Russell's slightly later book, *The Principles of Mathematics*, which was finished, as he tells us, on the last day of the century. Both authors were projecting further volumes of their works. And during this period, when Russell was working out the implications of Peano's symbolism, introducing Whitehead to it, working at solving problems in the logic of relations with the new concepts, and discovering new applications and new puzzles arising from them, the two men decided to collaborate on their further work. This first presented itself as a second volume of *The Principles of Mathematics*, but soon grew too large and complex, becoming instead the three volumes of *Principia Mathematica*.[3]

No passage of Russell's *Autobiography* is more vivid than his account of the first ten years of the twentieth century: the long struggle to solve the contradiction of the class which is not a member of itself; the long labors of writing, sending for the other's criticism, and then rewriting all three volumes of *Principia*, the many false dawns and defeats suffered in the course of the enormous labors; the intense concentration of thought required in the work. We know of the way in which each segment went through three versions: that of the author who had assumed responsibility for the writing of the segment, then that of the other author serving as critic and revising, and finally that of the original author putting it into final form. For Russell, the work was an agonizing mixture of intensity of thought and failure, a long journey through a dark tunnel in which he sometimes despaired of seeing any light, accompanied by near-suicidal moments;[4] for Whitehead, too it must have been agonizing, for he was carrying on his duties at the college and had to do his part of the work amid the pressures of reading examinations, directing dissertations, giving lectures, attending meetings, and writing reports.[5] It is notable that the correspondence which remains from this period, most of it from Whitehead to Russell, came in batches at term endings when Whitehead saw the opportunity to spend some days on the work, frequently apologizing for the delays in returning manuscripts. Of course much of the work of collaboration was done in visits of one to the other, and of this no record remains except as Russell mentions these visits and their outcomes in letters. But Whitehead's letters speak of points on which he is extremely full of praise, calling Russell's work beautiful, and points on which he is critical, frankly inquiring if the material Russell had sent is not open to this or that unwelcome interpretation or inference, and frequently recommending changes in the method of presenting the material where he finds Russell insufficiently explanatory or inconsistent in his method of exposition.[6] This correspondence, incidentally, needs a careful editing in conjunction with the segments of *Principia Mathematica* that are at issue both in the early letters commenting on parts of the original draft, and in the letters coming later that comment on desirable changes in the proofs. Such a task of collation and interpretation goes far beyond the scope of our discussion. The letters do show how intimate a collaboration the two men enjoyed and how free of any hesitation, indirectness, or apology Whitehead was in reacting to the material Russell sent.

The same ten years that saw *Principia Mathematica's* three volumes made ready for the publisher were years of intimate friendship between the Whiteheads and the Russells. Russell tells us that it was in 1901 that he had an experience of mystic illumination in the presence of Evelyn Whitehead's painful heart attack; later the same year, he discovered that he no longer loved Alys.[7] These two events may be linked, as Ronald Clark argues in his biography of Russell.[8] In any case, the change in the relations between Alys and Bertrand Russell began a period of personal suffering for both of them, Alys trying to regain her husband's love, and Russell veering between distaste for her clumsy, irritating ways and sorrow for the suffering he was helpless to avoid causing her. It must have been a strange and unhappy household when the Russells visited the Whiteheads. Alys and Bertie were indeed unhappy together: he longed for offspring; she blamed him to Evelyn for their childlessness and was miserable that he no longer loved her. Meanwhile, Evelyn confided to Russell her fears for Alfred's sanity, evident in his uncontrolled extravagance, and passed on to him Alys's comments. Russell (perhaps while suffering the pangs of unrequited and unexpressed love) tried to help Evelyn by giving her money unbeknownst to his closest friend, her husband. Russell was so agonized during this time that his journal reports days of despair over his marriage, his love, and his work, and nights wandering in the woods and contemplating suicide.[9] Yet in the letters that Whitehead wrote to Russell during this period all is calm, normal, benign. Usually he makes only minimal personal reference: tell Alys we are sorry to hear she was pelted with eggs at the meeting; Evelyn is very tired and is resting; one of the children is ill and he is worried, or is better and he is relieved; could the Russells visit at a certain time? "Affectionately ANW." In places Whitehead's letters are playful and in places tender. He pokes fun at himself for advising greater care with the formal apparatus in *Principia,* a switch from his usual advice, and, in congratulating Russell for what was thought to be a breakthrough on the contradiction, calls him "Aristoteles secundus." Later, in October 1916, when Russell was being prosecuted for his antiwar activities, Whitehead writes:[10]

> All right—we are always there—Don't be worried on that score for one
> moment. I shall come round and look you up Sunday morning—it will
> not matter if you are out, or engaged—anyhow I shall have a bus ride.
> Don't get up, if you take that morning in bed—you can chat recumbent
> unless you are vastly changed. But why not come here as Evelyn
> suggests, *very much better.*

If Clark is right, and Evelyn *was* the object of Russell's undeclared love, it is
difficult to believe that this would have been unknown to her or to Whitehead, and, in any case, reverberations of his friend's great unhappiness must
have come through to Whitehead. No echo of this appears in Whitehead's
letters, while those written to Russell by Evelyn and the three children
bespeak a warm and close friendship that gave Russell a status of "uncle"
that he enjoyed for many years.[11]

It was during the time when proofs were being read on the last volume of
Principia Mathematica, and the two earlier ones were already in print, that
Russell's personal life took a dramatic turn with his affair with Lady Ottoline
Morrell. Through the final rupture with Alys, the sustaining friendship
continued between the Whiteheads and Russell. Evelyn offered advice and
intervened with Alys. His new and absorbing interest, however, meant that
Russell spent less time with them, and he was not completely successful in
bringing Evelyn and Ottoline to be friends.[12] Yet in his letters to Ottoline he
reported visits with the Whiteheads, good discussions with Whitehead, and
concern over Whitehead's health. It was in January 1914 that Russell sent on
to Ottoline a draft of a paper Whitehead had written and sent to him, which
Russell thought showed incoherence and strange lapses of memory.[13] Soon
after this disturbing letter, however, the two men had a good discussion, and
later the same year they attended a congress in Paris together.

The frequent visits and the sharing of work went on and is recorded in the
Bertrand Russell-Ottoline Morrell correspondence. When Russell returned
to England after his visit to the United States, the war was imminent, and
both Russell and the Whiteheads were distracted by it in different ways.
Russell wrote to Ottoline Morrell: "When I got here [Trinity College] I found
a *very* war-like letter from Mrs. Whitehead, saying North [her son] wants to
enlist and she thinks he is right. I can't tell you how much I mind—I feel as if
my relations with the whole family could never again be quite the same. Next
to you they are the most important people in my life."[14]

Russell later judged that there were two sources of his separation from the
Whiteheads; one was the sharp divergence in their views of the war.
Whitehead felt that declaring war on Germany was the only honorable thing
Britain could do, in the light of the attack on her ally, Belgium; he believed

the atrocity stories and felt very deeply the danger to England. In a careful, painful letter he set forth his arguments against Russell's attack on the war.[15] The Whiteheads tried to keep their friendship untouched by this important difference in points of view, but Russell was frantically engaged in antiwar work, and they were involved in the anxieties of parents with two sons in combat. Notes of support and sympathy were exchanged when Russell was arraigned on charges stemming from his work for conscientious objectors, and when North Whitehead was wounded, and when Eric Whitehead was missing in action.[16] But the war left grave wounds in all their lives, and the deeply held opposing convictions could hardly be overlooked. In addition to this, Russell wrote in his *Autobiography* that Whitehead felt that Russell had preempted work that Whitehead had already done for the fourth volume of *Principia Mathematica* and had given it has own setting and interpretation, and that Whitehead was grieved by this. Russell reproduced the following letter as evidence.

> Twelve
> Elm Park Gardens
> Chelsea, S. W.
> Jan. 8th, 17

Dear Bertie

I am awfully sorry, but you do not seem to appreciate my point.

I don't want my ideas propagated *at present* either under my name or anybody else's — that is to say, as far as they are at present on paper. The result will be an incomplete misleading exposition which will inevitably queer the pitch for the final exposition when I want to put it out.

My ideas and methods grow in a different way to yours and the period of incubation is long and the result attains its intelligible form in the final stage, — I do not want you to have my notes which in chapters are lucid, to precipitate them into what I should consider as a series of half-truths. I have worked at these ideas off and on for all my life, and should be left quite bare on one side of my speculative existence if I handed them over to some one else to elaborate. Now that I begin to see day-light, I do not feel justified or necessitated by any view of scientific advantage in so doing.

I am sorry that you do not feel able to get to work except by the help of these notes — but I am sure that you must be mistaken in this, and that there must be the whole of the remaining field of thought for you to get to work on — though naturally it would be easier for you to get into harness with some formed notes to go on. But my reasons are conclusive. I will send the work round to you naturally, when I have got it into the form which expresses my ideas.

> Yours affectly
> Alfred N. Whitehead

*Before the war started, Whitehead had made some notes on our knowl-
edge of the external world and I had written a book on this subject in
which I made use with due acknowledgement of ideas that Whitehead
had passed on to me. The above letter shows that this had vexed him. In
fact, it put an end to our collaboration.*[17]

After the war, as the correspondence shows, contact between the two men
became infrequent and ceremonial; respect remained, and friendship. But
their paths in life, as well as their philosophic paths, diverged. In the period
framed by these letters—the first from Whitehead to Russell dated 1895,
speaking of Russell's fellowship chances, the last 1945, devoted to the peace
movement—two of the most important and interesting philosophic minds of
the century developed in interaction with, and reaction to, one another.

It is probably because of the great divergence of their later views that little
attention has been paid to what is common in the philosophies of the two
men. A. H. Johnson, for instance, in *Whitehead's Theory of Reality,* has a
chapter in which he compares Whitehead with other philosophers from Plato
to the positivists, but he has no mention of Russell.[18] Whitcheadians have
been thought of as process philosophers or philosophers of organism, and
this philosophy has been seen as opposed to the analytic strain, the limited
scope, and the atomistic assumptions of much contemporary philosophy;
Russellians, or anti-Russellian analysts, have viewed Whitehead as speculative and metaphysical, insufficiently analytic and precise.[19] Such a dichotomy is an almost given framework of thought in our time, and it has meant a
certain compartmentalization by virtue of which those who belong to one
tradition eschew the other and regard it as not being philosophy at all. Thus
there has been little study of the possible similarities and common methods
in the thought of Whitehead and Russell; since Russell's *Inquiry into
Meaning and Truth* (1940) and Whitehead's *Process and Reality* (1929) seem
so far apart, it has not been deemed worthwhile to look for common themes
in the work of their authors, even though they were once close collaborators.
This disregard has been sanctioned, as Victor Lowe has pointed out, by
Russell's having remarked that when he was in England, Whitehead was not
regarded as a philosopher but as a mathematician, and that Whitehead's
interest in philosophy did not develop until he went to America. Lowe
challenged the view and has made important contributions to the study of the
relationship of Whitehead and Russell.[20]

The differences between Whitehead's later thought and Russell's are
sufficiently marked, but the thesis here to be considered is that there are
large areas of agreement stemming from the period of their collaboration,

from the concept of philosophical method that they then shared, and from the common methodological techniques which were never abandoned, although the subject-matter and outcome of the methods were strikingly different. Perhaps the dichotomy of speculative versus analytic thinking is not so sharp as has been supposed by C. D. Broad and others.

6.2 *Collaboration on* Principia Mathematica

In 1898 Whitehead published the first volume of a projected two-volume book, *A Treatise on Universal Algebra*. He had been working for seven years on it, and it concerned developments in mathematics upon which Whitehead proposed to form the foundation of a systematic symbolization of mathematics: "The ideal of mathematics should be to erect a calculus to facilitate reasoning in connection with every province of thought, or of external experience, in which succession of thoughts, or of events can be definitely ascertained and precisely stated. So that all serious thought which is not philosophy, or inductive reasoning, or imaginative literature, shall be mathematics developed by means of a calculus."[21] This attempt to find such a calculus was to proceed by means of a generalizing of all extant algebras, and the first volume was concerned with analyzing and employing the work of pioneers in this field, principally Hermann Grassmann, Sir William Rowan Hamilton, and George Boole.[22] Whitehead retrospectively states, "My whole subsequent work on Mathematical Logic is derived from these sources."[23] In an article in the Library of Living Philosophers volume W. V. Quine gives an overview of the contents of this early work of Whitehead's and of the two articles that followed it in the extension and refinement of Boolean algebra, but Quine also notes the importance of Whitehead's acquaintance in 1900 with the new symbolism that Russell had learned from Peano and to which he then introduced an enthusiastic Whitehead.[24]

In the preface to the first edition of *The Principles of Mathematics,* dated December 1902, Russell records the way in which his interest developed in dynamics, through geometry, to logic. He describes how problems in the philosophy of arithmetic had posed insoluble problems before he accepted the realism and pluralism of G. E. Moore. He credits Peano with having introduced him to the method and symbolism of which he has made use in the book, and records that Gottlob Frege had anticipated much of his own work. His delay in becoming aware of Frege's writings and the discovery of the contradiction were the occasion of postponing the publication of his book. Russell refers his readers to the appendices for discussion of these topics. He looks forward to a second volume in which the topics discussed in the first volume will be given full strict symbolic treatment.

> The present work has two main objects. One of these, the proof that all pure mathematics deals exclusively with concepts definable in terms of a very small number of fundamental logical concepts, and that all its propositions are deducible from a very small number of fundamental logical principles, is undertaken in Parts II-VII of this Volume, and will be established by strict symbolic reasoning in Volume II. . . .
> The other object of this work, which occupies Part I, is the explanation of the fundamental concepts which mathematics accepts as indefinable.[25]

It is clear that this project overlaps with the project of Whitehead's *Universal Algebra,* and the acknowledgment of Whitehead's assistance in suggestions, encouragement, and proofreading indicates that the two were working together and found it natural to combine their efforts toward what had been two projected second volumes:

> The second volume, in which I have had the great good fortune to secure the collaboration of Mr. A. N. Whitehead, will be addressed exclusively to mathematicians; it will contain chains of deductions, from the premises of symbolic logic through Arithmetic, finite and infinite, to Geometry, in an order similar to that adopted in the present volume; it will also contain various original developments, in which the method of Professor Peano, as supplemented by the Logic of Relations, has shown itself a powerful instrument of mathematical investigation.[26]

When the two authors set out to complete *The Principles of Mathematics,* they found the topic larger than they had supposed, and they arrived at what they regarded as important ideas which solved some of the difficulties of the earlier work. Thus *Principia Mathematica* became a separate work in which they proposed to give "the greatest possible analysis" of the ideas of mathematical logic, to diminish the number of "undefined ideas and undemonstrated propositions," to develop the most precise, simple, and complete notation needed for those ideas, and to solve the paradoxes troubling mathematics and logic.[27] In the first part of the first volume, the primitive symbols and propositions were presented and propositions, propositional functions, classes, the class calculus, and the logic of relations were developed. Subsequent sections of the first volume and the second and third volumes provided full symbolic formulations and proofs of most of mathematics. The fourth volume was to have developed geometry and provided for the application of the methods and formulations of the work to concepts of space, time, and motion.

The philosophical and logical difficulties of *The Principles of Mathematics* were overcome partially by abandoning the realism of terms, classes, and propositions, which, as we have seen, was assumed in the earlier work. The theory of descriptions allowed an escape from that realism by providing an interpretation of nondenoting terms and of classes as incomplete symbols. The definition of the class specified only what would serve as values of the function without the class or its members having any ontological status; thus the unit class, the null class, and the "denoting concept" were no longer problems after the publication of "On Denoting." The theory of descriptions was given a precise formulation as part of the argument of *Principia*.

The theory of types adumbrated in the appendix of *The Principles of Mathematics* as a possible solution to the contradiction of classes not members of themselves was now given a precise form in which a proposition was prevented from including itself in its reference. The result was a "hierarchy" of classes in which first-order propositions referred only to what were not propositions, while second-order propositions referred only to first-order propositions, and so on.

The solution of the contradictions entailed that no statement of an order higher than the first could make a statement about *all* the properties of a class—for example, that Napoleon had all the properties of a great general. Yet in order to ground later parts of mathematics it must be possible, on pain of endless complications, to make such statements. Thus the axion of reducibility was required, asserting that statements could be made about *all* the properties of *a* "providing we remember that it is really a number of statements and not a single statement that could be regarded as assigning another property to *a*, over and above all properties."[28] As this axiom was not self-evident or demonstrable, it was accepted on pragmatic grounds, as leading to no known error and as being necessary for the further development of the system, including the important definition of identity. But neither the authors of *Principia* nor later logicians were entirely happy with the axiom or its employment.

In any case Whitehead and Russell did not claim that *Principia Mathematica* presented the only or the best possible system of primitive definitions and arguments, or that the theory of descriptions, the theory of types, or the axiom of reducibility were necessary to mathematical logic. They claimed them to be sufficient.[29] As we shall see in the next chapter, Russell had reason to abandon or at least revise some of the ideas included in the work.

In speaking of the ten years of work on *Principia Mathematica*, Russell remarks that Whitehead "left most of the philosophical problems" to him, and that, of the mathematical problems, Whitehead invented the symbols that were not Peano's, Russell did the work on series, and Whitehead did everything else. But because of the three workings-over of each part "there is hardly a line in all three volumes that is not a joint product."[30] This judgment is supported by the letters of Whitehead to Russell mentioned earlier. Since Russell's letters to Whitehead were destroyed, and no record (except the book itself) remains of their conversations, it is not easy to reconstruct the details of the debate that took place on various issues of the *Principia Mathematica*. We find Whitehead complaining that the order of exposition and the verbal explanations are not going to be easy for students to follow and telling Russell that "everything, even the object of the book, was sacrificed to making proofs look short and neat."[31] We also find Whitehead observing that in some explanations Russell requires a very narrow interpretation, counter to common sense, of the meaning of a word in one place, and then allows very rough and flexible meanings in other places:

> [undated, late 1905, or early 1906?]
> In reading your work I have the impression of an oscillation between extreme rigour where you expect the reader to take the symbols exactly as they have been defined generally, and extreme slackness in breaking through these general uses where a deviation appears obviously sensible to you. . . . One never knows if you are in your strict mood or your free-and-easy mood.

Whitehead goes on to say that the latter is the only means of working: "at the absolute beginning Frege may be right, but Peano is the practical mathematician and symbolist."[32] Whitehead also raises questions about the arguments and proofs at certain points where difficulties or differences appear. The correspondence shows that such difficulties arose over the dependent variable, over intension and extension, and over the relation of types of individuals.[33]

While *Principia Mathematica* was being written, both Russell and Whitehead published other articles and collaborated on and cross-criticized each others' work. Whitehead published two articles referring to the work he had previously done on universal algebra (published in 1899 and 1901); three articles of 1902, 1903, and 1904 which refer specifically to cardinal numbers and Peano's symbolism, the first crediting Russell with an entire section of the article; two articles on projective and descriptive geometry of 1906 and 1907 respectively, which may be thought to anticipate work to be part of the projected volume 4 of *Principia Mathematica;* and an article "On Mathematical Concepts of the Material World," in *Philosophical Transactions of the Royal Society of London* in 1906, where existing alternative concepts of space, time, and matter are criticized and analyzed.[34] This too may be taken as a part of the material being worked over by Whitehead and intended to become part of the fourth volume, which would include, according to

Russell, concepts of structure and the application of the ideas worked out in volumes 1, 2, and 3 to geometry and to the physical world.[35] (We will return to the previously mentioned article later in this chapter.)

Russell published a number of articles during the same period dealing with topics that are part of the work he was doing on *Principia Mathematica* and that were subsequently published there in complete form. These include an article of 1905, "On Denoting," which was the first statement of the theory of descriptions; "On Some Difficulties in the Theory of Transfinite Numbers and Order Types" and "The Theory of Implication," both of 1906; and "Mathematical Logic as Based on the Theory of Types" of 1908.[36]

In the years following the completion of *Principia Mathematica,* Russell and Whitehead collaborated in writing the section of the *Encyclopaedia Britannica* on mathematics for the edition of 1911; in the same year Whitehead published *An Introduction to Mathematics,* his "shilling shocker," in the Home University Series, lavishly praised by Russell.[37]

It seems apparent from what Russell says in different passages that the projected fourth volume of the *Principia Mathematica* was to be concerned with topics in geometry and in the application of the concepts of geometry to the basic concepts of space, time, and matter as these were used in science;

> The central problem by which I have sought to illustrate method is the problem of the relation between the crude data of sense and the space, time, and matter of mathematical physics. I have been made aware of the importance of this problem by my friend and collaborator Dr. Whitehead, to whom are due almost all the differences between the views advocated here and those suggested in *The Problems of Philosophy.* I owe to him the definitions of points, the suggestion for the treatment of instants and "things," and the whole conception of the world of physics as a *construction* rather than an *inference.* What is said on these topics here is, in fact, a rough preliminary account of the more precise results which he is giving in the fourth volume of our *Principia Mathematica.* It will be seen that if his way of dealing with these topics is capable of being successfully carried through, a wholly new light is thrown on the time-honored controversies of realists and idealists, and a method is obtained of solving all that is soluble in their problem.[38]

Russell goes on to say that the purely technical aspect of this project can be caried on only with the aid of mathematical logic and will be seen in full detail when Whitehead's work is published. A similar acknowledgment of Russell's debt to Whitehead without the reference to the by-then-abandoned volume 4 of *Principia Mathematica* may be found in the introduction to the second edition of *The Principles of Mathematics.*[39] "Dr. Whitehead, at this stage, persuaded me to abandon points of space, instants of time, and particles of matter, substituting for them logical constructions composed of events. In the end, it seemed to result that none of the raw material of the world has smooth logical properties, but that whatever appears to have such properties is constructed artificially in order to have them." A similar acknowledgment occurs in the foreword to the German edition of *The Problems of Philosophy*.

> Whitehead convinced me that "matter" is a logical fiction, that is, a piece of matter can be constructed as a system of connected events in various parts of the space-time continuum. There are various methods one can use to carry this through—the choice between them has been very difficult up to now. Whitehead gave one way in his [*An Enquiry Concerning*] *Principles of Natural Knowledge* [1919] and in [The] *Concept of Nature* [1920]; another way is presented in my book, *Our Knowledge of the External World*. [dated November 1, 1924][40]

With the aid of these published acknowledgments, with reference to Whitehead's own articles and books, and with recourse to the available correspondence, we can trace the development of the ideas that were to have been discussed in volume 4, the reasons for the decisions made with respect to them, and the similarity and difference between their final forms as they became an important part of the published works of both men, as we shall see.

As was mentioned earlier, Whitehead's articles published during the period of his work on *Principia Mathematica*, like Russell's of the same period, dealt with topics on which work was going forward for their joint project. Russell published on the theory of descriptions and the theory of types; Whitehead on geometry, a relational theory of space, and concepts of space, time, and matter in mathematical physics. In the latter work (1906), there are two main themes: the analysis of extant concepts of points, instants, and matter with critical remarks, and tentative approaches to different definitions. "The object of this memoir is to initiate the mathematical investigation of various possible ways of conceiving the nature of the material world. In so far as its results are worked out in precise mathematical detail, the memoir is concerned with the possible relations to space of the ultimate entities which (in ordinary language) constitute 'stuff' in space."[41] He goes on to say that this article depends on definitions offered in descriptive and projective geometry (these had been topics of previous articles of his); he indicates that his theory of interpoints, theory of dimensions, and "Concept V" are the chief matters of importance in the article. The first two theories mention definitions of points in space of two and three dimensions respectively, while Concept V brings together these technically formulated definitions of spatial points with concepts of instants of time and "objective reals" of which the "stuff" of nature is made up into one framework of interpretation:

> These [linear] concepts depart widely from the classical concept. The objective reals (at least those which, with the instants of time, form the field of the essential relation) have properties which we associate with straight lines, considered throughout their whole extent as single indivisible entities. These objective reals, which in Concept V are all the objective reals, will be called *linear objective reals.* Perhaps, however, a closer specification of the linear objective reals of these concepts is to say that they are the lines of force of the modern physicists, here taken to be ultimate unanalysable entities which compose the material universe but that geometry is the study of a certain limited set of their properties.[42]

At the end of the essay he suggests the possibility of identifying the point, for which he has offered a formal logical and geometrical definition, with an electron. The essay thus demonstrates the use of the method called "extensive abstraction" or "construction" in the definition of a point, which thus ceases to be the nonextended, arbitrary, defined concept of geometry, and to comprise logical, geometrical, and physical dimensions. The "method of extensive abstraction" is a version of the method of construction by which a term for which no denotative meaning can be supplied, or for which any definition appears unsatisfactory, can be replaced by the formulation of a series of propositions which make clear the context in which the term has meaning. This was discussed under the theory of descriptions presented in "On Denoting" earlier. Here, a mathematical construction replaces the problematic extensionless point, as earlier the "present king of France" was replaced by a series of propositions which gave the meaning of the proposition in which the phrase appeared without imputing existence to that royal person, or nonperson. A similar treatment is not given to time, however, and the notion of an "event" has not yet appeared. It is a first sketch.

The description of this article as providing a first sketch of what is needed in the treatment which Whitehead would eventually give to space, time, and matter is confirmed by his later letters to Russell. Writing to Russell in September 1911, Whitehead says:

> I hope to post the proofs at the same time as this letter, viz. before 5 or 6 o'clock when the mail departs. But last night when I should have finished them the idea suddenly flashed on me that *time* could be treated in exactly the same way as I have now got space (which is a picture of beauty, by the bye). So till the small hours of the morning, I was employed in making notes of the various ramifications. The result is a relational theory of time, exactly on four legs with that of space. As far

as I can see, it gets over all the old difficulties, and above all abolishes the instant in time, e.g. the present instant, even in the shape of the instantaneous group of events. This has always bothered me as much as the 'point' — but I have had to conceal my dislike from lack of hope. But I have got my knife into it at last. According to the theory, the time-relation as we generally think of it (sophisticated by philosophy) is a great cook up. Simultaneity does not belong to it. That comes in from the existence of the space-relation. Accordingly the class of all points in space serves the purpose of the instant in time. Also each object runs [?] its own time (properly so-called).

I don't pretend that this is an explanation of the theory. But I jot these notes down to let you see that the theory is rather far-reaching.

The fact is that with large objects — i.e. extended through long times and large spaces — their mutual relations become too complicated for simple logical statement. We break them up into small enough objects and then relations of a sufficient logical simplicity begin to appear. We push this process of paring away at the object to its ideal limit (marked of course by classes of thing tucked away in each other) and (with some cooking) we reach the ideal logical simplicity of time and space as usually conceived.

My root idea is that an object has essential extension in time as well as in space, and that there are time-parts of an object just as there are space-parts. In fact the time and space extensions are the object. The merely formal properties of time and space, as usually considered, arise from their being logical abstractions. The scientific universe arises from the research for objects which are always time-parts of yet greater objects.

The general result seems to me to help a naive realism.[43]

The analysis of space and time by means of the logical techniques of *Principia Mathematica* had already been mentioned as one of the philosophical benefits of mathematical logic by Russell in March 1911. Russell writes:

> From this [the new theory of number and of the continuum] follows a complete revolution in the philosophy of space and time. The realist theories which were believed to be contradictory are so no longer, and the idealist theories have lost any excuse there might have been for their existence. The flux, which was believed to be incapable of analysis into indivisible elements, shows itself to be capable of mathematical analysis, and our reason shows itself to be capable of giving an explanation of the physical world and of the sensible world without supposing jumps where there is continuity, and also without giving up the analysis into separate and indivisible elements.[44]

This anticipation by Russell, however, came when Whitehead had merely sketched out his method of extensive abstractions, and, indeed, the whole essay of Russell's is similar to *The Problems of Philosophy* in the general way it relates logic to physics.

An interesting precursor of later divergences in the philosophic outlooks of Whitehead and Russell can be read in the lengthy criticisms of the manuscript of *The Problems of Philosophy* which Whitehead wrote to Russell in August 1911.[45] These criticisms show that Whitehead, while disclaiming any status as a "professional philosopher" (a title to which in fact Russell at that time had almost as small a claim), had considerable knowledge of Kantian philosophy and was quite willing to tell Russell that his treatment was "not within a hundred miles of Kant."[46] Whitehead also displayed considerable acuity in his philosophical criticisms of inconsistencies and gaps in the argument. He asks, for instance, if Russell is assuming that perceived space is two-dimensional, a vital point in any criticism of an analysis of visual sense perception in which the only given elements of order are right and left, up and down, all other object-qualities being inferred, which Whitehead rightly judges to neglect psychological evidence of depth-perception. In *The Problems of Philosophy* Russell distinguished "knowledge by acquaintance" from "knowledge by description." By the former he understood the directly given, indubitable brown rectangular patches, the smooth, firm textures, and so on, from which is derived knowledge by description of the table. The ordering of successive and neighboring sensations yields by construction the table as an object. Yet, at the same time, the table is taken to be a real object from which reflected light causes our sensations of brown patches of certain shapes.

Whitehead's chief objection to *The Problems of Philosophy* seems to be directed at Russell's treatment of the perception of objects in terms of sense-data to which are added inferences to yield objects. He objects that we perceive colored, shaped, textured objects, not color, shape, and texture qualities from which the object is inferred. Moreover, Russell's view leaves the spatial location of objects in an anomalous position. Whitehead criticizes the refutation of solipsism by pointing out that Russell seems to be assuming the reality of space and the reality of the cat whose reality the solipsist is imagined to be doubting. His judgment: "As far as I can see all your objections are arrived at by making tacit presuppositions inconsistent with the position."[47]

Further objections are voiced to chapters dealing with idealism and with knowledge by acquaintance and knowledge by description; Whitehead points out that Russell assumes a public real space and an apparent private space of the percipient, and that in general the assumed causal connection which renders the perceiver's sense-data real as the product of his relation to the light, physical objects, and so forth might be open to a Berkeleyan interpretation.

It seems likely that Russell's analysis of experience in terms of sense-data, a turn away from naive to representative realism in which Russell followed Moore and which exposed both of them to the charge of phenomenalism, was the most serious objection that Whitehead had to a book which on the whole and for its purposes he judged to be good: "As a 'Message', I cannot praise it too highly." But he points out that Russell is writing while his views are in a state of transition; the ideas which are distinctively Russell's he thinks "excellent" but those in which Russell seems to be "repeating received ideas . . . I cannot follow." Russell's own elation with the book and his belief that it represented a new way of doing philosophy seems more in accord with the book's reception by the public, yet all of Whitehead's doubts regarding the validity of its argument seem justified. Russell does perform a sleight-of-hand with his "table," and certainly the whole view of sense-data, inferences, and physical objects leaves many questions unanswered, questions that Moore, Russell, and others were to wrestle with in succeeding years. I agree with Lowe that Whitehead was probably expressing his doubts about Russell's somewhat Humean analysis of experience, an analysis made under the current influence of Moore. This seems compatible with Whitehead's reactions to Russell's criticism of pragmatism in "Transatlantic 'Truth.'" In a letter of January 5, 1908, Whitehead writes to Russell:

> I always think that some of your best pieces of work are your statements of views which you do not hold—By the bye your article on Pragmatism does not quite convince me—perhaps because the alternative you dismiss without discussion (i.e. "no facts") seems to me by far their strongest thrust. You do not seem to me to touch a theory such as this:
>
>> The life of sensation and emotion (I don't know the technical terms) is essentially without thought and without subdivision. Objects are only for thought; they are the form by which thought represents the alien complex of sensation. As soon as I think 'I perceive the landscape', I am creating for the purpose of thought the objects 'I' and 'the landscape'—and so on, if I proceed to split up the landscape—Now as to truth—there are two essentially distinct indefinable harmonies which constitute the whole of truth (1) the self-consistency of thought with itself—this is logic: and (2) the consistency of thought with the non-rational complex of sensation—but this does not mean that the relations between objects should be thought of, as they are in fact, because the objects themselves are not in fact, they are merely in thought.
>
> Thus for truth the objects of thought are partly arbitrary within the

limits necessary to secure the two harmonies. I am quite prepared to hear that the pragmatist position as thus sketched is too hopeless to require refutation. All I mean is that I do not see how it is refuted on the lines laid down in your article.[48]

While it may be that Whitehead is here playing the devil's (that is, the pragmatist's) advocate, as his last remark may indicate, yet we find increasing divergence between the epistemological view to which Russell tied his use of logical method and the view of experience which Whitehead himself accepted.

From March 1911 on, Russell's letters to Ottoline Morrell give us an idea of what projects were central to his interest. He continually speaks of having useful discussions with Whitehead, of discussing space and time, of Russell's work on matter (Whitehead was working on the mathematical end of this and they hoped to meet in the middle Russell wrote in a letter of December 28, 1912).[49] In a letter postmarked January 19, 1913, Russell reports that he and Whitehead have agreed "to publish what is printed of *Principia Mathematica* at once in a thin volume (about 480 pages) and I have had to make the Table of Contents and List of Errata. . . . What remains to be done to the book is Whitehead's affair—his Manuscript won't be ready till the autumn at the earliest."[50] Thus it was that the third volume of *Principia Mathematica* was published in 1913, while Whitehead continued to work on the mathematical side of the problems of space, time, and matter, discussing them with Russell, who was also thinking of what he called the "psychological" aspects of the same topics.[51]

Early in 1914 there are two mentions of Whitehead's work on space and time in the letters to Ottoline. When Russell reported in January 1914 that he has received a manuscript on space from Whitehead, it is likely that this was the text of the paper which Whitehead read to Le Premier Congrès de Philosophie Mathématique in Paris on April 8, 1914, a paper printed as "La Théorie relationniste de l'espace."[52] In February of 1914, when Russell was preparing for his Lowell Lectures at Harvard to be given the following month, he reported to Ottoline, "[I] discussed time with Whitehead as I had got a result that struck me as odd, but he doesn't think it odd."[53]

Whitehead's view of space and time during this period can best be understood through the lecture of 1914. In it he begins by distinguishing four senses, or four kinds, of space: there is the apparent or perceived space of immediate experience; the apparent or perceived space that is filled in with unperceived elements (the space of common sense); the space of physics; and abstract space. This is an ascending order of abstractness, and the elements of construction which are unconscious in the case of the apparent space of commonsense objects become conscious constructions in the case of the world of physics and mathematics. There is an increasing stability, smoothness, and simplicity as we ascend the levels of abstractness. The fluidity of immediate experienced space is replaced by the space of permanent objects, then by the space of molecules and atoms, and finally by the space of events. (Here we find Whitehead using event language, apparently for the first time.) Whitehead criticizes the traditional assumptions concerning objects that rule out action at a distance (according to which there are no interactions of objects in space) and that legislate that no two bodies can be in the same place at the same time. These assumptions seem to require the further assumption of absolute space, but the contrary assumption presents difficulties as well. Whitehead argues that if a relational view of space be adopted, the point cannot be taken as a primitive, undefined simple. Points must be complex entities, logical functions of the relations between objects which constitute space.

In the relational theory of space it is not to be considered that physical bodies "first exist in space, then act upon one another directly or indirectly. Rather physical bodies are in space because they act upon one another and space is nothing other than the expression of certain properties of their interaction." Whitehead then goes on to supply the logical notions by means of which he plans to give a definition of a point. He goes through an analysis of the logic of relations, and shows how the relation of whole to part is to be fundamental to the construction of the class of points, lines, and surfaces. For apparent or perceived space, Whitehead thinks there may be minimum sensibilia, but for abstract space, any part has a part so there is infinite divisibility without paradox, because of the definition of the point by means of the inclusion series. The method of construction demonstrated in this article anticipates Whitehead's method in later publications; in the 1915 essay "Space, Time, and Relativity," for instance, a less technical presentation of the same point of view is given, event language is defended, and the analogy between the construction of points and the construction of instants is made. In the 1914 article, however, he stresses the aspects of immediate experience which make these constructions possible and concludes, "Our problem is, in fact, to fit the world to our perceptions, and not our perceptions to the world."[54]

In two essays of 1915 and 1916, "The Organisation of Thought" and "The Anatomy of Some Scientific Ideas," Whitehead gives a less technical and more philosophical treatment of the same material. In these essays he raises the question of how science as a set of well-defined logical concepts can represent the ill-defined chaotic stream of experience and have continuity with the kind of organization which commonsense experience of objects provides for the jumbled continua of experience. The level of philosophical sophistication, the reference to the techniques of logic (which are not used in the presentation but referred to), the presentation of the problem of the relation of science, common sense, and experience, make these essays parallel to Russell's *Our Knowledge of the External World*.[55] The chief difference seems to be that Whitehead's view of experience is not of collocations of sense-data or particulars which are the building blocks out of which objects are constructed (as in *Our Knowledge of the External World*) but of a variegated, continuous stream.

> So, finally, we conceive ourselves each experiencing a complete time-flux (or stream) of sense-presentation. This stream is indistinguishable into parts. The grounds of distinction are differences of sense—including within the term, differences of types of sense, and differences of quality and of intensity within the same type of sense—and differences of time-relations and differences of space-relations. Also the parts are not mutually exclusive and exist in unbounded variety.[56]

Again, in the same essay, "The world of present fact is more than a stream of sense-presentation. We find ourselves with emotions, volitions, imaginations, conceptions, and judgments. No factor which enters into consciousness is by itself or even can exist in isolation."[57]

The distinction between sense-objects and thought-objects is, like the distinction between apparent and abstract spatial relations in the 1914 essay, a distinction made by thought. Experience itself as ongoing is unconscious of its construction of objects, although it may consciously construct thought objects as is done in science and mathematics. In these essays Whitehead also acknowledges the realm of metaphysics and indicates that it must, at some point, be brought into relation to science and to experience. These essays, however, are less metaphysical than epistemological and programmatic of the forthcoming detailed treatment of the themes of sense, common sense, and science to be undertaken in *An Enquiry Concerning the Principles of Natural Knowledge* (1919) and *The Concept of Nature* (1920).

It seems, then, that we must consider the ideas of space, of time, and of objects, the analysis of events and of matter, as arising in the work of both Russell and Whitehead from their common concerns, joint discussions, and the work for volume 4 of *Principia Mathematica* which Whitehead carried close to completion and shared with Russell. Although the final volume of *Principia Mathematica* was never published, the work on which it was to have been based was published by Whitehead in the essays and books we have just been discussing, and by Russell in "The Ultimate Constituents of Matter," "The Relation of Sense-Data to Physics," and *Our Knowledge of the External World*.[58]

6.3 The End of the Collaboration

Our Knowledge of the External World, as we noted, contained in the preface a covering acknowledgment to Whitehead for the invention of the method of abstraction. The body of the text concerned itself with the same problems that were of interest to Whitehead: the relations of the worlds of sense, of common sense, and of science, and the kind of logical methods by which the defined entities of one could be understood in terms of the other. The 1914 article of Whitehead's on space set up the continuity in terms of degrees of abstractness but had little to say about the construction of moments of time or of units of matter, although the event language was already in use. In the original version of *Our Knowledge of the External World,* the philosophical public saw the first English version of the method invented and employed by Whitehead except for the tentative and incomplete version in the article of 1905–6, "The Mathematical Concept of the Material World." The currently most-used editions of Russell's *Our Knowledge of the External World* date from the 1920s and make specific references to Whitehead's two books of 1919 and 1920. Neither these books nor the articles of 1916 and 1917 were in print when Russell gave the Lowell Lectures and when the first edition of his book was published in June 1914. If we compare what Russell wrote in his book (and refrain from reading into it the later work of Whitehead), we find there are sharp differences between his treatment of Whitehead's method of abstraction and what Whitehead himself later wrote. Granted that Russell was more concerned with epistemology and that his presentation was intended to be more popular and less technical, yet there is a difference in the strong emphasis on sense-data and in the discussion of the construction of the object as being deliberate rather than "unconscious." This was what led to the widespread interpretation of the book as phenomenalist and must have seemed to Whitehead a serious misconstrual of his original method and its context. A full analysis of time as experienced and of instants as constructed, and a framework for a treatment of time which accommodates events, experienced durations, simultaneity, remembered time, and the requirements of physics is set forth. This seems to suggest, in accord with the correspondence, that Whitehead had already done the detailed work on points, referred to in Russell's letter of January 1914, and presumably also on the material in the paper read in Paris later that year. While the construction of instants was merely sketched out originally by Whitehead (in 1911) and worked on by both men, Russell's letter of February 1914 indicates he has discussed this new development with Whitehead just prior to his departure for Harvard and the delivery of the Lowell Lectures. In this book, as well as in Russell's two articles, "The Relation of Sense-Data to Physics" (January 1914) and "The Ultimate Constituents of Matter" (1915), Russell combines the method of construction (which owes much to Whitehead's method of extensive abstraction) with his own sustained struggle with the problem of making a transition from the private psychological space, time, and objects of individual percipients to the public and objective world of points, instants, and particles of matter. He uses the terms *particulars, sense-data, sensibilia,* and sometimes *event,* and tries to show how the combining of various perspectives of different percipients, the logical method of construction, and the excising of traditional notions of the independent reality of space, time, and matter make it possible to bridge the gap between perception and physics. We know from Russell's letters and manuscripts that these topics consumed much of his time and attention during the years 1911 through 1914 and that, while he borrowed freely from Whitehead's treatment of space, he also worked over the various alternative views of matter with alternative hypotheses. His treatment of the construction of instants of time in "The Relation of Sense-Data to Physics" was tentative and referred not only to Whitehead but to other writers as well. It seems impossible to pick out one part as Whitehead's work and one as Russell's. It should be noted as well that the method of extensive abstraction as Whitehead used it owed much to the method of description developed by Russell in 1905 and to their joint work in *Principia Mathematica.* The entanglement and interdependence of the themes of their work on this period is a natural outcome of an intimate collaboration; the trouble came where their views diverged and where one person spoke for the other without a full realization or report of the other's own particular point of view.

In short, this is what appears to have happened in the Russell-Whitehead collaboration: Up until 1914 it seems that they worked on parallel or overlapping lines and were able to work out any disagreements before the relevant parts of *Principia Mathematica* appeared, but when Russell gave and then published the lectures that comprised *Our Knowledge of the External World,* that material heavily credited Whitehead but did not accurately represent his point of view, least of all his view of experience. Whitehead, at this time, seemed still to call himself a "naive realist" and to be far from the atomistic, constructivist view of sensation and sense-objects which Russell advanced. While there are parallels between the attack on a body-mind dualism in Russell's "The Relation of Sense-Data to Physics," the rejection of the simple-minded acceptance of the independent reality of space and time in that essay and in "The Ultimate Constituents of Matter," and the criticism Whitehead made of the assumptions of science in *An*

Enquiry Concerning the Principles of Natural Knowledge and *The Concept of Nature,* the differences are nevertheless great. Whitehead's criticism is more thoroughgoing and includes Russell's contemporary dualism of subject and object in acquaintance (or at least the view that Russell expressed until 1921). Whitehead, on receiving a copy of *Our Knowledge of the External World* on August 28, 1914, wrote congratulations; but the note is included in an extended defense of Whitehead's position on the war as against Russell's. With respect to *Our Knowledge of the External World* he says:

> Yesterday the Open Court Co. sent me your book. Many thanks. You know what I think of it—but what a miserable time for publication. It will be a long time before questions of philosophy receive attention even in philosophical circles. The world will lose if it doesn't attend to some of your ideas. Meanwhile I shall be very busy—my own lectures have to be given, and also the lectures of my assistants who have been embodied in the Territorials or have gone abroad . . . I wonder where you are.[59]

More agonizing differences of opinion on the war were to follow, but the two men tried to retain the old friendship throughout.

In 1916 we find two letters from Whitehead to Russell attempting to arrange for Russell to read "The Organisation of Thought," which Whitehead had first read before the British Association for the Advancement of Science. On that occasion Whitehead had only one copy and was trying to set aside the time to read it to Russell. Apparently this plan failed, as a subsequent letter reports that the meeting went well and that Whitehead has been invited to give the same lecture before the Aristotelian Society and would like Russell's opinion first. Whether there was, on this occasion, a discussion of the ideas involved we cannot tell, as the letters from Russell to Whitehead have not survived for the most part. Nor do we know what Russell's reactions were to the other essays of this period when they were published in book form under the title *The Organisation of Thought* in 1917.

In 1917 Russell decided that he had done all he could in the service of peace and would return to philosophy. He proposed as a project completing the work for which *Our Knowledge of the External World* had been a sketch. Open Court refused him permission to use portions of *Our Knowledge of the External World,* but more significantly, Whitehead, as we have seen, refused him permission to employ the manuscript notes which Russell had previously consulted in working up *Our Knowledge of the External World.*[60]

From the vantage-point of the material considered here, it seems that Russell, in his note appended to Whitehead's letter, does not give due weight to the growing differences between the two philosophers, which meant that *Our Knowledge of the External World,* although crediting Whitehead generously for the original ideas, gave an interpretation of these ideas not in accord with Whitehead's own interpretation. As with Moore earlier and with Wittgenstein later, Russell's version of what he and his collaborator held did not necessarily represent the views of each equally well or please the other philosopher even when credit was given him. It is in the division of points of view that the collaboration necessarily foundered, though "vexation" may have had something to do with it. As to Whitehead's refusal to provide material—since in 1919 and in 1920 he published his own very carefully formulated—and very Whiteheadian—version of his ideas, it is understandable that in 1917 he wished to protect his almost-finished work. The contrast between these two books and what Russell did work on (in the absence of means of returning to matter and the physical world), that is, the lectures on *The Philosophy of Logical Atomism,* show how wide the gulf between the former collaborators had become. (At the same time, as we shall see, Russell's labors on *Theory of Knowledge* had been frustrated by the influence of, and subsequent criticism by, Wittgenstein.) That the division of their feelings about the war, and the loss of the Whitehead's son, were the causes of the end of their collaboration seems untenable; their paths had already grown apart, although the war made it more difficult for their friendship to survive in any vital form the end of their philosophical partnership. This aspect of their diminishing association is perhaps reflected in the preface to *An Enquiry Concerning the Principles of Natural Knowledge,* where Whitehead refers to the war and does not give credit to Russell for any contribution to the ideas of the book.[61] By this time, of course, much of the earlier discussion of the space, time, and matter of physics which had occupied both Russell and Whitehead before the war and would have been included in volume 4 of *Principia Mathematica* had been rendered obsolete by the work of Einstein. Whitehead, in particular, had been actively concerned with the alternative philosophical interpretations of relativity. (The special theory of relativity was published in 1905, the general theory in 1916.) It was not until 1927 and *The Analysis of Matter* that Russell would return to the philosophical discussion of physics and to the problems that were concerned with matter, space, and time.

6.4 Whitehead's Divergent Views

The philosophical outcome of the method of extensive abstraction—which Whitehead had originally proposed as a means of dealing with points, instants, and particles of matter, and of constructing a viable alternative to the logical impossibilities of real space, real time, and real matter—can be read in *An Enquiry Concerning the Principles of Natural Knowledge* and *The Concept of Nature.* As his letter to Russell indicated, the slow maturation of his thought resulted in a view far different from any he had shared with Russell and incorporated a more speculative element.

The originality of the new point of view can be seen in a passage from *An Enquiry Concerning the Principles of Natural Knowledge,* where he elaborates on the importance of relatedness in experience.

> The sense of action is that essential factor in natural knowledge which exhibits it as a self knowledge enjoyed by an element of nature respecting its active relations with the whole of nature in its various aspects. Natural knowledge is merely the other side of action. The forward moving time exhibits this characteristic of experience, that it is essentially action. This passage of nature—or, in other words, its creative advance—is its fundamental characteristic; the traditional concept is an attempt to catch nature without its passage.[62]

This passage shows Whitehead adopting a philosophical perspective encompassing nature as a whole, speculating about the characteristics which may be found to be pervasive, and refusing to isolate problems of philosophy, of physics, of geometry, of metaphysics, or of theory of knowledge. Action and duration appear as central concepts, and a critical perspective on other philosophies and on the presuppositions of science is to be developed from the standpoint of these concepts. *An Enquiry Concerning the Principles of Natural Knowledge* offers an extended mathematical and physical treatment of instants, points, and objects in terms of events along former lines. The theory that had been presented as a tentative analysis of different possible conceptual frameworks of space, time, and matter in the 1906 article, and that appeared as a technical treatment of points (with instants in the background) in 1914, and what appeared as a parallel treatment of points and instants in 1915, had become by 1919 a well-thought-out position that starts with temporal durations and constructs instants and points and event structures from the passage of durations.

In *The Concept of Nature,* the early chapters contain a celebrated critique of traditional concepts in philosophy and in science. Whitehead views the concept of substance as an unfortunate holdover from subject-predicate logic, which encouraged the belief in the substantive nature of subjects (a view Whitehead shared with Russell). But he also attacked the epistemological point of view from which perception was interpreted as direct awareness which yielded cognition. For him the perceived objects are cut out by thought from a perceptual flow not yet cognitive by a process which is unconscious. Here we have a position similar to that of William James, whom

Whitehead had earlier defended against Russell's criticism. In this respect Whitehead rejects the view that Russell held when he maintained the strict distinction between knowledge by acquaintance and knowledge by description, along with the subject-object distinction entailed by the subject's awareness of the object in knowledge by acquaintance, which had its own influence on the views Russell held in 1914. Whitehead includes a famous criticism of the Humean view that bases cause on spatial and temporal correlations, a view characteristic of the sensationalistic atomism that Russell shared with traditional British empiricism. He also attacks the causal theory of perception that regards the sense-object as the end of a causal chain leading from the object to the sense-organ, a linear view of a sequence of events in space-time which comports neither with Whitehead's view of nature nor with a Humean view of cause. The culmination of Whitehead's line of criticism is his attack on the "bifurcation of nature," in which he shows that the outcome of all these assumptions about substance, cause, and perception is to divide nature into the apparent and the real, mind and body, primary and secondary qualities.

> The reason why the bifurcation of nature is always creeping back into scientific philosophy is the extreme difficulty of exhibiting the perceived redness and warmth of the fire in one system of relations with the agitated molecules of carbon and oxygen, with the radiant energy from them, and with the various functionings of the material body. Unless we produce the all-embracing relations, we are faced with a bifurcated nature; namely, warmth and redness on one side, and molecules, electrons and ether on the other side. Then the two factors are explained as being respectively the cause and the mind's reaction to the cause.[63]

Whitehead goes on to suggest that such a framework of relations might be of space and time relations, and this is the locus of his proposal for a unitary process of nature conceived in terms of events within which both spatial and temporal relations can be formally defined, since the lived flow of durations is directly known. For his purpose it is necessary to give a detailed criticism of all other theories of space and time proposed or assumed as being compatible with the results of physics.

In the discussion of time in chapter 3 of *The Concept of Nature* there is much that is similar to the sketch given in *Our Knowledge of the External World* by Russell: the contrast between lived time, with its duration, or temporal thickness—the specious present of which one is aware—and constructed time, as made up of instants with no thickness—complex logical constructs to fit the purposes of science. This construction takes place by the extension of one duration over another, by the narrowing down of the defined instant by a series of enclosures. The transitive, asymmetrical relation is necessary for this definition. This is one on "all fours" with the earlier proposed treatment of points, and similar to Russell's treatment of 1914.

The difference between Whitehead's use of the method of extensive abstraction through enclosure series and Russell's use of the same method through a series of overlappings is not of great importance; Whitehead in *The Concept of Nature* regards the choice between the relation of overlapping and the relation of enclosure as arbitrary in the construction of points and instants. What is important is the philosophical framework in which this construction takes place. For Whitehead an event is defined as a unity not to be dismembered in terms of the three factors of time, space, and matter, but to be seen as retaining in itself a unity which is that of "passage" in nature, a passage which marks our experiencing of events. From the continuity of events, the characteristics of point-instants are constructed by the logical technique of extensive abstraction. There is thus no atomic structure and no maximum or minimum durations in nature.[64]

The discussion of the percipient event from the perspective of which durations are experienced, the cogredience of the "here" and the "now," seems similar to Russell's concept of perspective in "The Ultimate Constituents of Matter." However, the preeminence of passage and continuity in Whitehead's view, and his insistence that the correlation of perspectives is neither postulated nor to be regarded as a miracle unless one has already assumed the reality of nature in space at an instant, differentiate his view from Russell's. If space and time relations are structures of events constructed from lived durations, no problems of internal and external or subjective and objective can arise. If objects—the molecules, atoms, or electrons of science—are constructed as relatively permanent structures of the overlappings of time-space perspectives, then there is no need to regard these "entities" as physical, material, or in any traditional way substantive. Whitehead says "the theory of objects is the theory of the comparison of events. Events are only comparable because they body forth permanences."[65] Objects may be sense-objects, such as a certain shade of blue. These are relatively nontransient, existing in a situation in which the perceiver posits them as objects in such relations within that situation. Whitehead uses the term *ingression into nature* to express the way in which the sense-quality is related within nature in the situation, with the percipient event, and with the other related events in nature. When he goes on to analyze the perceptual object, he discusses how the habits built up on the basis of experience inform the way the body of the perceiver adjusts the color sense-object to the tactual sense-object, anticipating the warmth, roughness, and constraint of a worn coat from the perceived blue shape. This is not a function of judgment, but judgment enters in when the classification of kinds of objects occurs. Such judgments lead to the distinction of physical from delusive objects. This distinction involves the extent to which the sense-object is correlated with other sense-objects of the situation (the object is felt as well as seen and heard), and with other percipient events (it affects the other perceivers in the situation). Finally this leads Whitehead to the scientific objects:

> Thus the origin of scientific knowledge is the endeavor to express in terms of physical objects the various *roles* of events as active conditions in the ingression of sense-objects into nature. It is in the progress of this investigation that scientific objects emerge. They embody those aspects of the character of the situations of the physical objects which are most permanent and are expressible without reference to a multiple relation including a percipient event. Their relations to each other are also characterized by a certain simplicity and uniformity. Finally the characters of the observed physical objects and sense-objects can be expressed in terms of these scientific objects. . . . Scientific objects are the things in nature to which formulae refer.[66]

It is in this discussion of sense-objects, perceptual objects, and physical objects that the sharpest contrast between Russell and Whitehead can be seen. For the former, the atomistic sensationalism of the Humean tradition, with the sharp distinction between knowledge by acquaintance and knowledge by description, cannot avoid cutting the sense-data (even with the additional of sensibilia) from the structure of nature as object, referring the sense-data to the subject, and the structure of nature to the object. Moreover Russell's view requires the continuities and stabilities (i.e., the most marked characteristics of those situations in which Whitehead describes the percipient event), the relations, and the objects to be constructed by a conscious logical technique. This seems to leave Russell dangling between a view of representative realism, with its sharp dualism of subject-object, cause-effect, and body-mind, and a phenomenalism of sense-data which seems to flirt with solipsism or Berkeleyan subjectivism.

Most noticeable of all are the differences between Russell's attempt to use extensive abstraction as a logical technique to formulate the relations between experience, common sense, and science and Whitehead's development of that same theme. Whitehead is reaching for a philosophy of nature, and, in his books of 1919 and 1920, he makes theory of knowledge a concern subsidiary to the main theme of a view of nature within which all these kinds and aspects of experience and knowledge can be related. Russell, on the other hand, never moves far from his epistemological interest.

Back in 1913–14, when Russell and Whitehead were still planning a joint fourth volume of *Principia Mathematica,*Russell's work might have developed in a way that would not overlap with Whitehead's. This would have happened if, first, the book on theory of knowledge had not run into a destructive storm of criticism from Wittgenstein, as we shall see in the following chapter, and if the original plan for Russell's Lowell Lectures, which was to concern "The Search for Wisdom" or "The Search for Insight," had been followed. (The change in plan was due to the terms of the trust, by which a proposed lecture on "The Place of Good and Evil" was disallowed. It was to have been the capstone of the lectures, incorporating much of the material that Russell and Ottoline Morrell had originally written as "Prisons."[67]) Just as Moore drew Russell apart from Whitehead with respect to sense-data, so Wittgenstein drew Russell away from Whitehead with respect to logic and philosophy in relation to logic. These influences account for the sharp divergence of Russell's work between 1917 and 1921, during the time Whitehead was working on the two major books we have been discussing. Russell's two important works of that period were "The Philosophy of Logical Atomism" (1919) and *Introduction to Mathematical Philosophy* (1921). It is interesting to speculate on what direction his work would have taken had Whitehead provided the notes he wanted. With a large part of his theory of knowledge still not reconstructed after Wittgenstein's critique, and with the way to the philosophy of matter blocked, Russell turned to the theme of "The Philosophy of Logical Atomism," which shows the high-water mark of Wittgenstein's influence, and to an introductory, nontechnical presentation of the development of mathematical logic. It is this latter book that traces the influence of various logicians on the development of the subject-matter. Whitehead is referred to in the text as "my friend and collaborator Dr. A. N. Whitehead," and in several different passages a point is made of attributing the work on specific topics of *Principia Mathematica* to Whitehead. The references are to the work on fractions, on complex numbers of a higher order as of importance to geometry, and on limits and continuity of functions as not requiring number. The single tentative reference to Wittgenstein refers to his view of logic with respect to tautologies.[68]

In Whitehead's writings of the early 1920s, chiefly *The Principle of Relativity* (1922) and *Science in the Modern World* (1925), there is much that is of interest to Russell and overlaps his own work. The other results of Whitehead's extraordinary philosophical activity during the years at Harvard were of less interest to Russell, who regarded them as speculative, semi-mystical, and panpsychist in tone. He confessed that there was much in them that he never succeeded in understanding. Russell's own work in the 1920s is close to Whitehead's in interest if not in its conclusions: *The Analysis of Mind* of 1921 and, in particular, *The Analysis of Matter* of 1927.

The first of Russell's two books is concerned primarily with theory of knowledge and behavioristic psychology and contains no references to Whitehead's work. Yet we might expect that the new themes introduced would bring Russell closer to Whitehead, as some of the chief epistemological points on which we have seen them to be divided are points on which Russell makes a complete change. He does this under the influence of William James and the New Realists, and with the help of psychology; but the rejection of the subject as a term in the analysis of the knowledge relation, the rejection of the metaphysical dualism of mind and matter with the adoption of "neutral monism," the rejection of the sharp distinction between knowledge by acquaintance and knowledge by description, and the recognition of unconscious inferences and habitual interpretations as part of the given in experience—all these suggest a view closer to the one Whitehead held in *An Enquiry Concerning the Principles of Natural Knowledge* and in *The Concept of Nature*. Russell uses the language of "particulars" and views these, on the one hand, as the units grouped in classes through successive times and, as such, the basis of the construction of the data of perception; and, on the other hand, as the units grouped as classes through simultaneous observations and, as such, the basis of the construction of the entities of physics. Particulars include both some that are perceived, as in sensation, and some that are not perceived, such as occur in places where there happen to be no perceivers. In this sense the particulars function in a way similar to the "sensibilia" of his earlier work. However, these same particulars are, in themselves, neutral as to mind or body, and as to perception or physical reality. Russell tells us that if particulars are grouped longitudinally, that is, through time, they form "biographies" and the correlations of these biographies are formulated as the laws of psychology. The same particulars grouped laterally, that is, as at a moment of time, and simultaneously arranged in space, form the events of which the "matter" of physics is constructed, and of which the laws of physics are correlations. Russell's concern in *Analysis of Mind* is to explain all the phenomena of what was formerly called "consciousness"—sensation, imagination, memory, thought, belief, and desire—according to this philosophical hypothesis. In this way he hopes to cut through the "materialistic" assumptions of psychology, which no longer fit with the dematerialized matter of current physics, to a view that will be equally at home with body and mind, matter and thought.

In doing this, however, Russell is not able to weld together into one kind of "stuff," one neutral reality, the "stuff" of the particulars; just as there are entities discussed by physics that are never experienced, so there are entities discussed by psychology that are not equally physical, such as images. The very distinction of successive times and simultaneous spaces reinforces the dualism. Further, the framework in which Russell explains perception and the physiological basis of "psychic" functions is built on the body, on the causal theory of perception, and on the location of "places" where the body is and where the perceived object is. Even though we are cautioned against giving the usual commonsense dualistic and realistic interpretation to this language, so that we do not assume objective space and time, and causes operating from "here" to "there" or from "object" to "consciousness of object," it is very difficult to follow the argument of the *Analysis of Mind* without pushing Russell's interpretation back either into a bifurcated nature and dualistic epistemology, or into a thoroughgoing phenomenalism. Both interpretations have been defended by commentators on Russell. It seems clear that he means to retain the method of construction of objects and of instants and points which was set forth in *Our Knowledge of the External World*, but to do so in a framework of his new "neutral monism." In attempting this, his object, if not his attainment, makes his work parallel to the more metaphysically oriented work of Whitehead. It is in the book on matter that the similarities and contrasts become more apparent.[69]

6.5 Matter, Space, and Time: Two Views

The *Analysis of Matter* is devoted to the discussion of the relation of physics to perception and perception to physics, for Russell argues, "We must therefore find an interpretation of physics which gives a due place to perceptions; if not, we have no right to appeal to empirical evidence."[70] The problem has three aspects: a logical one that asks "What deductive structure will serve the needs of physics?" An epistemological one that asks "What facts and entities do we know of that are relevant to physics and may serve as its empirical foundation?" And an ontological one that asks "What are the ultimate existents in terms of which physics is true (assuming that there are such)? What is their general structure? And what are the relations of space-time, causality, and qualitative series respectively?"[71] Russell answers the first question by providing a logical structure based on "particulars," the second in terms of a causal theory of perception, and the third in terms of events. In all three, Whitehead's previous analyses are an important resource. There are more references to Whitehead than to any other person in the index of the book, and credit is frequently given, approval expressed, and, in certain crucial matters, a contrary position argued for. In the latter case, then, the main incompatibility of viewpoints is clear.

In general, Russell approves Whitehead's taking the same problems as central to his work, approves his use of a logical mathematical method, agrees with the main lines of his solution, agrees with his masterly analysis of the history of science and with his detection and rejection of the fallacy of the "bifurcation of nature." Russell disagrees, although tentatively, with Whitehead's interpretation of Einstein's way of formulating the outcome of the theory of relativity. In chapter 8, "Geodesics," Russell presents three views of relativity, Einstein's, Eddington's, and Whitehead's. According to Russell, in all three interpretations the scientific results of Einstein's work are accepted, but various modes of formulating these results have different philosophical interpretations. Whitehead argues against the others that it is preferable to maintain a Euclidean geometry and to use the concept of a field of force to accommodate Einstein's theory, in preference to the use of what Russell calls a "variable geometry," Euclidean or non-Euclidean, as suits the requirements of the specific formulation. Whitehead justifies this position by pointing out that our experience requires, and nature exhibits, a uniformity of structure. The point for Whitehead is not that non-Euclidean geometry is unacceptable, but that a uniform geometry ought to be possible. This would also have the effect of keeping the logical structure of geometry separate from the varying empirical demands of the description of the natural world. That is, for Whitehead, it is epistemologically, logically, and metaphysically preferable to adopt the realism of his view of nature as opposed to the idealism that Einstein adopts. Russell says he does not see that it matters which interpretation is adopted so far as the analysis of physics is concerned; it would be a matter of convenience, and he finds Einstein's formulation more convenient. He wonders if Whitehead is making some kind of assumption of the reasonableness of nature, but postpones further discussion of the epistemological issues.

Part II of the *Analysis of Matter* concerns epistemological issues in the relation of perception to physics. Russell warns us that his view is to diverge from Whitehead's:

> It is by means of mathematical logic that Dr. Whitehead has been enabled to make his immense contribution to our problem. But, greatly as I admire his work, which I place far above anything else that has been written on the relation of abstract physics to the sensible world, I think there are points—and not unimportant points—where his methods break down for want of due attention to psychology and physiology. Moreover, there seem to be premisses in his construction which are

derived rather from a metaphysic than from the actual needs of the problem. For these reasons, I venture to think that it is possible to obtain a solution less revolutionary than his, and somewhat simpler from a logical point of view.[72]

The first criticism that Russell makes of Whitehead is in relation to the latter's argument against the position that there are different kinds of space—visual space, tactual space, and so forth. Whitehead argues that adopting this view would also lead to spatial time, visual time, etc., and thus to the whole stream of experience falling into parts. This tendency follows from making space dependent upon the relations between figures, and carried to its logical conclusion would make it a miracle that in one room the visual and tactual newspaper would make its appearance simultaneously. Russell argues that the difference of the two views is partially due to a terminological difference but that it is proper to make both space and time orders based on correlations; that such correlations are not miraculous depends on the causal theory of perception. After all, visual and tactual and all other images are within the physical space of the brain, and the correlations of visual and tactual sensations occur simultaneously, that is, within one time. It seems that here Russell is challenging an assumption Whitehead makes about experience—that is, that the interrelatedness is not patched together but is given with its own duration and extension, visual and tactual spaces being abstractions from it. On the other hand, Whitehead's view challenges one Russell appears to hold, which is that there is, after all, physical space, for example, where the head itself is, and that we can trace the various psychological spaces back to this causally, and that there is a time, within which experienced events either are or are not simultaneous.[73]

There are several other passages in this section of the *Analysis of Matter* where Russell attributes views to Whitehead that he himself finds unacceptable; there is no full discussion of the issues nor a documentation of Whitehead's views; however, these passages indicate Russell's perception of the divergence of the positions from which they approach their common problem.

In discussing the causal theory of perception, Russell points out that in such matters there is no possibility of logical proof:

> A certain collection of facts is known to me by perception and recollection; what else I believe about the physical world is either the effect of unreasoning habit or the conclusion of an inference. Now there cannot be any logical impossibility in a world consisting of just that medley of events which I perceive or remember, and nothing else. Such a world would be fragmentary, absurd, and lawless, but not self-contradictory. I am aware that, according to many philosophers, such a world would be

self-contradictory. I am aware also that, according to other philosophers, what we perceive is not fragmentary, but really embraces the whole universe—what is fragmentary is only what we perceive that we perceive . . . the second is that of Bergson and (perhaps) of Dr. Whitehead.[74]

. . . . What grounds have we for inferring that our percepts and what we recollect do not constitute the entire universe? I believe that at bottom our main ground is the desire to believe in simple causal laws.[75]

These passages are followed by Russell's familiar argument for the likelihood of the existence of the external world, of the existence of other persons, and of the acceptability of their testimony, and, hence, (on the basis of correlations) of the account of perception in terms of causal laws. Ultimately these strategies provide for Russell an escape from the unacceptable alternative of subjectivist, phenomenalistic solipsism.

It seems likely that the views of perception in this part of *Analysis of Matter* are opposed not by a radical mysticism on Whitehead's part but by the latter's rejection of the atomistic and subjectivistic pattern of Russell's interpretation of sense-perception that Whitehead finds to follow from mistaken assumptions, including the bifurcation of nature. Whitehead instead takes experience to be marked by just the unities and "objects" which we meet there.

A more substantive and technical point of divergence is discussed in chapter 28, "The Construction of Points"; here Russell takes issue with Whitehead's construction of points and events in terms of an enclosure series. He argues that Whitehead is thus committed to the position that there is no minimal extension for an event. Russell adds that psychology may well find that there is a minimum perceptible event and that such a minimum seems compatible with the theory of quanta in physics. Similarly, Russell contends that either there must be a maximum length for something that one would call an event or the event must itself have a complex structure made up of parts. For Russell events are defined as simple, and therefore they must last for only a few seconds, as otherwise they would have parts. By a similar argument, if Whitehead defines a point by means of an enclosure series which has no limit, the point must have no minimal extension. For his part, Russell defends his proposal of a relation of overlapping as the basis of such a definition, and develops, in two chapters, the mathematical implications of his definitions.

Russell's criticism of the way in which Whitehead constructs points and instants, or "events," leaves some questions unanswered. Why does Russell identify the *experienced event*, which Whitehead describes as having temporal thickness, duration, and, specifically as not being a knife-edge present, with the *constructed scientific point-instant events* which have been so made, by means of extensive abstraction, as to have the characteristics of smoothness, uniformity, and infinite divisibility required by science but not found in experience? It is only of the former that one would ask what psychology has to say about the minimal length of an event, and only of the former that one would say that it could endure at most a few seconds. But it is of the latter that one may ask if it is appropriate for it to have an internal structure, and it is of the latter that one can ask whether Whitehead's relation of enclosure, of whole covering part, is inferior or superior to Russell's relation of overlapping. Hence when Russell warns that his major criticism of Whitehead's treatment of time, space, and matter concerns his neglect of physiological and psychological data,[76] it is difficult to evaluate this criticism. One may say that Whitehead intends to take experience as given and to show how objects of common sense and of science, and science's concepts of points, instants, are constructed from this material by logical techniques, and that Whitehead does not conceive himself to be required to relate this to the data of physiology and psychology, except insofar as their objects, including the physical head with its bones, nerves, and so on is one such construct. For Russell, it may be necessary that, through the assumption of the causal theory of perception, the data of physiology and psychology are fed back into the events to establish an underlying "real" space and "real" time that are fundamental. It is not so for Whitehead.

The only other references to Whitehead in the *Analysis of Matter* refer to the holism implied in his maintaining that the given percipient events from which the construction of point-instants starts embrace "passage" and wider interrelations of temporal, spatial, and personal contexts than Russell's view would allow. This, to Russell, smacks of mystical pantheism. Without referring to a specific passage, Russell attributes to Whitehead the view that "different events which constitute a group . . . are not *logically* self-subsistent, but are mere 'aspects,' implying other aspects in some sense which is not merely causal or inductively derived from observed correlations."[77] Similar criticisms are made of Whitehead's views in a review of *Science and the Modern World,* in which Russell agrees with his rejection of the "fallacy of simple location" as this was accepted in the seventeenth and eighteenth centuries, but demurs at Whitehead's alternative:

> However, the new start which he advocates is suggested by Bergson rather than by the technical needs of physics. He is not content with substituting simple location in space-time for simple location in space and time. He regards everything as having aspects everywhere, which

are apparently not separate entities related to the thing, but genuine parts of the thing itself. And he argues that the ultimate conception is that of "organism."[78]

In effect, Russell admires Whitehead's philosophy of science, but rejects the elements of "mysticism" with which Whitehead connects it, but which Russell regards as separable from it. The two views come to fundamental opposition: Russell is inclined to attribute the difference to a speculative and mystical tendency on Whitehead's part; his own analysis shows the tendency toward atomism. Their philosophical differences may be connected, as Russell suggests, with temperamental differences in their angle of vision: "He [Whitehead] said to me once: 'You think the world is what it looks like in fine weather at noon day; I think it is what it seems like in the early morning when one first wakes from deep sleep'"[79] Although in the context Russell is attributing to Whitehead the awakening of Russell to the need for a technique of mathematical logic to "dress up" his "higgledy-piggledy world" in "Sunday clothes," there is a sense in which their perspectives remained marked by such a difference.

During the twenties, one other event occurred that linked the two philosophers by way of their common past. The second edition of *Principia Mathematica* was published in 1927, with a new introduction and new appendixes. These changes were influenced by the work of Wittgenstein and by the cooperation of F. P. Ramsey (whose opinion of their worth was not very favorable, however). Whitehead had inserted in *Mind* the following note:

> The great labour of supervising the second edition of the *Principia Mathematica* has been solely undertaken by Mr. Bertrand Russell. All the new matter in that edition is due to him, unless it shall be otherwise expressly stated. It is also convenient to take this opportunity of stating that the portions in the first edition which correspond to this new matter were due to Mr. Russell, my own share in those parts being confined to discussion and final concurrence. The only minor exception is in respect of #10, which precedes the corresponding articles. I had been under the impression that a general statement to this effect was to appear in the first volume of the second edition.[80]

Whitehead was now settled into a chair of philosophy at Harvard University, where his work became increasingly more metaphysical, and there was, thereafter, little discussion between the two men. Their friendship remained, and a few letters survive, but their students and others who have studied their work since 1927 received the impression that their philosophies are as far apart as it is possible for two contemporary philosophies to be. In fact it is even accepted that each philosopher was a pioneer and leader of contrasting modes of philosophizing, called analytic on Russell's side and speculative (or process philosophy) on Whitehead's. But as we look at their work side by side, seeing influences, interactions, and specific reactions and oppositions, a different picture of the pattern of philosophical development has become clear.

6.6 Russell and Whitehead as Analytic Philosophers

What makes a philosopher analytic? It seems that analysis refers specifically to a method of philosophizing, a method variously described as passing from what is vague, complex, apparently true, to what is clear, precise, simple, known to be true or false. Such methods have traditionally followed the model of mathematics, whether it be Plato's dialectic, Descartes's rules for the understanding, or the logical techniques derived from *Principia Mathematica* and its successors by philosophers such as Rudolf Carnap and W. V. Quine. To this company clearly belong both Russell and Whitehead, themselves pioneers in the development of the application of logical techniques to philosophic problems. As we have seen, the impression is false that Whitehead and Russell were mathematical logicians together, but that Russell was the philosopher, and Whitehead only a mathematician until he came to the United States and became converted to mystical philosophy. In all of Whitehead's work from beginning to end there is a concern with a generalized logical method, and the imprint of the mathematical model is a permanent one; nor was he ever unconcerned with philosophical problems.

Whitehead and Russell share another important aspect of their philosophizing which more than anything else may set them apart from contemporary analytic philosophy: both want to describe nature in the most general terms possible, and in doing so they make use of the physical sciences, their data and their concepts alike. For both men a major concern of their careers, as we have seen, was the attempt to bridge the gap between what experience shows us, what common sense has us believe, and what physical theories reveal about the structure of the world. For both this meant using their analytical tools to dissect the concepts of space, time, matter, and cause.

To this project Russell added a lifelong concern for the problems of theory of knowledge and for the analysis of language, whereas for Whitehead the major philosophical concern was the description of nature in metaphysical as well as physical terms, although Whitehead, too, was interested in meaning and knowledge. It would not be misleading to refer to both as empiricists, but they differed widely in their concepts of experience. For Whitehead, the lived-in, naively presented experience was marked by continuity, variety, instability, passage, infused throughout with meaning, feeling, and action. For Russell, although he came to recognize that the data of "pure" sensation had to be analyzed out of given perceptual experience, experience was of sense-data, separate color-patches, sounds, smells, and so forth, which come to us "encrusted" with habitual interpretations. Only spatial ordering of up and down, right and left, and temporal orderings of earlier and later or simultaneous are in any fundamental sense given, and the "leading on" aspect of experience, its feelings and drives, can be separated off as another topic from ground-level epistemology. This basic difference in their concepts of experience explains much about the differences of the two men, as it does about the different kinds of "empiricists" in our own time. But at least for neither of them did physiology and psychology remain out of bounds for philosophy, since for both, although in different ways, the data of these sciences could contribute to the total view of man's experience in the natural world.

Aside from their conflicting views of experience and the greater speculative reach of Whitehead's description of nature, it is striking how little does divide the two philosophers. Certainly each was significantly influenced by the other. His involvement with Russell in *Principia Mathematica* taught Whitehead the use of logical techniques which he might not otherwise have worked out, and the general strategy of *Principia Mathematica,* with Russell's theory of descriptions, must be seen as contributing to the method of extensive abstraction and the work on space, time, and matter which occupied him throughout his career. Russell acknowledges that the main ideas of applying the techniques of *Principia Mathematica* to space, time, and matter were Whitehead's, but of course his own version was strikingly different. Once again, Russell absorbed and made his own a distinctive part of a contemporary's original work. The problems that came from the attempted fusion of the Moorean aspects of Russell's thought with the Whiteheadian are part of the ongoing story, presenting, as we shall see, a crisis when confronted with Wittgenstein's totally different point of view.

7
Russell and Wittgenstein

MUCH HAS BEEN WRITTEN about the relationship between two of the leading philosophers of the twentieth century; Russell has given several accounts of the influence that Wittgenstein had upon his own thinking, in *My Philosophical Development,* in his *Autobiography,* and in the introductory essay in the Library of Living Philosophers volume devoted to his philosophy.[1] In addition there is an ever-increasing literature on this relationship.[2] In many of Russell's publications of the second decade of the century, he credited Wittgenstein with originating ideas for which Russell was the first spokesman. The letters of Wittgenstein to Russell and the "Notes on Logic," based on Wittgenstein's presentation of his own thoughts, were given circulation by Russell. On the other hand, Wittgenstein has left no written account of their collaboration beyond the critical references in his later work to the position that he himself took in the *Tractatus Logico-Philosophicus* and that he shared to some degree with Russell in that period.[3] Impressions which Wittgenstein's students and friends received concerning the relationship of the two philosophers are now being corrected as archival material becomes widely accessible.[4] Scholarly work on early versions of the *Tractatus* and the publication of Russell's hitherto unpublished book on theory of knowledge are contributing to a fuller view of their interrelations,[5] although ample opportunities for dispute and interpretation remain.

7.1 Russell in 1911

When he met Wittgenstein, Russell was thirty-nine and lecturing at Cambridge on the foundations of mathematics and on logic. He had finished his labors on *Principia Mathematica,* which was being published at the rate of one volume a year, the first having appeared in 1910. He was still collaborating with Whitehead, for whom volume 4 of the *Principia Mathematica* was a responsibility not yet discharged. But essentially Russell was feeling relief after the ten years of concentration on the "big book" and was casting about for his next major task. His personal life had taken a decisive turn when, after years of self-denial and difficulty in his first marriage, he became the lover of Lady Ottoline Morrell in March 1911. With her he was thinking along the lines of ethics and religion, working with her on a book on the release of the self from "prison" through the salvation of philosophy. His interest in politics remained lively, and the companionship of students and colleagues at Cambridge was delightful to him.[6]

So far as his philosophical work was concerned, he had completed two papers for the Aristotelian Society, one on particulars and universals, and one on knowledge by acquaintance and knowledge by description; he had given three papers in France in March 1911; and he had written the popular book in the Home University Library series (which he referred to as "the shilling shocker") *The Problems of Philosophy*.[7] None of this work was of the technical logical kind, and, even prior to the influence of Wittgenstein, Russell had expressed to Ottoline doubt as to whether he could ever return to technical work of any importance in philosophy. This doubt seems to have stemmed from feeling "burned out" as far as mathematical logic was concerned.[8] This may have been a passing mood, perhaps partially engendered by Ottoline Morrell's doubts about her ability to share his work, for it is clear from other letters that he enjoyed the discussions with his students and welcomed their contributions to technical logical projects.[9]

Beyond the themes of religion and ethics, explored in writing he termed "inspirational," Russell's interest was centered on the development of a new realist position that he called "analytic realism," on problems of the use of logical techniques in philosophical methodology, specifically in relation to matter and to sense-data, and on general problems of theory of knowledge. For Russell in 1911, philosophy leaned heavily on the results of science; both physics and psychology provided data for the philosopher, and the analysis of scientific concepts was an appropriate philosophical task. At this time Russell viewed logic as of primary philosophical importance; the most general a priori logical truths provided premises for philosophy; the inventory of logical constants and logical entities provided data for philosophy; the method of analysis of logic provided the method by which the philosopher could move backward from the conclusions of science to its empirical premises, or forward from the data of sensation to the construction of commonsense and scientific objects and concepts. During this period Russell called himself not an empiricist but an "analytic realist," and his method he termed that of "logical atomism." The tenor of his thought was optimistic and comprehensive; he viewed the methodology of logic as capable of both identifying adequate premises and providing constructive techniques that would knit together science, common sense, and empirical data with logic.[10] That Russell held this view of logic is often forgotten, perhaps because it is most clearly expressed in a paper published in French and not translated until 1913, when he had already modified the view of logic that it contained.[11]

In the analysis of propositions, which became a central problem for Wittgenstein and himself, Russell had already had some difficulties. In *The Principles of Mathematics,* he had held that terms were real, and the implication of this realism was that the proposition, in some extended sense, is itself an entity or constellation of entities, in a sense similar to that of Meinong's *Objektiv.*[12] In Russell's 1904 study of Meinong the ultimacy of the proposition was asserted and its property of truth or falsehood, was compared to the ultimacy of the fact that some roses have the property of being red and some of being white. It will be recalled that this was the high-water mark of Russell's propositional realism.[13] But the invention of the theory of descriptions destroyed the necessity of a term or a proposition realism, with its uncomfortable subsistent false propositions and subsistent fictitious entities (which Russell regarded as the consequences of Meinong's position and of his own view before 1905). Following the new way of interpreting "incomplete symbols," as Russell called the seeming names that were the names of nothing, and the introduction of a technical means of restating propositions containing such apparent anomalies as *the present king of France* or *the golden mountain,* he was led in *Principia Mathematica* to refer to the proposition itself as an incomplete symbol.[14] Yet this way of treating it made the general propositions of logic, with their universal truth, different from other propositions, and it appeared to make the proposition, whether logical or empirical, purely verbal. This was troublesome to Russell, as some of Whitehead's remarks in correspondence and his own remarks in unpublished material show.[15] He tried different analyses of judgments and propositions, and it was this crucial theme that emerged as decisive in his discussions with Wittgenstein two years later. He described a complex as that to which a relational proposition refers. The proposition *This pen is red* refers to the complex of pen and color, while the symbol *xRy* refers to the complex xRy. While the complex has its own order and unity, it is also analyzable in terms of its constituents, so that if, in fact, the proposition is in error, that error can be analyzed as due to an erroneous combination of terms that do not relate to one another in a complex as they are said to be related by the proposition.[16] This analysis avoids conferring upon the proposition a psychological meaning as the verbal form of a judgment, and it escapes the Meinongian necessity of postulating referents for false judgments, yet it preserves the realism required by a correspondence theory of truth. This treatment of propositions, however, was not so clearly and sharply perceived that Russell did not often slip over from taking the proposition as a symbol to taking it as a meaning, or as itself a complex.[17] These themes can be seen emerging early in the discussions of Wittgenstein and Russell and are crucial in Russell's final coming to terms with Wittgenstein's criticisms and views.

7.2 *The Encounter with Wittgenstein*

At the time Wittgenstein came to Cambridge he was twenty-two and had studied engineering in Berlin and aeronautics in Manchester. He had become interested in the foundations of mathematics and had read Frege's treatise and Russell's *The Principles of Mathematics*. It has been suggested that it was Frege who directed Wittgenstein to study with Russell. Wittgenstein was already registered for the fall term at Manchester when, on October 18, 1911, he presented himself to Russell as a prospective student. The biographies of Wittgenstein have portrayed him as unhappy, unsure of himself and of what he wanted to do, and as eager to study mathematical logic with Russell.[18]

Russell, as usual, wrote an account of his daily life to Ottoline Morrell and described how a meeting of the Universal Suffrage Society in his rooms was interrupted by the appearance of an "unknown German" who spoke very little English but refused to speak German. Russell wrote, "He turned out to be a man who had learnt engineering at Charlottenburg, but during his course had acquired, by himself, a passion for philosophy of mathematics and has now come to Cambridge on purpose to hear me." The gratification at being thus selected by someone from abroad as an expert on mathematical logic is evident when the account continues: "I went to my lecture where I found my German duly established. I lectured very well, owing to excitement and insufficient preparation. I am much interested in my German and shall hope to see a lot of him."[19]

Russell's letters to Ottoline during the fall term of 1911 reveal an increasing interest in Wittgenstein and a growing estimation of "his German's" ability. Wittgenstein's perversity in argument is referred to humorously: "My German ex-engineer, as usual, maintaining his thesis that there is nothing but asserted propositions. . . . My German was very argumentative and tiresome. He wouldn't admit there was not a rhinoceros in the room." Wittgenstein, now identified as an Austrian, was said to be "very literary, very musical, very mannerly . . . very intelligent." Russell reported Wittgenstein's interest in devoting his life to philosophy, and Russell's own feeling of responsibility in advising him. Russell recognized his student's instability, but more and more felt sure that he had ability of a high order. Moore, whose lectures Wittgenstein attended in the spring term of 1912, agreed with Russell's estimate, while W. E. Johnson refused to continue coaching Wittgenstein in logic because he was so argumentative.[20] At the end of the spring terms of 1912, Russell wrote in his daily letter about Wittgenstein:[21]

> March 17 [#388]
> Wittgenstein came and stayed until after twelve. We had a close equal passionate discussion of the most difficult point in mathematical philosophy. I think he has *genius*. In discussion with him I put out *all* my force and only just equal his. With all my other pupils I should squash them flat if I did so. He has suggested several new ideas which I think valuable. He is the ideal pupil—he gives passionate admiration with vehement and very intelligent dissent. He spoke with intense feeling about the *beauty* of the big book, said he found it like music. That is how I feel it, but few others seem to. Our parting was very affectionate on both sides. He said the happiest hours of his life had been passed in my room. He is not a flatterer, but a man of transparent and absolute sincerity. I have the most perfect intellectual sympathy with him—the same passion and vehemence, the same feeling that one must understand or die, the same sudden jokes breaking down the frightful tension of thought.
>
> He is far more terrible with Christians than I am. . . . He abominates ethics and morals generally; he is deliberately a creature of impulse, and thinks one should be. What he disliked about my last chapter [of *Problems of Philosophy*] was saying philosophy has *value;* he says people who like philosophy will pursue it, and others won't, and there's an end of it. *His* strongest impulse is philosophy.
>
> When he left I was strangely excited by him. I love him and feel he will solve the problems that I am too old to solve—all kinds of vital problems that are raised in my work, but want a fresh mind and the vigour of youth. He is *the* young one hopes for. But, as is normal with such men, he is unstable and may go to pieces. His vigour and life is such a comfort after the washed-up Cambridge type. His attitude justifies all I have hoped about my work. He will be up again next term.

From this time on Wittgenstein and Russell were less student and teacher, and more close friends and collaborators. The letters of Wittgenstein to Russell fill the gaps between terms and refer to personal as well as philosophical matters. Russell worried about Wittgenstein's mental anguish during periods of depression, feared he might commit suicide, recommended hot chocolate, gave him advice which, Russell wrote to Ottoline made him sound to himself like a "puny compromiser":[22]

Sept 5, 1912 [#566]

Then I gave him sage advice, not to put off writing until he had solved *all* the problems, because that time would never come. This produced a wild outburst—he has the artist's feeling that he will produce the perfect thing or nothing—I explained how he wouldn't get a degree or be able to teach unless he learnt to write imperfect things—this all made him more and more furious—at last he solemnly begged me not to give him up even if he disappointed me. I *love* his intransigeance. He makes me feel myself a puny compromiser. But I have such a strong protective feeling towards him that I find it hard to be as reckless for him as he is for himself, though he is quite right.

Russell enjoyed having Wittgenstein as a student and envisioned him as his successor at Cambridge. Their intellectual collaboration began, however, to run into difficulties. Wittgenstein's new ideas were difficult for Russell to understand, and became less improvements of what had already been accomplished in mathematical logic than they were an overturning of its basic ideas. Russell never doubted the importance of what Wittgenstein was doing, even when he did not fully understand it, but Wittgenstein had many doubts about Russell's work. He thought writing on religion, on ethics, and on epistemology was not really philosophy, and he deprecated Russell's work in these areas. He came to criticize much that Russell had done and was trying to do—a criticism that affected Russell deeply. Russell reported that he had become much more skeptical in philosophy under Wittgenstein's influence.[23] This skepticism and the philosophical and logical considerations on which it was based, exercised a lasting influence on Russell's work, as we shall see.

On a personal level there were problems, too. Russell gradually became aware of the differences between them and of the way in which he failed to be to Wittgenstein what Wittgenstein wanted him to be.[24] In a letter to Ottoline he wrote:

[postmarked June 1, 1913] [#793]

Wittgenstein affects me just as I affect you—I get to know every turn and twist of the ways in which I irritate and depress you from watching how he irritates and depresses me; at the same time I love and admire him. Also I affect him just as you affect me when you are cold. The parallelism is curiously close altogether. He differs from me just as I differ from you. He is clearer, more creative, more passionate; and I am broader, more sympathetic, more sane. I have overstated the parallel for the sake of symmetry, but there is something in it.

From their meeting in October 1911 until the writing of Russell's manuscript on theory of knowledge in May and June 1913, Russell's letters and the notes from that period (now in the Bertrand Russell Archives) show us that he was working on the problem of matter, how to give a logical analysis of it and relate it to sense-data, and on the concept of cause. He reported to Ottoline Morrell that Wittgenstein liked much of what he was doing.[25]

In the summer of 1912 Wittgenstein wrote to Russell that he was working on the problem of the apparent variable.[26] He raised questions about atomic propositions and reported that he was working on the problem of a new form of proposition. His and Russell's work are evidently parallel, as we find references to many of the same problems in Russell's manuscript notes. A fragment of this period that indicates that Russell's concept of logic was undergoing change is entitled "What is Logic?" and is dated, by his letter to Ottoline Morrell, September 1912. In this sketch he raised difficulties with the definition of a proposition: if a proposition is a judgment, it is too subjective and psychological; if it is an *Objektiv,* as in Meinong, there must be false objectives as well as true ones; if it is a form of words, it cannot be the concern of logic. A complex is what corresponds to a true proposition, but not to a false one. A form of a complex is what is in common among a number of complexes in which each constituent may be substituted and the complex remain. This is proposed as the subject of logic. "Logic = the class of logical complexes." But Russell found fatal objections to this definition, since if one is substituting in a symbol, it is always possible symbolically, but what would it mean to substitute in a complex when the result is not a complex? (Presumably this applies when the substitution produces a false or nonsensical rather than a true proposition.)[27]

In January 1913 Wittgenstein wrote from Vienna, where he remained during his father's final illness, that he was getting clearer about "the complex problem," that he was wondering if qualities, relations, all could be copulae. (Apparently he, like Russell, was searching for a single form for all propositions.) He believed, he said, that a proper theory of symbolism could make the problems of logic easier, eliminate the theory of types, and prevent the possibility of symbols for different things being substituted the wrong way round (if symbolism was such that only predicates could be substituted for predicates, only subjects for subjects, for example).[28] In an ingenious and persuasive reconstruction of the development of Wittgenstein's criticisms of the logic of *Principia Mathematica* and the application of these criticisms to Russell's work on theory of knowledge, S. I. Sommerville argues that in the letters to Russell of this period, Wittgenstein was struggling to overcome inconsistencies in *Principia Mathematica's* definition of the proposition in relation to the ramified theory of types as put forth there. This has to do with the role of logical constants, the limitation of propositions to apparent rather than real variables, and hence a disagreement with Russell's argument in that work.[29] Russell's sketch shows that he also is trying to work out an alternative to some of the concepts of the *Principia*.

7.3 Theory of Knowledge: The 1913 Manuscript

In May of that year, 1913, Ottoline had left England, and Russell began his work on theory of knowledge; an outline had been needed for the syllabus for the course he would teach at Harvard University the following spring, and he had begun to see this as a major undertaking, bringing together and providing a foundation for his work on the concept of matter and on the analysis of sense-data. He reported to Ottoline that it would have three main parts: acquaintance, judgment, and inference; that it might run to five hundred pages, and that the constructive part, on matter, might constitute another book.[30] On May 7, Russell set to work on writing it. Within approximately one month, until he stopped writing June 7, he completed 350 manuscript pages and reached the end of the first two portions of the first part of the work. This work has been reconstructed: the first 142 pages of the manuscript which have not been found have been identified as the articles in the *Monist* of 1914-15, pages 143 to 350 constituting chapters 7, 8, 9 of Part I, and chapters 1 through 7 of Part II: the third portion of the manuscript, which was to have dealt with inference and the constructive part, was apparently never written.[31]

In the letters to his absent lover we can trace Russell's progress in writing the book, a progress he reported with delight and enthusiasm in the beginning. On May 8 he had completed the chapter on "The Preliminary Description of Experience" (*The Monist* article of that title of January 1914), and was going on to the "refutation of James" (William James's neutral monism was discussed under the title "On the Nature of Acquaintance. II. Neutral Monism," in *The Monist* of April 1914). On May 11 he had written fifty-five pages on the criticisms of James, and had gone on to his own view of consciousness; on May 13 he was puzzling over "the present time" (this evidently became "On the Nature of Acquaintance. III. Analysis of Experience" in *The Monist*, July 1914). By the following day he had finished eighty pages and was thinking of sensation and imagination, and two days later he had written 110 pages and completed the work on sensation and imagination ("Sensation and Imagination" in *The Monist* of January 1915). On the 17th he was working on the analysis of our knowledge of time and had completed it by May 19 ("On the Experience of Time" in *The Monist*, April 1915). On May 21 he reported that he had finished with the part of the work that dealt with particulars and was ready to start on acquaintance with universals. This completed portion of the work consists in the six missing manuscript chapters, that is, the portion appearing in *The Monist* articles.[32] It should be noted that a fourth *Monist* article, "Definitions and Methodological Principles in Theory of Knowledge" of October 1914, does not appear as a topic in the letters. Various explanations may be advanced for some discrepancies between the reported work in the letters and the extant articles, including the possibility of revisions when the manuscript was prepared for publication in the form of articles. However, the general development of the argument meshes with the continuation of that argument as it can be read in the manuscript portion of the book.[33]

May 20 was noted in the letters not only as the day on which the work moved on to the topic of acquaintance with universals but also the day that Wittgenstein had come to him with a "refutation of the theory of judgment which I used to hold."[34] This theory, which Russell referred to as the one he "used to hold," was presented in different forms in the period preceding his work on theory of knowledge, in *The Problems of Philosophy,* and in *Philosophical Essays.* Russell called this the multiple relation theory of judgment, and it was intended to present a realist correspondence theory of truth which would avoid the postulation of entities corresponding to false judgments and the idealist subjective account of judgment. If Othello believes that Desdemona loves Cassio, this can be analyzed as a relation, that of belief, holding between the subject, Othello, and the various constituents of the judgment, that is, between Othello and Desdemona, Othello and Cassio, Othello and love. If the belief is true, the three constituents are related to one another as the judgment says they are; if it is a false belief, each of the constituents is real, but the relation is not as the belief postulates it to be. We are not told in the letters what Wittgenstein's criticism was, but we can speculate that the reference to his former theory indicates that Russell felt it would not affect his current work; it may well have had to do with the difficulty referred to by Wittgenstein in his letter of substituting "the wrong way round," a topic addressed by Russell in the following chapter, and with the difference of level of the two "verbs," a part of the theory of judgment treated differently by Russell in his subsequent discussion. Both criticisms by Wittgenstein appear in "Notes on Logic," as we will see.[35]

After Wittgenstein's visit of May 20, Russell began to work on the next chapter of his book, titled "On the Acquaintance Involved in Our Knowledge of Relations." The first problem that Russell refers to in this chapter has to do with the awareness of the *form* of the relation, that is, of the way it is known that *A before B* has the same form as *C before D.* A closely related problem is how it is recognized that *A before B* is the same form, if it is the same form, as *B after A*. Then there is a problem, one that Russell had puzzled over before, or the "sense" of the relation, that is, what it is about an asymmetrical relation that indicates that it holds from A to B, but not from B to A. In this chapter Russell concluded that there is such a thing as being directly acquainted with relations as constitutive of complexes. Not all relations may be such direct objects of acquaintance, for some may be known by their similarity to relations which are the objects of acquaintance. We are acquainted with something that could be called the "form of a relation," that which is in common in *A before B, C before D,* and *B after A*. This form is itself an object of acquaintance, but the usual way of symbolizing relations does not fully represent the form of a relation. The perception of a relation as embedded in a complex, and of complexes as resembling one another in containing a relation, are also topics discussed in this chapter.[36]

It is apparent that not all problems are solved and that further problems lie ahead when Russell must pass from relations, or relational complexes, known by acquaintance to those understood. It is also clear that the way of differentiating one term from another, and terms from relations, also symmetrical from asymmetrical relations is yet to be worked out. Here we can infer, I believe, that Wittgenstein had raised the problem of how an atomic complex such as *xRy* could tell us how the order, sense, and identity of those constituents are to be read. These problems are preliminary in the sense that the theory of judgment turns on the theory of relations, and Russell has indicated that he was aware that here the symbolism for relational complexes needed revision to meet Wittgenstein's criticisms and his own difficulties. It seems that those revisions would have to do with complicating the symbolism for relations in some way that would require the symbols to mean *A before B* and *not B before A;* to mean *before* as the relation, and *A* and *B* as the terms, *not A* as the relation, and *before* as the term. The form would have to be abstract and an object of acquaintance in itself, not dependent on one knowing something of the relation of precedence in time prior to one's acquaintance with the particular instance of a preceding complex. At the same time, the symbolism for such a form would have to provide specific directions about how it is to be read in identifying terms, relation, symmetry, and so forth. At least it seems that Russell believed such measures could render his theory invulnerable to the problems of relations which he described and which are probably the ones Wittgenstein raised against his "former theory."[37]

Another set of difficulties that Russell had to face concerned the relation of judging itself. The problems discussed above might be said to be internal to the relational complex, and it is this complex that is judged. Even more serious objections were raised by Wittgenstein concerning Russell's treatment of judgment itself. Perhaps Russell thought that his new way of symbolizing relations would allow his theory of judgment to meet the difficulty Wittgenstein raised about the two verbs. (Russell wrote to Ottoline Morrell that he had a new treatment of judgment much superior to his former treatment.[38]) Wittgenstein said that Russell's theory of judgment put on the same level the relational verb internal to the complex judged (for example, the verb *loves* as relating Desdemona and Cassio) and the verb of the relation of judging itself (for example, the relation of believing holding between Othello and the elements of his belief). It must be wrong, according to Wittgenstein, for the many-one relation of believing to break up and come between the elements of the belief or judgment for which the proposition is an object. (This criticism was expressed in the "Notes on Logic" of October 1913, but I am assuming it would have constituted a major part of the May 20 comments, since it applies to the earlier version of Russell's multiple-relation theory of truth.) Russell's concern with the problem of a realist theory of truth, which had led him to the many-one relation of judgment in the first place, made him unwilling to give up this theory. He thus attempted to use a different and more complicated way of formulating relations and a new way of symbolizing the relation of judgment in the hope of escaping the problems he was facing. This appears in chapter 1 of Part II of the unpublished manuscript, but depends as well on some important ideas contained in chapter 9 of Part I, the discussion of acquaintance with logical data.

In the latter chapter, Russell argues that there must be something that can be called acquaintance with "logical objects." He admits that it is difficult to find such a direct experience of acquaintance with abstract forms, but argues that it must occur. His reasons are that it would be impossible for someone acquainted with the terms and the relation of a dual relational complex, taking each as a separate object of acquaintance, to understand what it would mean for these to be put together in a complex unless he had had experience of the abstract logical form of a dual complex. If one were acquainted with Plato and Socrates and with the relation of precedence, but not with the complex "Socrates precedes Plato," one would not be able to understand that proposition unless one were acquainted with the logical form of a dual complex, that is, xRy.

This "extended" view of acquaintance must be understood in the light of several premises in Russell's thought. One premise is the sharp distinction between acquaintance, a two-term relation of direct awareness by the subject of an object without the possibility of error, and description, an indirect knowledge derivative from acquaintance and liable to error. If no logical data are among the objects of acquaintance, then logic can have no error-free premises. Another premise of Russell's epistemology is the view that logic consists of purely formal, general, and nonempirical propositions. He usually conveyed the nature of logic by showing how a proposition that refers to a specific empirical content can have its terms and its relation replaced by variables until only the form remains — thus *Socrates precedes Plato,* by substituting variables, becomes *xRy,* a purely general and hence logical proposition. (Sommerville believes that this view of logical propositions is inconsistent with other definitions of propositions in *Principia Mathematica* and was, in itself, a main target of Wittgenstein's criticism, but there is no direct evidence for this.[39]) A third premise, which is connected with the other two, is that "every proposition we can understand is composed of constituents with which we are acquainted."[40] This means, of course, after a suitable analysis has been performed; propositions may contain descriptive terms, but these are reducible by logical techniques to their bases in acquaintance. From these three premises it follows that logic itself, as a body of self-evident and purely abstract propositions involving logical terms, can only be possible if there is such a relation as acquaintance with logical data. The assumptions involved, and the enumeration of logical forms, have consequences in the further analysis of judgment that occupied Russell in Part II of the unpublished book. In a letter dated May 24, the day following a second Wittgenstein visit, Russell told Ottoline Morrell that he had embarked on judgment, that he had a new way of dividing the subject — "quite new and much more searching than the traditional division."[41] He had made an abstract of the second part and begun to write, and a number of new and important ideas had occurred to him. (It may be speculated that the new ideas are partly represented by the diagram of the understanding of a relation, on the reverse of which is an outline of the second part of the book, which may be the abstract referred to.[42]) From that date until May 30, Russell wrote the chapters dealing with understanding, judgment, and belief (pages 191 to 273 of the manuscript). On May 26, after Russell had been at work for three days on his new view of understanding, Wittgenstein came a third time and was shown the new work:[43]

> Tuesday [May 27, 1913, postmarked May 28] [#787]
> Wittgenstein came to see me — we were both cross from the heat. I showed him a crucial part of what I have been writing. He said it was all wrong, not realizing the difficulties — that he had tried my view and knew it wouldn't work. I couldn't understand his objections — in fact he was very inarticulate — but I feel in my bones that he must be right, and

that he has seen something I have missed. If I could see it too I shouldn't mind, but as it is, it is worrying, and has rather destroyed the pleasure in my writing. — I can only go on with what I see, and yet I feel it is probably all wrong, and that Wittgenstein will think me a dishonest scoundrel for going on with it.

In the first part of the chapter which introduces the second part of the book, Russell attempts to define a proposition; his difficulties stem from several problems already encountered. Are we to define the proposition in terms of the relation it bears to a subject — the degree of doubt, conviction, or whatever else it may be that links it to a particular subject? Or can we view this as not essential to the nature of the proposition, assuming that the same proposition may have different psychological contexts? If the proposition is not to be defined in relation to a subject, perhaps it can be defined in terms of its linkage to a referent of some kind. Russell introduces a lengthy discussion of Meinong, the *Annahme,* the *Objektiv* (he rewrote this passage, shifting slightly in his interpretation of Meinong, to emphasize the difference between two levels of presentation and of representation[44]). Again he finds this view lacking, in that it will fit true propositions but not false ones. He then discusses the opinion that a proposition is an incomplete symbol, requiring a context for its interpretation, a view close to that of *Principia Mathematica.* He finds no satisfactory definition of a proposition, and leaves the questions unanswered.[45]

Russell's main topic is the logical form of a proposition, the analysis of the common form of the relation of *what* is believed, or understood, or doubted, to the *subject,* a relation different from that of acquaintance, which is a two-term relation. The basic distinction between acquaintance and understanding is outlined, and the distinction between atomic and molecular propositions is set forth.

Russell returns to the example of *A precedes B.* This time the proposition *A precedes B* is used as an example of the relation of understanding between the subject and the object, when the object is a proposition and hence may be false or true. Although he had concluded that it was necessary that we be acquainted with the form of a dual complex in order to understand such a proposition, it had not been clear how the form of a dual complex would enable one to know what order of the terms was intended. The problem is this: "When we were discussing relations, we said that, with a given relation and given terms, two complexes are 'logically possible'. But the notion of what is 'logically possible' is not an ultimate one, and must be reduced to something that is *actual* before our analysis can be complete."[46]

This problem was solved by rephrasing the proposition: an atomic proposition stating a relation between terms in a complex is formulated as *A precedes in the complex* $\propto$, where $\propto$ is a sequence-complex.[47] Since *A* and $\propto$ differ logically, it is impossible to substitute these the wrong way round, since *The complex $\propto$ precedes A* is meaningless. For Russell this formulation seemed to avoid Wittgenstein's problem of the form needing to prevent wrong-way-round substitution. Sommerville suggests that it was this suggestion that may have occasioned Wittgenstein's irritation and the remark that "he had tried this and it hadn't worked." Sommerville sees Russell's idea of the reformulation of the atomic relational proposition as very like the suggestion in Wittgenstein's letter of making all atomic propositions into propositions with copulae. This proposal would put relations and predicates within the copula—a suggestion that Wittgenstein saw as unworkable because it put two different levels or types of symbols within the atomic proposition.[48] If this interpretation is correct, Russell must either have failed to understand Wittgenstein or to have rejected the criticism, as he goes on in the same vein in the succeeding chapter. At any rate, Russell used this new formulation, but to avoid the complications of asymmetrical dual complexes which were not essential to the analysis of the understanding of a dual relational complex, he used the example of a symmetrical relational proposition, *A and B are similar.* From the analysis of previous chapters we know that understanding such a proposition involves acquaintance with A, with B, and with similarity, and with the general form of a symmetrical dual complex. How the three constituents and the form are brought together in the relation of understanding is what Russell takes as the problem addressed in this chapter.

The questions that Russell poses and tries to answer show that the concerns of this chapter touch on a topic of his and Wittgenstein's inquiries and on points where Wittgenstein was likely to have criticized Russell's "former" theory of judgment (my interpolations are indicated within square brackets).[49]

(1) What can we mean by the "form" of a complex? [Note that the manuscript shows that *complex* here replaced *proposition*. Did Russell make that substitution in order to try to make the question less logical and more epistemological in order to avoid Wittgenstein's criticisms?]

(2) Can we, by bringing in the "form" or in any other way, make the "proposition" an entity, i.e. not a mere incomplete symbol, but something which can subsist on its own account, and not only as a fictitious constituent of certain mental complexes? [This was an old problem for Russell, though Wittgenstein's criticism may

have made the status of the proposition more questionable than ever.]

(3) How can we be sure that acquaintance with the "form" is involved in understanding a proposition? And finally,

(4) What is the logical structure of the fact which consists in a given subject understanding a given proposition? [This last question was the only problem raised by Wittgenstein that Russell specifically acknowledged.]

The answer to the first question is that it may be possible to state in the most general terms the structure that makes the form of a group of complexes of the same form have that same form; for instance, the form of a dual complex may be *something has some relation to something*. This answer is similar to Russell's attempted formulation in "What Is Logic?"

The second question received an answer by generalizing under the symbol *U* any relation of a subject to that which is understood, believed, doubted, or so forth. The subject is symbolized by *S;* the complex itself receives the symbol γ; the form of the complex *something has some relation to something*, by substituting variables for the *somethings* and *some relation*, becomes "xRy". This process produces a form that can be identified as the proposition and that is said to be neither merely linguistic nor merely psychological: "There is a U and an S such that U (S,x,R,y,γ)."[50]

With respect to the third question Russell argues, against his own "former" view, that it is insufficient to explain the understanding of a relational complex by assuming that one can understand each term and the relation separately and depend upon the sense of the relation to unite and order the complex. He now believes it necessary that there should be an understanding which includes that of the form of the complex, i.e., "something and something have a relation." The terms, the relation, and the form of the relation must all be involved in understanding such a complex.

The fourth question brings Russell to the real nub of the difficulty that Wittgenstein's criticisms of the "former theory" forces him to face—that is, how is he to give an analysis of the form of judgment or belief? Russell returns to his formulation of the relation of understanding and attempts to refine it so that no objections—concerning the ambiguity of the form, or the possibility of wrong-way substitution, or of a mixing of the relation of understanding with the attributed relation between the terms of the object complex—could be raised. It seems that this is his answer to Wittgenstein's first criticisms; for he points out that the various constituents of the five-term complex must enter into the complex in different ways and that one cannot be substituted for the other except under restrictions imposed by the form of the relation itself (as A and B could be substituted for each other in the symmetrical relation of similarity in his example). The resultant diagram Russell calls "the map of the five-term complex involved in a subject understanding that A and B are similar."[51] This diagram and the accompanying explanation occur in Russell's unpublished *Theory of Knowledge: The 1913 Manuscript* (p. 118).

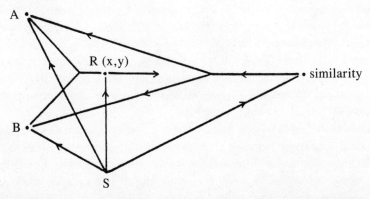

In this figure, one relation goes from *S* to the four objects; one relation goes from *R(x,y)* to similarity, and another to *A* and *B*, while one relation goes from similarity to *A* and *B*. This figure, I hope, will help to make clearer the map of our five-term complex. But to explain in detail the exact abstract meaning of the various items in the figure would demand a lengthy formal logical discussion. Meanwhile the above attempt must suffice, for the present, as an analysis of what is meant by "understanding a proposition."

In the next chapter, "Analysis and Synthesis," Russell completed his mechanism for formulating relational complexes by devising ways in which alternatives of positions of terms, kinds of terms, and determinations of substitutions could be indicated in the form of the symbols, rather than having to be read off from the way in which a standard set of symbols could apply to a given referent-complex. The problem involved in the analysis of such complexes is the following: "it makes a difference whether the complex is one which is determinate as soon as its form and its constituents are given, or whether it is one which even then may be one of several."[52] Russell tries to show how one may go from the logically possible (relations possible within one form) to the actual (the specific characteristics of the relation which are intended). In this analysis he makes use of the concept of permutation-groups.

Permutation-groups occur when, for a certain group of terms within a complex, nothing in the form prohibits an interchange of terms, but a lack of symmetry in the relation that relates them gives a different meaning when that substitution does occur. Russell's way of formulating displays these possible groups and allows additional specifications that limit the substitution of terms and narrow the logically possible to the actual relation intended. This is complicated and ingenious and earned a commendation from Wittgenstein, if, as seems compatible with our interpretation here, this is what Wittgenstein was referring to in his "Notes on Logic" when he said[53] "Just as people used to struggle to bring all propositions into the subject-predicate form, so now it is natural to conceive every proposition as expressing a relation, which is just as incorrect. What is justified in this desire is fully satisfied by Russell's theory of manufactured relations." Russell did not return to this way of formulating relational complexes, so that this phrase of Wittgenstein's remained mysterious, as the footnote to the 1969 edition of "Notes on Logic" explains.

The chapter on "Analysis and Synthesis" continues with an application of the kind of analysis proposed for a simple spatial complex, the letter T, and concludes with a list of problems which are postponed, referred to as belonging to logic rather than theory of knowledge, or acknowledged as beyond Russell's ability to solve. These are "purely logical problems": "How is the meaning of a complex name such as 'aRb' determined when the meanings of the simple constituent names are known? What is meant by 'a is part of aRb'? What is meant by 'aRb consists of a and R and b united in the general form of a dual complex'?"[54] The lack of solutions to these problems may reflect a response to Wittgenstein's insistence that the new theory of judgment was still vulnerable to his criticisms.

In the following two chapters of the manuscript, other examples of the understanding of complexes and other examples of the relations of a subject to a complex, such as believing, doubting, and so on, are analyzed. Again and again Russell returns dissatisfied that no "objective" or "purely formal" definition of the proposition has been developed. The upshot of the view of judgment is that it is, as it was before, a multiple relation of the subject to the constituents of the judgment, but that these constituents are united with the form of the relation:[55]

> When a certain subject understands a proposition and when he believes it, the two complexes differ, according to us, solely in the fact that understanding and believing are different relations: belief in the proposition results from substituting believing for understanding in the complex which is the understanding of that proposition. But understanding a proposition, if our previous theory on this point bore any resemblance to the truth, is a complex of a wholly different form from acquaintance, except in the one case of understanding a pure logical

form. Both belief and understanding, except in this one case, have not a single object, the "proposition", but have a plurality of objects, united with the subject in a *multiple* relation. Thus although there is a neutral attitude, namely understanding, which gives complexes having the same logical form as beliefs, yet this attitude is fundamentally different from that of . . . acquaintance.

Russell's attempt to amend his theory of relations and of judgment to meet Wittgenstein's criticisms could scarcely be called a success. In a letter written May 27, three days after he had begun work on judgment, Russell told Ottoline of Wittgenstein's criticisms, although he did not describe them, and said that, although he felt the criticisms were serious he could not understand them and felt the only thing he could do was to press on. One can speculate that Russell, having believed he had met the criticisms of his former theory presented on Wittgenstein's first visit by the new elements in his theory of judgment presented in the second part of his book, was worried by the fact that Wittgenstein still felt it to be unsatisfactory. Russell did keep on with his writing until he reached the end of Part II. His letters show the struggle he faced in trying to cope with these criticisms. First he thought he could leave them to one side and work around them, then he thought that even if they were just, they would not destroy the value of his work (possibly he decided the criticisms could belong to logic rather than to epistemology). Finally, by June 20 he admitted, "It makes a large part of the book I meant to write impossible for years to come probably."[56]

In June, while Wittgenstein was in Cambridge, Russell referred to several "bad times with him," and, finally, he gave up writing as term time and Wittgenstein made it impossible. He spoke of postponing the work rather than abandoning it. But when the term was over he went on a walking tour in Italy and returned to begin preparing the Lowell Lectures to be delivered at Harvard the following spring. In looking back on his manuscript, he wrote, "It falls apart just where Wittgenstein said it did."[57]

7.4 Wittgenstein's Criticisms and New Ideas

In the meantime Wittgenstein was in Austria and wrote to Russell that he could put his objections to his theory of judgment in this way: "I believe it is obvious that, from the proposition 'A judges that (say) a is in the Re[lation] R to b', if correctly analyzed the prop[osition] '$aRb.\mathrm{V}.\sim aRb$' must follow directly *without the use of any other premiss.* This condition is not fulfilled by your theory."[58] This letter was apparently written in June; in July Wittgenstein wrote that he was sorry his criticism of Russell's theory of judgment "paralyzed" him, and that it could only be put right by a correct theory of propositions.[59]

In August, on his way to Norway, Wittgenstein came to see Russell—Wittgenstein had done very good work and practically solved the problems he had been working at, Russell wrote to Ottoline Morrell.[60] Later, in October, Russell gave Lucy Donnelly a lively account of his attempt to dissuade Wittgenstein from going into seclusion alone in northern Norway:[61]

> October 19, 1913
>
> Then my Austrian, Wittgenstein, burst in like a whirlwind, just back from Norway, and determined to return there at once, to live in complete solitude until he had solved *all* the problems of logic. I said it would be dark, and he said he hated daylight. I said it would be lonely, and he said he prostituted his mind talking to intelligent people. I said he was mad, and he said God preserve him from sanity (God certainly will). Now, Wittgenstein, during August and September, had done work on logic, still rather in the rough, but as good, in my opinion, as any work that ever has been done in logic by anyone. But his artistic conscience prevents him from writing anything until he has got it perfect, and I am persuaded that he will commit suicide in February. What was I to do? He told me his ideas, but they were so subtle that I kept forgetting them. I begged him to write them out, and he tried, but after much groaning said it was absolutely impossible. At last I made him talk in the presence of a short-hand writer, and so secured some record of his ideas. This business took up the whole of my time and thought for about a week.

By this time the full seriousness of Wittgenstein's new ideas in terms of both his theory of knowledge and his logic must have been plain to Russell. We have an indication that even while he was working on his manuscript in late May he tried out Wittgenstein's new way of looking at propositions, on the back of a canceled manuscript sheet, page 197.[62] After Wittgenstein left for Norway, Russell had the notes of the stenographer typed up and sent to him there. Further correspondence between them referred to points in the notes. Russell later prepared a set of these notes with some editing and rearrangement to present to his class in logic at Harvard in the spring.[63] What had not been apparent until the unpublished manuscript was available for study was that the "Notes on Logic" which were derived from this dictation of Wittgenstein's related directly to the unpublished manuscript, responding to and reflecting ideas in that book and, also, to the conversation that the two men had had about it. It need not be assumed that Wittgenstein had a copy of the manuscript in his possession, or that he had read all of it; we do know that he had read the part on judgment, at least. But the ideas in the book were those that he and Russell had discussed, hence the notes provide a valuable reflection on both sides of the divergence of their views at this period.

The main points in the "Notes on Logic" which refer to themes in Russell's unpublished manuscript are referred to in the sequel. The two main themes are criticisms of the viewpoint of Frege and Russell on the nature of logic and logical propositions, with detailed discussion of some of the points on which Wittgenstein is particularly critical, and the statement of the basis of his own view of logic, which he contrasts with that of Frege and Russell. The critical portion of the notes contains several main themes, including a sharp distinction between philosophy and all other disciplines; philosophy is said to be on a different level from natural science — the latter describes empirical subject-matter, while philosophy designates something entirely different, "over or under, not beside" the sciences. Philosophy "consists of logic and metaphysics, the former as its basis." Epistemology is said to be the philosophy of psychology.[64] These statements not only identify what Wittgenstein was working at himself (and achieved in the *Tractatus Logico-Philosophicus*), but also they specifically reject what Russell regarded as the nature of philosophy, encompassing the descriptions provided by science and making logic and epistemology contiguous. For Russell, theory of knowledge has been a foundation on which logic and scientific methodology in philosophy are grounded.

As regards the nature of logic itself, Wittgenstein says that logic is not a deductive system deriving its validity from proofs resting on primitive propositions as envisaged in *Principia Mathematica;* it is purely descriptive. What Wittgenstein appears to mean by this is that logical propositions show in their form their truth or falsity without any recourse to postulates from which they are derived or features of the world to which they might be taken to refer. It seems that at this time Russell may not have been entirely clear about the difference between this view of logic and his own with respect to logical propositions. For Russell logical propositions give the form of logical possibilities, the most fundamental a priori truths, and this is why logical data are included among elements of acquaintance in the manuscript. But for Wittgenstein neither these functions nor this status are appropriate; the propositions of logic are self-sufficient, tell us nothing about the world, and simply exemplify in their form their own logical status.

This theme is connected with another subject matter of the notes: the sharp distinction between logical and empirical truth. It was concern with the correspondence theory of truth that had led Russell to cling to the multiple relation theory of judgment. But Wittgenstein was not concerned with that problem any more than with the compatibility of logical forms with the analysis of space, time, or matter, or the coherence of an epistemological distinction between acquaintance and description with the knowledge of logical truths or inferences. Russell's aim of fitting together in a complete theory of knowledge accounts of sensation, of truth, and of logic was alien to Wittgenstein, but for Russell this aim was so important that it was impossible for him to defer the logical problems he saw Wittgenstein to be raising, because theory of knowledge and logic could not be separated.[65] Hence Wittgenstein's criticisms and new ideas were vital to both men, and his characterization of epistemology as the philosophy of psychology was tantamount to a rejection of Russell's entire book.

Wittgenstein's remarks in the "Notes on Logic" about the way in which the terms of atomic propositions have been interpreted as names, and how this has led to the mistaken idea that such propositions are themselves names and to the further error of considering the terms of logical propositions as names of "logical objects," were clearly directed at Russell's manuscript. On the point of constituents of propositions being taken to be names, we saw that it had been a characteristic Russellian doctrine that all propositions we can understand are composed of symbols which are either themselves names of objects of immediate acquaintance or can be reduced by an analysis, on the model of the theory of descriptions, to such terms. This produces the status of a "name" for every term in the proposition: predicates, relational terms, real variables, and what Russell had called logical constants. Wittgenstein had been critical of logical constants and real variables as constituents of logical propositions and had seen difficulties, as had Russell, in the whole concept of the atomic proposition. Here he points out that it is impossible to treat all these items as names on the same level, for then one can only distinguish them as being on different logical levels because of the referents one happens to know they have. Furthermore, Russell compounds the difficulty by treating the combination of such elements in an "atomic proposition" as itself a name for a complex. Hence the proposition xRy (an atomic proposition) is a name for the complex xRy and can be analyzed into its constituents, in which x is a name for x, R for R, and y for y. A further aspect is that it can be argued that there must be knowledge of the acquaintance kind with such elusive entities as the form of a complex *something has some relation to something*. And terms such as V or $\supset$ are similarly names for logical objects. All this Wittgenstein rejects, arguing that there can be but one kind of fundamental name-symbols, which must be interpreted consistently, and no other kind of name must be confused with it, nor can any other level of complexity also be named. One must not just invent name-symbols ad hoc.[66]

These doctrines of Russell's manuscript of the theory of knowledge seem to be the targets of many of the remarks in Wittgenstein's "Notes on Logic."

It is clear that if one eliminated the analysis of the relational complex, the form of the relation, the name status of both its constituents, and the complex itself from the seventh chapter of Part I, and found the resultant treatment of atomic propositions unsatisfactory, a heavy blow would be dealt to Russell's whole enterprise. On the logical side, it has been argued by Sommerville that this criticism works havoc on the role of the atomic proposition in Russell's logical scheme, and especially on the theory of types.[67] (However, there is little evidence of such a dislocation in Russell's presentation of logic at this time.)

There are several remarks in the notes specifically referring to Russell's theory of judgment. Several of these repeat remarks made in letters to Russell but are more explicit in the notes.[68] One has to do with the contention that Russell's theory of judgment would not make it nonsensical to say that the table penholders the book. Here the point is that the introduction of the symbolism xRy is arbitrary through failure to identify which item in the complex is the relation and which are the terms, something a proper symbolism would make clear. (Of course, only a completely different view of the nature and function of a symbolism could answer this criticism, and it is plausible that Russell, with his way of making variables replace names as a means of constructing a purely logical proposition, would find this criticism difficult to understand.) It seems that Russell might have first interpreted the criticism, as offered of his "former theory of judgment," to mean that the symbolism did not sufficiently tell us the "sense" of the relation or direct us to discriminate between a term and a relation. If this is the case it would explain why Russell thought the new way of dealing with relation as *A precedes in the complex* $\propto$ would solve the problems in part, while the invention of permutative/nonpermutative and homogeneous/heterogeneous relations with corresponding symbolism would do the rest.[69] But this did not meet Wittgenstein's objections, as the "Notes" make clear. The problem with naming constituents and complexes at the same time, and the unsatisfactory habit of inventing newly defined symbols to solve problems, are relevant here.

One of the most decisive criticisms of Russell's theory of judgment was Wittgenstein's insistence that what is asserted, judged, or doubted must stand alone as a proposition; the proposition is that which is doubted, asserted, or believed, and this aspect of the proposition, which Russell read as introducing a new relation between the subject and the proposition and its constituents, *U,* violates this principle. Wittgenstein held that the two verbs must be distinguished—that is, the verb of judging, and the verb internal to what is judged. Perhaps Russell thought he had met this objection to his "former theory" by his new formulation, in which the U is clearly outside the proposition judged and differently symbolized from the verb internal to what is judged, doubted, and so forth: U(S,x,R,y,γ). But this did not meet Wittgenstein's objection—for he says in the "Notes" that whether the proposition is asserted, doubted, or believed is as irrelevant to the proposition itself as is its number. The verbs of understanding around which Russell built the second part of his work are psychological and cannot be treated as relations in the proper sense since they cannot be said to hold between one term and another, as does the relation within the relational proposition. "There is no *thing* which is the *form* of a proposition, and no name which is the name of a form. Accordingly we can also not say that a relation which in certain cases holds between things holds sometimes between forms and things. This goes against Russell's theory of judgment."[70]

It is clear that this statement of Wittgenstein's refers to the theory of judgment of the manuscript, since in all his prior writing Russell did not introduce into his analysis of judgment the form of the complex as a separate element of what is judged (see diagram, page 151). Another remark in the notes also refers to the later theory of judgment—that is, the reference to "Russell's manufactured relations." In the context it shows how seriously Wittgenstein's criticism affected Russell's entire treatment of propositions: "Just as people used to struggle to bring all propositions into the subject-predicate form, so now it is natural to conceive every proposition as expressing a relation, which is just as incorrect."[71] As we saw when this was quoted previously (page 152), it seems to refer to Russell's newly devised symbolism for relational complexes that allowed the form of the symbolism to eliminate all possible alternative interpretations of the relational complex, of a given number of terms in a given relation by the addition of symbols for position and assignment. Wittgenstein seems to be saying that the means used by Russell to distinguish among possible relational complexes is justifiable, but it would not be justifiable to extend this symbolism to apply to predication or to other forms of propositions. Also the introduction of the form of the relation as one of the elements of the judgment-complex is unsatisfactory. Wittgenstein also hits at Russell's new theory of judgment by asking, if judgment itself is a relation between the subject and the proposition, how is it that a term of this relation can be negated, something that cannot occur within the complex itself? That is, it makes sense to deny a proposition but not to deny a term.[72] "It is easy to suppose only such symbols are complex as contain names of objects, and that accordingly '$(x,\phi)\phi x$' or '$(\exists x,y)\ xRy$' must be simple. It is then natural to call the first of these the name of a form, the second the name of a relation. But in that case what is the meaning, e.g. of '$\sim(\exists x,y).xRy$'? Can we put 'not' before a name?

The year 1913 was an important one in the philosophical development of both Wittgenstein and Russell. For Russell the unpublished manuscript was the expression of his earlier doctrines brought together in a synthesis which he hoped would give the basis for further work in philosophizing in the epistemological mode as *Principia Mathematica* had given the basis for further work in the mathematical and logical mode. Russell always looked at his work as tentative and provisional and did not draw back from publishing work in which he knew there were unsolved problems, anticipating that in philosophy, as in science, further inquiry would push forward to the solution. Yet in this case Wittgenstein's criticisms produced an obstacle so fundamental that, as Russell said, he came to believe that it made his work impossible for probably years to come. The difficulty lay in the very concept of what logic is and what it can tell us, and in the corresponding possibility of synthesizing logical themes and techniques with areas of sense experience, scientific theory, and psychological-epistemological analysis. We shall see him struggling in the years from 1913 to 1919 to bring his understanding of Wittgenstein's insights and criticisms together with his own ideas of what philosophy is and how it works. He must also have perceived to some extent that much of what he had accomplished in mathematical logic was also affected, as Sommerville argues; yet, so far as his *Introduction to Mathematical Philosophy* is concerned, the changes are not great, and it is not until the second edition of *Principia Mathematica* that the extent of the changes is evident. Between the 1913 manuscript with its criticisms and the second edition of *Principia Mathematica* of 1927 are the important works of the "logical atomism" period. The years between 1913 and 1919 show the "first wave" of Wittgenstein's influence on Russell.

7.5 *Wittgenstein's Influence: The First Wave*

During World War I, in fact from the fall of 1913 to the fall of 1919, there were only brief notes and no philosophical interchange between the two men, although several of Russell's publications give credit to the ideas of Wittgenstein. For example, in *Our Knowledge of the External World*, Russell writes, "In pure logic, which, however, will be briefly discussed in these lectures, I have had the benefit of vitally important discoveries, not yet published, by my friend Mr. Ludwig Wittgenstein." In a later edition of the book, a footnote gives credit to Wittgenstein's *Tractatus Logico-Philosophicus* for the origin of the idea of denying the existence of logical constants, an idea already present in Wittgenstein's "Notes" of 1913, as we have seen.[73] A

note added to the fourth *Monist* article that was based on the early part of the
unpublished manuscript refers to Wittgenstein as pointing out the problem of
what the logical form of the relation of judgment to what is judged must be,
but it is ambiguous whether Russell is referring here to a problem he thinks
himself to have solved, or one that was pointed out but not solved.[74] A note
added to "Knowledge by Acquaintance and Knowledge by Description" for
the 1917 publication refers briefly to the criticism of the theory of judgment
put forth in that essay and requiring "modification" because of Wittgenstein's criticism.[75] In *Introduction to Mathematical Philosophy,* written
while Russell was in prison for his antiwar efforts and published in 1919, he
discusses briefly Wittgenstein's view that logical propositions are tautologies
and the implications of this view for logic and mathematics.[76] (This seems to
indicate that he had not grasped or had not accepted the important new
insights in logic discussed between them for which he gave generous credit to
Wittgenstein in 1913.)

But the work that both acknowledges and shows the influence of what
Russell understood Wittgenstein's work to be is the lectures entitled "The
Philosophy of Logical Atomism," given in 1918 and published in *The Monist*
of 1919.[77] Russell introduces the lectures thus:

> The following articles are the first two lectures of a course of eight
> lectures delivered in London in the first months of 1918, and are very
> largely concerned with explaining certain ideas which I learnt from my
> friend and former pupil Ludwig Wittgenstein. I have had no opportunity
> of knowing his views since August 1914, and I do not even know
> whether he is alive or dead. He has therefore no responsibility for what
> is said in these lectures beyond that of having originally supplied many
> of the theories contained in them.

In quoting this passage in *My Philosophical Development,* forty years later,
Russell goes on to say that he first adopted the term *logical atomism* to
describe his philosophy in those lectures.[78] As we have seen, Russell used
the term before he was influenced by Wittgenstein, but the meaning he gave
it in 1918 no doubt owed something to later additions suggested by Wittgenstein's discussions and "Notes." The method is clearly set forth in the article
of 1911, and the early discussion in the 1918 lectures of philosophical data and
the method of philosophical analysis seems to have little in common with any
of the writings or reported words of Wittgenstein. It is also true that many of
the positions attributed to Wittgenstein are put forward by Russell tentatively
and with reservation. (We know, for instance, from the "Notes on Logic" that
Wittgenstein held that a negative atomic proposition referred to a negative
fact;[79] this was not held by Russell prior to "The Philosophy of Logical

Atomism" and it was not held later, but in those lectures it is put forth, although with no very great conviction.)

If we try to disentangle the Russellian and Wittgensteinian themes in "The Philosophy of Logical Atomism," we will find that the atomic-molecular distinction, the analysis of atomic propositions in terms of constituent names, the stress on the use of an artificial language as revealing or suggesting features of reality by the kinds of terms that seem inevitably to be employed in it, and, most significantly, the description of the analytic method in philosophy clearly originated with Russell, whether he said so or not. On the other hand, the dropping out of the subject's relation of belief or judgment to what is believed in favor of treating the proposition as unaffected by this relation; the lack of emphasis on sense-data or acquaintance; the change in the method of treating the truth or falsity of atomic propositions in terms of pointing to or away from the fact; the true-false-schema, which was the nucleus of the truth-table method of dealing with the derivation of molecular propositions and of testing logical truth by the logical form of the proposition—all these can be traced to their origin in the "Notes on Logic" and the letters of Wittgenstein.

In addition, it should be pointed out that the very generous credit given to Wittgenstein tends to obscure the continuity of these lectures with Russell's earlier work, while the lack of contact between the two men may explain Russell's impression that the position he set forth was closer to Wittgenstein's than in fact it was.

So far as Wittgenstein was concerned, the "Notes" reveal his use of Russell's work as a reference-point against which he was developing his own very different ideas. These ideas were sharpened and formulated in contrast to the mistakes that he took Russell to be committing. Perhaps it is not too much to say that the very weaknesses of Russell's unpublished theory of knowledge were a demonstration of some of the "impenetrable thickets" to be avoided in his own work. The notes on logic dictated at Russell's behest in the fall of 1913 and the notes dictated to Moore in the spring of 1914 seem to have in them the nucleus of the work which occupied him from then until he completed the *Logisch-philosophische Abhandlung* in the closing months of World War I.

In this period his contacts with Russell were minimal; there were the letters mostly concerned with the further amplification of the critical points Wittgenstein had made in discussion with Russell, and later written down in the various sets of notes. Some of the correspondence between them, and that between Russell and Ottoline Morrell, reveal personal conflicts between the two men. In the spring of 1913 the meetings in which the theory of knowledge manuscript was discussed were stormy; Russell writes of their being "cross from the heat" and of "bad times with Wittgenstein." Russell's analysis of their relationship as being comparable to that between Russell and Ottoline Morrell tells us that the intemperate devotion and demands of Wittgenstein received a cooler response than the latter wished. On February 17, 1914, Russell wrote to Ottoline Morrell that he had received a letter from Wittgenstein: "[It said that] he and I are so dissimilar that it is useless to attempt friendship, and he will never write to me or see me again. I dare say his mind will change after a while. I find I don't care on his account, but only for the sake of logic. And yet I believe I do really care too much to look at it. It is my fault—I have been too sharp with him."[80]

The letter from Wittgenstein was apparently destroyed by Russell, but subsequent letters from Wittgenstein show that the older man had written in a friendly or apologetic vein, and Wittgenstein left the door open for further philosophical contact, although the basic differences of value were said to be irreconcilable. More letters and books were exchanged, and the lack of personal contact was because of Russell's visit to the United States from March to late June 1914, and the outbreak of war in August 1914. Russell devoted most of his energies to opposing the war, while Wittgenstein was working on logic during the time he was serving in the Austrian army. Through the war years brief messages were relayed through friends in neutral countries, and when the war ended Wittgenstein wrote to Russell from a prisoner-of-war camp concerning his completed book. But it was not until 1920 that they were able to meet and discuss their philosophical ideas again.

7.6 Wittgenstein's Influence: The Second Wave

The "second wave" of Wittgenstein's influence on Russell came after World War I, when Russell had the opportunity to read the work (in its original German) which was to become *Tractatus Logico-Philosophicus* and to meet Wittgenstein in The Hague for a week's discussion of it. In a letter to Ottoline Morrell, Russell reported his impressions of Wittgenstein and something of their discussion.[81] From this source, and from Wittgenstein's letters to Russell at the time, we have the impression that the conference was fruitful and reassuring to Wittgenstein, who had agonized that not one person would understand his solution to the problems of philosophy. Russell reported surprise at finding Wittgenstein so "religious" and his manuscript tinged with the "mystical." The former referred to Wittgenstein's reported experiences during the war when he read Tolstoy and was deeply impressed by him and by the ideal of a religious commitment; the latter referred to the final portions of the book in which Wittgenstein stressed what could not be said. Russell coupled these two elements as being new and, to him, surprising and unwelcome. Nevertheless, it was agreed that Russell would assist in the publication of the book by writing an introduction.

In letters following their meeting, Wittgenstein implored Russell to hurry with the introduction, but when he received it he became deeply dissatisfied and, in spite of his eagerness to get the book into print, and in spite of his confidence that without Russell's introduction it might well be impossible to have it published, he withdrew the introduction. It is understandable that the terse, epigrammatic style of the book would seem to Russell to require an introduction which would give the reader a context of the kind of problem with which its author was concerned. It was natural that Russell's interpretation of that context would follow his knowledge of the kind of questions in philosophy of logic that had given rise to their former discussions and that were the background for the themes discussed in the book. But Russell's attempt to provide this kind of context was bound to provoke distaste in Wittgenstein, who had once told Russell that this type of explanation was like pulling apart a flower with muddy hands. The extent to which the dissatisfaction was due to Russell's failure to appreciate the important themes of the book, to a lack of understanding revealed in the introduction, is a matter of interpretation. Certainly Russell's insight was selective. It is also likely that Wittgenstein, whose intransigence Russell had once admired, was inclined to wish his ideas to be adopted in their entirety as the final truth that he saw them to be, or rejected as nonsense, rather than treated with judicious reservation and withheld commitment. In any case, after initially rejecting the introduction, Wittgenstein gave up trying to have his book published, retired to the village school where he was to teach, and left the matter in Russell's hands, to publish the book if he wished.[82]

Russell left for China and asked Dorothy Wrinch, a friend and former student, to arrange for the publication of Wittgenstein's book if she could. There followed the publication of the original text in a German periodical, *Annalen der Natursphilosophie,* and later that of the English translation with German on facing pages by C. K. Ogden with the cooperation of Wittgenstein and Russell. Wittgenstein was gratified to have the book in print and accepted Moore's suggestion of the title *Tractatus Logico-Philosophicus.* It was arranged that Wittgenstein would visit the Russell family, which now included a wife and two children, in Switzerland in the summer of 1924. As it turned out, the meeting between Wittgenstein and Russell took place in Innsbruck, and it seems to have marked the end of their personal friendship and philosophical collaboration. Russell referred only briefly to some irritation Wittgenstein felt about their accommodation; some commentators have inferred a quarrel. But it seems likely that the wide divergence of their temperaments, interests, and convictions, of which both had been aware, combined with the long break in any close interaction, made their former friendship impossible. In fact, Wittgenstein, explaining to his friend von Ficker why the latter should postpone his visit to Vienna to see him, wrote that he had to spend a few days to meet his English acquaintance *(Bekannt)*. After Wittgenstein returned to England, their contacts were few: Russell reviewed with Wittgenstein the work on mathematics for which he recommended that Wittgenstein receive support from Cambridge University, sat as part of his examining committee for a Cambridge degree, and saw him infrequently at philosophical meetings.

The record of the influence of the Wittgenstein of the *Tractatus* on Russell's thought can be traced in the explicit arguments and acknowledgments of the second edition of *Principia Mathematica* of 1927, in *The Analysis of Matter* also published in 1927, and in the extended critical argument of *Inquiry into Meaning and Truth* of 1940. In addition, a retrospective summary of this influence and of Russell's second thoughts appeared in *My Philosophical Development* of 1959.[83]

In the introduction to the second edition of *Principia Mathematica*, changes are listed in the new edition; some of these are attributed to Wittgenstein and some to Frank Ramsey, identified by Russell as a follower of Wittgenstein. These alterations include the elimination of any distinction between real and apparent variables, a matter on which Wittgenstein had been critical since the earliest correspondence with Russell (1912–13); Russell also lists the elimination of the assertion of a propositional function, again a matter on which the "Notes on Logic" is critical. An important point discussed in appendix C is the axiom of reducibility, which had originally been included as a necessary but not fully justified postulate by the authors of *Principia*. Russell said that since he and Whitehead had regarded this as something of a "blot" on their system, it seemed advisable to explore the possibility of working out Wittgenstein's suggestion for making the axiom superfluous. This, too, had been an early target of Wittgenstein's criticism. It involved the proposal that all functions of a proposition be treated as truthfunctions, and that a function occur in a proposition only through its values. Russell worked this proposal out in some detail, as it would fit into the argument of the *Principia,* but retained some reservation about its adequacy.[84] Later, in *My Philosophical Development,* Russell expanded on Ramsey's later contribution to this proposal, which made clear that all propositional logic is to be treated extensionally, and, although this seems somewhat arbitrary, Russell concluded that it would not involve as many fatal consequences to other parts of mathematics and logic as the original Wittgensteinian version of the *Tractatus* entailed. In the second edition, he left the matter unsettled, but presented this different view of mathematical logic as an alternative that might be promising. There is a tone of detachment in Russell's description of different possible ways of dealing with the problems of mathematical logic, a tone indicating that it is not important to his philosophy.

Similarly, he answered Kurt Gödel's discussion of his work in the Library of Living Philosophers volume with the bare remark that he, Russell, had done no work in logic for many years. He was not similarly disengaged in answering philosophical critics.

Several other points in the introduction to the second edition of *Principia Mathematica* are reminiscent of the *Tractatus:* the denial that propositions are names; the proposition treated as a fact itself, and, in contrast, as something that is true or false according to some rule; the treatment of logical propositions as logically true or false by the rule of symbolism according to which they are formulated (as tautologies or as contradictions); the distinction by which individuals serve as subjects of propositions, and verbs and subjects cannot be substituted for one another. All these are positive influences of Wittgenstein's work in the *Tractatus*. The discussion of the inventory of forms of propositions, the reservations about possible non-truth-functional propositions, the retention of the earlier concept of identity: all these recall the earlier Russell of the unpublished manuscript, even during this period of strong Wittgensteinian influence. The limitations of Russell's acceptance of Wittgenstein's ideas are indicated in Ramsey's letter to Wittgenstein concerning the second edition of the *Principia*.[85]

> I have done little except, I think, made out the proper solution rather in detail of *some of the contradictions which made Russell's Theory of Types* unnecessarily complicated, and made him put in the Axiom of Reducibility. *I went to see Russell a few weeks ago,* and am reading the manuscript of the new stuff he is putting into the *Principia*. You *are quite right that it is of no importance; all it really amounts to is a clever proof of mathematical induction without using the axiom of reducibility.* There are no fundamental changes, identity just as it used to be. *I felt he was too old: he seemed to understand and say "yes" to each separate thing,* but it made no impression so that three minutes afterwards *he talked on his old lines. Of all your work he seems now to accept only this: that it is nonsense to put an adjective where a substantive ought to be which helps with his theory of types.* [Ramsey's emphasis]

In *My Philosophical Development,* Russell expressed even more reservations about the principle of extensionality and about Wittgenstein's view of identity. The concept of the isomorphism of fact and proposition, which was influential on Russell from the time of the "Notes on Logic" onward, is said to have been an excess, since modified by both Russell and Wittgenstein.[86] (It must be mentioned that the basic notion of some correlation of the structure of the proposition and the structure of the fact is present in Russell's 1913 unpublished manuscript and his seminar notes on the theory of knowledge of the spring of 1914, as well as in Wittgenstein's "Notes on Logic" of the fall of 1913.)

One recurrent theme in Russell's references to Wittgenstein is the report of the suffering that Russell experienced when he had to accept Wittgenstein's view that mathematical logic consisted only of "different ways of saying the same thing." The status of logical truths as tautologies dethroned Russell's a priori and universal logical truths, which, although admittedly empty of empirical content, nevertheless provided the basis of methodological security and the premises of universal forms of possibilities which philosophy employed. Hence the criticism that Wittgenstein launched against Russell's theory of knowledge in 1913 was grounded in the emerging view of logic as not significant philosophically in the way Russell had believed it to be. This destroyed the link by which Russell intended to pass from acquaintance with the forms of a relational complex, via a relational theory of judgment, to atomic propositions, and then, by the use of logical techniques, to molecular propositions and the application of logical argument to the concepts of science. The new view of logic also made all logical premises unavailable for epistemological use and made the "proofs" of logic empty of philosophical meaning. For Wittgenstein, the chief significance of his own criticism was in clearing the way for what he perceived as the final solution of the logical, and hence metaphysical, problems which he and Russell faced. But for Russell the grand scheme of an ultimate scientific and philosophical synthesis became impossible. That faults had been found in the theory of types was of less significance, and, if this was to be a matter only for logic, it became of less concern to him, for he essentially gave up his own work in an area in which he now felt insecure himself and believed to be irrelevant to his philosophical interests.

But the consequence of the Wittgensteinian view of logic not only dealt blows to his philosophy as a whole and caused him to abandon all remnants of the logical realism of *The Principles of Mathematics,* but it also entailed the notion of a sharp distinction between logical and empirical truth. This distinction, the dichotomy of the logical, analytic, syntactical, and a priori, as opposed to the empirical, factual, synthetic, and a posteriori, became an accepted premise of logical positivists (and logical empiricists) and dominated one branch of philosophical analysis from the 1920s until after World War II. Neither Wittgenstein nor Russell, who were claimed as its fathers, acknowledged their offspring, but this distinction was part of the impact of Wittgenstein which left Russell's philosophy incapable of achieving any final synthesis.

In *The Analysis of Matter* of 1927, Russell reviewed the historical distinction between the analytic and the synthetic, and he concluded:

> We must ask ourselves, therefore: What is the common quality of the propositions which can be deduced from the premisses of logic?
>
> The answer to this question given by Wittgenstein in his *Tractatus Logico-Philosophicus* seems to me the right one. Propositions which form part of logic, or can be proved by logic are all *tautologies*—i.e. they show that certain different sets of symbols are different ways of saying the same thing, or that one set says part of what the other says.[87]

Russell goes on: "Knowledge is said to be a priori when it can be acquired without requiring any fact of experience as a premiss; in the contrary case, it is said to be empirical."[88]

The acceptance of the tautologous character of logical propositions and the attendant distinction between logical and empirical truth may be seen as a permanent impact of Wittgenstein upon Russell—some would say it was the destruction of Russell's philosophy of logic.[89] In contrast to this conversion, and to some of Russell's responses to the *Tractatus*, there are many aspects of Wittgenstein's thought that were always antithetical to Russell's philosophical point of view. It is these which have emerged more emphatically in recent perspectives. The distinction in the *Tractatus* between showing and saying and the consequent interdiction on the use of a metalanguage were not seen as part of what Wittgenstein was saying about logic in 1913 and were regarded by Russell as a "mystical" element for which he saw no justification either within the text of the *Tractatus* or outside of it. Yet to many interpreters this doctrine is part and parcel of Wittgenstein's concept of logic and of philosophy, certainly at this period and perhaps later as well. This was neither appreciated nor accepted by Russell, even at the time of the high tide of Wittgenstein's influence.

7.7 Divergence

The limitation of philosophy to a concern with logic and its metaphysics early in Wittgenstein's career, and to a clarification of the way philosophers knock their heads against the limits of language in his later career, were both alien to Russell's concept of philosophy. In the days when Wittgenstein was Russell's student, he was reported to have held that the realm of feeling and impulse could not be talked about, and this included ethics, religion, and aesthetics.[90] At the same period, Russell had plans to extend philosophical methodology to all problems that philosophers had ever considered, to show definitively how they could be solved, or else that they could not be solved.[91] Wittgenstein and Russell disagreed concerning the relevance of theory of knowledge to the domain of philosophy in those days; Wittgenstein regarded it as derivative from psychology and of little philosophical import and deprecated Russell's concern for it, while Russell regarded it as a core and foundation for work in logic and in scientific conceptual analysis. Russell continued to labor in psychology and to relate it to his theory of knowledge, a topic he kept in the foreground.[92] To him science and philosophy were intimately related in the analysis of scientific concepts by philosophy, in the adumbration of new hypotheses for science by philosophical constructions, and in the use of information from science in building viable philosophical concepts, such as space, time, and cause. For Wittgenstein, the two realms of science and philosophy were separate; philosophy cannot tell us how things are, and science cannot clarify our ideas or our language.

For Russell, the Wittgenstein of the period after World War I had passed into a mystical religious realm lacking either discipline or reason, and there, he guessed, might lie the end of their friendship.[93] Their final judgments on each other were harsh. In 1946 Wittgenstein is reported by Norman Malcolm to have remarked, "Russell isn't going to kill himself doing philosophy now."[94] Russell, for his part, remarked:

> The earlier Wittgenstein, whom I knew intimately, was a man addicted to *passionately intense thinking,* profoundly aware of difficult problems of which I, like him, felt the importance, and possessed (or at least so I thought) of true philosophical genius. The later Wittgenstein, on the contrary, seems to have grown tired of serious thinking and to have invented a doctrine which would make such an activity unnecessary.[95]

In the divergence of these judgments, or rather, in their mutual antipathy, can be read the split in the analytic movement since the World War II. Those who have followed Russell have picked out some of his work and moulded it into compatibility with a view he did not himself accept. Such philosophers as Ayer, Quine, and Carnap have given generous credit to Russell's insights but followed courses not of his choosing. The later Wittgenstein rejected much of what he and Russell had found important in the period of the *Tractatus:* the use of an artificial language, the conviction that a single model of meaning could be found, that ordinary speech and ordinary language, though "in order" for ordinary purposes, required reform or reformulation for the purposes of logic, the search for definitive forms. That rejection continues in Wittgenstein's students. Those who followed Wittgenstein in his later years have looked at Russell through the eyes of their mentor as a false prophet unable to see the error of his ways, and necessitating that a whole generation of readers and students be purged of the false concepts which still afflict philosophers guilty of "subliming the language."

The followers of the first party tend to look only at Russell's contributions to logic and his use of the method of construction; for this reason much of the secondary material on Russell emphasizes issues in logic that go back to *Principia Mathematica* (a fate that Whitehead has not shared). On the other hand, the followers of the second party have treated Russell as a kind of *bête noire* and look only at that part of his philosophy which has to do with his influence on or by Wittgenstein. There are signs of a change; both philosophers are now historical figures, and the number of those who feel a personal loyalty to either of them is now small. Further research in the archival materials lately made available has removed some misconceptions and opened up new lines of inquiry in which historical and textual accuracy is a guiding principle, and in which fresh philosophical insights guide the interests of the researchers.

8

Russell and the Pragmatists

The INTERACTIONS BETWEEN RUSSELL and the various pragmatists whom he met and with whom he had philosophical exchanges were of a different nature from those between Russell and the philosophers who were his close friends and collaborators, Moore, Whitehead, and Wittgenstein; it was adversarial in nature. This was true also for Russell's interactions with the idealists; the difference was the fact that he had gone through a stage of neo-Hegelianism himself. In the case of pragmatism he began as and remained an opponent for whom their position was alien; this did not change although, in the course of his own development, changes in his thought brought him closer to the pragmatic position than he recognized, as we will see. Russell became acquainted with William James and Charles Sanders Peirce when he made his first visit to the United States in 1896. Later he heard reports of Peirce's ideas from Lady Victoria Welby, who tried to arrange for Peirce to visit England, hoping to bring him and Russell together to discuss theory of meaning. Peirce read Russell's *Principles of Mathematics,* and his annotated copy is in the archives of Harvard University. Although each respected the logical achievements of the other, their interactions were minimal.[1] With respect to William James, Russell continued a correspondence with him, met him at various times when James came to England, and wrote numerous reviews of his works. He held James in the highest regard and learned much from his work, although he remained very critical of his theory of truth.[2] John Dewey and Russell first met in 1914 when Russell lectured at Harvard. Later they were in China at the same time; later still, during World War II when Russell was denied his appointment at City College of New York University by court action, they corresponded about the protest against this action.[3] But the two philosophers were not close friends, nor were they ever able to satisfy each other in the presentation of philosophical issues in their extended controversy. The less well-known pragmatist, F. C. S. Schiller, was an acquaintance of Russell's, and the two had many exchanges in letters and in conversation over a twenty-year period while Schiller taught at Oxford.[4]

Through all the interactions with these various pragmatic writers, Russell remained an intransigent critic of their point of view. For their part, the pragmatists generally expressed dismay at what they regarded as Russell's consistent misunderstandings of their position. At times it seemed to them that a rapprochement between the two positions was at hand; but this never materialized. It is interesting that the rather contemptuous attitude sometimes expressed by Russell, especially toward the pragmatic theory of truth, still seems to be widely shared in Britain. Although it has been apparent to many commentators that there is much in common between the pragmatic theory of meaning and the "don't look for the meaning look for the use" motif in current British philosophy, and although the emphasis on context in twentieth-century writers, including Wittgenstein and Gilbert Ryle, is similar to that of pragmatism, British philosophers have, for the most part, been uninterested in the American school.[5] Sometimes this has been attributed to the malign influence of Schiller, said by his colleagues to have been a "bounder"; sometimes it has been attributed to the low level of American culture reflected in American pragmatism. In part the lack of interest may be due to the influence of Russell himself, who reviewed the main writings of the pragmatists as they were published. The British attitude is reflected in the surprised appreciation expressed by A. J. Ayer in *The Origins of American Pragmatism:* "In going through his [Peirce's] works in detail I found so many points of difficulty and interest that I was drawn into writing about him at much greater length than I had intended. When the same turned out to be true of James, I decided that the first half of my plan was enough to be going on with; critical examination of the philosophy of these two great pragmatists." Ayer does not explain his omission of G. H. Mead and Dewey from his survey of American pragmatism, but he refers to the events that first brought Peirce to the notice of "English philosophers, who until then derived their mainly unfavorable ideas of pragmatism from the more popular and polemical writings of James and Schiller."[6]

8.1 Russell and Schiller

Of the three pragmatists with whom Russell had exchanges, Schiller was the one for whom the polemical exchange of letters was a continuing interest and activity. In many ways Schiller and Russell were alike: both had quick and sometimes savage wit; both were irreverent in their attitudes toward entrenched academic respectability; both enjoyed a good argument. Their correspondence is a delight and also sheds light on the way in which persistent efforts failed to resolve differences between the pragmatic and the Russellian positions.

Schiller was teaching at Corpus Christi College in Oxford when he and Russell first came in contact. Whether or not he was a "bounder" (according to the dictionary "a cheerfully ill-bred person"), it is clear that he must have been a very uncomfortable colleague for the other philosophers at Oxford. His written work and letters abound in attacks on F. H. Bradley, then the major figure at Oxford, on Joachim, and on John Cook Wilson, a classical scholar and rival in the teaching of logic at Oxford. Nor were these attacks gentlemanly polemics beginning with "I beg to disagree with my learned colleague"; they must have earned Schiller a good deal of dislike. In the preface to his 1903 *Humanism: Philosophical Essays,* Schiller prophesies the imminent demise of idealism and the coming of a new and better philosophy (the one the essays espouse): "The ancient shibboleths encounter open yawns and unconcealed derision. The rattling of dry bones can no longer fascinate respect nor plunge a self-suggested horde of fakirs in hypnotic stupor. The agnostic maunderings of impotent despair are flung aside with a contemptuous smile by the young, the strong, the virile."7

On other occasions the references are directed to individuals. It is no wonder that Russell is reported to have said, "I have always thought that he rather enjoyed being hated by the other Oxford philosophers."8 That propensity for contention is remarked by William James in letters to Schiller. James replies to Schiller's suggestion that Bradley's criticism of pragmatism be answered; James is amused that Bradley has treated James himself but not Schiller with kindness because, he writes, "you are too bumptious," and he recommends that Bradley's criticism be ignored. Schiller, however, writes a long polemical retort to Bradley, and James, reacting to the retort, complains that the article was too detailed, too sharp in tone—"But you, for the pure pleasure of the operation, chase him [Bradley] up and down his windings, flog him into and out of his corners, stop him and cross-reference him and counter on him, as if required to do so by your office."9

Schiller's views were variously termed by him *personalism, humanism, voluntarism,* and *pragmatism.* The first of these terms refers to Schiller's thesis that the intellectualist tradition of philosophy has assumed that the person of the philosopher makes no difference to the philosophical inquiry, whereas Schiller held that there is abundant evidence that the individual's interests, desires, purposes, and biases have a strongly determinative effect on what and how he studies. In his view that fact need not lead us to despair that all thought is subjective and hence flawed, but it should lead us to see that through the psychology of inquiry we can bring to bear scientific evidence that will help us see how people think, enhancing the barrenness of logic with the richness of the study of individual psychology. Schiller's most common appellation of his own position is *humanism,* and this reflects his emphasis on a standard of truth and of value which is set within the limitations of human inquiry and human goods; it would avoid the intellectualist fallacy of seeking an objective, abstracted truth-in-itself or good-in-itself too remote from human concerns to be grasped or lived by ordinary mortals. Schiller believes that if we look at ordinary human inquiry—for instance, that actually carried out by scientists—as it unfolds, wrestling with confusing questions, making false starts, uncovering fresh problems, we will have a better theory of knowledge than if we take the finished results of science and, abstracting from them, make a logical and perfect pattern of the truth-unfolding process. In quoting Protagoras's "Man is the measure of all things," Schiller makes the point that there is no ultimate and final truth or good "out there" by reference to which (if we could ever reach it to make such a reference) our own puny ideas can be warranted; we make our truths and our goods as we go along, and it is that rambling, incoherent, but purposeful process that we need to study. This brings him to *voluntarism,* the view that a person's own will and own efforts can make the future, can affect what events come to be. In this aspect of his thought, he holds a common ground with Bergson's view of evolution and, as has been pointed out, is a precursor of Sartrean existentialism.[10]

> I have long thought that I was really much nearer to the ideal of dispassionate intellectualism and pure contemplation than any of those who professed it. Which was of course my reason for rejecting it—just as Plato attacked poetry because he was incurably poetic, and the ascetic attacks pleasures because they appeal to him too strongly. In virtue of this temper, and the discipline by which it was acquired, I perceived that it was ultimately *impossible* to "escape from one's own personality." If, therefore, personality is vitiation, everything, from the purest mathematics downwards, is tainted beyond redemption. Ergo our only hope is that personality may be a good not an evil, or at least may be turned from the one into the other by being consciously recognized and controlled systematically. Voilá the genesis of my "humanism."[11]

It is evident that all these themes in Schiller's thought have much in common with that of pragmatism; he himself said that he had developed many of his ideas before reading James in the early 1890s. The similarity of the ideas of Peirce, James, Schiller, and, later, Dewey was marked; Schiller identified himself as a pragmatist and argued for a common theory of truth and of meaning.[12] As a critic of idealism, Schiller welcomed Russell as an ally who shared the opposition to monism and to the abstract version of a single ultimate truth, and was, as were Schiller and James, inclined to pluralism. It turned out, however, that this alliance by no means included a nonaggression pact.

It has sometimes been suggested that Russell misunderstood Dewey's theory of truth because of James, and James's theory of truth because of Schiller, a kind of "halo effect" convincing Russell that the subjectivist implications of Schiller's theory, and the religious implications of James's theory, were present also or were implicitly allowed in Dewey's more scientific view. This judgment requires qualification, as we shall see, but it is true that Schiller's version of the pragmatic theory of truth was the first topic discussed between Russell and Schiller when their correspondence began.

The correspondence that has survived begins with a letter of Schiller's, dated November 30, 1902, in which he continues an argument begun in discussion of the same evening in which he and Russell had participated. The correspondence continued in spurts, often stimulated by a publication or a public discussion, until 1925. During those years the two men must have met often or been in the same company; the Aristotelian Society, the Moral Science Society at Cambridge, meetings at Oxford are mentioned in the letters. For five years, beginning in 1905, Russell lived part of each year at his home in the environs of Oxford. In addition to letters, there are numerous reviews—by Russell of Schiller's books and those of the other pragmatists, by Schiller of Russell's 1921 *The Analysis of Mind,* and Russell's response to it. There is also a three-part discussion on meaning that took place between Russell, Schiller, and Joachim at the Aristotelian Society meetings of 1919–20. The letters reveal an articulate and ardent defense of his own ideas by Schiller, and insistent inquiries as to what Russell means by some of his propositions; on Russell's part there is considerable effort to answer, to clarify, and to specify differences. It seems that they were never close friends but long-term acquaintances for whom personal references were appropriate as to vacation plans, political events of the moment, and so forth. Russell's letters sometimes reveal impatience at Schiller's insistence on answers, and Schiller acknowledges that he is aware of irritating Russell and of putting forth ideas that he knew Russell would reject. On the whole the correspondence is lively and friendly; Schiller felt secure enough in Russell's esteem to request a letter of support in his (ultimately unsuccessful) application for a chair at Oxford.[13] Toward the end of the period of their interaction Russell writes: "Dr. Schiller's article dealing with me . . . . is a model of philosophical discussion: the points which he discusses are fundamental, and the divergences between him and me which he notes concern vital problems."[14] It is apparent that mutual respect and interest in the same region of problems kept the correspondence alive and allow us the expectation of learning something from it concerning the development of their positions.

The topics discussed in the exchange of letters beginning at the end of 1902 have to do with theory of truth. Russell had maintained that if Schiller is to define the true as the advantageous, he must claim that this definition is itself true in the traditional correspondence sense. This was a criticism often made by Russell in later discussions—that pragmatism implicitly assumes the traditional meaning of "truth" to apply to its own statements about truth. But Schiller points out that this technique can be as well used by him against Russell as it can the other way around. So if Russell gives a definition of truth in terms of independent correspondence with fact, Schiller can point out that Russell has implicitly assumed that this definition is advantageous and thus true in Schiller's sense. But Schiller goes on to reject such arguments as "logic-chopping" and to point out that what he means is that all inquiry and all propositions are propounded for the sake of some practical advantage, some real consequence to follow from them. Hence Schiller's claim is that the truth of a proposition cannot be held to be a priori but must be tried out and verified in terms of consequences in experience, and he denies Russell's apparent claim that a logical valuation of true or false must belong to a proposition independently of its usefulness or of the future course of inquiry. Such a valuation is the *outcome* of the inquiry.

In a long response, Russell assumes that Schiller has given up the claim that *true* means *advantageous* and admits that any definition of truth may turn out to be circular. He transfers his attention then to Schiller's statement that propositions having "no relation to practical life have no meaning" and denies this to be true, in any except the trivial sense that it might derive from the original definition, that the true is the advantageous. Russell does go on to maintain that any discussion of the *value* of beliefs is psychological and hence has nothing to do with the prior notion of the *truth* of propositions, and that the advantage of true propositions is merely sociological and historical and therefore just as irrelevant to truth. Russell again tries to trap Schiller into a circular argument by claiming that Schiller's meaning is that an individual inquirer will judge a proposition *p* to be true if he judges it to be advantageous to so believe it, but whether it *is* advantageous to believe that proposition to be true must be established by another appeal to the advantageousness of that criterion of advantageousness, and Schiller is, therefore, committed to assuming that some such circular reasoning is performed by anyone prior to his accepting even the most obvious and natural of beliefs. In his reply, Schiller makes the point that he did not claim to be giving a definition of truth, but simply stating something about the tendency people have to reject as false what turns out to be misleading or irrelevant to the concerns of the inquiry, and to accept as true that which works out to the advancement of the inquiry. He claims, against Russell, that logic ought not to be divorced from psychology and that the study of human nature is relevant to logic, and that of logic to the study of human nature. He attempts a different formulation of his point of view that he hopes will lead Russell to understand it. There is at least one letter missing of Russell's to Schiller, and the last of the series is a despairing letter of Schiller's in which he feels that Russell is changing his, Schiller's position so that what Russell draws out of it is valid, but in doing this he has changed the issue and the meaning, and a new start would have to be made to clarify the issue.[15] But no letters have been found that would intervene between those of early 1903 and those of 1906.

We have seen that during the first ten years of the century Russell was much concerned with the theory of truth, and that he passed from the assertion of the independence and objectivity of truth expressed in *The Principles of Mathematics* of 1903 and "Meinong's Theory of Complexes and Assumptions" of 1904, where the transcendence of truth and falsity was expressed, to the multiple-relation theory of belief and the correspondence theory of truth expressed in the *Philosophical Essays* of 1910. In 1904, just after Schiller's and Russell's first exchange, the latter had come to hold that some propositions are true and some are false, just as some roses are red and some are white, but he acknowledged problems with the reality of negative propositions which are affirmed, with denied affirmative propositions, and with the denial of unasserted propositions.[16]

In the course of the next few years, Russell wrote several papers on the theory of truth, in addition to his published reviews of Joachim and of Schiller and the other pragmatists. One of the papers was read at the Moral Science Society, November 2, 1906, and became, it seems, his Aristotelian Society address of December 6, 1906 (one which elicited enthusiasm and a request for a copy from Schiller). In this paper Russell rejects the idealist theory of truth and puts forward two possible realist theories of truth: the first, that truth is a quality of belief in fact (a correspondence theory); the second, that truth is a quality of a nonmental complex called a proposition. The decision regarding which of these two views is better is left in doubt; the latter may be identified as Russell's old theory of 1904; the former as a view which is gradually emerging and being refined to its complete form in the essay "On the Nature of Truth and Falsehood" in *Philosophical Essays* (1910).[17]

Another paper, which exists in manuscript in the Bertrand Russell Archives and which is undated, gives an extensive criticism of both the idealist and the humanist concepts of truth. The criticisms made of Schiller's view are similar to those expressed in the earlier letters, and very close to those contained in a review of Schiller's *Studies in Humanism* in *The Nation* of March 2, 1907.[18] Both the review and the paper employ an extended example of the belief that the express train has just passed as an example of the kind of simple and indubitable truth that Schiller's theory overlooks in the interests of discussing unsettled, doubtful beliefs requiring inquiry and risky commitments and involving portentous consequences. The similarity of parts of the paper and the review (there are closely corresponding sentences in different segments of the paper and the review), the internal references in the paper to a 1906 article of Schiller's and to the 1906 book on truth by Joachim, suggest that it may have been written in 1907. This dating seems also to fit in with the fact that a crossed-out paragraph in the paper refers to truth as a property of propositions independent of their being known or believed and confesses that Russell does not know exactly what is meant by calling such propositions true. (This suggests that a similar hesitancy in the 1906 paper may now have been overcome.) The conclusion still has a tentative character, however; after two missing manuscript pages Russell concludes:

> I conceive, then, that the world consists of many things, any two of which have certain relations and do not have certain others. That they have any of the relations they do have, or do not have any of the relations they do not have, are facts; that they have any of the relations they do not have, or do not have any of the relations they do have, are the opposite of facts, which we may call fictions. Facts are true, and fictions false, quite independently of any one's ever knowing them or thinking about them. Neither the one nor the other is mental: they are *objects* of beliefs and disbeliefs, but the objects which are before the mind are not themselves mental, except in the case of introspection. When we believe a fact, we believe correctly; when we believe a fiction, we believe erroneously.

Having raised the objection that objective fictions may strain one's acceptance of his theory, and finding no answer to that, Russell concludes that it is not "essential to admit the objectivity of fictions; by a suitable theory of belief, the objectivity of facts can be made to suffice."[19]

Thus the manuscript seems to provide the clue to his later work, which links the theory of truth with the theory of belief. In this manuscript the full form of the 1910 theory is foreshadowed, but many more difficulties lay ahead for Russell's theories. Yet as always, the fact that he had not yet solved the difficulties of his own theory did not restrain him from voicing the objection to Schiller's theory that it did not recognize the objectivity of fact and that truth depended on fact, not on a truth claim made by a belief. "Hence Mr. Schiller can speak of a *proposition* as having a 'claim' to truth; but this, surely is mythical language. It is we who make a claim to truth; the fact or non-fact that is the object of our judgment does not make a 'claim' . . . it merely is a fact."[20]

In a letter responding to Russell's review of his book, Schiller makes use of the "express train":

> I could not but recognize that marvel of *human* ingenuity and addition to 'reality', your 'express train', as it whizzed past me going a mile a minute on the Nation's business. It would infallibly have blown off my cap of darkness, as I stood on my platform, if I had not long ago given up wearing such things, when I found they did not fit me. It was however a close shave and I am glad we avoided a collision, and as you may be uncertain as to whether you touched me, you may be glad to know that you only just grazed the anti-intellectualist flag with which I was incautiously signalling.

Schiller goes on to say that all truths are dubitable, in the sense that one would not want to affirm of any truth that it could not be doubted at some time and under some circumstances. Again he tries to point out that in speaking of a belief "working" he did not intend to use the term for any consequences other than those of cognitive value. He also protests that humanism is not subjectivist, but his letter ends with appreciation for the generous criticism, to be accounted for by their both being "heretics."[21]

In the January 2, 1908, issue of *The Albany Review,* Russell published a well-known article on pragmatism entitled "Transatlantic 'Truth'"; this had been read earlier as a paper at Oxford (October 23, 1907), and it later appeared under the title "William James' Conception of Truth" in *Philosophical Essays* (1910).[22] Schiller was present at the original presentation of this paper, and it elicited praise from him. He felt Russell had moved from his original position and, in his treatment of induction, had granted a major point to the pragmatists. With respect to the definition of *working,* Schiller, in a letter of this period, differentiates his view from that of James and clarifies the meaning of the term for Russell:

> The difference between us about "working" is possibly a misapprehension due to the facts that (1) we have emphasized so much the psychological side of *all* working, and (2) taken it in too generic a sense. As to (1) it is true I think that James always speaks psychologically (which is why he is so ready to admit that the absolute "works"), but I have always conceived the problem as logical as well. I have always (?), that is, joined to my protest against the divorce of logic and psychology

assertions of the normative functions of a logic which grows naturally out of the psychological nature of the cognitive process. Only (2) one had to convince logicians that they could not simply ignore the human aspects of knowing, before going into details as to the various modes of "working" in various fields of the criteria of validity and proof within them, and also the possibilities of conflicts between working values.[23]

Schiller goes on to express readiness to specify his meaning more fully, and also comments that Russell has overlooked the psychological side of religious belief in his comments on James. Three months later, after reading the article in print, Schiller commented that it is "the best, best written and best-tempered criticism we have encountered up to date."[24]

In 1909 Russell published a major article entitled "Pragmatism," in which he reviewed six recent works, James's *Will to Believe and Other Essays* and *Pragmatism;* Schiller's *Humanism: Philosophical Essays* and *Studies in Humanism;* Dewey's *Studies in Logical Theory;* and *Essays, Philosophical and Psychological in Honor of William James, Professor in Harvard University,* by his (James's) colleagues at Columbia University. Most of the article, however, is devoted to James and to Schiller, with little reference to the two last books. Apparently, he sent proofs of the article to Schiller, who replied with congratulations and appreciation—"on the whole I don't complain of your criticisms"—and with several closely written pages of response to the criticisms.[25]

Much of Schiller's commentary concerns Russell's criticisms of "The Will to Believe," and he is surely right in finding a misrepresentation in Russell's claim that the pragmatists confuse believing a hypothesis and acting upon it. It also seems to Schiller a strained interpretation of that essay to conclude, as Russell does, that it justifies any and every belief being held with full force even in the absence of evidence, and therefore that it increases rather than decreases the risk of intolerance and persecution. Schiller also objects that Russell has misunderstood James and himself when he takes their dictum that truth is a species of good to mean that the good and hence truth is whatever satisfies desire.

Russell writes that the errors of pragmatism with respect to truth rest on its confusion of two senses of meaning—a causal sense, as when clouds mean rain, and the linguistic sense in which *pluie* means *rain*. In attempting to elucidate the meaning of *truth* they have hit on the first rather than the second sense of *meaning*. Schiller responds:

You *don't* say what you think it is, and it part of our case that there is no other than the pragmatic. We have not made this point very prominent so far, because we have hope that some one on the other side would come forward with a coherent account. But I am growing confident that this won't happen because it can't. Admitting then your distinction as to the two "meanings" in the abstract, we have in this case only one, viz, the causal meaning of truth. As no one can tell what truth means per se, we are entitled to say it means what it means in relation to action, when the illusion that it means something other has been uprooted from the mind.[26]

Schiller also objects to Russell's attributing to him the reintroduction of the rejected distinction of real and apparent in Schiller's assuming that some facts could be altered. Schiller says, in effect, I certainly can try to alter facts since I don't regard them as absolute or ultimate, but that does not mean I have created the two realms you attribute to me. Schiller also objects to Russell's attributing to pragmatism a convenient form of skepticism, and his specific quotations from Russell's article identify shifts in terminology which alter the pragmatists' meanings unfairly; the shifts from "liable to revision" to "capable of improvements," from "rest securely" to "be lazy," appear in Russell's text as published unaltered. Schiller is also stung by the brief reference to his having conducted a poll on the beliefs held concerning immortality—a kind of survey that would be useful to moral studies, though it indicated no disposition to use such methods to settle questions of truth or value. Russell's final thrust, attributing to the pragmatist a love of struggle for its own sake and an encouragement of the use of force to settle disputes in the absence of any objective or outside arbiter of differences of opinion, draws from Schiller the predictable historical observation that it has been in the service of various kinds of absolutism that the persecution of heresies and the use of force to ensure assent have been undertaken, and that pragmatism's commitment to free inquiry works to halt persecution. He passes in silence over Russell's final rejection of any view which confines itself to the human and the natural, and Russell's comment that this humanism is not for one who seeks release from the prison of life on this planet. In sum, it seems that Schiller was rather generous in his acceptance of the article as "animated by a spirit of fairness."

In a letter acknowledging the volume of essays of 1910, which contained a reprint of the same article, Schiller, noting no changes in it, again protests Russell's assumption of the existence of "independent" facts. He also points out that neither he nor James confused different varieties of satisfactions or justified the indiscriminate exercise of the "will to believe." It seems that the dialectic of discussion and letter writing surrounding Russell's reviews of the pragmatists had little effect. James, too, as we shall see, was discouraged by the misunderstandings inherent in the reviews or engendered by them.

Schiller, however, seemed always hopeful of further developments in Russell's view and of some meeting of minds between them. Perhaps, as certain references suggest, he looked on Russell as a fellow heretic and was ready to welcome his criticism in contrast to his real enemy, the absolutism enthroned at Oxford. It might also be conjectured that Russell's chapter "On the Nature of Truth and Falsehood" in *Philosophical Essays* was recognized by Schiller as an advance over Russell's previous espousal of the independence of fact, or of the proposition as itself true or false. In the 1910 essay, the amended theory of truth defined it as pertaining to beliefs in which the many-one relation of the believer to the components of the belief corresponded to the relation of the components of the fact.

How far Russell still was from a pragmatic position can be seen in the correspondence and publications of 1912; one important segment of this material concerns the publication, criticism, and defense of Schiller's *Formal Logic*. When Russell first received this book, he wrote to Ottoline Morrell in anger at Schiller's "impertinence" in publishing such a work, *Principia Mathematica* having just come out, and adding that Schiller was incapable of doing mathematical logic and unaware of the fact. His acknowledgment of the receipt of the book is correspondingly cool; "I agree with you that traditional formal logic is rot, but beyond that suppose I shan't agree with much."[27] Schiller in turn hopes that, in spite of obvious disagreement, "I can't help suspecting that in the end the intellectual kosmos also will turn out to be *round* so that possibly, if we each go straight on in our own way, we may one day meet to our mutual surprise and delight."[28] Russell was surprised at how much he did find to agree with, but, as his review in *The Nation* (May 18, 1912) shows, he still had many criticisms. Having paid tribute both to Schiller's attack on the traditional logic derived from Aristotle and still taught as a literary subject in many universities, and to the value of his insistence on the freshness and inventiveness necessary for inquiry, Russell goes on to convict Schiller of failure to understand and appreciate recent developments in formal logic from Boole onward, developments that have replaced the old classic tradition, then to accuse him of inconsistency in both condemning and admiring the syllogism, and to reject the subjectivist and humanist tone of the work.[29] Schiller, in acknowledging the review, tells Russell that he is overly optimistic in thinking traditional logic "dead" while it is still dominant in the teaching at Oxford and many other universities and still appears in currently acclaimed texts. He feels it unfair to stress the literary aspect of Schiller's background when he is using psychology and biology in his logic and is trying to do justice to a description of the scientific method as it is actually used.

As to the charge of "subjectivism" we shall probably never agree: I have often told you that it is *not* subjectivism but psychology, and that you can't abstract from the psychological side in all *known objects,* simply because there is a *knowing process* involved in getting to them, . . . likewise I venture to predict that you will never be able to conceive the difference between "truth" and "error" until you consent to consider the process of discriminating them.[30]

Later in the same month Schiller writes to Russell giving him information about the way questions on logic were answered on Oxford examinations and detailing the lack of understanding and knowledge of mathematical logic in general and the work of Russell in particular. How, he asks, do you contrive to live on both sides of Plato's chasm?[31]

In a comment on Russell's critical article on Bergson, Schiller protests both Russell's insufficient understanding of the psychological aspects of experience as lived, and his bias toward mathematics. "Your article seems to me to have the defect of all your criticisms of biologically and psychologically minded thinkers, viz, that you speak statically from a stand-point which accepts as final the present products of man's secular struggle to conceptualize his immediate experience."[32]

In an interesting series of letters from October 30, 1912, to January 2, 1913, Schiller attempts to clarify some points in Russell's logic, under the stimulus of Russell's article on cause. Only Schiller's letters survive, but the questions he raises within the context of a psychology of inquiry are clearly irrelevant to the formal context of *Principia Mathematica* within which Russell answers. Schiller wants to know what a "propositional function" is and how it can be said to be always or necessarily "true," and he wants to compare a logical language with other languages.

The exchange proves frustrating for both philosophers: Schiller accuses Russell of neglecting the most interesting and important problems by failing to see matters from any point of view other than his own, and maintains that his own interests are more extensive than Russell's. Schiller writes, "[I am] sorry my persistence annoys you . . . the more so as I feel we are not getting any forrader." He adds, though, that it is not his fault. He calls for specific references in Russell's work and defends himself against the charge of entertaining confusions due to "metaphysical dogmas." In the final letter of this series, Schiller says he is going to study Russell's references. "No doubt, as you suggest, we are all growing old and fossilizing, but the process seems to me to be essentially psychological and to have nothing to do with 'axioms' or 'logic.' "[33] As this correspondence coincides in time with the excitement

Russell felt over the work in logic done with Wittgenstein, it is perhaps not surprising that no permanent enlightenment for either philosopher followed from this aspect of their correspondence. During the years of the war, and of Russell's problems in the wake of Wittgenstein's onslaught, there seems to have been little contact with Schiller. One letter concerns Britain's war policy, and two letters have to do with Schiller's application for the chair of logic at Oxford.[34]

Two letters from Schiller to Russell early in 1919 welcome a turn toward psychology in the latter. Russell had sent a copy of an article and a copy of the prospectus of his lectures, possibly lectures that became *The Analysis of Mind,* and Schiller comments: "I was glad to note that you have now got interested in psychology at last, and (it seems to me) on the right lines. I infer both from the article and from the syllabus that the approximation to pragmatism which I predicted years ago has made great progress. And as you have, with the utmost candour, analyzed your bias and incidentally that of many others I predict further acceleration." Schiller goes on to remind Russell that James, like Schiller himself and Dewey, was really scientifically minded and to appeal to Russell not to convict him on the basis of some theologians' interpretation of him.[35]

Some of the 1919 correspondence refers to the projected symposium in which Russell, Schiller, and Joachim were to debate "The Meaning of Meaning." Any hopes for an easy rapprochement between the newly psychologized and debiased Russell and the humanism and pragmatism of Schiller seemed doomed to disappointment, as the two contributions reveal apparently irreconcilable differences.

Schiller's contribution is a response to Russell's "On Propositions: What They Are and How They Mean" of the preceding year.[36] That baffling juxtaposition of logical atomism, with its isomorphism of the bare proposition and the fact, and the behavioristic analysis of belief and judgment presents itself to Schiller as suggesting that for Russell meaning is a relation of object and image. While they are in agreement that the meaning does not attach to the word as such or to the object as such, Schiller protests the undue importance given to visual images, which are neither necessary nor even always important to meaning, he believes. He also protests the viewpoint of an outside versus an inside perspective on meaning, apparently attacking the behaviorism of Russell's psychology, and the preference for the viewpoint of the spectator over that of the actor. For Schiller meanings are demands made on experience; they are a universal stream of experiences which are vital, personal, communicated, and relative to the whole personality, not to the intellect alone. Moreover, as against Russell, Schiller asserts the intimate connection of meaning and value—objects acquire both as a result of the activities of persons and their communications.

It is odd to read Russell's response, accusing Schiller of ignoring the history of the individual and asserting that the essence of meaning lies in the causal efficacy of that which has meaning, then describing how the meaning of a word is derivative from the habit grown up around the corresponding image. He agrees that words are an improvement over images as far as communication of meaning is concerned but says he was speaking of the psychological and physiological origins of meaning. As we have seen already, this is in sharp contrast to Russell's earlier theory of meaning.

As for the issue of the internal versus the external perspective, Russell converts it into a dispute between Schiller's affirmation of the existence of unobservable entities such as the self or the conscious subject, and his own agnosticism concerning them and attempt to construct a psychology of meaning without them. "My object has been to endeavour to construct a theory of meaning after the model of scientific theories, not on the lines of traditional philosophy. It is this, at bottom, that causes the divergence between Dr. Schiller's views and mine." To refer to such "unobservable entities" in Russell's sense as being "experienced from within," as does Schiller, is for Russell an indefensible use of the word *experience*. Russell reemphasizes the behaviorist aspect of his new theory of meaning in defining "signs" as "sensible" (or imaginal) phenomena which cause actions appropriate, not to themselves, but to something else with which they are associated." In referring to mnemic causation he then extends this definition to a general definition of meaning. The motif that developed later in *The Analysis of Mind* is clearly evident:

> We may therefore lay down the following definitions:—(1) A "sign" is an occurrence which, through mnemic causation, has mnemic effects (not, in general, other effects) appropriate (from the point of view of the animal's instincts and desires) to some other occurrence or set of occurrences with which it is apt to be associated.
> (2) In such a case, the other occurrence or set of occurrences is the "meaning" of the occurrence which is a sign.[37]

The failure of Russell's new interest in psychology to bring his concepts of knowledge, of truth, and of logic closer to agreement with Schiller's pragmatism and humanism is evident in the last exchange of which we have any record between the two philosophers. This occurred in the review of Russell's *The Analysis of Mind* published by Schiller in the May 25, 1922, issue of *The Journal of Philosophy* (pp. 281–92), and in Russell's response in the same journal.[38] In his review Schiller welcomes Russell's concern with psychology and his recognition of its intimate connection with philosophy. He detects Russell's basic assumptions, which to Schiller are distortive, especially the assumption that it is always possible to seek for the "simple" or the "elements" among data that for Russell do not constitute a continuum. Also, Schiller says, Russell's analysis is not intended as a factual psychological account of the mental life but is an idealized construct which is made up to meet the theoretical needs of his philosophy. The result is far from a de facto account of what the minds of plain men are and contain; rather it is an artificial and sophisticated creation of his own ingenuity employing, as required, the findings of behaviorist psychology. Schiller believes the author should be closer to the facts and more aware of alternative psychological theories.

Although he gives credit to behaviorism for its success in describing and explaining ranges of external behavior and notes its affinity to pragmatism, Schiller goes on to offer a defense of an introspective and humanistic psychology. But by starting with discrete data of particulars of sensa, Russell, like Hume before him, finds it impossible to construct the unity of the self, of one's own experience, of the subject, all of which Russell had begun by forswearing.

Russell's perspectives and biographies are welcome to Schiller insofar as they break up the unity of the physical object. He also welcomes the abandonment of pure sensations and the data of acquaintance and Russell's recognition of the interpreted whole which is perception, although, in his opinion, Russell has not gone far enough in this direction. However, Schiller believes that there are elements in experience that coagulate around an "I" or a "self" and that Russell has not recognized these.

It is interesting that Russell begins his response to Schiller's review by enunciating what he had hinted at earlier in his dealings with him, that there may be fundamental divergences between points of view concerning which no arguments are possible. "He and I are agreed, I think, that it is impossible to produce arguments on either side of the questions which divide us. Philosophies which differ radically necessarily involve different logics, and therefore can not be proved or refuted by logic without question-begging. Accordingly, the remarks which I shall have to make will be of the nature of rhetoric rather than logic."[39] Russell goes on to set up the dichotomy between their philosophies as that between Hume on the one hand and romantic rebellion on the other, the head on the one hand, the heart on the other, the analytic and scientific on the one hand, the literary and the search for the one or the continuum, on the other. In this opposition Russell stands with the first alternative of each pair, Schiller with the second. Specifically,

Russell says he can find no experience of activity such as Schiller attributes to a self; moreover Russell defends the method of analytic construction attacked by Schiller as scientific and denies that it cannot lead to the construction of a unity simply because it begins with units. After rebutting certain specific points of Schiller's comment, he concludes by pointing out that he himself is only following James's lead in abandoning the "subject," while Schiller is maintaining it because what appeals most to Russell in James is what appeals least to Schiller.

It is easy to agree with Russell that his response is largely rhetorical, but less easy to agree that this is all that the case admits of; many accommodating words passed between Schiller and Russell, and their evident intent to understand each other need hardly be wrecked on the rock of inexpungeable temperamental differences. Surely, further arguments could be given regarding what is or is not found in experience, on psychologies, on the validity of respective arguments about the theory of truth and about logic. One feels that Russell's rejection of Schiller, while it may have a temperamental basis, cut short any grounds that could have been found for agreement. Is this the case with James and Dewey as well? In a sense Schiller's prophecy came true, for Russell had come to accept many of Schiller's points on which they had earlier diverged: his acknowledgment that experience is not the data of immediate acquaintance but the growth through memory and habit of certain attitudes of expectation is more pragmatic and Schiller-like than his earlier view; his theory of truth, although still realist, is now based on a correspondence of facts and beliefs, and the independently real and true (or false) proposition with its status as an entity has been abandoned. He has found it necessary to piece out the logical form of the proposition with a psychological analysis of belief and language. The irony is that, although in these respects Russell and Schiller did seem to approach each other (having gone round the "Kosmos" from opposing directions), they now pass each other without meeting, Schiller insisting on complementing behaviorism with an introspective view of the self, Russell rejecting the self and consciousness in the light of neutral monism.

8.2 Russell and James

It is noticeable that in his interactions with Schiller, Russell treated him with comradely unconcern over the niceties of compliments and courtesies; they were not intimate friends, yet there was no reserve or formality in their relationship. Schiller seemed remarkably free from rancor or resentment under what seemed, at times, to be unfair criticism. Perhaps he preferred critical review by Russell, whom he respected, to total snubbing by his Oxford colleagues—better to be insulted than ignored.

Russell's relations with William James were of a very different nature. The two had met before making their major contributions in print, and they had some correspondence during 1908 and 1909 which has survived.[40] These letters do not indicate any degree of intimacy, but even so they have, on the whole, a friendly and affable tone. The articles Russell wrote which concerned James always expressed great admiration for James's gifts as writer, psychologist, and philosopher, but were also extremely critical. The obituary for James that Russell contributed to *The Nation*[41] was similarly appreciative; his respect, however, did not prevent him from attacking pragmatism. James, unlike Schiller, was outspoken in rejecting Russell's criticisms, charged him with unfairness, and responded to those criticisms in print in vigorous fashion, striving as Schiller had done to correct specific misunderstandings and challenging Russell's own assumptions. He attacked Russell's logical method, advising him to "say good-bye to mathematical logic if you wish to preserve your relations with concrete realities!"[42] To this Russell replied rather mildly that he was "not wholly inclined to dispute the wisdom" of James's statement about mathematical logic. "Standing for Parliament gave me more relations with concrete realities than a lifetime of thought."[43] This was a sharp contrast to Schiller's attempt to find an accommodation with Russell's logic. Russell tried to improve his understanding of pragmatism between the 1908 and 1909 articles; James, however, found that Russell was still far from the mark.[44]

We have already seen some aspects of Russell's criticism of the pragmatic theory of truth. The main outlines of this criticism are clear in all of the early articles which Russell wrote on the subject.[45] His view might be paraphrased by saying that he found partial good and absolute evil in these views. The partial good was that the pragmatists rejected any nonempirical theory of truth based on the coherence of beliefs with one another, as did Russell; they took the possibility of error seriously, as the coherence theory did not; they properly stessed the role of verification in the testing of doubtful truths; and their analysis therefore was appropriate to certain kinds of situations in which evidence is derived from induction, in which truth is not obvious, and in which subsequent experience can be expected to shed light on the truth in question. It was this approval that had rejoiced Schiller, who said that it was no small thing for Russell to concede the entire area of induction to the pragmatist.

Russell's limited praise, however, has to be put in the context of his total disapproval of the rest for its import to be fully realized. The rejection of the coherence theory, for Russell, could only be properly realistic if one accepted his assumption that some independent reality or realm of facts exists, that it has certain characteristics unaltered by our knowing or not knowing them, and that it is by corresponding with this independent realm that a belief is true. At the time that he began writing about James's and Schiller's theory of truth, Russell held that truth *itself* had an objective existence in this realm of facts. This view, or variants of it, persisted in Russell's thought even when other aspects of his theory that originally supported it were changed, as we have seen. Not only truth but also error must have such an independent existence, so that, while it is admirable for the pragmatist not to ignore the *possibility* of error, yet he fails to recognize the independence, the obstinacy, and the unsurmountable nature of falsity. This is evident in the unduly subjective and relativistic view taken by James in religion, for instance, and, in general, in the pragmatic assumption that there may be cases when one may properly treat a belief as true when in fact it may be in error.

As for the importance of verification, Russell insists that while the pragmatist correctly describes the methods and criteria employed in checking doubtful beliefs, they fail to distinguish between the *criterion* of truth and the *meaning* of truth. It is Russell's assumption, based on the postulated objectivity of truth, that how one comes to know the truth must be different from what the truth in itself is. Thus, there are many propositions which are true because they correspond with fact, but are believed for the wrong reasons, and there are others which are objectively true or objectively false, even though we have no evidence in regard to which they are. In Russell's mind this demonstrates the need for distinguishing the meaning of truth from the criterion of truth.

This need is reinforced by Russell's pointing out that there are many other kinds of truth in addition to those to which the pragmatist refers. He distinguishes between obvious truth and doubtful truth. Obvious truth, such as the redness of the rose which I see in front of me, the passing of the express train, the self-evidence of the law of noncontradiction—all these are true without doubt or the necessity of proof, and Russell believes this kind of truth has a very important role to play in the theory of knowledge. This kind of obvious truth the pragmatist cannot consider, since his theory is centered around the truths that are the subjects of inquiry. And Russell argues that whatever definition of truth be adopted, it must be one equally well adapted to all kinds of truth. The pragmatists have been interested in the way the truth-value assigned to certain beliefs changes both in the mind of the individual and in the social history of inquiry, and, Russell admits, they have given a good description of what he calls "the natural history of beliefs."

However, what *happens* to a truth is not the same as its *being* a truth. In drawing attention to the way certain beliefs come to be accepted as fitting in with, satisfying the interests of, and being useful to the inquirer in question, the pragmatist is telling only an incidental part of their story, a part belonging to either psychological or sociological history.

There is another aspect to Russell's early criticisms of pragmatism that also survives into later criticisms, and this is his turning of pragmatism's theory of truth against itself. This is done in several ways, not all of them compatible with each other. First, Russell quotes a specific statement made by an individual pragmatist concerning truth, treats the statement as a definition in which the definiendum "truth" is taken as intended to be equivalent to the alleged definiens. The definition is then taken to license substitution of the definiens for the definiendum in any case, and various absurd consequences are shown to follow.[46] For example:

According to the pragmatists, to say 'it is true that other people exist' *means* 'it is useful to believe that other people exist'. But if so, then these two phrases are merely different words for the same proposition; therefore when I believe the one I believe the other. If this were so, there could be no transition from the one to the other, as plainly there is. This shows that the word 'true' represents for us a different idea from that represented by the phrase 'useful to believe', without destroying the meaning commonly given to the word 'true', which meaning, in my opinion, is of fundamental importance, and can only be ignored at the cost of hopeless inadequacy.

Another of Russell's arguments is to set up a regress. "Is it true that the Pope is infallible?"[47] For the pragmatist, this means: Does the belief in the infallibility of the Pope lead to satisfactory consequences? Then it is either true or not true that the belief in the infallibility of the Pope leads to satisfactory consequences, and this in turn requires us to investigate whether the alleged satisfactory consequences in which the truth of the belief in the Pope's infallibility are said to lie are themselves truly satisfactory, and so on. Sometimes Russell leaves the argument with the unacceptable regress; sometimes he points out that the pragmatist clearly does not or cannot mean this, and therefore must mean: Does the belief in the infallibility of the Pope lead to satisfactory consequences in the "old-fashioned" or nonpragmatic sense of truth? For this reason Russell often claims that the pragmatist must have two theories of truth, his own in terms of the initial response, and the traditional, in terms of knowing whether in fact the initial response is, or is not, satisfactory. Again, in a similar situation, and assuming that the traditional correspondence theory of truth is in fact involved, he points out that it is harder to know if it is true that the consequences of a belief are satisfactory than to know if the belief is true.

One of the most common criticisms of the pragmatist theory of truth made by Russell is the supposed ambiguity of the "satisfactoriness of consequences." There may be many ways in which the consequences of holding a belief may be satisfactory or unsatisfactory. Sometimes Russell infers that this means that pragmatists reject any unpalatable truths; sometimes that they wish to submit truth-claims to a study of the number of people who assent to or reject the truths, sometimes that biological survival might be a test of satisfactoriness, or that long-run political expediency might be. Russell's criticisms of James on this point are closely tied to his criticism of the latter's religious views, which he takes to justify his charges against assessing the satisfactoriness of the consequences of a belief in terms of psychological comfort. This leads Russell to the sweeping interpretation of pragmatism in terms of humanistic, subjectivist, Nietzschean, evolutionary, and politically authoritarian concepts.[48]

James was not without answers to the challenges to his theory of truth; these can be read in letters to Russell, in the marginal notes on "Transatlantic 'Truth,'" and in his reply to Russell in "Two English Critics." In his letter on the subject, James is patiently explanatory; in his marginal comments he liberally annotates Russell's statements about what he says or means with "silly" or "rubbish" or with more specific corrections of misstatements. In the article and letter, James counterattacks, attempting to show, not what specific points are in error, but what are the root causes in Russell's own assumptions, and how these come out in his criticism.

> Instead of being one universal relation *sui generis* called "truth" between any reality and an idea, there are a host of particular relations varying according to special circumstances and constituted by the manner of "working" or "leading" of the idea through the surrounding experiences of which both the idea and the reality are part.
>
> It is *particularly* of these experiences that I have always had in mind when I have called the working "Practical," for only with particulars and concretes do we have particular relations. One ought thus *to be able to define empirically* what the truth-relation *consists in* in every instance, and some will probably find it different in most instances.
>
> The ordinary conception makes the same abstract thing in every possible instance. Direct verification by sensible presence is one kind of leading. When no kind of verification is possible to us it seems to me that the question of our idea being true is irrelevant except as meaning accord with some enveloping authority who *has* the verification which we are cut off from, and our accord with that observer has itself to be defined *pragmatically.* I imagine these views are Schiller's.[49]

This letter appears to refer to the article "Transatlantic 'Truth.'" The first paragraph seems to refer to Russell's comment that the pragmatic theory neglects certain kinds of truths. James is saying that he does not seek, or believe possible, one universal definition of truth which is the same for each case—the idea of the leading-on character of ideas allows him to adapt the pragmatic concept of truth to such cases as direct sensory experience, which Russell had called obvious truths, as well as to cases where no verification is possible. To claim an absolute truth-value for propositions in the absence of any verification would seem to mean that one was referring to some transcendental experience within which the truth was verified. James, in another letter responding to the *Edinburgh Review* article, writes that the pragmatist does not end up regarding as true what he wishes to be true because "no pragmatist forgets that *concretely* our wish to square our selves with hard *fact* may be irreconcilable with our other wishes."⁵⁰

In his article "Two English Critics," James's chief thrust is against what he calls Russell's "abstractionist" logic.⁵¹ He counters some of Russell's regressive and circular logical gambits by pointing out that when the pragmatist speaks of the evaluation of a belief by means of the goodness of its consequences, this cannot be converted into the consideration of a different belief—that is, the belief that such and such consequences are good. In pointing out the good-consequences aspect of truth, the pragmatist is not setting up a logical definition, or a logical criterion, but pointing out "the lurking motive inside every truth claim." In a similar vein, James says that Russell converts every belief into a belief about pragmatism itself; when the pragmatist says that when a belief is judged true, it works, this does not mean that the belief in question is about its working.

As for the pragmatist theory of truth justifying the belief in the existence of something that does not exist, James calls this "the usual slander." Of course, if something does exist, there will be observable consequences of its existence, and it is in terms of these that belief in its existence would need to be justified, according to pragmatism. The real difficulty with the argument in question is the logical technique that Russell employs. He first assumes, as we have seen, that in speaking of *truth* the pragmatist is offering an exact and absolute definition of the word, that the definition thus offered is then assumed to be substitutible in all contexts for the word *truth,* and that absurd consequences are then shown to follow from such substitution. But it is just this kind of analytic single, unvarying, and exact definition that the pragmatist does not regard as possible; some of what Russell takes to be definitions are actually generalizations which it is illicit to convert. If truth is a species of good, that does not mean that if anything is a good it is also true, for instance.

James concludes by pointing out the slipperiness of the terms *proposition* and *fact*. In one context one may speak of *the fact that* . . . , and this usage would be equivalent to *the proposition that* . . . . But when Russell speaks of facts which just are and have the characteristics they have independent of their being known, believed in, or having statements made about them, it is a simple step to treat propositions in the same way, as without relation to belief, human inquiry, or knowledge. In that case you end with the strangeness of propositions which just are true or false the way roses are red or white. James points out the obvious anomaly of this way of regarding propositions, a consideration that calls for some clarification on Russell's part of his own view of truth and falsity. James connects this with similar positions held by Moore and Meinong.

One of James's early and most famous essays, "The Will to Believe," stirred the most prolonged and negative reaction in Russell of any of James's writings. It has been maintained that it was James's view of religion that turned Russell against pragmatism and caused his life-long and decisive reaction against the pragmatic theory of inquiry and its definitions of truth and knowledge. Whether or not this is the case (and it seems somewhat unlikely in view of the early controversy with Schiller), Russell made it clear that James's view of religion and the pragmatic theory of truth were intimately connected. In the 1908 article "Transatlantic 'Truth,'" after a general discussion of the pragmatic theory of truth, Russell makes specific reference to James's view of religion.

> It is chiefly in regard to religion that the pragmatist use of 'truth' seems to me misleading. Pragmatists boast much of their ability to reconcile religion and science, and William James, as we saw, professes to have discovered a position combining the merits of tender-minded-ness and tough-mindedness. The combination is really effected, if I am not mistaken, in a way of which pragmatists are not themselves thoroughly aware. For their position, if they fully realized it, would, I think, be this: 'We cannot know whether, in fact, there is a God or a future life, but we can know that the belief in God and a future life is true.' [In the margin James commented "silly!"] This position, it is to be feared, would not offer much comfort to the religious if it were understood, and I cannot but feel some sympathy with the Pope in his condemnation of it.[52]

Russell goes on to argue that James has said that if belief in the Absolute has consequences useful to life, it is so far forth true, and Russell says this must mean that the consequences flow from believing that the Absolute is a fact, but we can scarcely be convinced of the Absolute's factuality on the basis that it would be useful to life to believe in its existence. The pragmatic philosophy can give no reasons other than psychological ones for belief in the existence of God, and this turns out to be merely a play on the word *true*. With respect to Russell's reference to the hypothesis of the factuality of the Absolute, James writes marginally "this is all rubbish." He says, "The coincidence of the true with the emotionally satisfactory becomes of importance for determining what may count for true, only when there is no other evidence. Surely, *other satisfactions being equal* in two beliefs, Mr. Russell himself would not adopt the less emotionally satisfactory one, solely for that reason. It seems to me a man would be a fool not to adopt the *more* satisfactory one."[53] This strong reaction to Russell's criticism of the will to believe brought a reference in a letter to Russell to the "calamitous" criticisms he had made of "The Will to Believe." James goes on: "My doctrine deals explicitly with our concrete relations with a world where we can only get *probability* in cosmic matters, and where, concretely, belief is a variable of which the willingness to act is the sign without being the measure. (I mean very little more belief may let loose all the action possible.) You treat me as one ignoring probabilities and treating hypotheses for which there is *no* evidence." James refers to Russell's own essay "A Free Man's Worship" as an example of all that James justifies in "The Will to Believe," but says that Russell turns and rends it.[54]

To this complaint Russell returns a soft answer, praising *A Pluralistic Universe*. He comments that James's first "demand of God is to love him"; Russell's is to worship him. "I do not desire familiarity lest it breed contempt." He will try to correct his abuse of abstraction and his treatment of pragmatism. He goes on to say, "The pragmatic difference that pragmatism makes to me is that it encourages religious belief, and that I consider religious belief pernicious . . . a prejudice fed by history, and current politics." He says this because he does not want to pretend to be "solely influenced by intellectual considerations."[55]

The exchange of letters leaves many questions unanswered—if Russell admits that his view, as well as that of James, has origins in emotional responses to religion, how can he consistently take an "objective, fact-determined, suspense-of-judgment" position? How is the theme of "A Free Man's Worship" different from that of "The Will to Believe"?

Some clues to the answers to these questions may be provided by the second discussion of James's view of religion, which followed the correspondence and attempted to fulfill Russell's promise to be fair to pragmatism. In the article "Pragmatism" of April 1909, Russell begins his discussion with a detailed presentation and criticism of "The Will to Believe." He makes a point of recognizing the option to believe whole-heartedly in one of two possibilities when there is no evidence on which to decide the matter, and when the option is forced, vital, and momentous, thus limiting the discussion in the way that James himself did. He also restates James's view that to decide to disbelieve, or to suspend judgment, is as much an option or risk with an unsupported belief as is the option to believe, and that this justifies the taking of the risk of error over the risk of missing the truth when the consequences of the former are better. However, in setting up the risk of truth versus the risk of error as logical alternatives, Russell is scarcely fair to James's claim that it is only justified when other satisfactions are not jeopardized, since he says that "the legitimate conclusion from this argument would be . . . we ought to believe both alternatives; for in that case we are sure of 'knowing' the truth, since it is by no means impossible to believe two contradictory propositions." Russell concludes that this essay is a valuable introduction to pragmatism: "Some practice in the will to believe is an almost indispensable preliminary to the acceptance of pragmatism; and conversely pragmatism, when once accepted, is found to give full justification of the will to believe." Russell in his "commonsense criticism" finds a confusion between action and belief (one may be forced to act as if one knew one alternative to be true but without intellectual assent to the "belief" upon which one acts), a confusion between entertaining an hypothesis and acting on it. James's requirement of belief in the absence of evidence when momentous issues are involved, and when one alternative belief has consequences more satisfying than the other, appears to justify the reinforcement of beliefs prevalent in one's culture, and to justify an intolerant temper in religion that a rigorous apportionment of belief to evidence would leave open.[56] It is not surprising that James found this attempted correction inadequate; in a footnote to "Two English Critics," James refers to the *Edinburgh Review* article and says, "As far as his discussion of the truth-problem goes, although he has evidently taken great pains to be fair, it seems to me that he has in no essential respect improved upon his former arguments."[57]

In a segment of his obituary for James, Russell refers to James's philosophy of religion, which urges "that any religion, so long as it is useful in promoting happiness or virtue is to be considered 'true' in the times and places of its utility." Russell comments that such a utilitarian basis of religion will seem inadequate to many and that, although it promotes sympathy to different viewpoints, as is shown in *The Varieties of Religious Experience,* "to say that this suffices to prove that their beliefs were in any way *true* will remain a paradox to many."[58]

Russell retains throughout the discussion his stand that there is just one truth, objective, independent of our knowledge, and unrelated to our inquiry or our desires or life purposes. This truth either does or does not include the existence of God; if the former, religion is true, if the latter, false. Russell combines this traditional view of religion with his allegedly traditional view of truth. His own attitude is not without its contradictions. Intellectually, he should retain an uncommitted agnosticism, but in fact it is as difficult for Russell as it is for anyone else to hover between worship and nonworship. Since he has contempt for many of the arguments in favor of the existence of God, and since (as he admits to James), he has political prejudices against historical religions, his final attitude is an ambivalent combination of several perspectives: a recognition of the impossibility of marshaling evidence sufficient to justify belief in the existence of a God who would satisfy his yearning for something greater than the human to hold in awe; a lively criticism of and rejection of religious arguments and institutions; Russell's assumption is that the religious attitude is one of contemplation of whatever carries a warrant of truth, rather than an attitude of risk-taking necessary as a basis of action. This all follows from his insistence that religious belief is a matter of intellectual assent to propositions such as "God exists" and must be judged by the same standard as any other belief. Yet his own attitudes are themselves not strictly in accord with this assumption. It seems that none of the offered analyses of the differences between Russell's philosophy and that of pragmatism resolve the differences between them: not James's explanation of the difference between tough-minded and tender-minded philosophers; not Russell's diagnosis of pragmatism as either springing from the delight in struggle or from an optimism which refused to recognize the limits of human knowledge or achievement, or as an evolutionary, romantic emphasis on continuity.

With respect to the third issue of importance in the interaction between Russell and James the situation is very different. From the beginning, Russell found much that was instructive and attractive in James's psychology. From *The Principles of Psychology* (1890) to "Does 'Consciousness' Exist?" (1904) James's neutral monism spoke appealingly to Russell in its psychological acuteness, its empirical realism, and its modest, antidualistic metaphysics. As time went on, more and more of this appeal is evident in the acknowledged and unacknowledged transitions from the Russell of "Knowledge by Acquaintance and Knowledge by Description" to the Russell of *The Analysis of Mind*.

The earliest element of James's thought to be incorporated into Russell's thought was the distinction between acquaintance and description which James had set forth in *The Principles of Psychology*. For James it was the differentiation between the immediacy of directly present experience which is what it is and carries with it the givenness of the "buzzing blooming confusion," and the indirectness and constructed relations of knowledge by description. This distinction was adapted by Russell for his own purposes. Knowledge by acquaintance became the direct two-term relation in which the components of experience were directly denoted or named, in which there was a guarantee that no error could creep in because there was no interpretation. Knowledge by description became the interpreted, constructed, and inferred knowledge by which components of the proposition which did not name could be restated as constructions from the named components. On this level there is error, judgment, and a scope for epistemological analysis. In *The Problems of Philosophy* the two levels of knowledge became the groundwork of an empirical and realist epistemology. There were many obvious differences, however, between Russell's view and that of James. For the latter the immediate was not cognitive but precognitive, as yet unanalyzed; it was not given in units of sense-data as was Russell's; it was error-free because it lacked any kind of cognitive status; it was the continuity of qualitative flow. Knowledge by description could not be linked to acquaintance in the same way by James and Russell: not only did James's analysis precede Russell's, but for James relational elements emerged within the given experience and came to be formulated in terms of the practical bearings that it required. Nor was there any sharp distinction for James, as there was for Russell, between the logically given and the sensory given. For Russell, with the demands of the elements of logical theory before him, the logically simple, primitive, and self-evident required some unimpeachable cognitive status. For James, conceptual structures, whether perceptual, scientific, mathematical, or logical, arose to meet the needs of experience and its inquiries; they were provisional, partial, and corrigible.[59]

Two aspects of experience stressed in *The Principles of Psychology* to which Russell often referred, and of which he made extensive use in his early analyses of experience, were those of attention and of "the specious present." James had not invented either of these psychological concepts, of course, and he himself gives credit to earlier treatments in psychological literature. But for Russell James's presentation was decisive. The concept of time was an ever-recurring problem for Russell beginning in the period when he and Whitehead were struggling with the application of logical techniques to the construction of instants of a physical time series. For Russell it would fit the Humean analysis of experience to think of durationless events with position in a time series in terms of simultaneity and succession, each event saturated with its specific sense qualities. It might even be possible to demarcate "here" and "now" and "I," and relations of "right" and "left" and "up" and "down," corresponding to the "now" and "then" of the event series. However, the "then" and "succession" posed a problem: how could a present event which is a "now" have a "then" within it? And if the durationless event explained sensation, what of memory?[60] Is the former moment which is remembered really here and now, or here and now in some secondary sense? How about errors of memory? How about our impressions of ongoing sequences, such as a tune? Russell came to believe that, whatever the requirements of the events of physics might be, experienced time was not of "knife-edges" but of "saddle-backs"; the specious present had an earlier and a later within it and faded backward into the past and forward into the future. As the teacher says, "Read chapter three for a test tomorrow," the "three" is simultaneous with the first chime of the clock, and the earlier part of the sentence, "Read chapter," is still present as earlier, the second chime is emerging as the latest part of the present, and the second chime and the word "tomorrow" became the earlier part of the present, as the first part of the sentence has receded beyond the horizon of the present. A series of overlapping presents represents the experience of time as duration. The Jamesian influence is not only acknowledged but can be clearly distinguished in Lecture V of *Our Knowledge of the External World* and in "On the Experience of Time."[61] It is noteworthy, however, that James's present emerges and fades while Russell's marches by steps of simultaneity and succession.

With respect to the concept of attention, this appears as a marked addition to the earlier analysis in *The Problems of Philosophy,* for instance, where sense-data and perceptions incorporating interpretation are distinguished, but where the givenness of the sensory particulars is related to a subject, which is thought of as contributing no more than passive awareness. In the 1913 analysis, attention is seen to play a role in the selection of the focus of the present experience, which is the "here" and "now" clearly apprehended, in contrast to the elements present but unattended to. It was necessary to bring in attention to explain why some elements of a given experience are vivid and consciously apprehended while others are ignored. It was also useful to explain which elements of the immediate memory of the earlier elements of the present experience are selected for retention while others are lost. As Russell strove always to incorporate whatever psychological data were available to him, he had given attention an important role.[62] He did not appear to notice, in 1913, that attention already compromises the two-term indubitable relation of awareness by contributing an element due to the interest of the observer, rather than the presented data. It was only a short step to recognize other contributions — of memory, expectation, and habit, and also to acknowledge the errors or biases that might accrue to the experience through the one-sided interest due to attention. But this was to come later and represented a further shift toward pragmatism in Russell's analysis of experience.

One of the most interesting and important aspects of the interaction between Russell and the pragmatists has to do with his reactions to "neutral monism." This term was used by James to name his particular way of circumventing the body-mind problem in philosophy. The position is called "monism" because James rejected the dualism of body and mind, a dualism which had been associated with realism concerning the knowledge relation; James was attempting a nondualistic realism. The position is called "neutral" because, unlike other alternatives to a body-mind dualism, it rejects the monism implicit in idealism, which explains body in terms of mind, and the monism of materialism, which explains mind in terms of body. In this sense the position is neutral concerning mind and matter. James related his theory to his particular form of "radical empiricism" and to the leading-on character of experience which is part of his pragmatism.[63] It was also related to James's rejection of an entity called *consciousness*. These various themes appear in Russell's discussion—particularly the metaphysical neutralism and the rejection of consciousness. Neutral monism was adopted by several of the American realists and aroused interest as a basis for a possible synthesis of physics and psychology.

One of the reasons that this theme is of great interest in Russell's thought is that the concern with neutral monism, and the shift in his view of it, occurred between 1913 and 1921, during the same period that Russell's major shift in the emphasis of "logical atomism" occurred. It is defensible to assert that commentators on Russell have been overconcerned with his logical atomism, partially because of its link with Wittgenstein, and have paid insufficient attention to this other aspect of his thought, an aspect that had more enduring repercussions in his work, and which was also intimately related to Wittgenstein's influence. Another reason for the neglect of the influence of neutral monism in Russell's philosophy may be the confusion created by the fact that he first radically criticized the position, then softened parts of that criticism, and, finally, adopted neutral monism without providing answers to his own earlier difficulties. One commentator notes that if one did not know the dates of the writings, one could construct a scenario in which Russell first adopted the position, and then abandoned it on the basis of the criticisms advanced in "On the Nature of Acquaintance."[64] In fact, some such confusion seems to have influenced Robert Charles Marsh in his comments introducing the essays of that series when he edited *Logic and Knowledge*.[65]

Neutral monism, as Russell understood it, was connected with three distinct but interrelated topics: the analysis of sensation (the dropping out of the subject); the analysis of belief (the pragmatic denial of the independent object of belief); and the body-mind problem (the denial that there are minds and bodies with two different kinds of reality and two kinds of causal laws). In the first discussion of neutral monism in "On the Nature of Acquaintance," attention was on the first topic, since Russell had in mind what he regarded as a satisfactory theory of belief. The references to the elimination of body-mind dualism were favorable, and it is evident that constructing correlations of sense-data into psychological laws and parallel laws of matter would fit in with his program of that time.

In the second discussion of neutral monism in "The Philosophy of Logical Atomism" and in "On Propositions: What They Are and How They Mean," attention was on the second topic, the analysis of belief in the context of logical atomism and the problem of the form of the fact relating belief to what is believed. This period corresponds to Russell's interest in psychology and intensive reading in gestalt, physiological, and behaviorist psychologies.

The third context of discussion in *The Analysis of Mind* has as its central focus the third topic of neutral monism, the elimination of body-mind dualism, although here, in the final stage of the discussion, all three of the topics are addressed to some extent.

There seem to be three chief areas in which neutral monism, as Russell presents it in his "On the Nature of Acquaintance," fails as an adequate theory. It must be remembered that Russell included among persons holding this position American realists (E. B. Holt, R. B. Perry, and W. P. Montague) and a phenomenalist (Ernst Mach). Hence although in his presentation of it he ties it to James's theory of the pragmatic view of experience, other references are to philosophers whose views of experience differed from that of James. His first doubts concern whether all elements of "the mental life" might properly be treated as neutral. He sees it as counting against neutral monism that there might be such items as imaginings and abstract ideas for which no physical correlates could be shown. In the same way there must be a difference between a color seen and a color not seen, a difference "not consisting in relations to other colors . . . but more immediate." Russell regards this as a weakness because he interprets neutral monism to imply that everything in experience must be equally physical and psychological.

The second category of difficulty lies in the elimination of the subject from the relation of acquaintance; in one way this is welcome because Russell, like Hume, finds it difficult to experience the subject. But in another way he feels that the subjective pole of the acquaintance relation is required. For instance, there is such a thing as the experiencing of an experiencing, and how could this be if there were no subject doing the experiencing? No doubt this does not mean that the subject must be defined as a mental existent, but it does mean, Russell argues, that there must be a subject end of the experiencing relation. Another difficulty, and, one feels, the most important, comes in the failure of neutral monism to acknowledge the importance of the immediate experiencing of the *here* and *now* and the *I*. These terms represent a certain focus of attention as experience moves on: the first two referring to what is immediately present to the subject, the third to whoever is the subject in the experience. How could these basic foci of attention in experience be explained if not in the relation of the subject to the objects of the subject's immediate awareness? Russell does not see how to dispense with a relational view of awareness without sacrificing this immediate awareness, which is not only part of experience but, in his analysis, is also an important part of the epistemological warranty for empirical knowledge. He recognizes that for James immediacy does not have cognitive status, but he finds it impossible to see how this can be omitted.

The third category of difficulty came in the analysis of belief or judgment; Russell, quoting Montague, finds that neutral monism is committed to the doctrine that both true and false judgments have objects, and thus their theory of error involves them in the postulation of an unreal domain of reality. He admits, however, that this might be circumvented. Throughout the analysis he refers forward to his own view, which, he says, when it is discussed, will present a better analysis of the matter than does neutral monism. Hence he regards the two views as competing, and that of neutral monism as eliminated not so much by its own unredeemable errors as by being shown to be less satisfactory in comparison with a better analysis, that is, Russell's own. For instance, he struggles with the problem of whether two subjects can know the same reality. On the one hand, it is certainly desirable to have a theory in which two different observers can see the same object, and this is permitted by neutral monism; on the other hand, it seems apparent that one's theory should also accommodate the fact that one observer cannot have access to another observer's observation of the common object, and this Russell feels neutral monism cannot admit.

In his summary of neutral monism, Russell lists the following major problems, while conceding that many topics involved must be taken up in the later portions of the book that was to be. These are the assumptions that whatever I experience must be part of my mind (no two-term relation of acquaintance) and that things cannot be immediately present to the mind at a moment but can be known only through relations with other objects known; the theory of belief involves difficulties with error; there is no adequate way of dealing with things not in time (abstractions); neutral monism neglects the knowledge of truths; and (more fatally) there are difficulties with *here, now,* and *I.*

> For these reasons—some of which, it must be confessed, assume the results of future discussions—I conclude that neutral monism, though largely right in its polemic against previous theories, cannot be regarded as able to deal with all the facts, and must be replaced by a theory in which the difference between what is experienced and what is not experienced by a given subject at a given moment is made simpler and more prominent than it can be in a theory which wholly denies the existence of specifically mental entities.[66]

We have seen that the criticisms leveled by Wittgenstein at Russell's theory of belief and judgment caused him to abandon his book on the theory of knowledge, and although he went ahead and published the early chapters as papers, including "On the Nature of Acquaintance," those criticisms affected the whole scheme of the book, driving a wedge between the analysis of acquaintance and the constructive synthesis of the concepts of science and of common sense which was to have been the culmination of the entire structure. What Russell did was to work at a sketch of the synthesis *(Our Knowledge of the External World),* but the link that was to have brought together the sensory and the descriptive, the immediate and the judgmental, was defective. This gap in his theory of knowledge is evident in the lectures given at Harvard.[67] Publications from 1913 on give credit to Wittgenstein for pointing out the problem of the form of a fact to be used in analyzing belief, but no analysis is provided to solve the problem. During the war years, Russell had Wittgenstein's notes to work on, and when he returned to active philosophizing with the lectures on "The Philosophy of Logical Atomism," he used what he believed himself to have learned from Wittgenstein. The first three lectures give the outlines of the forms of facts and of propositions, their respective constituents, and the new definition of the truth of a proposition as pointing toward or away from a fact. In Lecture IV, however, Russell is forced to tackle the problem of the form of propositions of the kind "I believe that. . . ." He cannot follow Wittgenstein's dictum that "S believes that p" is the same in meaning as "p," since this molecular form is not truth-functional. What is the proper analysis of its form? Before giving his own answer to this question, Russell presents what he calls Dewey's and James's neutral monist theory of belief.

The presentation and the criticism of neutral monism in "The Philosophy of Logical Atomism" are definitely odd; in the first place, neutral monism (the view that there are not two different kinds of stuff, material and mental), behaviorism (the interpretation of psychological terms in terms of behavior), and the pragmatic concept of truth (what is true is what leads to success) are pushed into one argument, a process which would not be entirely to the liking of all the philosophers on whom he is commenting. Russell then characterizes the pragmatic theory of belief as having as its model the belief in persons or objects, rather than, as in his own model, the belief "that such and such." This theory of belief, attributed to James and Dewey, not only does not fit all kinds of belief but also commits those men to nonexistent objects in the case of false beliefs. This is a similar criticism to the one offered in "On the Nature of Acquaintance," and it is puzzling, since it is difficult to see what there is in the writings of James or Dewey that would lead to this interpretation. One might suppose that belief as commitment to act in a certain way, or as a hypothesis for action, would have misled Russell, particularly with his interpretation of James's view of religion in mind. At any rate, it is difficult to see how this theory of belief can be attributed to the pragmatists in the same breath as an explanation of error in terms of the failure of a certain line of action to which one had committed oneself. In the same passage, for instance, Russell goes on to give as an example the belief that a train leaves at 10:25, and what it leads to in missing or catching the train.[68]

After this rather off-hand and casual presentation of neutral monism and what is wrong with it, Russell concludes: "I do not myself feel that that view of things is tenable. It is a difficult one to refute because it goes very deep and one has the feeling that perhaps, if one thought it out long enough and became sufficiently aware of all its implications, one might find after all that it was a feasible view; but yet I do not *feel* it feasible."[69] Russell goes on to say that on the basis of Ockham's razor he finds neutral monism most attractive, but that he has difficulty believing it. Referring to his earlier criticisms, he says, "I should really want to rewrite them rather because I think some of the arguments I used against neutral monism are not valid. I place most reliance on the argument about 'emphatic particulars.'" Russell does not say in what respects his earlier arguments against neutral monism were invalid, but simply repeats the "emphatic particular" argument and concludes that he does not see how neutral monism can deal with *this*.[70]

When Russell develops his own theory of belief, he tries a new version of the multiple-relation theory of belief that stresses that the two verbs, one interior to the belief and the other that of the believing itself, must be put on two different levels (*pace* Wittgenstein). Hence if Othello believes that Desdemona loves Cassio, the first verb "believes" is "propositional" and the second verb, "loves," is internal to the belief, and the two verbs are on two levels. But Russell argues against Wittgenstein that the proposition cannot be treated as an independent entity. No real solution is offered, but a description is given of the problem, a legacy of his earlier difficulties in theory of knowledge. So Russell admits that "one has to be content on many points at present with pointing out difficulties rather than laying down quite clear solutions."[71]

In the final lecture of the series, Russell returns again to the discussion of neutral monism in its "metaphysical" aspect as licensing the constructions of physics and psychology without dichotomy between body and mind. He advises that such constructions as this theory calls for could only be carried out with the aid of the logical techniques that he has been discussing. He says he cannot tell whether neutral monism is true or false, but that he feels more and more inclined to feel that the difficulties might be solved. He mentions two difficulties: that of the form of belief, which might be taken care of by behaviorism, and that of the "emphatic particulars," but this argument is so delicate and subtle that he cannot be sure it is not in error. The conclusion is a confession of ignorance.[72]

In his "On Propositions: What They Are and How They Mean," Russell once again returns to the topic of belief and reviews some of the concepts of neutral monism, but here he uses behaviorism as a proposed answer to the problems of belief and produces some criticisms of neutral monism. On the whole, however, a behaviorist-neutral monist theory of belief is to be used in conjunction with a Wittgensteinian theory of propositions. The criticisms and difficulties cited are not spoken of as insuperable — J. B. Watson may be wrong in restricting thought to the larynx; James may be wrong in thinking there are no entities belonging to the physical and not the psychical, or the psychical and not the physical. The way is open for *The Analysis of Mind,* and the once-rejected "neutral monism" and behaviorism come in to fill, through psychology, the epistemological gap that had opened up with the difficulties of the 1913 version of the multiple-relation theory of belief.

It is now possible to see how Russell's earlier strictures against neutral monism were turned into an adoption of it. With respect to his problems about entities that might be psychological but not physical, or physical but not psychological, he merely amended neutral monism, detaching it from James's "pure experience" (which he said had a "lingering taint of idealism") and making particulars neutral, while allowing some to belong only to the correlations of physical laws (i.e., unobserved particulars, similar to the earlier "sensibilia") and others, notably images, to belong only to the correlations of psychological causal laws.[73] With respect to the problems about belief, Russell adopted a modified form of behaviorism, amending the undue materialism of Watson's view and joining it to the correlations of observed particulars of neutral monism. The difficulties with the "emphatic particulars" are not mentioned in *The Analysis of Mind,* nor does *this,* or *here,* or *I* figure in the analysis of sensation in that book. In part, this difficulty proved to be less important because Russell gave up his claim that immediate experience is cognitive, accepting Dewey's position that any perceptual experience incorporates into itself habits of response, expectations, and memory.[74] So far as Russell's assumption of a tie-up between neutral monism, behaviorism, and the pragmatic theory of truth was concerned, he cut that connection and instead linked neutral monism and behaviorism with a correspondence theory of truth in which the needs of action explained the preference for truth, but the truth itself consisted in the correspondence of the belief with fact.[75] Hence the neutral monism that Russell had footnoted to James was adopted in *Analysis of Mind.* The new Russellian theory depended less on James's leading-on of ideas from one part of experience to another, less on radical empiricism, and not at all on the pragmatic theory of truth. In thus giving his own version of a neutral monist view of experience, Russell was doing what other American realists such as Perry had also done. Russell was also, perhaps unknowingly, wedding new truth to old in incorporating older parts of his own theory of knowledge with new elements taken from James, and such a marriage is in the Jamesian tradition. James might well forgive Russell for changing the meanings of his philosophical terms, as Peirce had *not* been willing to forgive James. It might, in a sense, be termed a partial conversion to pragmatism on Russell's part: but if so it was a conversion that mitigated not at all the rigors of Russell's opposition to the pragmatic theory of truth and to the work of the third pragmatist to be the target of his criticism, John Dewey.

8.3 Russell and Dewey

James died in 1910; Schiller's interactions with Russell ceased, apparently, with their exchanges in the early 1920s; but Dewey lived until 1952, so that his interactions with Russell lasted through the span of Russell's philosophical career until 1948. They did not have close personal exchanges or correspondence, but they made many references to each other's work and several explicit criticisms. The tendency was for each philosopher to come to represent a position antithetical to the other; Dewey remained *the* pragmatist for Russell; Russell for Dewey was *the* defender of what he called "analytic realism." This fact, along with the persistent misunderstandings of each other's positions, obscured the great areas of agreement between their points of view. Although Russell included *Studies in Logical Theory* in his review of pragmatism of 1909, no specific mention was made of the book. Russell writes only that "Professor Dewey, of Columbia University, is also to be reckoned among the founders of pragmatism. His writings are more technical and less popular than those of James and Schiller, but on certain points his exposition is perhaps preferable to theirs."[76] In a separate review of the same volume, Russell comments that Dewey's view of knowledge is "Kantian."[77] In 1916 Dewey published a volume of essays of which several were devoted to a criticism of analytic realism, and one in particular dealt specifically and in detail with Russell: the book was *Essays in Experimental Logic,* and the essay, "The Existence of the World as a Logical Problem," was directed at Russell's *Our Knowledge of the External World.* In 1919 Russell reviewed Dewey's book and responded in full to this essay.[78] In 1921 Russell's *The Analysis of Mind* adopted many pragmatic tenets with respect to psychology and epistemology, among them the view that immediate experience could not claim to be direct veridical knowledge, and this he attributed to Dewey, as we have seen.[79] Thereafter there was little philosophical interchange until 1938. In that year Dewey published *Logic: The Theory of Inquiry,* in which one chapter was devoted to a criticism of "Immediate Knowledge," a view he attributed to Russell.[80] The following year Russell wrote a critical review of the book as a contribution to *The Philosophy of John Dewey,* the Library of Living Philosophers volume.[81] Again, in his *An Inquiry into Meaning and Truth* (1940), Russell joined issue on several topics with contemporary philosophers, among them Dewey,[82] who responded with an article of 1941, "Propositions, Warranted Assertibility and Truth," in *The Journal of Philosophy.*[83] In his later books, *Human Knowledge, Its Scope and Limits* and *A History of Western Philosophy,* Russell again made critical references to pragmatism and to Dewey.[84] The volume of Dewey and Arthur F. Bentley, *Knowing and the Known* (1949), also contained critical references to Russell.[85] It cannot be said that the disagreements were resolved or even noticeably clarified for the participants, but for us they are useful in seeing the directions in which their respective philosophies were moving and some of the issues that came to seem, at least, to be watersheds between their two different positions.

On the personal level, the two men first met in 1914 when Russell was lecturing at Harvard. He reports in his letters to Ottoline Morrell that he liked Dewey and found him to have a large, slow, philosophical mind, that in a discussion with him and Perry, Dewey seemed clearly to catch the point of Russell's problems with "this" (which may have had to do with one of the criticisms Russell made of neutral monism), and, in retrospect, Russell judged Dewey as one of the two most impressive people he encountered in

America.[86] They met again in China in 1920, when both addressed the educational conference at Changsha. The man who interpreted for both of them reported that Dewey always spoke from notes which the interpreter had had an opportunity to study and translate in advance, but that Russell spoke ex tempore and often in technical terms, and thus it was difficult to translate for him. (Russell tells how he was pressed into service at the conference soon after his arrival in China, so presumably he had little time to prepare, and, in fact, he gave four lectures and three speeches in the course of twenty-four hours.)[87] Russell had been invited to China as one of the three world-famous living philosophers of the day.[88] Later, during the same visit to China, Russell, Dora Black, and the Deweys formed part of the expatriate English-speaking group in Peking. In some of their exchanges Russell found the Deweys very irritating in their political views and attacked them vigorously in a letter to Ottoline. When Russell became desperately ill, however, Dewey was summoned, and whatever the truth of the stories surrounding their relations in Peking, it is clear that Russell's gratitude to the Deweys was sincere.[89] Later, in the 1940s, during the period when Russell was criticizing Dewey, the latter became involved in the defense campaign against those working for Russell's ouster from City College when Russell was ruled unfit to teach mathematical logic because of his views on marriage.[90] When, in the end, the defense failed, Dr. Albert Barnes hired Russell at Dewey's suggestion as a lecturer at his foundation. This arrangement eventually terminated in Russell's dismissal by Barnes and a lawsuit by Russell against Barnes, which Russell won. The lectures became *A History of Western Philosophy* (1945), a book which, as Russell tells us, was the foundation of his financial solvency during the postwar years. There are several letters extant in which Dewey refers to Russell; he expresses the view that Russell was "petulant" about Dewey's writing in the wake of Dewey's early criticism of *Our Knowledge of the External World*. In others Dewey finds something "willful" in Russell's misunderstanding in spite of Dewey's efforts to make his views clear.[91] Whatever the causes, personal or impersonal, one would have to agree that there was a failure to understand, and that on both sides of the controversy.

It is my contention that, contrary to the disputants' impressions, there is a great deal in common between the two philosophies, that over the years each was coming closer to the other's position, and had not prejudice interfered, analytical pragmatism might have appeared on the scene earlier than in fact it did.

In the exchange concerning "The Existence of the World as a Logical Problem" and in Russell's 1919 review of the book in which it appeared, the issues have to do with the claim for immediate knowledge, Russell's treatment of data, the legitimacy of the epistemological problem of the reality of the external world, and the concept of knowledge implied in the discussion. Dewey claims that the problem of the existence of the external world is one created by, and one to which the answer is provided by, the terms in which the problem is set. Russell, he believes, asks how we are to infer to a commonsense world from the knowledge provided by the immediate data of sense. But in describing his experience in terms of these immediate and self-evidently known visual, auditory, and other data, Russell has already made assumptions about the connections of these data with sense organs and has assumed that such data have a position in a time order and has claimed their yieldings as knowledge. In opposition to this, Dewey argues that such data as Russell describes are the products of refined analysis, while the immediacy of sense does not constitute knowledge. We are just where we are with the given crude unanalyzed experience, and there is no problem here of the reality of the external world. For Dewey, data are those items of knowledge selected as relevant to particular inquiries; they may be observations, or the products of previous inquiries, but their status as data is in terms of their being taken as given for the purposes of the inquiry in hand, not as having a status as data for all inquiries. Knowledge also refers to the findings of specific inquiries. In *Essays in Experimental Logic,* Dewey castigates all realisms, both of the analytic kind and that of others, for making knowledge a universal idea and for making cognitive relations universal and constitutive of the whole of the relation of knower and known, instead of taking it as only one among a number of relations by which the organism functions with and in its environment.[92]

In his 1919 review, Russell disavows many of the positions attributed to him by Dewey, including the self-evidence of immediate sensory knowledge and the existence of data which are psychologically as well as logically and epistemologically prior in the knowing process. Russell agrees with Dewey that the immediately given is vague and must be tested; that is why data for him are not psychologically primitive (he is not interested in the experience of babies or monkeys), but logically primitive. Data are those elements of knowledge that have passed the test of analysis. Russell also claims that Dewey has misunderstood him in attributing to him the view that perception is itself knowledge; the problem that Dewey has missed is that of passing from the uninferred to the inferred. Russell says he had held that it is the inferred, not the uninferred, which has a reference to sense organs and to a time order.

It appears that Dewey in his role as a critic of Russell was sharing the difficulty of the "shifting target." The Russell of *The Problems of Philoso-*

phy and of *Our Knowledge of the External World* did begin with sense-data as psychologically as well as logically primitive. It is also difficult to see how sense-data in that period could be said not to be given as connected with sense-organs. But Russell here may be referring to the "constructions" of *Our Knowledge of the External World;* if so, does not passing from the uninferred to the inferred rely on given sense-data? It seems that Russell's earlier position had been considerably modified in the interim and was no longer open to the same criticisms.

According to Russell's argument, Dewey has neglected the Humean problem of a fundamental skepticism and has blandly made causal and other inferences. At the end of the review, Russell confesses a bias favorable to the neutral monist and behaviorist aspects of Dewey's view but unfavorable to the pragmatism and instrumentalism of the position. Pragmatism, he adds, is too closely allied to superstitious theology and too inclined to find true what is pleasant to believe. Although he exempts *Essays in Experimental Logic* from this judgment as being scientific in tone, Russell still finds that Dewey's instrumentalism is antagonistic to his own bent toward contemplation and the desire to escape from oneself. Russell says that it is true that the "knowledge" of the external world is there, but the problem is of its validity, and this problem is not one that he invented, but is one that Dewey ought to find legitimate and take seriously.[93]

Although, as we have seen, Russell has now moved to a position closer to that of James and Dewey when it is a question of the content or the reference of a belief rather than of its origin, the older view, that the content of a belief consists in a complex and its relations, is asserted against behaviorism and pragmatism. Truth and falsity are defined in terms of whether the belief, and the proposition in which it is expressed, point toward the fact or away from the fact. This is said to be a view different from, and better than, the pragmatic position that belief is always concerned with what exists. An uneasy alliance of a theory of propositions and logic due to the influence of Wittgenstein and a psychological treatment of belief due to the influence of J. B. Watson and James can be seen in "The Philosophy of Logical Atomism" and "On Propositions: What They Are and How They Mean." On the theory of truth, Russell is still antipragmatic and holds to the independence and reality of fact beyond the causal relation to inquiry. He now accepts as belief images as well as verbal expressions, describing what constitutes believing as a belief-feeling allied to the emotions. This way of dealing with the "propositional verb" obviates some of the difficulties of the earlier conception and allows the belief-content and the truth or falsity of belief to be treated according to a traditional correspondence theory of truth.[94]

When Russell answered Dewey in 1919, he did so as a prisoner being punished for his antiwar efforts during World War I, when they returned to the discussion of their philosophical differences, a second world war was in progress. In the years between, their careers had been curiously parallel: both had been vitally interested in political and social questions, writing books advocating liberal social democracy; both had lectured and traveled widely abroad; both had run experimental schools and written on progressive education; both were currently addressing themselves to systematic philosophical questions—Dewey having written *Experience and Nature, Art is Experience,* and *Logic: The Theory of Inquiry,* Russell having served as a lecturer in American universities and begun developing the text for *An Inquiry into Meaning and Truth,* his first major philosophic work since the 1927 *The Analysis of Matter.*[95]

In his *Logic* Dewey interprets Russell's position as a kind of antithesis of his own. He rejects the abstractness and lack of connection with concrete inquiries which he considers Russell to be advocating for logic, and he attacks the doctrine of immediate knowledge, which he attributes to "analytic realists." Dewey argues that abstract patterns of thought such as are characteristic of mathematics and symbolic logic belong within inquiry, in that phase where abstract symbols are related to one another; these symbol-systems feed back into the ongoing of inquiry as logically formulated possibilities for hypotheses.[96] There is a clear-cut difference between the definition of logic given by Dewey and that of *Principia Mathematica.* Russell himself, however, had shifted in his notion of the significance of logical truth. He no longer regarded such truths as data, or as philosophically fundamental premises, as once he had. Following Wittgenstein, he looked on logic as consisting of tautologies, and hence, for the most part, irrelevant to philosophy. Here again there might be less disagreement between the two philosophers than either of them realized.

On the other matter, much of what Dewey says about immediate knowledge is otiose, since Russell had not held that immediate experience was cognitional for many years. Yet there is some point in the criticism in the sense that, although Russell had disowned knowledge by acquaintance and the immediate self-evidence of sensory immediacy, yet he continued to hold that something in the immediate perceptual experience was significant as a touchstone for knowledge. This became clearer in *An Inquiry into Meaning and Truth.* Hence Dewey was partly out-of-date, yet had a point to make in contrasting his own position with Russell's.

The issues between the later philosophies of the two men come out most clearly in the two essays in the Library of Living Philosophers volume, *The*

Philosophy of John Dewey.[97] In his article on Dewey's logic, Russell remarks that nothing in Dewey's book corresponds with what *he* would call logic, but that many questions on theory of knowledge are raised. Because of Dewey's setting of inquiry within a problematic situation, Russell finds that there is something holistic and Hegelian in his position, since no limits have been set to the scope of the situation. Although he agrees with Dewey's attack on immediate knowledge, he finds no description of the role perception and immediacy play in inquiry. A more complete causal and behaviorist account of perception is required, Russell believes.

In relating his logic to inquiry, and in defining inquiry as a transformation of subject-matter in which propositions are merely tools, Russell believes that Dewey, like Marx, sees philosophy as a means of changing the world rather than a means of understanding it. He finds in Dewey no way of distinguishing inquiry from any other form of practical activity.

Russell notes that Dewey uses the term *truth* only once in his text, and on that occasion he quotes Peirce's definition: "The opinion which is fated to be ultimately agreed to by all who investigate is what we mean by truth, and the object represented by this opinion is real." This, and a second, similar quotation from Peirce, are all Dewey says on the subject of truth, except that he prefers the term *warrantedly assertible.* Russell then proceeds to draw from Dewey's statements all the absurd or unacceptable consequences that they might be made to yield: truth might be what the last man left alive believes; or, if truth is defined in terms of the allaying of doubt, suicide or alcohol might be successful and hence true; or a brass band might succeed in settling doubt and thus be true. When the definition is taken in terms of success in inquiry—that is, in the obtaining of the desired effects—Russell finds the term *success* equally susceptible of unwanted meanings. Russell concludes that the pragmatic theory of truth has the familiar weaknesses he has already attributed to it in his criticism of Schiller and James, "the usual slander."[98] He ends with a confession of a temperamental bias against a view such as he regards pragmatism to be, which denies that knowledge can be sought for its own sake or can be relished as a purely intellectual joy, but sees it only as a means towards "better dinners" and "more rapid locomotion."

In his response to his critics at the end of the Library of Living Philosophers volume, Dewey expresses irritation at Russell's reiteration of the theme that pragmatism is connected with American industrialism and commercialism, and repeats his denial that the pragmatist theory of inquiry makes knowledge instrumental to action, quoting his own words to the effect that any experimental theory of inquiry seeks effects in terms of the confirmation or disconfirmation that follows on the actual operations directed by the hypothesis in question.

Dewey also points out the pluralistic and individualized character which he has always attributed to situations to show that Russell is mistaken in his "holistic" interpretation. He also contends that Russell, in complaining that Dewey tells us nothing about what objects of knowledge are before they are inquired into, assumes that such objects have characters prior to and independent of the inquiry. But for Dewey, when something is proposed or presents itself as an object of inquiry it is already an object of previous knowledge. Hence such independent objects will not fit the scheme of ideas within which Dewey works.

With respect to the criticisms of the pragmatic theory of truth, Dewey points out that the proviso in his own definition that the consequences which serve as a test be "operationally instituted" and such as to "resolve the specific problem evoking the operations" is neglected by Russell. Russell's criticism attributes his own meaning to Peirce and Dewey — for instance, that the outcome which establishes truth means that *here and now* some proposition is true in terms of long run future inquiry, and that propositions are the subject-matter of inquiry. Neither of these is their view.

Like James, Dewey finds Russell unable to understand the pragmatic theory of truth because he retains and reads into it the presuppositions of his own theory, while Russell for his part finds the same weaknesses in Dewey that he found in James.[99]

In the *Inquiry*, Russell has two passages in which he takes issue with Dewey, one having to do with data, the other with truth. In neither case is the criticism new, but in both cases he contrasts another contemporary view with his own views on the same subject; Dewey's is only one of the contemporary alternatives considered. In relation to data, Hans Reichenbach's position is reviewed; there are also criticisms of Otto Neurath and Rudolf Carnap. There is a common realist strain in all these criticisms, and especially in the ones of Dewey. With respect to data, Russell says that Dewey denies their importance and that he not only rejects the status of observation or perception as itself knowledge, but also goes further and finds it unnecessary to make elements of new perceptual experience into fresh data for inquiry. It is against this position that Russell urges the importance of the epistemological premises that directly express and indicate immediately given perceptual experience. If one does not have such an influx of fresh perceptual data, one is left revolving endlessly among already established beliefs, and one's only touchstone for knowledge is the coherence of those already established beliefs with one another. Here, again, he hints at the Hegelian influence and the holistic tendencies in Dewey.

Undoubtedly it was this stress on the importance of propositions directly occasioned by immediate perception that led Dewey to claim that Russell had not really given up immediate knowledge, as he claimed to have done. In any case, the dispute between them on this point seems unnecessary; of course, Dewey calls *data* materials selected as relevant to the solution of a given problem, while Russell calls *data* beliefs or propositions having a certain status in an epistemological ordering. But both philosophers, as empiricists, must provide a role for direct observation to play in inquiry; if Russell's perceptual premises could be amalgamated with Dewey's material means of inquiry, then they could have both the input of fresh experience and the relevance to inquiry that is required. Each is emphasizing a different aspect of the observational component of inquiry.

On the matter of truth, in the *Inquiry* Russell again restates his objections to replacing the traditional term *true* with Dewey's *warrantedly assertible;* after reviewing the different ways in which it is possible to interpret the meaning of *warrantedly assertible*—in terms of the satisfaction of the consequences of the belief, the settlement of an unsettled inquiry, and the agreement of investigators, Russell concludes that Dewey is faced with a dilemma: either he is stuck with a view in which historical, sociological, biological, or psychological successes are the judges of the truth-value of a proposition, or he is tacitly assuming the "old" view of truth all the time. Further, Russell reviews the implications of Dewey's view in terms of its inroads on the law of excluded middle, which Russell wishes to retain and which pragmatic logic would exclude, since not all propositions have truth-value in their role in inquiry if there is no way that they can be tested in that inquiry. Russell again defends an "old-fashioned" correspondence theory, with its tie to two-valued logic, its assumptions of facts beyond and independent of inquiry, and its implication that there are many propositions that are true or false, although they are forever inaccessible to inquiry that would allow us to know them.[100]

In a further article, "Propositions, Warranted Assertibility and Truth," Dewey expands his response to Russell, pointing out in accordance with the details of his theory of inquiry what these terms mean and how they are different from Russell's. For Dewey, a proposition is never evaluated as true or false; it is taken as providing relevant information in the inquiry into a topic other than its own validity. As such, it is *proposed* as relevant. A judgment will emerge at the end of an inquiry as warrantedly assertible on condition that the judgment, as a hypothesis, has been tested according to established procedures and in terms of the solution required for the specific problem in hand, and has been found to answer the need of the inquiry in question. This, as Dewey argues, is what is meant by the experimental method. Dewey makes the two relevant points that separating judgments, as warranted, from propositions, as true, cuts the connection between the definition of truth and actual inquiry, and that Russell is committed to an abstract and barren formal logic which is not tied to the way operations of inquiry are actually conducted.[101]

Here again, in retrospect, it seems that there is room for both philosophers' opinions; if Dewey and Russell could accept the placing of abstract logical techniques and operations within the context of the manipulation of meanings on an abstract level, as part of the process of inquiry (as Dewey placed mathematics in *Logic: The Theory of Inquiry*) they might agree on this. For there is not any real opposition between formal and psychological logic — both recognized the importance of what the other was doing; it was just that what one called "logic" the other called "mathematics," and what the other called "logic" the first called "induction and the conduct of inquiry." Again, with respect to truth and knowledge, the dispute over what was to be called a "proposition" is surely not in itself a vital and never-to-be-settled dispute. But the tenacity of Russell's clinging to a realist correspondence theory of truth in the face of both adversaries, such as Dewey was seen to be, and allies, such as Ayer, put a stop to Russell's further movement in the direction of pragmatism. Yet when one considers the history of the relations between Russell and the individual pragmatists which we have been reviewing in this chapter and disregards Russell's polemical drawing of sharp dichotomies, it is apparent that from the time of the 1913 manuscript to that of the 1948 *Human Knowledge,* Russell, in fact, conceded more and more points to the pragmatists and came closer and closer to their position. He could not travel the route of mere formal analysis, as he conceived Wittgenstein to be doing, nor the route of a nonscientific uncriticized common sense as he conceived Moore to be doing, nor the route of a panpsychistic speculative metaphysics, as he conceived Whitehead to be doing. More and more, the patient inspection of experience brought him first, to abandon the subject, as had James; second, to abandon the claim that sensation is knowledge, as had Dewey; third, to recognize the importance of the "encrustation of habit, memory, and expectation"; fourth, to recognize the importance of psychology and what it contributed to the understanding of the way beliefs developed and language was used, as had Schiller; and finally, to appreciate the scientific temper and commitment, as had James and Dewey. Dewey, too, had moved closer to Russell without recognizing it; his earlier strictures on all theories of knowledge were replaced by a Deweyan theory of knowledge (in the *Logic*), and this "theory of inquiry," as he called it, had a place for formal logic. Dewey's logic was not, like Schiller's, a protest against antique methods and assumptions; it was an attempt at a genuine synthesis, reinterpreting Aristotle and Mill and others in the context of a pragmatic logic of wider scope than any earlier logic. Russell's clarity and grasp of contemporary logic could have helped Dewey. Dewey's interpretation of a role for formal logic to play in inquiry (not as merely different ways of saying the same thing) would have offered some unity to Russell's dichotomized world. In fact, the role of logic in inquiry, as Dewey saw it, would accord very well with Russell's remark that "modern logic . . . has the effect of enlarging our abstract imagination, and providing an infinite number of possible hypotheses to be applied in the analysis of any complex fact."[102]

But this was not to be; for Russell, for whatever reasons, could not accept the naturalistic and humanistic tone of Dewey's, or anyone else's pragmatism. As he wrote in 1919, even when pragmatism was not allied to pernicious theology, it lacked the piety toward what was larger than human, the commitment to pure intellect and truth for its own sake, which were basic commitments to Russell. In *My Philosophical Development,* in a chapter entitled "Retreat from Pythagoras," Russell confesses to having abandoned his view of the "prison of the self" and the need for some perspective larger than human:

> I still think that truth depends upon a relation to fact, and that facts in general are non-human; I still think that man is cosmically unimportant . . . but I no longer have the wish to thrust out human elements from regions where they belong. . . . I think of sense, and of thoughts built on sense, as windows, not as prison bars. . . . We view the world from the view of the *here* and *now,* not with that large impartiality which theists attribute to the Deity.[103]

In spite of this modification of his earlier aspirations for philosophy, Russell's antagonism to pragmatism remains; he calls it "cosmic impiety." Dewey's emphasis on continuity, a view of experience that held *truth* with its nose to the scientific grindstone but liberated *nature* and *experience* to envelop and contain—all this was antithetical to Russell's "prejudice toward analysis," his view of experience as confined to successions of complexes of sense qualities, and his insistence on the ultimacy of truth and the limitations of nature and experience. So it is with some regret that we find the same old statements about pragmatism in *A History of Western Philosophy,* and the same old opposition to analytic realism in *Knowing and the Known.*[104]

9

The Legacy of the Dialogue

IN THE YEARS OF the Second World War and the following decades Russell's interactions with philosophers were not restricted to those with Dewey. In *An Inquiry into Meaning and Truth* he discussed critically a number of positions taken by logical empiricists such as Rudolf Carnap, Hans Reichenbach, Otto Neurath, and A. J. Ayer, setting his own position in contrast to theirs.[1] In 1944 *The Philosophy of Bertrand Russell* was the occasion of exchanges between Russell and his critics, in this case largely devoted to the removal of misunderstandings of his position. Some of the contributions to this volume of the Library of Living Philosophers were recognized by Russell as scholarly and illuminating, as in the case of the article by Morris Weitz, for example.[2]

Russell published *A History of Western Philosophy* (1945), *Human Knowledge: Its Scope and Limits* (1948), and *Human Society in Ethics and Politics* (1954).[3] He also became involved in discussions with British philosophers of the emergent linguistic schools represented by the later Wittgenstein, Gilbert Ryle, and J. L. Austin, among others. Russell responded with polemical articles to the criticism of these philosophers, including J. O. Urmson's attack in *Philosophical Analysis,* P. F. Strawson's criticism of his theory of descriptions in "On Referring," and G. F. Warnock's critique in "Metaphysics in Logic." These articles, and a trenchant review of Gilbert Ryle's *The Concept of Mind,* were reprinted in *My Philosophical Development* (1959), along with a retrospective view of the development of his own philosophy.[4] Russell also became involved in a sharp dispute over the decision on the part of the editor of *Mind* to refuse to review Ernest Gellner's *Words and Things* (1959), a slashing attack on ordinary language philosophy for which Russell wrote the introduction.[5] In the three volumes of Russell's *Autobiography* much attention is paid in the first two volumes to his own philosophical life and his interactions with other philosophers.[6] In addition

there were several occasional pieces, obituaries, biographical sketches of
other philosophers, and continued correspondence with colleagues and
aspiring students. He assisted liberally in the preparation of *Logic and
Knowledge* (1956), for instance. His letters show a generous attention to the
appeals of scholars and students of his work, even amid the increasing
burdens of his efforts for world peace, which came to absorb more and more
of his time during the last two decades of his life.

9.1 Russell's Methods of Argument

Before discussing those issues in current analytic philosophy to which these
later exchanges are relevant, some cumulative impressions of Russell's way
of dealing with his philosophical interlocutors are appropriate. One's first
impression must be of the sheer volume of published and unpublished
material which Russell directed toward other philosophers. Not only did
Russell read widely in all major European languages and on a wide variety of
subjects and review books across this full range but he also carried on a lively
correspondence with a large number of persons working in science, mathematics, logic, and general philosophy. The volume of this correspondence is
staggering. The surviving reviews, reading notes, and correspondence attest
to a very large investment of time and energy, and indicate that for Russell
this was an important part of his intellectual life.

   One also receives the impression that on the whole Russell's study of the
work of other philosophers was neither sketchy nor superficial, although he
did sometimes fail to understand exactly or appreciate sufficiently their
positions. Not only were his reading notes extensive, but also the questions
he raised in letters and in reviews were cogent and often pursued in further
correspondence, especially if the philosopher in question complained of
being misrepresented.

   It is often noted—and this impression is reinforced by this study—that
Russell was unusually open to influence by others, and often generously gave
credit to other philosophers for having originated his most recent ideas or for
having caused an amendment of his old ones. Alan Wood, for instance, sees
Russell as overly generous in this respect. Our study seems to show that this
habit reflected the reality of the way his ideas developed and was neither too
modest nor overly punctilious.[7]

   One intriguing aspect of his philosophical dialogues is the emergence of a
picture of Russell as a very disconcerting respondent. At times early
enthusiastic agreement turns to withdrawal or critical rejection; this must
have been a shock to a philosopher such as Meinong, who in 1904 was

acclaimed but judged to be insufficiently realist in his treatment of propositions, and in 1905 was criticized as affirming the reality of referents beyond
the proper bounds of existence. Often Russell rushed in ahead of his
collaborator to publish ideas they had discussed together, and, in giving
credit to that collaborator, he also gave the impression, which might well
have been false, that the ideas Russell put forth were also those of the
collaborator. Was Moore entirely comfortable with having the full weight of
the philosophical basis of *The Principles of Mathematics* placed on his
shoulders? Moore's unpublished review of that book suggests that he may not
have been. We know that Whitehead was unhappy with the presentation of
Our Knowledge of the External World as representing work that he and
Russell had in progress. To criticize a position which one's opponent has held
in the past, and then to be told that that opponent no longer holds it is
disconcerting. In this respect Russell was both a victim and an offender.
Joachim and Dewey both criticized Russell and found his response to be that
he did not maintain the position that they criticized. But Dewey also
protested that Russell had criticized a position that Dewey did not hold. It
was also disconcerting to Russell's interlocutors to be told that he could show
their positions to be false, although he cheerfully admitted that he did not
have a better position immune to criticism to offer as a replacement. Hence
Bradley's remark that if Russell found that the logic of *The Principles of
Mathematics* resulted in a contradiction, it might be appropriate for him to
question the basis of a logic which had such an outcome, rather than to use
that logic as a basis of criticizing the thought of others.

The forms of argument used by Russell in his polemical exchanges also
deserve comment. Often, as happened with Bradley, a challenge to his first
sweeping criticism brought Russell back to a more careful statement and
more modest charges. He would frequently admit that there might be
junctures in the argument where it dissolves into a claim by each person that
their own insight is right, the other's wrong. Russell speaks of the possibility
in such a situation of using a *reductio ad absurdum* argument, a device
whereby Russell's wit gave him a decided advantage. The basic argument he
recommends, although he admits it cannot always be used conclusively, is to
show that the position of one's opponent leads to contradictions or has as
consequences some unacceptable tenets (unacceptable either because they
conflict with other positions that the opponent cherishes or because they
conflict with common sense). A special form of the reductio argument shows
that the opponent is driven into an infinite regress if that position is accepted.
Another form of argument is to show that, of the different possible positions
on the issue in question, one's own position has advantages over any others,

those of one's opponent included. The advantages may be in terms of consistency, agreement with science, agreement with common sense, or agreement with experience.

We have seen Russell use all of these argument forms against his opponents: idealists are led into an infinite regress if they hold that a relation is a predicate of the terms related; pragmatists are led into an infinite regress when they hold that a belief is true if it is satisfactory, for they must ask if it is true that it is satisfactory; Meinong is led into accepting the contradictory consequences of postulating nonexistent existences; Frege must accept the unhappy consequence of having an ad hoc distinction between two kinds of referents of propositions of the same form where one expression is fictional, the other not. In many cases the opponents protest that Russell's imputed absurdities or unwelcome consequences followed from reading into their theories positions he himself held. Russell himself had similar arguments used against him: *implication, identity,* and *negation* must mean for Russell what everyone else means by them, and, in that case, his logic is seriously flawed. Russell cannot have commonsense objects "constructed" and at the same time accept a causal theory of perception; therefore he is contradicting himself.

Given the difficulties in the use of such techniques in philosophical debate, can philosophical interchanges be useful, move the discussion forward, or be conclusive? At one point it seemed that Russell might be willing to claim that the techniques of formal logic, as employed in a truly scientific philosophy, could enlist agreement by showing that a problem is solved or by showing that the problem is not solvable. But this early Leibnizian hope faded. At other times, Russell seems ready to admit that, in some cases, there may be a temperamental bias that affects philosophers in a debate and that cannot be overcome by argument. Russell admits a bias against the humanism of pragmatism, against the "fuzzy" outlines of Whitehead's world, against the holism he finds in idealism and in some aspects of pragmatism. In spite of such "prejudices," however, Russell enjoyed philosophical debate, and it was important to him, as his participation over many decades indicates. Such discussion can show one the limits of one's own position, suggest alternatives, and stimulate and test new ideas.

In this respect, as we have seen, the work of other philosophers was an important resource for Russell in developing his own philosophy, and we have seen how the work of others caused emendations and changes in his own point of view. One may be warned of pitfalls through others' problems; one can clarify and formulate one's own position against the alternatives presented by other philosophers. As we have seen, this was a customary approach for Russell; an example is the presentation of his theory of denoting against the alternatives of Meinong and Frege. In this case the interest is not historical but is instrumental to the solution of one's own problem. Once one has arrived at a satisfactory solution, all other alternatives are forgotten, including one's own earlier opinions—"bygone lucubrations," as Russell called them.[8]

If we contrast Russell's dialectical habits with those of present-day philosophers, several differences appear. He had a much larger range of interactions with philosophers whose positions were very different from his own than do contemporary philosophers who commonly debate only with others of closely similar views on fine points within that perspective. This may be partly due to the exponential increase in the volume of philosophical literature, which defies efforts to encompass all of it. Russell himself was also partly responsible for this narrowing because of his stress on the similarity of philosophy and science in technical, piecemeal, cooperative inquiry.

9.2 Writing on Russell

The body of writing on the thought of Russell is considerable and continually growing; it comprises several different kinds of work. The largest amount of secondary material is concerned with themes related to his logic; every logician who hopes to further the comprehensiveness and accuracy of that field starts from *Principia Mathematica* and must deal with its accomplishments and its difficulties as a prelude to original work. For the most part the attempt to criticize, defend, amend, or replace the logical structure of *Principia* has gone on without participation from either Russell or Whitehead. As we have seen, the second edition of *Principia* attempted to respond in minimal fashion to newer work of Wittgenstein and F. P. Ramsey, but the more usual response of Russell is that of his reply to Kurt Gödel to the effect that he has not worked for nearly two decades in this area and that he no longer feels it to be of philosophical relevance.[9]

Another portion of the literature on Russell has been the attempt of logical positivists to carry out the method and program of Russell's view of philosophy as they understood it and as they linked it with what they thought was presented in Wittgenstein's *Tractatus*. Russell was sympathetic and interested in this work and recognized these philosophers as followers and fellow travelers, but he was also in disagreement with them on several points.

A third body of work on Russell took its historical roots from pre-Russell Oxford philosophy, from the later Wittgenstein, and from an interpretation of

G. E. Moore. This work was devoted largely to the Russell of the years before 1920 and was concerned with the critical destruction of the claim of logical atomism to be a valid or fruitful form of philosophy. These attacks on Russell included Urmson's criticism of analytic philosophy, Strawson's criticism of the theory of descriptions, Black's and Ryle's criticisms of the theory of meaning of the kind attributed to Russell, and the criticisms of Russell's alternatives to Frege and Meinong discussed earlier in this book. These criticisms and Russell's counter-criticisms seem to be more like confrontations than dialogues based on reciprocal understandings, but they are relevant to the current state of analytic philosophy.

A fourth kind of study of Russell's work is now beginning to take shape: this is no longer a dialogue between Russell and his philosophical allies or adversaries but between scholars of different persuasions who are going back to the texts of Russell's books and papers and using the newly available historical materials to reconstruct, reinterpret, and make useful its content. In this category, a good example would be the work of the American Grover Maxwell, who takes his cue from the Russell of *The Analysis of Matter.* Similar work is being done on Europe, for example by Jules Vuillemin, and these labors, in conjunction with the contemporary reassessment of the analytic movement and its history may well lead to a considerable difference in the view that the twentieth century takes of itself and of the role of Russell in developing its patterns of thought.[10] Certainly the appearance of *The Collected Papers of Bertrand Russell* and the archival resources which they employ are already altering our view of him and his philosophy.

In addition to evaluating the place of philosophical interchanges in Russell's own methodology, it is important to ask how the dialogues here surveyed have had an influence in the history of twentieth-century analytic philosophy. This is especially the case at a time when writers are asking whether the analytic movement has run its course and is bankrupt, or indeed whether philosophy, as we have known it, is at an end. If the confidence that truth could be gained and philosophy improved by the exchange of views and arguments among philosophers signifies anything, it must be that in spite of temperamental bias, circular argument, or polemical ploys, some new insights emerge from such interactions, and some difference is made in the course of serious thought. If the analytic philosophy of which Russell was a pioneer has a value today, some philosophical progress should be evident. To see to what extent this may have been the case, it will be useful to look at some of the issues raised repeatedly among Russell's disputants to see whether such issues are now dead or still vital, and if new versions of analytic philosophy have been affected or can profit from them.

9.3 Philosophy after Russell

The earliest issues discussed by Russell had to do with metaphysical problems: external versus internal relations, pluralism versus monism, transcendent versus immanent objects of knowledge. These issues raised in the dialogue with idealists have a dated air about them. Within analytic philosophy the tendency has been to say that such issues are outside the scope of knowledge—speculative, poetic, but not cognitive. Idealism versus realism is no longer debated as between two conceivably sound positions. That is not to say that coherence, internal relations, and monistic systems have not found a home in other philosophical traditions, such as that of phenomenology. But in this respect the debates between Russell and Moore on one side and Bradley and Joachim on the other are no longer possible. Although Russell himself was an active participant in such debates, he was himself partly to blame for their end. His sharp distinction between philosophy that is concerned with ethical and religious implications and philosophy that is analytic and scientific was taken to put the former out of bounds for analytic philosophy. The end of such debates is partly due to the triumph of a verificationist theory of meaning and truth in the hands of pragmatic naturalists and logical empiricists, for whom the outcome of speculative and metaphysical debate can make no difference and hence is of no interest. In this respect, analytic philosophy has taken a turn away from idealism and also from traditional metaphysics. Some recent writers have argued from the analysis of the way language works and the way things must be said to the necessity of metaphysical presuppositions. The analytic methodology of such writers as Strawson, however, is strikingly different from that of more traditional speculative philosophy.

With respect to mathematical logic, as we have seen, Russell was one of those who first presented this as philosophically significant. At one time the logical realism he entertained required that logical truths contribute to philosophy. Although he later modified this position, he continued to recommend the logical symbolizing of philosophical arguments in order to avoid the errors inherent in ordinary language and to achieve precision. His and Whitehead's own contributions were responsible for much of the appeal that the new "scientific" method made to philosophers of the logical positivist tradition. The method of construction used to build the world of science and common sense from the data of sense with the tools of logic was an impressive model, influential in Carnap's and Nelson Goodman's constructionist projects and retained by Russell himself in *The Analysis of Matter* and *The Analysis of Mind*. There is a sense in which the working out of a philosophical theory in terms of its symbolic formulation is still a fruitful one; it is used, for instance, in the event-ontologies that owe much to the heritage of Russell's method of construction. But the logical empiricists' philosophical interpretation of *Principia Mathematica* itself, and their view of the role of symbolic logic in philosophy, were much influenced by the Wittgenstein of the *Tractatus,* as was Russell's later view. In this context, logical empiricists saw logical "truths" as syntactical, showing in their form their consistency or inconsistency. The question of the inferences that could be made from the importance and role of certain kinds of symbolic expressions to "what there is" became a point of discussion and then division among analytic philosophers from Russell on. Quine's early view that "to be is to be the value of a variable," his discussion of ontology under the title (borrowed from Russell) "What There Is," Carnap's concept of the choice of a symbolic language in terms of convenience rather than ontological commitment—all these issues stemmed from those first raised by Russell. But because Russell himself saw philosophy as aiming at providing truths, he resisted the view that a science, however sophisticated, that told us only different ways of saying the same thing could be of major significance for philosophy. His disappointment at the emptiness of logic and his acceptance of the distinction between analytic truth and empirical probability came from Wittgenstein. Russell continued to hold that logical language is necessary to philosophy in providing precision, and that it allows us to infer something about the nature of the world, for example, we may infer the relational character of the world from the necessity for any logic to have a relational schema. He also continued to reject the idea of any logic as a theory of inquiry, in spite of the psychological elements introduced into his own analysis of propositions.

A different aspect of the early work in logical theory concerned what might be called "theory of reference," and, as we saw in an earlier chapter, this gave rise to a major body of philosophical literature in the interpretations of Meinong, Frege, Russell, and their arguments. Here again Russell passed from a distinction between indicating (denoting) and meaning (describing), parallel to the epistemological distinction between knowledge by acquaintance and knowledge by description, to a much more complex logical, psychological, and philosophical theory based on a hierarchy of languages, minimal vocabularies, egocentric particulars, and logically proper names. For the most part it was his earlier work which has elicited comment, emendation, and revised theories, and this is reflected in the work of such diverse philosophers as P. F. Strawson, John Searle, Leonard Linsky, Saul Kripke, Terence Parsons, Peter Geach, and many others.

One of the areas in which the most progress has been made in post-Russellian analysis has been the development of formal systems of syntactics and semantics. Russell praised Carnap's contributions, which he recognized as making important advances in precision and sophistication. Russell was less aware of and less influenced by the progress made by linguistic analysts who did not use the logical mode of Carnap but whose work was closer to that of natural language. Where ordinary-language analysis was castigated by Russell as idle and pointless in its attention to everyday speech, the more scientific approach of logical empiricists was welcomed for its clarity and completeness. Yet Russell also reserved a doubt as to whether Carnap was not making philosophy excessively linguistic, so to speak. Alter all, the point of philosophy, for Russell, is to describe the world, not merely to describe the way we talk about the world. In spite of Russell's reservations about the "linguistic turn" in philosophy, his own work was an important part of that turn. The very problems of *Principia Mathematica* which elicited the distinction between proposition and propositional function, the theory of types, and the theory of descriptions stressed the degree to which logic was concerned with "expressions" rather than entities, and this, in addition to the *Tractatus,* led to the linguistic interpretation of logic and eventually of philosophy.

The analytic philosophers such as Carnap, A. Tarski, and their contemporary descendants who employ a formal mode of argumentation are following in Russell's footsteps, or at least in the path he recommended, by using logical symbols for philosophical arguments. Terseness, univocal meanings, freedom from the misleading metaphysics embedded in ordinary speech, explicitness of rules governing the use of symbols: these advantages have been persuasive to a large number of twentieth-century philosophers. But the later Wittgenstein and many philosophers who followed earlier logical models going back to Aristotle have argued that the use of an "artificial language," such as symbolic logic, renders the meanings of life into mathematics and thus distorts and diminishes the richness of meanings and the presuppositions which ordinary languages used in real-life situations possess naturally. From natural language the philosopher can learn more than he can from a set of schemata invented in order to have a simplicity and consistency which a living language does not and ought not to have. This issue of philosophical methodology, whether or not to use symbolic formulations in philosophical argument, developed into a major split within twentieth-century analytic philosophy.

Another set of topics appearing again and again in Russell's discussions with his contemporaries is what might be called "the analysis of experi-

ence." Under this description we can include some questions about immediate experience: whether or not it is cognitive as given; whether it is marked
by easily distinguishable sense-data, such as colored patches, sounds of
specific pitch and volume, and so forth; whether as given, or as analyzed, the
presence of some form of experiential reference confers epistemological
status of greater reliability, of incorrigibility, or of probability; whether it is
appropriate to analyze experience in terms of subject, act, content, object, or
some set of these terms; whether and how dreams and imaginary experiences
differ from those of waking "real" observation; how commonsense objects
are related to colored patches; how particles of matter, light rays, and so forth
are related to those patches. The range of these problems reminds us of the
many twentieth-century philosophers who have discussed them from the
time when Russell and Moore first posed their own epistemological problems
in the language of sense-data to the present day. As we have seen, Russell
changed his mind on many of these issues, and argued on many of them
against James, against Dewey, against Whitehead, and against Meinong.
Later Russell debated with A. J. Ayer, although they both agreed that basic
observational propositions were fundamental to our knowledge. Some of the
questions Russell raised would be judged to be more psychological than
philosophical today, and this partially explains the difference of opinion
between Ayer on the one hand, and Moore and Russell on the other. Russell
gave more and more ground to psychology than he had earlier, but he still
insisted that no theory of knowledge could be adequate unless the contributions of basic perceptual premises were provided for in the system: he
claimed that pragmatism, for instance, did not make such a provision.

   The recent explicit challenge to what is now called "foundationalism," the
attempt to establish incorrigible elements of experience as epistemological
premises, undermines the project shared by Russell and Moore and followed
by Ayer and others. In *Sense and Sensibilia* J. L. Austin argues that the
tortuous effort to find some way of formulating units of experience as error-
free had led to the creation of the technical vocabulary and puzzles of *sense-
data,* a sign that something had gone wrong when ordinary language had no
trouble with *its* natural vocabulary of perception.[11] Among empiricists
today, many find the kind of analysis of experience practiced by Russell
hopelessly out-of-date. Even moving from sense-data to observation-sen-
tences does not save this early motif of analytic empiricism from impinging
on the realm of science. Philosophers can be concerned only about the form
of sentences or the legitimacy of inferences from observations to lawlike
generalizations. Few philosophers in the late twentieth century follow
Russell in holding that it is appropriate for philosophers to use the outcome of

physiological, physical, and psychological sciences as valuable data in the theory of knowledge.

The most divisive issue emerging in the various controversies we have recounted is that of the definition of truth and its relation to what is known and what is believed. As we have seen, Russell did battle against the coherence theory of idealism and the various forms of the pragmatic theory of truth, and even had difficulties with the theories of Meinong and Moore, the philosophers who most closely agreed with him. In the course of these debates he shifted from the view of truth as a characteristic of propositions independent of what is known or believed to the view that knowledge means "true belief" and that beliefs are true or false independently of whether or not we judge them to be true, but only in respect to their correspondence with facts. Hence empirical method and scientific induction are the best we can do in determining the truth of our beliefs. In this context, verification is the most important tool, yet what truth *is* is different from our reasons for believing it. On this rock foundered all chances of reaching agreement with pragmatists or with logical empiricists, both of whom defined truth in terms of some concept of verifiability. What is the point, they asked, of speaking of a belief as true or false if there is no way of ascertaining which it is? But Russell replied that it *is* either true or false that it snowed on Manhattan Island in the year A.D. 1, even if there is no possible way of knowing whether in fact it did snow, or even of estimating the probability of snow falling on the island in that year.

In the light of the discussion of the role of experience, the status of scientific truth and its relation to philosophy is of great importance. For Russell science is the paradigm of knowledge, and as he often mentions, the vastness of the physical universe dominates his imagination. He thought the task of philosophy to be the description of the world. For him science could help philosophy by providing theories as data for philosophy; philosophy could help science by inventing new hypotheses and by analyzing the results of science in terms of events and perception. It seemed a "cosmic impiety" to reduce the scale of our understanding to the human and to the best that we can do in the way of inquiry. Yet science and philosophy can never claim final truth; the truth of our time becomes the falsity of another. But for Russell the world is there to be known, and if knowledge changes, truth abides.

Like Russell, his early colleagues thought philosophy should aim at the description of the world. For Whitehead, philosophy could synthesize the sciences and bring that synthesis into relation with our own experience. For Moore, the description of the world rested on common experience and commonsense language. While logical empiricists and pragmatists disagreed with Russell's theory of truth, they agreed in thinking of science as the paradigm of knowledge and in finding that of significance for philosophy. For the logical empiricists it was the task of science, not of philosophy, to describe the world. But the precision and caution of science served as a model for philosophy, and philosophy was concerned with the analysis of scientific methods, scientific laws, and scientific concepts. For pragmatists, the importance of science is that its method of inquiry can be generalized to apply to *all* human inquiries, including the philosophical.

For the Wittgenstein of the *Tractatus Logico-Philosophicus,* philosophy does not stand beside or overlap the realm of science, and everything that can be known of the world is the domain of science. For the later Wittgenstein, the sole task of philosophy is the curing of the confusions and bewilderments that philosophy falls into through its "subliming" of language. Other analysts have different ideas concerning the task of philosophy: It may be a game played with words; it may be a means of uncovering tacit presuppositions *behind* our use of words; it may be a way of eliciting truths from habits of language usage; it may be a flight of imaginative insight yielding felt satisfaction, if not the hard currency of truth.

The restriction of philosophy to a realm different from that of science has created problems for both. Within philosophy of science there has grown up a skepticism about whether science itself *can* describe the world, or whether it merely reflects the dominant paradigm of the historical and cultural context. Whatever science is able to do or not do, it seems that if philosophy and science are separated, there is no truth left for philosophy to tell. The threat of a philosophy with no task to perform is expressed by Frank P. Ramsey: "I conclude that there really is nothing to discuss; and this conclusion corresponds to a feeling I have about ordinary conversation also. It is a relatively new phenomenon, which has arisen from two causes which have operated gradually through the nineteenth century. One is the advance of science, the other the decay of religion; which have resulted in all the old general questions becoming either technical or ridiculous."[12] Ramsey offers as an example of the emptiness of philosophy a talk of Russell's on "What I Believe": Ramsey says that what Russell believes about the world is really physics and that what he believes about ethics is really psychology. For Ramsey, Wittgenstein may be right that philosophy is nonsense, but wrong if he thinks it "important nonsense."

A loss of meaning in philosophy, a sense in which there is no task for philosophy to perform which is of importance, and no truth for it to reveal, is not an uncommon malady of twentieth-century philosophy, and it afflicts analytic philosophy both from within, as in the case of Ramsey and

Wittgenstein, and from without, as in the case of the attacks by such critics as Herbert Marcuse, who, in *One-Dimensional Man,* finds analytic philosophy empty of human meaning, narrow, technical, and sterile.[13] The problem of a contentless "pursuit of truth" and of the narrowness of philosophical analysis has led to various attempts to use that analysis as a tool for the discussion of policy questions, such as abortion or punishment, and to the conception of philosophy as not so much a claim to knowledge or an analysis of knowledge as a kind of illumination or, as Richard Rorty calls it, "edification."[14]

In fact the difficulties encountered by analytic philosophy have led to widespread defection from analysis. Some philosophers, such as Alan Donagan, have turned to the model of speculative philosophy; some have sought to extend the scope of philosophy into realms such as linguistic analysis and technical probability theory, which, while still methodologically analytic, had previously been considered not part of the subject-matter of philosophy. J. J. Katz and Richard Jeffrey are examples of this tendency. A recent collection of essays, *Post-Analytic Philosophy,* includes criticisms of the limitations of analytic philosophy such as those of Thomas Nagel and Hilary Putnam; it also includes under its title types of philosophical discourse closely allied to history, cultural commentary, and literary criticism.[15]

9.4 *The Future of Analysis*

In finding philosophy to be without subject-matter with Ramsey, or to be moving into a postanalytic phase with the editors of the collection just referred to, it may be that we are writing a premature obituary for twentieth-century analytic philosophy. It might be that saying that analytic philosophy is "dead" means only that there is no single dominant tradition that can be identified today. The apparent simplicity of the analytic realism of Russell in the early years of our century has given place to a number of different kinds of analytic philosophy. All owe something to Russell; some have followed the turns of his thought more closely than others. Within the range of these alternative kinds of analysis, it may be possible to find a version that does not lead to an impasse, emptiness of content, or triviality.

On the place of formal logic in philosophy, the schism between the view that such logic should be excluded as too far from the way we speak and live and too close to mathematics, and the opposing view that any philosophical work that is not or cannot be symbolically formulated is defective, seems unbridgeable. But these views need not exclude one another. Surely it can do no harm to try to clarify a muddled idea or argument by putting it into symbolic form; on the other hand, logical schemata would be empty without application to the situations, judgments, and actions of everyday experience and the common language in which we have learned to talk about them. Perhaps a reconciliation between those who use symbolic language in philosophy and those who reject it would be more likely if the analytic-synthetic distinction were abandoned and a wider philosophical context invoked. If logic is conceived as a method of inquiry, analytic pragmatists, scientifically-minded empiricists, and perhaps other kinds of analysts, including those influenced by the later Wittgenstein, can find a place for the calculus of classes, of propositions, and of probabilities, and for an analysis of concepts, presuppositions, common sense, and scientific and metascientific inquiries as well. An area of concern in theory of knowledge and philosophy of science that was of interest to Russell and is still vital today is that of probability theory and induction as these bear on the evaluation of belief. Such work promises to assume an increasing importance in philosophy.

A basic empiricist and realist orientation seems comfortable to most philosophers today; this orientation, as Roderick Chisholm suggests,[16] may be the common background of Anglo-American analytic realism and of Continental phenomenology and realism. If we could follow the trend of interpreting empiricism as meaning that *all* philosophical inquiries have their starting-points, their outcomes, and their warrants in experience, we should be able to say of some types that they fit experience less well than others. What philosophy best fits experience is an open question and a direction for research. If to this empiricism is added a continuity of philosophical and scientific inquiry, we may follow both Russell and some of his interlocutors. One wonders why a sharp territorial division should be laid down between science and philosophy, with truth attributable only to science. Let us take an example. If, at one point in time, the problem of destructive personalities is identified as ethical or religious, is it impossible for it later to become a medical one because of advances in brain chemistry? The tacit acceptance of a philosophical concept of substance may have formerly inhibited the progress of atomic physics; it required a liberal dose of philosophical analysis to unstop the conceptual bottleneck for the scientists. Again, on the outer reaches of human groping into the "warp and woof" of the universe, a Russell or a Whitehead may make an educated philosophical guess that will someday bear scientific fruit. Or perhaps in our time, when human survival is gravely threatened, Russell's words may appeal to us as human beings more than as citizens, patriots, or professional philosophers; for sometimes the words of philosophers have been heard. At any rate, a flexible partnership between philosophy and science would seem to free science from having to live up to an ideal of the achievement of objective, unanimous, universal truth that is independent of all contexts, and to free philosophy from biting its lip every time it is tempted to make a judgment that claims more than logical or linguistic content.

A traditional concern of philosophy from the time of Socrates to the present day has been the attempt to arrive at a universal, univocal, exception-less definition of a concept. Russell strove to craft such a definition of truth, as we saw, in spite of the protests of pragmatists. Current discussions also search for such definitions of truth and knowledge, and the terms *coherentism, fallibilism,* and *verificationism* reproduce older arguments. But the later Wittgenstein and his followers, unconsciously echoing the pragmatists, said, "Don't look for the meaning, look for the use." It seems that giving up the search for universal definitions might move the discussion to more specific contexts and free philosophy from its so far fruitless fixation on formulating *the* definition of *cause, knowledge,* or *truth.*

It is likely that from the perspective of the twenty-first century we will be better able to see what elements of permanent value to philosophy have emerged from the give-and-take between Bertrand Russell and his contemporaries. Meanwhile, we can have enough confidence in the process of philosophical discussion to follow their examples and to seek to move the issues of our day forward to greater clarity and, perhaps, to areas of greater agreement.

Notes
Bibliography
Index of Names
Index of Subjects

Notes

1. Introduction

1. Bertrand Russell, *Mysticism and Logic and Other Essays* (London: Longmans, Green & Co., 1918), 29–31. Bertrand Russell, *Our Knowledge of the External World as a Field for Scientific Method in Philosophy* (Chicago: Open Court Publishing Co., 1914), preface.

2. C. D. Broad, "Critical and Speculative Philosophy," in *Contemporary British Philosophy,* 1st ser., ed. J. H. Muirhead (London: George Allen & Unwin, Ltd., 1924). For a discussion of the interpretation of Russell's philosophy as unstable see Elizabeth R. Eames, *Bertrand Russell's Theory of Knowledge* (London: George Allen & Unwin, Ltd., 1969), chap. 1.

3. Rudolf Carnap, "Intellectual Biography," *The Philosophy of Rudolf Carnap,* vol. 10, The Library of Living Philosophers, ed. Paul Arthur Schilpp (Chicago: Open Court Publ. Co., 1963), 13–14. J. O. Urmson, *Philosophical Analysis* (Oxford: Clarendon Pr., 1956), chaps. 9 and 10.

4. Alan Wood, "Russell's Philosophy," in Bertrand Russell, *My Philosophical Development* (New York: Simon and Schuster, 1959), 273.

5. See chaps. 4 and 5, below.

6. Russell, *Our Knowledge of the External World,* 8.

7. Bertrand Russell, "On Denoting," *Mind,* n.s. 14 (1905):473–93. Reprinted in *Logic and Knowledge,* ed. Robert Charles Marsh (London: George Allen & Unwin, Ltd., 1956).

8. Bertrand Russell, "Knowledge by Acquaintance and Knowledge by Description," *Proceedings of the Aristotelian Society,* n.s. 11 (1910–11):108–28, reprinted in *Mysticism and Logic and Other Essays* (London: Longmans, Green & Co., 1918).

9. Bertrand Russell, *A Critical Exposition of the Philosophy of Leibniz with an Appendix of Leading Passages* (Cambridge: Cambridge University Press, 1900), xii.

10. I. Grattan-Guiness, *Dear Russell-Dear Jourdain: A Commentary on Russell's Logic Based on His Correspondence with Philip Jourdain* (London: Gerald Duckworth & Co., Ltd., 1977). Ronald W. Clark, *The Life of Bertrand Russell* (New York: Alfred A. Knopf, 1976). Ludwig Wittgenstein, *Letters to Russell, Keynes and Moore,* ed. G. H. von Wright (Oxford: Basil Blackwell, 1974). The Collected Papers

of Bertrand Russell (London: George Allen & Unwin, Ltd.), Vol. 1, *Cambridge Essays 1888–89,* ed. Kenneth Blackwell, Andrew Brink, Nicholas Griffin, Richard A. Rempel, and John G. Slater, 1983. Vol. 7, *Theory of Knowledge: The 1913 Manuscript,* ed. Elizabeth Ramsden Eames with Kenneth Blackwell, 1984. Vol. 8, *The Philosophy of Logical Atomism and Other Essays, 1914–19,* ed. John G. Slater, 1986. Vol. 9, *Essays on Language, Mind and Matter, 1919–26,* ed. John G. Slater with the assistance of Bernd Frohmann, 1988. Vol. 12, *Contemplation and Action, 1902–14,* ed. Richard A. Rempel, Andrew Brink, and Margaret Moran, 1985. Vol. 13, *Prophecy and Dissent, 1914–16,* ed. Richard A. Rempel with Margaret Moran, 1988.

2. *Russell and the Idealists*

1. Bertrand Russell, "My Mental Development," *The Philosophy of Bertrand Russell,* vol. 5, The Library of Living Philosophers, ed. Paul Arthur Schilpp (Evanston and Chicago: Northwestern Univ., 1944), 10–11; Bertrand Russell, *Autobiography,* vol. 1 (London: George Allen & Unwin, Ltd., 1967), chap. 5; Bertrand Russell, *My Philosophical Development* (New York: Simon and Schuster, 1959), chap. 4; G. E. Moore, "An Autobiography," *The Philosophy of G. E. Moore,* vol. 4, The Library of Living Philosophers, ed. Paul Arthur Schilpp (Evanston and Chicago: Northwestern Univ., 1942), 13–16.

2. Harry Ruja, "Principles of Polemics in Russell," *Inquiry* 11 (Fall 1968):282–94.

3. C. N. Keen, "The Interaction of Russell and Bradley," *Russell: Journal of the Bertrand Russell Archives* 3 (1971):7–10; Carl Spadoni, "Russell's Rebellion Against Neo-Hegelianism" (Ph.D. diss., Univ. of Waterloo, Ontario, 1977).

4. G. E. Moore, "The Nature of Judgment," *Mind,* n.s. 8 (1899):176–93.

5. Russell, *The Philosophy of Leibniz.* See especially chap. 4.

6. Bertrand Russell, "On the Relation of Number and Quantity," *Mind,* n.s. 6 (1986):326–41; Bertrand Russell, *An Essay on the Foundations of Geometry* (Cambridge: Cambridge Univ. Pr. 1897); Bertrand Russell, "On the Notion of Order," *Mind,* n.s. 10 (1901):30–51; Bertrand Russell, "Is Position in Space Absolute or Relative?" *Mind,* n.s. 10 (1901):293–317; Bertrand Russell, "Recent Work on the Principles of Mathematics," *International Monthly* 4 (July 1901):83–101; Bertrand Russell, "Sur la Logique des relations avec des applications à la théorie des series," *Revue de Mathématique* 7 (1901):115–36, 137–48; Bertrand Russell, "On Finite and Infinite Cardinal Numbers," *American Journal of Mathematics* 24 (Oct. 1902):378–83; Bertrand Russell, "Théorie générale des séries bien-ordonnées," *Revue de Mathématiques* 8 (1902):12–43; Bertrand Russell, *The Principles of Mathematics* (Cambridge: Cambridge Univ. Pr., 1903).

7. Bertrand Russell, "Meinong's Theory of Complexes and Assumptions," Parts 1,2,3, *Mind,* n.s. 13, nos. 50–52 (1904):(50) 204–19, (51) 336–54, (52) 509–24; Bertrand Russell, "On Denoting," *Mind,* n.s. 14 (1905):473–93; Bertrand Russell, "Sur la Relation des mathématiques à la logistique," *Revue de Métaphysique et de Morale* 13 (Nov. 1905):906–16; Bertrand Russell, "On Some Difficulties in the Theory of Transfinite Numbers and Order Types," *Proceedings of the London Mathematical Society* 2 (March 1906):29–53; Bertrand Russell, "The Theory of Implication," *American Journal of Mathematics* 28 (April 1906):159–202; Bertrand

Russell, "Les Paradoxes de la logique," *Revue de Métaphysique et de Morale 14* (Sept. 1906):627–50; Bertrand Russell, "On the Nature of Truth," *Proceedings of the Aristotelian Society,* n.s. 7 (1906–7):28–49; Bertrand Russell, "Mathematical Logic as Based on the Theory of Types," *American Journal of Mathematics 30* (May 1908): 222–62; Bertrand Russell, *The Problems of Philosophy* (London: Williams and Norgate, 1912).

8. Bertrand Russell, "The Monistic Theory of Truth," in Bertrand Russell, *Philosophical Essays* (London: Longmans, Green & Co., 1910). All citations are to the paperback edition (New York: Simon and Schuster, 1966). See section 2 of the essay. See also Russell, *Principles of Mathematics,* 221–26.

9. F. H. Bradley to Bertrand Russell, Nov. 6, 1900; Russell to Bradley, Nov. 16, 1900. Bertrand Russell, "On Denoting," in Bertrand Russell, *Logic and Knowledge,* ed. Robert Charles Marsh (London: George Allen & Unwin, Ltd., 1956), 43. All letters from Bradley to Russell here quoted are in the Bertrand Russell Archives, McMaster University, Hamilton, Ontario, Canada; letters of Russell to Bradley are in the archives of Merton College, Oxford; copies at McMaster. F. H. Bradley, *The Principles of Logic,* 2 vols. (Oxford: Oxford Univ. Pr., 1883). F. H. Bradley, *Appearance and Reality* (Oxford: Clarendon Pr., 1893).

10. Russell, *Principles of Mathematics,* 47–52.

11. Ibid., chap. 26 for the discussion of both monadistic and monistic interpretations of relations.

12. Ibid., part 4 is concerned with order, as are many of the articles of this period; see nn. 6 and 7, above.

13. Russell, "The Monistic Theory of Truth," 141–42.

14. Russell, *Principles of Mathematics,* 446–55. Points in space are discussed in the context of the criticism of a mentalistic analysis of geometry. The entire text reflects the interpretation of propositions as real. See p. xix for definition.

15. Ibid., xviii. See also G. E. Moore, "The Refutation of Idealism," *Mind,* n.s. 12 (1903). Repr. in G. E. Moore, *Philosophical Studies* (London: Routledge & Kegan Paul, 1922).

16. Russell, *Principles of Mathematics,* introduction to 2d edition, x. For a full statement of the realism of this period see Russell, "Meinong's Theory of Complexes and Assumptions."

17. For Joachim's criticisms see Harold H. Joachim, *The Nature of Truth* (Oxford: Clarendon Pr., 1906), 44–49. See also the exchange of letters between Joachim and Russell, especially Joachim's letters tentatively dated Sept. 13, 1903, and Sept. 5, 1904. Joachim's letters are in the Bertrand Russell Archives; Russell's in the archives of Merton College with copies at McMaster.

18. Russell, "On the Nature of Truth"; see n. 7, above.

19. Russell's reviews of Joachim's book are: Bertrand Russell, "What Is Truth?" *Independent Review* (June 1906):349–53; "The Nature of Truth," *Mind* 16 (1907):528–33. G. E. Moore's review is "Mr. Joachim's *Nature of Truth,*" *Mind* 16 (1907):229–35. Joachim's reply to Moore, "A Reply to Mr. Moore," *Mind* 16 (1907):410–15.

20. Joachim, *The Nature of Truth,* 42.

21. Ibid., 46–48.

22. Ibid., 50.

23. Russell, "The Nature of Truth"; Joachim to Russell, May 21, 1906.

24. Russell, "The Nature of Truth," 532–33.

25. See Moore's review and Joachim's response, cited in n. 19, above.

26. All arguments referred to are from "The Monistic Theory of Truth," cited in n. 8, above.

27. Russell, *Philosophy of Leibniz,* 50n, 60.

28. The correspondence between Bradley and Russell began with Bradley's letter to Russell in response to the Leibniz book (this letter is missing—June 21, 1901, is the date of the first letter in the collection), and continues to Sept. 25, 1914. Russell's begins with a response to the missing letter of Bradley's Nov. 16, 1900 and continues to Jan. 30, 1914, with an additional letter of Nov. 20, 1922, acknowledging the receipt of Bradley's *Essays on Truth and Reality.*

29. Bradley to Russell, April 11 and April 20, 1910, published in Russell, *Autobiography,* 1:199–200.

30. Russell to Bradley, Oct. 29, 1909.

31. F. H. Bradley, "On Appearance, Error, and Contradiction," *Mind,* n.s. 19 (1910):154–85; Russell, "Some Explanations in Reply to Mr. Bradley," *Mind,* n.s. 19 (1910):373–78; Bradley, "Reply to Mr. Russell's Explanations," *Mind,* (1911):74–76. The bulk of Bradley's criticisms are contained in his *Essays on Truth and Reality* (Oxford: Clarendon Pr. 1914). chaps. 9 and 10.

32. Russell, *Principles of Mathematics,* 47.

33. Russell, *My Philosophical Development,* 61–62.

34. Bradley to Russell criticizing *Principles of Mathematics,* Feb. 4, 1904.

35. Russell to Bradley responding to criticisms and containing five pages of detailed notes, Feb. 11, 1904.

36. Ibid.

37. Russell responded to Bradley's criticisms with respect to assertion and negation in a letter of April 9, 1910. For his later problems with assertion and negation, see "Meinong's Theory of Complexes and Assumptions," where he struggles with the question of whether it is the same to assert a negative proposition and to deny an affirmative proposition, and how the proposition as unasserted can be distinguished from the proposition as denied; see above, pp. 000–000. Later he took a different view of negative propositions as corresponding to negative facts in "The Philosophy of Logical Atomism"; see *Logic and Knowledge,* 213–16. But later still, in *An Inquiry into Meaning and Truth* (London: George Allen & Unwin, 1940), Russell treated negative propositions as disappointed expections, 81, 162, 211–12.

38. See letter of Russell to Bradley, April 9, 1910, and Russell's published comments in "Some Explanations in Reply to Mr. Bradley," 376–77.

39. See letters of Bradley to Russell of Feb. 4, 1904; Feb. 17, 1904; Oct. 21, 1907; also "On Appearance, Error, and Contradiction," *Mind:*180–81. For Russell's response, see letter of Feb. 11, 1904. See also Joachim, *Nature of Truth,* 48–50.

40. For the treatment of class in *Principles of Mathematics,* see chaps. 6, 10, and appendixes A and B.

41. For Bradley's problems with Russell's view of classes, see his letter to Russell of Feb. 4, 1904, and *Essays on Truth and Reality,* 283–86.

42. Russell, "Some Explanations in Reply to Mr. Bradley," 376.

43. Bradley to Russell, Oct. 21, 1907; Russell to Bradley, Oct. 29, 1907; also

Russell, "Monistic Theory of Truth," 143–46.

44. Ibid., 138–39. See Bradley's response in "Coherence and Contradiction," in *Essays on Truth and Reality,* chap. 7.

45. Bradley, ibid., 302–3; Bradley, "Reply to Mr. Russell's Explanations," 74. Russell letter to Bradley, Mar. 2, 1911.

46. Russell letter to Bradley, Dec. 11, 1904, discusses impossibility; Russell to Bradley, April 9, 1910, discusses necessity and possibility; see also "Some Explanations in Reply to Mr. Bradley," 374.

47. Russell, "Some Explanations in Reply to Mr. Bradley"; Russell, "The Monistic Theory of Truth" in *Philosophical Essays,* 130–39; Bradley's response *Essays on Truth and Reality,* 291.

48. Bradley, *Essays on Truth and Reality,* 253–54.

49. Bradley, "On Truth and Coherence," in *Essays on Truth and Reality,* chap 7.

50. Bradley to Russell, Feb. 4, 1904, refers to the presentation of Russell's theory of truth as incomplete; Russell in response refers to "Meinong's Theory of Complexes and Assumptions," for a further development. It is in this series that true and false beliefs are said to differ as do red and white roses (see below). Joachim based his criticism of the Moore-Russell theory of truth on this position, but by 1906 Russell had already modified his position, as is evident in his 1906 paper to the Aristotelian Society.

51. Russell, "On the Nature of Truth and Falsehood," in *Philosophical Essays;* references in the following pages are to this essay.

52. Bradley, "Reply to Mr. Russell's Explanations," 76.

53. Harold H. Joachim letter to Bertrand Russell, May 6, 1906. As we shall see, Schiller made a similar comment claiming cooperation with Russell in opposing idealism.

54. Russell, "Some Explanations in Reply to Mr. Bradley," 377.

55. A. J. Ayer, et al., *The Revolution in Philosophy* (New York: The Macmillan Publ. Co., 1965), 42–43.

3. Russell and Moore

1. Russell, *Philosophy of Leibniz,* preface to 1st edition, xv; Russell, *The Principles of Mathematics,* preface to 1st edition, xviii: "on fundamental questions of philosophy, my position in all its chief features, is derived from Mr. G. E. Moore." Similar attributions to the influence of Moore are made in Russell's articles of this period; see n. 6, chap. 2, above. For other references to Moore, see B. J. Lucas, "Moore's Influence on Russell," *Russell: Journal of the Bertrand Russell Archives* 1 (1971):9; this article consists of listings of references to Moore in Russell's early work. The present note lists only those in which clear indication is given by Russell of a debt to Moore. Russell, *The Problems of Philosophy,* preface v.

2. Bertrand Russell, "The Elements of Ethics," in *Philosophical Essays* (London: Longmans, Green & Co., 1910), n. 1. There are also five footnote entries in *Principles of Mathematics* referring to Moore.

3. Bertrand Russell, "My Mental Development," in *The Philosophy of Bertrand Russell,* 12. G. E. Moore, "An Autobiography," in *The Philosophy of G. E. Moore,* 13–16. Russell, *Autobiography,* 1: 64, 73, 134–35; 2: 60.

4. A. J. Ayer, *Russell and Moore: The Analytical Heritage* (Cambridge, Mass.: Harvard Univ. Pr., 1971).

5. L. Susan Stebbing, "Moore's Influence," in *The Philosophy of G. E. Moore,* 517–18.

6. Russell, *Autobiography,* 1: 64.

7. Moore, "Autobiography," in *The Philosophy of G. E. Moore,* 13–16.

8. Paul Levy, *G. E. Moore and the Cambridge Apostles* (London: Weidenfeld and Nicholson, 1979), 196–97, 204–7.

9. Bertrand Russell, "The *A Priori* in Geometry," *Proceedings of the Aristotelian Society* 3 (1896):97–112; Bertrand Russell, "On the Relation of Number and Quantity"; Bertrand Russell, *German Social Democracy* (London: Longmans, Green & Co., 1896); Bertrand Russell, *An Essay on the Foundations of Geometry.*

10. Russell to Moore, Oct. 19, 1897.

11. Russell to Moore, July 20, Sept. 13, Oct. 14, Dec. 1, 1898.

12. G. E. Moore, "Freedom," *Mind,* n.s. 6 (1898):179–203. See S. P. Rosenbaum, "G. E. Moore's *The Elements of Ethics,*" *The University of Toronto Quarterly* 38 (April 1969):214–32.

13. G. E. Moore, "The Nature of Judgment."

14. Ibid., 179.

15. G. E. Moore, "Necessity," *Mind* n.s. 9 (July 1900):289–304. For Russell's article see n. 6, chap. 2, above.

16. G. E. Moore, "Critical Notes: *An Essay on the Foundations of Geometry,*" *Mind* n.s. 8 (1899):397–405.

17. Ibid., 399.

18. Bertrand Russell, *My Philosophical Development,* 39. See also Russell to Moore, July 18, 1899, where Russell says he agrees with it in all important points and then corrects some of Moore's remarks about points in space and infinite series.

19. G. E. Moore, "Identity," *Proceedings of the Aristotelian Society,* n.s. 1 (1900–1901):103–27.

20. Russell, *Principles of Mathematics,* 221–26.

21. See n. 1, above. See also Russell to Moore, April 30, 1900, June 9, 1900, June 29, 1900, August 21, 1900.

22. Moore, "Identity," 107–8.

23. Russell to Moore, May 9, 1900, August 16, August 21, 1900.

24. Russell to Moore, Mar. 6, Mar. 17, 1903.

25. G. E. Moore, *Principia Ethica* (Cambridge: Cambridge Univ. Pr, 1903); Bertrand Russell, "Review of Mr. G. E. Moore's *Principia Ethica,*" *Independent Review* 7 (March 1904):328–33; Russell to Moore, Oct. 10, 1903.

26. G. E. Moore, "The Refutation of Idealism," *Mind* (October 1903):433–53. G. E. Moore, "The Nature and Reality of Objects of Perception," *Proceedings of the Aristotelian Society,* n.s. 6 (1905–6):68–127; both published in *Philosophical Studies.*

27. Russell to Moore, Dec. 17, 1904.

28. Russell to Moore, Dec. 23, Dec. 29, 1904; Moore to Russell, Oct. 25, 1905.

29. See Moore's reference to an unpublished review, "The Philosophy of G. E. Moore," 15.

30. G. E. Moore, unpublished review of *The Principles of Mathematics,* Bertrand

Russell Archives.

31. Russell to Moore, May 2, 1905.

32. Russell, *The Problems of Philosophy,* v.

33. G. E. Moore, *Some Main Problems of Philosophy* (London: George Allen & Unwin, Ltd., 1953) preface, 8.

34. Russell, "Knowledge by Acquaintance and Knowledge by Description," in *Mysticism and Logic.*

35. G. E. Moore, *Ethics* (London: Williams & Norgate, 1912).

36. See below for discussion of the influence of Wittgenstein on Russell.

37. Their respective autobiographies in the Library of Living Philosophers volumes report the influence of Wittgenstein on each philosopher.

38. Russell's criticisms of James during this period occur in "Transatlantic 'Truth'," *The Albany Review* 2 (Jan. 1908):393–410; "Pragmatism," *Edinburgh Review* 209 (1909):363–88; "On the Nature of Acquaintance—Neutral Monism," *Monist* 24 (1914):161–87. Moore's criticism occurs in "Professor James' 'Pragmatism'," *Proceedings of the Aristotelian Society,* 8 (1907–8):33–77, reprinted in *Philosophical Studies.*

39. Russell, *Our Knowledge of the External World.*

40. G. E. Moore and G. F. Stout in "Symposium: The Status of Sense-Data," *Proceedings of the Aristotelian Society,* 14 (1913–14) 355–80; and G. E. Moore, "Some Judgments of Perception," *Proceedings of the Aristotelian Society* (1918–19) 1–29. Both reprinted in *Philosophical Studies.*

41. Moore, "Reply to My Critics," *Philosophy of G. E. Moore,* 627–67.

42. G. E. Moore, "The Conception of Reality," *Proceedings of the Aristotelian Society,* n.s. 18 (1917–18):101–20, and "External and Internal Relations," *Proceedings of the Aristotelian Society* (1919–20):40–62. Both in *Philosophical Studies.*

43. G. E. Moore, "An Analysis of Mind," *Times Literary Supplement,* London, Sept. 29, 1921, 622. Russell to Moore, Oct. 2, 1921. Bertrand Russell, "Analytic and Synthetic Philosophers," *The Nation and the Athenaeum* 31 (July 15, 1922):538–39.

44. Rosenbaum, "G. E. Moore's *The Elements of Ethics.*"

45. Russell, *Mysticism and Logic,* preface, v.

46. George Santayana, "The Philosophy of Mr. Bertrand Russell," in *Winds of Doctrine: Studies in Contemporary Opinion* (New York: Charles Scribner's Sons, 1913). Originally published in *The Journal of Philosophy, Psychology, and Scientific Methods* as "The Study of Essence," 8, no. 3 (Feb. 3, 1911):57–63; "The Critique of Pragmatism," 8, no. 5 (March 2, 1911):113–24; and "Hypostatic Ethics," 8, no. 16 (Aug. 3, 1911):421–32.

47. Russell, "Reply to Criticisms," *Philosophy of Bertrand Russell,* 720–25, G. E. Moore, "Reply to My Critics," *Philosophy of G. E. Moore,* 537–54.

48. Russell, "On the Notion of Cause with Application to the Free Will Problem," in *Our Knowledge of the External World.*

49. Russell's criticism in letter of Nov. 25, 1899; Moore's response in letter of Nov. 30, 1899.

50. Russell, "On the Notion of Cause," *Proceedings of the Aristotelian Society,* n.s. 13 (1912–13), reprinted in *Mysticism and Logic.* James Mark Baldwin, *Dictionary of Philosophy and Psychology,* 1902, reprinted 1940. The definitions of cause and effect in vol. 1:164–67 are close to those of Hume.

51. Ibid., vol. 2, 716–18 for Moore's definition of truth and falsity.

52. Moore, *Some Main Problems of Philosophy,* chap. 15.

53. See n. 42, above. Russell to Moore, Feb. 10, 1921.

54. Bertrand Russell, "Analytic and Synthetic Philosophers," *The Nation and the Athenaeum* 31 (July 15, 1922):538.

55. G. E. Moore, "Russell's 'Theory of Descriptions,'" in *The Philosophy of Bertrand Russell,* reprinted in *Philosophical Papers* (George Allen & Unwin, Ltd., 1959). See also Russell's response in "Reply to Criticisms" in LLP.

56. G. E. Moore, "Is Existence a Predicate?" *Proceedings of the Aristotelian Society,* supplementary vol. 15 (1936), reprinted in *Philosophical Papers.* See also G. E. Moore, "Wittgenstein's Lectures 1930–33," in *Philosophical Papers.*

57. G. E. Moore, "Four Forms of Scepticism," in *Philosophical Papers.* This article was based on lectures given in the United States, 1940–44.

58. Ibid., 226.

59. Bertrand Russell, "The Influence and Thought of G. E. Moore," *The Listener* (April 30, 1959):755–56.

4. *Russell, Frege, and Meinong Before 1905*

1. Bertrand Russell Archives, Mills Memorial Library, McMaster University, Hamilton, Ontario, Canada, Russell's notes and letters from Meinong; Gottlob Frege, *Nachgelassene Schriften und Wissenschaftlicher Briefwechsel,* ed. Gottfried Gabriel, Hans Hermes, Friedrich Kambartel, Christian Thiel, Albert Veraart, 2 vols. (Hamburg: Felix Meiner, 1976); Gottlob Frege, *Philosophical and Mathematical Correspondence,* abridged from the German edition by Brian McGuinness, trans. Hans Kaal. Alexius Meinong, *Philosophenbriefe aus der Wissenschaftlichen Korrespondenz von Alexius Meinong mit Franz Brentano (et al.)* (Graz: Akademische Druck— und Verlagsanstalt, 1965); Alexius Meinong, *Gesamtausgabe,* ed. R. Haller and R. Kindinger, 8 vols. (Graz: Akademische Druck—und Verlagsanstalt, 1968).

2. List of Meinong's and Russell's published responses and letters arranged chronologically:

(1) Meinong, *Über die Bedeutung des Weberschen Gesetzes,* Beitrage zur Psychologie des Vergleichens und Messens (Hamburg and Leipzig: Voss, 1896). Issued as a supplementary volume to *Zeitschrift für Psychologie und Physiologie der Sinnesorgane.*

(2) Russell, review of above work, *Mind,* n.s. 8 (1899):251–56.

(3) Meinong to J. S. Mackenzie, referring to Russell's review, Sept. 16, 1899. Bertrand Russell Archives, McMaster University.

(4) Meinong, "Über Gegenstände höherer Ordnung und deren Verhältnis zur inneren Wahrnehmung," *Zeitschrift für Psychologie und Physiologie der Sinnesorgan* 21 (1899):82–272.

(5) Meinong, "Abstrahieren und Vergleichen," *Zeitschrift für Psychologie und Physiologie der Sinnesorgane* 24 (1900):38–82.

(6) Meinong, *Über Annahmen* (Leipzig: Barth, 2d ed. 1910, 1st ed. 1902). This book was issued as a supplementary volume to *Zeitschrift für Psychologie und Physiologie der Sinnesorgane.*

(7) Russell, "Meinong's Theory of Complexes and Assumptions." See n. 6,

chap. 2, above.

(8) Meinong to Russell, December 7, 1904, Bertrand Russell Archives.

(9) Meinong, contribution to cooperative volume (#11) published 1904 "Über Gegenstandstheorie," sent to Russell separately with letter (#8).

(10) Russell to Meinong, Dec. 15, 1904, in Meinong, *Philosophenbriefe,* 137 (acknowledges #9).

(11) Meinong, et al., *Untersuchungen zur Gegenstandstheorie und Psychologie* (Leipzig: Barth, 1904).

(12) Russell, review of #11, *Mind,* n.s. 14 (1905):530–38.

(13) Russell, "On Denoting," *ibid.*

(14) Meinong, *Über die Erfahrungsgrundlagen unseres Wissens,* Abhandlungen zur Didaktik und Philosophie der Naturwissenschaft. Band I, Heft 6 (Berlin, 1906).

(15) Russell's review of #14, *Mind,* n.s. 15 (1906):412–15.

(16) Meinong to Russell, Oct. 24, 1906, Bertrand Russell Archives, sends item #18.

(17) Russell to Meinong, Nov. 5, 1906, in Meinong, *Philosophenbriefe,* 137–38.

(18) Meinong, *Über die Stellung der Gegenstandstheorie im System der Wissenschaften* (Leipzig: Voigtlander, 1907).

(19) Russell, review of #18, *Mind,* n.s. 16 (1907):436–39.

(20) Russell, letter to Meinong, Nov. 5, 1907, in Meinong, *Philosophenbriefe,* 138.

3. List of Frege's published work, Russell's relevant publications, and correspondence between them arranged chronologically based on Frege, *Philosophical and Mathematical Correspondence.* See n. 1, above.

(1) *Begriffsschrift, eine der arithmetischen nachgebildete Formalsprache des reinen Denkens* (Halle a.s. 1879). English trans. in T. W. Bynum (ed.), *Conceptual Notation and Related Articles* (Oxford: Clarendon Pr., 1972).

(2) "Anwendungen der Begriffsschrift," *Jenaische Zeitschrift für Naturwissenschaft* (hereafter *JZN*) 12 (1879): supplement 2, 29–33. For English trans., "Applications of the 'Conceptual Notation,'" see (1).

(3) "Über den Zweck der Begriffsschrift," *JZN* 16 (1883):supplement, 1–10. For English trans., "On the Aim of the 'Conceptual Notation,'" see (1).

(4) *Die Grundlagen der Arithmetik* (Breslau, 1884). English trans. by J. L. Austin, *The Foundations of Arithmetic* (Oxford: Basil Blackwell, 1950).

(5) Review of *Das Princip der Infinitesimal-Methode, und seine Geschichte,* H. Cohen, *Zeitschrift für Philosophie und philosophische Kritik* (hereafter *ZPPK*) 87 (1885):324–29.

(6) "Über formale Theorien der Arithmetik," *JZN* 19 (1886): Suppl. 94–104. English trans., "On Formal Theories of Arithmetic," in *On Formal Geometry and Formal Theories of Arithmetic,* trans. Eike-Henner W. Kluge (New Haven: Yale Univ. Pr. 1971).

(7) "Funktion und Begriff," *der Jenaischen Gesellschaft für Medizin und Naturwissenschaft* 9:1 (Jena: Verlag Hermann Pohle, 1891). English trans. "Function and Concept" in P. Geach and M. Black, *Translations from the Philosophical Writings of G. Frege,* 2d ed. (Oxford: Basil Blackwell, 1960).

(8) "Über das Tragheitsgesetz," *ZPPK* 1018 (1891): 145–61. English trans., "On the Law of Inertia," by H. Jackson and E. Levy in *Studies in History and Philosophy of Science* 2 (1971–72):195–212.

(9) "Über Sinn und Bedeutung," *ZPPK* 100 (1892):25–50. For English trans., "On Sense and Reference, see (7).

(10) "Über Begriff und Gegenstand," *Viertel jahresschrift für Wissenschaftliche Philosophie* 16 (1892) 192–205. For English trans., "On Concept and Object," see (7).

(11) *Grundgesetze der Arithmetik,* vol. 1 (Jena: Verlag Hermann Pohle, 1893). Partial English trans. by M. Furth, *The Basic Laws of Arithmetic* (Berkeley: Univ. of California Pr., 1964).

(12) "Le nombre entier," *Revue de Métaphysique et de la Morale* 3 (1895):73–78. English trans., "The Whole Number," in *Mind* 79 (1970): 481–86.

(13) "Kritische Beleuchtung einiger Punkte in E. Schröder's Vorlesungen über die Algebra der Logik," *Archiv für systematische Philosophie* 1 (1895):433–56. For English trans., "A Critical Elucidation of Some Points in E. Schroeder's *Algebra der Logik,*" see (7).

(14) "Lettera del Sig. G. Frege all 'Editore," *Revista di Matematica (Revue de Mathématiques)* 6 (1896–99):53–59.

(15) "Über die Begriffsschrift des Herrn Peano und meine eigene," Berichte über die Verhandlungen der Königlich Sächsischen Gesellschaft der Wissenschaften zu Leipzig, Mathematische-Physische Klasse 48 (1897):361–78. English trans. "On Herr Peano's Begriffsschrift and My Own," by V. H. Dudman, in *Australian Journal of Philosophy* 47 (1969):1–14.

(16) *Über die Zahlen des Herrn H. Schubert* (Jena, Verlag Hermann Pohle 1899).

(17) Russell to Frege, June 16, 1902, in Frege, *Philosophical and Mathematical Correspondence,* 130.

(18) Frege to Russell, June 22, 1902, ibid., 131.

(19) Russell to Frege, June 24, 1902, ibid., 133.

(20) Frege to Russell, June 29, 1902, ibid., 135.

(21) Russell to Frege, July 10, 1902, ibid., 137.

(22) Russell to Frege, July 24, 1902, ibid., 138.

(23) Russell to Frege, July 28, 1902, ibid., 139.

(24) Frege to Russell, Aug. 3, 1902, ibid., 142.

(25) Russell to Frege, Aug. 8, 1902, ibid., 143.

(26) Frege to Russell, Sept. 23, 1902, ibid., 145.

(27) Russell to Frege, Sept. 29, 1902, ibid., 147.

(28) Frege to Russell, Oct. 20, 1902, ibid., 149.

(29) Russell to Frege, Dec. 12, 1902, ibid., 150.

(30) *Grundgesetze der Arithmetik,* vol. 2 (Jena, Verlag Hermann Pohle 1903). Partial English translation, see (11).

(31) Frege to Russell, Dec. 28, 1902, ibid. Frege, *Correspondence,* 152.

(32) Russell to Frege, Feb. 20, 1902, ibid., 154.

(33) Russell, *The Principles of Mathematics.* Preface dated Dec. 1902, but appendix A on the work of Frege added later. Latter contains reference to items (1), (4), (6), (7), (9), (10), (11), (13), (15), above.

(34) Frege to Russell, May 21, 1903; Frege, *Correspondence,* 156.

(35) Russell to Frege, May 24, 1903, ibid., 158.

(36) Frege to Russell, Nov. 13, 1904, ibid., 160.

(37) Russell to Frege, Dec. 12, 1904, ibid., 166.

(38) Alfred North Whitehead and Bertrand Russell, *Principia Mathematica,* 3 vols. (Cambridge: Cambridge Univ. Pr.; 1 [1910], 2 [1912], 3 [1913].

(39) Frege to Russell, Sept., 6, 1912, Frege, *Correspondence,* 170 (acknowledges receipt of vol. 2).

4. Leonard Linsky, *Referring* (London: Routledge & Kegan Paul, 1967).

5. John R. Searle, "Russell's Objections to Frege's Theory of Sense and Reference," *Analysis* 18 ((1957–58): 137–43; reprinted in E. D. Klemke, *Essays on Frege* (Urbana: Univ. of Illinois Pr., 1968), 337–45.

6. J. N. Findlay, *Meinong's Theory of Objects and Values,* 2d ed. (Oxford: Clarendon Pr., 1963), chap. 11, especially 331–37.

7. Herbert Hochberg, "Russell's Attack on Frege's Theory of Meaning," *Philosophica* 18 (1976):9–34.

8. Gilbert Ryle, "Intentionality-Theory and the Nature of Thinking," in Rudolf Haller, ed., *Jenseits von Sein und Nichtsein* (Graz: Akademische Druck—und Verlaganstalt, 1972).

9. Rudolf Carnap, "Empiricism, Semantics, and Ontology," *Revue Internationale de Philosophie* 4, no. 11 (1950):20–40; W. V. Quine, *The Roots of Reference* (Lasalle, IL: Open Court Pub. Co., 1973); Nelson Goodman, *The Structure of Appearance,* 2nd ed. (Indianapolis: Bobbs Merrill, Inc., 1966).

10. Gustav Bergmann, *Logic and Reality* (Madison: The Univ. of Wisconsin Pr., 1964); Reinhardt Grossman, *The Structure of Mind* (Madison: The Univ. of Wisconsin Pr., 1965).

11. Donald Davidson, "Causal Relations," *Journal of Philosophy* 64 (1967): 691–703; reprinted in Myles Brand, ed., *The Nature of Causation* (Urbana: Univ. of Illinois Pr., 1976); Jaegwon Kim, "Causation, Nomic Subsumption, and the Concept of Event," *Journal of Philosophy* 70 (1973):217–36.

12. Karel Lambert, "Being and Being So," and Jaako Hintikka, "Knowledge by Acquaintance—Individuation by Acquaintance," in *Jenseits von Sein und Nichtsein.*

13. Terence Parsons, "A Meinongian Analysis of Fictional Objects," *Grazer Philosophische Studien* 1 (1973):73–86; R. Routley and V. Routley, "The (Logical) Importance of Not Existing," *Dialogue* (Canada) 18 (1979):129–65; Richard Routley, *Exploring Meinong's Jungle and Beyond* (Canberra: Australian National Univ., 1980). Terence Parsons, *Nonexistent Objects* (New Haven: Yale Univ. Pr., 1980).

14. Janet Farrell Smith, "Theory of Reference and Existential Presuppositions in Russell and Meinong" (Ph.D. diss., Columbia Univ., 1975). This study contains an interesting and thorough discussion of the issues between Meinong and Russell.

15. P. F. Strawson, "On Referring," *Mind* 59 (1950); reprinted in *Essays in Conceptual Analysis,* ed. Anthony Flew (London: Macmillan & Co., Ltd., 1960). (This essay has been frequently anthologized.) Russell, "Mr. Strawson on Referring," in "Some Replies to Criticism," in *My Philosophical Development,* 238–45. See also discussion in Linsky, *Referring,* 90–99.

16. Hans D. Sluga, "Frege's Alleged Realism," *Inquiry* 20 (1977):227–42.

17. Edgar Morscher, "Von Bolzano zu Meinong: zur Geschichte des Logischen

Realismus," in *Jenseits;* Hans Schermann, "Husserl II. *Logische Untersuchung und Meinong's Hume-Studien,"* in *Jenseits.*

18. Roderick M. Chisholm, "Editor's Introduction," in *Realism and the Background of Phenomenology* (New York: The Free Pr., 1960).

19. Chisholm's own work serves as an example of this interest; see Roderick M. Chisholm, *Perceiving: A Philosophical Study* (Ithaca: Cornell Univ. Pr., 1957).

20. Russell, *The Principles of Mathematics*, 43.

21. Ibid. Chap. 5 discusses denoting concepts; chap. 6 is concerned with intentional and extensional treatments of classes and problems of class membership.

22. Russell discusses his problems with philosophy of mathematics in the introduction to the second edition of *The Principles of Mathematics;* his opposition to empiricism emerges in the discussion of geometry on p. 373 and 374 of that book. For a general antiempiricist position, see "Meinong's Theory of Complexes and Assumptions," note 2 (7) above in Bertrand Russell, *Essays in Analysis,* ed. Douglas Lackey (New York: George Braziller, 1973), 22.

23. For an autobiographical account of this period of Russell's intellectual life see *My Philosophical Development,* chaps. 7 and 8; see also "My Mental Development," in *The Philosophy of Bertrand Russell;* for a list of articles published during this period see the bibliography in Schilpp, *The Philosophy of Bertrand Russell* 749–54.

24. For acknowledgments to Peano, see *The Principles of Mathematics,* xvi, 10–13; for criticisms see 27–32, 68. For debt to Frege see xvi.

25. Russell, *My Philosophical Development,* 70–75. See also the preface to *Principles of Mathematics.*

26. Russell to Frege, June 6, 1902. See n. 3 (18) and (19), above. in Frege, *Correspondence,* 130, 131, respectively. Frege to Russell, June 22, 1902.

27. Russell, *Principles,* appendix A, discussion of Frege, appendix B, discussion of contradiction and proposed solution.

28. For discussion of denoting concepts, *Principles,* 55–56; for discussion of Frege's "Sinn" and "Bedeutung," ibid., 502; for Frege's discussion of Russell's concept of the proposition, *Correspondence,* 162–65, Nov. 13, 1904. See n. 3 (36), above.

29. Russell recommends "Sinn" and "Bedeutung" to Meinong, Dec. 15, 1904. See n. 2 (10), above.

30. Russell's problem with the "sense" of names, appendix A, *Principles,* 502–3.

31. Russell's problems with "Gedanke," ibid., 502ff; *Correspondence,* 155–66. See n. 3, (32), (34), (35), (36), above.

32. Frege, *Correspondence,* 162–65, n. 3 (36), above.

33. Frege, *Correspondence,* Russell on truth-value as referent, 149–51, n. 3 (29), above; Frege's response, 152–53, n. 3 (31), above; Russell's misunderstanding of truth-value as referent, 134–36.

34. On the confusion of sign with thing signified, Frege, *Correspondence,* Frege's criticism, ibid., 149–50, n. 3 (28), above; on Russell's criticism of Frege as unduly psychological, *Principles,* 503.

35. Frege on functions, objects, and concepts, "Funktion und Begriff" "Über Begriff und Gegenstand," n. 3 (7), and (10) above respectively. Russell's report,

Principles, 505–7.

36. Frege on function and argument, n. 3 (10), above, in Frege, *Philosophical Writings,* tr. Geach and Black, 44–55.

37. Russell's objections to restriction of concept as subject and Frege's use of inverted commas, *Principles,* 507, 510.

38. Frege on function as unsaturated, *Correspondence,* 160–61, n. 3 (36), above. Russell on function as unsaturated, ibid., 166–69, n. 3 (37), above.

39. Rulon S. Wells, "Frege's Ontology," *Review of Metaphysics* 4 (1951):537–73; reprinted in *Essays on Frege,* ed. Klemke, 8.

40. For relation of proposition to "Annahme" see Frege, *Correspondence,* Russell, 159, n. 3 (35), above, Frege, 163, n. 3 (36), above.

41. Russell, *Principles,* 76ff.

42. Ibid., preface, xix; chap. 6, above.

43. Ibid., 522.

44. For a discussion and comparison of Russell and Frege at this period, see Jules Vuillemin, *Leçons sur la première philosophie de Russell* (Paris: Librairie Armand Colin, 1968), 195f; P. T. Geach and Max Black, eds., preface to Frege, *Translations from the Philosophical Writings of Frege* (Oxford: Basil Blackwell, 1952); P. T. Geach, "Quine on Classes and Properties," and P. T. Geach, "On Frege's Way Out," W. V. Quine, "On Frege's Way Out," in *Essays on Frege,* 479–514; 502–6; 485–501, respectively.

45. Russell, *Principles,* appendix B, 523–28.

46. "Frege on Russell's Paradox," tr. of appendix, vol. 2 of *Grundgesetze der Arithmetik,* in Geach and Black, *Philosophical Writings,* 253–65.

47. Ibid., 243.

48. See n. 44, above.

49. Robert Sternfeld, *Frege's Logical Theory* (Carbondale and Edwardsville: Southern Illinois Univ. Pr., 1966), chap. 7.

50. Weber's Laws (E. H. Weber) are described by William James in *Principles of Psychology,* 2 vols. (New York: Henry Holt Co., 1890), 1, 537. See n. 2 (1), above.

51. See n. 2 (1) through (7), above.

52. Meinong, "Gegenstandstheorie," translated as "Theory of Objects," in Chisholm, *Realism and the Background of Phenomenology.* See n. 2 (9), above.

53. Ibid., 83–86.

54. Alexius Meinong, *Über Emotionale Präsentation* (Vienna: Kaiserliche Akademie der Wissenschaften, 1917), tr. by M. L. Schubert-Kalsi as *Emotional Presentation* (Evanston, IL: Northwestern Univ. Pr., 1972). See "An Attempt to Make the Notion of Content More Precise" in that volume.

55. Russell, "Meinong's Theory of Objects and Assumptions," in Douglas Lackey, ed., *Essays in Analysis,* 59–68; see n. 7, chap. 2, above.

56. Ibid., 25–27.

57. Ibid., 54.

58. Ibid., 67–68.

59. Ibid., 63–64.

60. Ibid., 45–46.

61. Ibid., 56–57.

62. Ibid., 74–75.

63. Ibid., 75.
64. Ibid., 76.
65. Ibid.
66. Russell, n. 2 (12) above. Review of *Gegenstandstheorie.*

5. *Russell, Frege, and Meinong: 1905 and After*

1. Russell, *My Philosophical Development,* 83.

2. There are a large number of discussions of Russell's criticisms of Frege, including those in A. J. Ayer, *Russell and Moore: The Analytical Heritage;* Ronald Jager, *The Development of Bertrand Russell's Philosophy* (London: George Allen & Unwin, Ltd., 1972); Michael Dummett, *Frege: Philosophy of Language* (London: Gerald Duckworth & Company, Ltd., 1973). In addition see Searle and Hochberg (nn. 5 and 7, chap. 4, above), Chrystin E. Cassin, "Russell's Discussion of Meaning and Denotation: A Re-examination," in *Essays on Bertrand Russell,* ed. Klemke; P. T. Geach, "Russell on Meaning and Denotation," *Analysis* 20 (1959):53–62; M. Brian McMahon, "Russell's Denoting Relation," *The Personalist* 57:4 (1976), 345–50; S. Blackburn and A. Code, "The Power of Russell's Criticism of Frege, 'On Denoting', pp. 48–50," *Analysis* 38 (1978):65–77. See also the response to this last article in the same issue by P. T. Geach and further discussion in vol. 39 of *Analysis.*

3. All references to "On Denoting" refer to its appearance in Bertrand Russell, *Logic and Knowledge,* 49–56, n. 2 (13), chap 4, above.

4. Willard Van Orman Quine, *From a Logical Point of View: Logico-Philosophical Essays* (Cambridge: Harvard Univ. Pr. 1953) 1–2.

5. See nn. 5 and 7, chap. 4, above.

6. Russell, "On Denoting," 46, second footnote.

7. Ibid., 49–50.

8. Frege, *Correspondence,* 152; n. 3 (31), chap 1, above.

9. Ibid., 153–54.

10. Ibid., 72–81, appendix, Philip E. B. Jourdain, "Gottlob Frege." See also Grattan-Guinness, *Dear Russell-Dear Jourdain.*

11. Ibid., Jourdain, 78; Frege's answer, 79–80.

12. Ibid., 81–84.

13. Ibid., 74.

14. Ibid., 191.

15. Victor Lenzen records the importance given to Meinong in "Bertrand Russell at Harvard, 1914," *Russell: Journal of the Bertrand Russell Archives* 3 (1971):4–6. See also Lenzen's notes from the seminar in manuscript form in the Bancroft Library, University of California, Berkeley. For the 1913 manuscript on theory of knowledge see Bertrand Russell, *Theory of Knowledge: The 1913 Manuscript,* ed. Elizabeth R. Eames and Kenneth Blackwell, *The Collected Papers of Bertrand Russell,* vol. 7 (London: George Allen & Unwin, Ltd., 1984). The influence of Meinong on Russell in this work is argued for by Douglas Lackey in "Russell's 1913 Map of the Mind" in *The Foundation of Analytical Philosophy,* Midwest Studies in Philosophy, vol. 6, ed. Peter Finch, et al. (Minneapolis: Univ. of Minnesota Pr., 1981).

16. Bertrand Russell, "On the Nature of Acquaintance," *Monist* 24 (Jan., Apr.,

July 1914):1–16, 160–87, 435–53; reprinted in Russell, *Logic and Knowledge,* 124–74.

17. Russell, *Theory of Knowledge: 1913 Manuscript,* 108–13, 232, and appendix B. 1., 195.

18. Ibid., 152–53. "The theory in question has, however, been held; for example, there is an author who states it in the following terms. . . ." Russell goes on to quote a 1904 article without mentioning that the author in question is Russell himself.

19. Ibid., 160–64.

20. Bertrand Russell, *The Analysis of Mind* (London: George Allen & Unwin, Ltd., 1921) 14–18, 163–64, 262–63.

21. Nicholas Griffin, "Russell's 'Horrible Travesty of Meinong,'" *Russell: Journal of the Bertrand Russell Archives* (1977):39–51. The reference is to Findlay, *Meinong's Theory of Objects and Values,* xi–xii. See also Ronald Suter, "Russell's 'Refutation' of Meinong in 'On Denoting,'" *Philosophy and Phenomenological Research* 217 (1967):511–16. See also Elizabeth R. Eames, "Russell's Study of Meinong," *Russell* (1972):3–6.

6. Russell and Whitehead

1. Russell, "My Mental Development," *The Philosophy of Bertrand Russell,* 8, 12, 13. Russell, *Autobiography,* vol. 1, chap. 6, 127–30; vol. 2, 65, 78, 235, 257. A. N. Whitehead, "Autobiographical Notes," *The Philosophy of Alfred North Whitehead,* Vol. 3, Library of Living Philosophers, ed. Paul Arthur Schilpp (Evanston and Chicago: Northwestern Univ., 1941), 10–11.

2. Alfred North Whitehead, *A Treatise on Universal Algebra,* vol. 1 (Cambridge: Cambridge Univ. Pr., 1898).

3. Russell, *The Principles of Mathematics,* preface to 1st ed., 4. Whitehead and Russell, *Principia Mathematica,* see n. 4 (38), chap. 4 above.

4. Russell, *Autobiography,* vol. 1, chap. 6. Bertrand Russell, *My Philosophical Development* chaps. 7 and 8.

5. Letters from A. N. Whitehead to Bertrand Russell, Bertrand Russell Archives, McMaster University; for example, May 25, 1904, March 9, 1908. See also letters from Russell to Morrell, Harry Ransom Humanities Research Center, University of Texas at Austin; for letters mentioning how busy Whitehead was, see, for example, Russell's letters of Oct. 6, 1911, and Sept. 3, 1912.

6. Whitehead to Russell, Sept. 28, 1903, mentions that some of what Russell has written offends against the rules of symbolism, but in other respects is "exactly what is wanted." Also see below, n. 32.

7. Russell, *Autobiography,* vol. 2, 145–46.

8. Ronald W. Clark, *The Life of Bertrand Russell,* 84–89.

9. Russell, *Autobiography,* vol. 1, chap 6. See also Russell's diary in the Bertrand Russell Archives, McMaster University.

10. Whitehead to Russell, Oct. 20, 1916.

11. Russell to Morrell concerning the closeness of Russell to the Whiteheads: #8 (March 3, 1911), #149 and #150 (July 15, 1911, and July 17, 1911). For Russell's relations with Whitehead's children see letters of May 8, 1911, May 9, 1911, and the description of Russell's walking tour with North and Eric, summer of 1913.

12. On the relation of Evelyn Whitehead to Ottoline Morrell, see Russell to Morrell, #7 and #8 of March 28, 1911.

13. Russell to Morrell, #963 Jan. 2, 1914.

14. Russell to Morrell, #1070 Aug. 14, 1914. Quoted in Clark, *The Life of Bertrand Russell*, 248–49.

15. Whitehead to Russell, April 16, 1916. In part the letter reads: "I am miserable at differing from you on so great a question. I cannot see what other course was open to us than the one which we actually took." There follows a defense of the necessity of Britain declaring war on Germany. The letter concludes "I wonder where you are." It is signed "Yours affectionately, Alfred N. Whitehead." Quoted in Clark, *The Life of Bertrand Russell*, 249.

16. The Whiteheads to Bertrand Russell in regard to Russell's arrest and subsequent trial and conviction: June 4 and 5, 1916, Sept 14, 1916, April 1, 1918.

17. Russell, *Autobiography*, vol. 2, 78.

18. A. H. Johnson, *Whitehead's Theory of Reality* (Boston: Beacon Pr., 1952), chap. 7.

19. For a discussion of this dichotomy, see Richard M. Rorty, "The Subjectivist Principle and the Linguistic Turn," in *Alfred North Whitehead: Essays on His Philosophy*, ed. George L. Kline (Englewood Cliffs, NJ: Prentice Hall, 1963).

20. Victor Lowe, "The Development of Whitehead's Philosophy" in *The Philosophy of Alfred North Whitehead*, a careful study that includes the relation between Russell and Whitehead. See also Victor Lowe, "A. N. Whitehead on His Mathematical Goals: A Letter of 1912," *Annals of Science* 32 (1975):85–101.

21. Whitehead, *A Treatise on Universal Algebra*, v.

22. Ibid., viii.

23. Whitehead, "Autobiographical Notes," *The Philosophy of Alfred North Whitehead*, 9.

24. W. V. Quine, "Whitehead and the Rise of Modern Logic," in *The Philosophy of Alfred North Whitehead*.

25. Russell, *The Principles of Mathematics*, 2d ed., xv.

26. Ibid., xvi.

27. Whitehead and Russell, *Principia*, 1.

28. Ibid., 55.

29. Ibid., preface to first edition, vi.

30. Russell, *My Philosophical Development*, 74.

31. Quoted from a letter of Whitehead to Russell in *Autobiography*, vol. 1, 151.

32. Whitehead to Russell, undated, from end of 1905 to early 1906. Bertrand Russell Archives.

33. Discussion of dependent variable, Feb. 26, 1906; of intension and extension, June 16, 1907; of types and individual, Jan. 6, 1908. These are a few examples from the letters of Whitehead to Russell during the period of their working on *Principia Mathematica*.

34. The following items are listed in the bibliography of Whitehead's publications for this period (from *The Philosophy of Alfred North Whitehead*, 706–8): "Sets of Operations in Relation to Groups of Finite Order," abstract only published, *Proceedings of the Royal Society of London* 64 (1898–99), 319–20. "Memoir on the Algebra of Symbolic Logic," *American Journal of Mathematics* 23, no. 2 (1901):139–

65, and no. 4 (1901):297–316; "On Cardinal Numbers," *American Journal of Mathematics* 24, no. 4 (1902):367–94: "The Logic of Relations, Logical Substitution Groups, and Cardinal Numbers," *American Journal of Mathematics* 25, no. 2 (1903): 157–78; "Theorems on Cardinal Numbers," *American Journal of Mathematics* 26, no. 1 (1904):31–32; "The Axioms of Projective Geometry," *Cambridge Tracts in Mathematics and Mathematical Physics,* no. 4 (Cambridge: Cambridge Univ. Press, 1906).

35. Russell, *My Philosophical Development,* 99. See also Whitehead to Russell, Oct. 12, 1909, for topics on which he was working and which were apparently to be part of vol. 4.

36. For references see n. 7, chap 2, above.

37. Alfred North Whitehead, *An Introduction to Mathematics,* Home University Library of Modern Knowledge (London: Williams and Norgate, Ltd., 1911).

38. Russell, *Our Knowledge of the External World,* 7–8.

39. Russell, *Principles of Mathematics,* 2d ed., 1927, xi.

40. Ibrahim Najjar and Heather Kirkconnell, "Russell's Foreword to the First German Translation of *The Problems of Philosophy,*" *Russell: The Journal of the Bertrand Russell Archives* 17 (1975), 27–29.

41. Alfred North Whitehead, "On Mathematical Concepts of the Material World," *Philosophical Transactions of the Royal Society* (1906), reprinted in *Alfred North Whitehead: An Anthology,* ed. F. S. C. Northrop and Mason W. Gross (New York: The Macmillan Co., 1953), 11.

42. Ibid., 32.

43. Whitehead to Russell, Sept. 3, 1911.

44. Bertrand Russell, "The Philosophical Importance of Mathematical Logic," trans. P. E. B. Jourdain, *Monist* 23 (October 1913):481–93. (Originally given as a paper to a conference of L'École des Hautes Études in Paris, March 1911. Published as "L'Importance philosophique de la logistique," *Revue de Métaphysique et de Morale* (May 1911):281–91.)

45. Victor Lowe, "Whitehead's 1911 Criticism of *The Problems of Philosophy,*" *Russell: The Journal of the Bertrand Russell Archives* 13 (1974):3–11.

46. Ibid., 7.

47. Ibid., 6.

48. Whitehead to Russell, Jan. 5, 1908.

49. Russell to Morrell, Dec. 28, 1912.

50. Ibid., #675, Jan. 19, 1913.

51. Ibid. In an undated letter cataloged as #950, Russell speaks of reading a "pile of manuscripts" of Whitehead's. The catalog number would lead one to date the letter as late 1913.

52. Alfred North Whitehead, "La Théorie relationniste de l'espace," *Revue de Métaphysique et de Morale* 23 (May 1916):423–54. The paraphrase of the contents of this article is based on a translation by Elizabeth R. Eames.

53. Russell to Morrell, #982, Feb. 2, 1914.

54. See n. 52, above.

55. Alfred North Whitehead, "The Organisation of Thought," *Report of the 86th Meeting of the British Association for the Advancement of Science* (1916):355–64, reprinted as chap. 6 in *The Organisation of Thought* (London: Williams and Norgate,

1917) and as chap. 8 in *The Aims of Education and Other Essays* (New York: The Macmillan Co., 1929). Current references are to the last mentioned book. Alfred North Whitehead, "The Anatomy of Some Scientific Ideas," first published as chap. 7 in *The Organisation of Thought,* subsequently published as chap. 9 of *The Aims of Education,* to which current references apply.

56. Whitehead, *The Aims of Education,* 128–29.

57. Ibid., 133.

58. Russell, *Our Knowledge of the External World;* Bertrand Russell, "The Relation of Sense-Data to Physics," *Scientia* 16 (1914):1–27; Bertrand Russell, "The Ultimate Constituents of Matter," *Monist* 25:3 (1915)399–417 both articles reprinted in *Mysticism and Logic.*

59. Whitehead to Russell, Aug. 28, 1914.

60. See above, p. 103–4.

61. Alfred North Whitehead, *An Equiry Concerning the Principles of Natural Knowledge* (Cambridge: Cambridge Univ. Pr., 1919), preface.

62. Ibid., reprinted in Northrup and Gross, 168.

63. Alfred North Whitehead, *The Concept of Nature* (Cambridge: Cambridge Univ. Pr., 1920), reprinted in Northrop and Gross, 220–21.

64. Ibid., chap. 3.

65. Ibid., 281.

66. Ibid., 291.

67. A. Lawrence Lowell to Russell, June 6, 1913. Quoted in Russell, *Theory of Knowledge: 1913 Manuscript,* xxiii. Letter in Bertrand Russell Archives.

68. Bertrand Russell, "Philosophy of Logical Atomism," *Monist* 28 (1918):495–527; 29 (1919):32–63, 190–222, 345–80. Bertrand Russell, *Introduction to Mathematical Philosophy* (London: George Allen & Unwin, Ltd., 1919). References to Whitehead occur on pp. 64, 76, and 107. The reference to Wittgenstein occurs on p. 205n.

69. Russell, *The Analysis of Mind;* Bertrand Russell, *The Analysis of Matter* (London: George Allen & Unwin, Ltd., 1927). Compare the interpretation of the two books by W. T. Stace, "Russell's Neutral Monism," in *The Philosophy of Bertrand Russell* with Russell's own comments, 702–3; also with Elizabeth R. Eames, *Bertrand Russell's Theory of Knowledge,* chap. 4.

70. Russell, *Analysis of Matter,* 4.

71. Ibid., 9.

72. Ibid., 138.

73. Ibid., 144–46.

74. Ibid., 199.

75. Ibid., 200.

76. Ibid., 292.

77. Ibid., 247.

78. Bertrand Russell, "Science, Relativity and Religion," *The Nation and Athenaeum* 39 (May 29, 1926):206. The above article is a review of Alfred North Whitehead, *Science and the Modern World.* Lowell Institute Lectures, 1925 (New York: The Macmillan Co., 1925).

79. Bertrand Russell, *Portraits from Memory* (New York: Simon and Schuster, 1956), 39.

80. Alfred North Whitehead, "Note," *Mind* 35 (1926):130.

7. *Russell and Wittgenstein*

1. Russell, *My Philosophical Development,* 110–27. Russell, *Autobiography,* 98–101. Russell, "My Mental Development," *The Philosophy of Bertrand Russell.*

2. Clark, *The Life of Bertrand Russell,* 206. B. F. McGuinness, "Bertrand Russell and Ludwig Wittgenstein's 'Notes on Logic,'" *Revue Internationale de Philosophie* 26 (1972):444–60. G. H. von Wright, "Historical Introduction" to Ludwig Wittgenstein, *Prototractatus,* ed. B. F. McGuinness, T. Nyberg, G. H. von Wright, trans. D. F. Pears and B. F. McGuinness (Ithaca, N.Y.: Cornell Univ. Pr., 1971), 3–34. Kenneth Blackwell, "Wittgenstein's Impact on Russell's Theory of Belief," (Master's thesis, McMaster Univ., 1974). D. F. Pears, "The Relation Between Wittgenstein's Picture Theory of Propositions and Russell's Theories of Judgment," *Philosophical Review* 86 (April 1977):177–96.

3. Ludwig Wittgenstein, *Philosophical Investigations,* ed. G. E. M. Anscombe and R. Rhees, trans. G. E. M. Anscombe (Oxford: Basil Blackwell, 1953, 2d ed., 1958), 638–47.

4. For example, Ludwig Wittgenstein, *Letters to C. K. Ogden with comments on the English translation of the Tractatus Logico-Philosophicus,* ed. with intro by G. H. von Wright (Oxford: Basil Blackwell, 1973). The letters clarify the part played by Wittgenstein in the publishing of the first English translation of the *Tractatus Logico-Philosophicus* and dispel the impression that the edition did not have Wittgenstein's approval or participation. Ludwig Wittgenstein, *Tractatus Logico-Philosophicus* (London: Routledge & Kegan Paul, 1922). See Georg Henrik von Wright, "Biographical Sketch," in Norman Malcolm, *Ludwig Wittgenstein: A Memoir* (Oxford: Oxford Univ. Pr., 1958), 12. The relationship of the two versions of the "Notes on Logic" is now clear: see McGuinness, "Bertrand Russell and Ludwig Wittgenstein's 'Notes on Logic,'" cited above.

5. See *Prototractatus,* n. 2, above. Also see Kenneth Blackwell and Elizabeth Ramsden Eames, "Russell's Unpublished Book on Theory of Knowledge," *Russell: Journal of the Bertrand Russell Archives* 19 (1975):3–18. Elizabeth Ramsden Eames, "Introduction," *Theory of Knowledge: The 1913 Manuscript.*

6. Russell, *Autobiography,* 1, 201–14. See also the letters of Russell to Morrell.

7. Bertrand Russell, "On the Relation of Universals to Particulars," *Proceedings of the Aristotelian Society,* n.s. 12 (1912):1–24. Russell, "Knowledge by Acquaintance and Knowledge by Description."

8. Russell to Morrell, #286, Dec. 11, 1913. *Autobiography,* vol. 1, 153.

9. Russell, Morrell, March 7, 8, 1912.

10. Bertrand Russell, "Le Réalisme analytique," *Bulletin de la Société française de Philosophie* 11 (1911):153–82.

11. Russell, "The Philosophical Importance of Mathematical Logic." See also "Logic as the Essence of Philosophy," in Russell, *Our Knowledge of the External World.*

12. Russell, *The Principles of Mathematics,* chap. 4.

13. Russell, "Meinong's Theory of Complexes and Assumptions." see pp. 84–86 above.

14. Whitehead and Russell, *Principia Mathematica,* 1 "Introduction," chap. 2, section 4.

15. Bertrand Russell, "What Is Logic?", 220.011430 Bertrand Russell Archives. Whitehead to Russell, May 5, 1906. Bertrand Russell Archives. "False propositions are a great difficulty to me. You say — and this seems sense — there is only the fact that Caesar is dead, and there is not in addition the truth of the proposition 'Caesar is dead' — but then what the devil is there in respect to 'Caesar is not dead'!"

16. Russell, "On the Nature of Truth and Falsehood," 153–56.

17. Ibid., 155. Truth is predicated of belief, judgment, and statements. Although the discussion concerns *beliefs,* in fact, Russell shifts from referring to the judgment that *Charles I died in his bed* to the judgment concerning Charles's death, and bed; see p. 155 in particular. See also "Knowledge by Acquaintance and Knowledge by Description" in *Mysticism and Logic,* 218–29.

18. Von Wright, "Biographical Sketch," 4–6.

19. Russell to Morrell, #225, Oct. 18, 1911.

20. Russell to Morrell, between Oct. 18, 1911 and March 19, 1912.

21. Russell to Morrell, #388, March 17, 1912.

22. Russell to Morrell, #565, Sept. 5, 1912.

23. Russell to Morrell, #459, May 12, 1912.

24. Russell to Morrell, #803, June 10, 1913.

25. Russell to Morrell, #460, May 22, 1912.

26. Wittgenstein to Russell, R2. Cambridge June 22, 1912. Also R. 5 (Aug. 16, 1912) in Wittgenstein, *Letters to Russell, Keynes and Moore.*

27. Russell, "What Is Logic?"

28. Wittgenstein to Russell, R9, Jan. 1913, *Letters to Russell, Keynes and Moore.*

29. S. I. Sommerville, "Types, Categories, and Significance" (Ph.D. diss., McMaster Univ., 1979).

30. Russell to Morrell, #768, May 8, 1913. Quoted in Russell, *Theory of Knowledge: 1913 Manuscript,* xxiii.

31. Blackwell and Eames, "Russell's Unpublished Book on Theory of Knowledge."

32. See Russell's letters to Morrell during May and June of 1913 for accounts of the progress of the work and topics discussed.

33. Eames, "Introduction," see n. 5, above.

34. Russell to Morrell, #782, May 21, 1913. For discussion of "former" theory see Russell, "On the Nature of Truth and Falsehood," in *Philosophical Essays.* See pp. 29–30, above.

35. Ludwig Wittgenstein, "Notes on Logic," Sept. 1913 in Ludwig Wittgenstein, *Notebooks 1914–1916,* ed. G. H. von Wright and G. E. M. Anscombe (Oxford: Basil Blackwell, 1969), 96.

36. Russell, *Theory of Knowledge: 1913 Manuscript,* chap. 7 of Part I.

37. See n. 34, above.

38. Russell to Morrell, #785, May 24, 1913.

39. Sommerville, "Types, Categories, and Significance," appendix A.

40. Russell, *The Problems of Philosophy,* 91.

41. Russell to Morrell, #785, May 24, 1913.

42. Russell, *Theory of Knowledge: 1913 Manuscript,* appendix A.4., 187.

43. Russell to Morrell, #787, May 28, 1913.

44. Russell, *Theory of Knowledge: 1913 Manuscript,* 107–08, 232.

45. Ibid., 115–16.

46. Ibid., 111.

47. Ibid., 111–12.

48. Sommerville, "Types, Categories, and Significance," appendix A.

49. Russell, *Theory of Knowledge: 1913 Manuscript,* 113. For "former" see p. 145–46, above.

50. Ibid., 115.

51. Ibid., 117–18.

52. Ibid., 122.

53. Wittgenstein, "Notes on Logic," 103.

54. Russell, *Theory of Knowledge: 1913 Manuscript,* 128.

55. Ibid., 137.

56. Russell to Morrell, #811, June 20, 1913. Nicholas Griffin has pointed out that this letter followed a meeting with Wittgenstein and his mother and, possibly, a clarification of the full impact of Wittgenstein's criticisms. See Nicholas Griffin, "Russell's Multiple Relation Theory of Judgment," *Foundations of Logic Conference,* Univ. of Waterloo, April 1982.

57. Russell to Morrell, #900, Oct. 24, 1913.

58. Wittgenstein to Russell, R. 12, June 1913, in *Letters to Russell, Keynes and Moore.*

59. Ibid., R. 13.

60. Russell to Morrell, #858, Aug. 29, 1913.

61. Russell to Donnelly, Oct. 19, 1913.

62. Russell, *Theory of Knowledge: 1913 Manuscript,* appendix B.1, "Props." 194–99.

63. See n. 2, above. McGuinness, "Bertrand Russell and Ludwig Wittgenstein's 'Notes on Logic.'"

64. Wittgenstein, "Notes on Logic," 93.

65. Russell, *Theory of Knowledge: 1913 Manuscript,* 46.

66. Wittgenstein, "Notes on Logic," 99, 104.

67. Sommerville, "Types, Categories, and Significance," appendix A.

68. Wittgenstein, "Notes on Logic," 96, 99–103.

69. Blackwell, "Wittgenstein's Impact on Russell's Theory of Belief," 77. Blackwell argues that Russell's theory of judgment in the theory of knowledge manuscript was not vulnerable to Wittgenstein's criticism.

70. Wittgenstein, "Notes on Logic," 99.

71. Ibid., 103.

72. Ibid., 104.

73. Russell, *Our Knowledge of the External World,* 9. For acknowledgment to the *Tractatus Logico-Philosophicus,* see 213.

74. Russell, *Theory of Knowledge: 1913 Manuscript,* 46.

75. Russell, *Mysticism and Logic,* 221.

76. Russell, *Introduction to Mathematical Philosophy,* chap. 18.

77. Russell, "The Philosophy of Logical Atomism," reprinted in *Logic and*

Knowledge. For reference to Wittgenstein see *Logic and Knowledge,* 177.

78. Russell, *My Philosophical Development,* 113.

79. Wittgenstein, "Notes on Logic," 94–95.

80. Russell to Morrell, #929, Feb. 17, 1914.

81. Russell to Morrell, #1542, Dec. 20, 1919. Wittgenstein, *Letters to Russell Keynes and Moore,* R. 43, R. 4, R. 45, R. 46.

82. Ibid., R. 48.

83. Whitehead and Russell, *Principia Mathematica.* Russell, *The Analysis of Matter.* Russell, *An Inquiry into Meaning and Truth.* Russell, *My Philosophical Development,* chap. 10.

84. Whitehead and Russell, *Principia Mathematica,* 2d ed., Introduction to the Second Edition, xiv.

85. F. P. Ramsey to L. Wittgenstein, Feb. 20, 1924 in Ludwig Wittgenstein, *Letters to C. K. Ogden,* 85.

86. Russell, *My Philosophical Development,* 113–19.

87. Russell, *Analysis of Matter,* 171.

88. Ibid., 173.

89. J. Vuillemin, *Leçons sur la première philosophie de Russell* 237–40.

90. Russell to Morrell, #388, March 17, 1912.

91. Russell, *Our Knowledge of the External World,* 7–9, 68–69.

92. For Russell's use of psychology during the period of Wittgenstein's influence, see "On Propositions: What They Are and How They Mean" (1919) in Russell, *Logic and Knowledge.* The primary example of the use of psychology is Russell's *Analysis of Mind* of 1921.

93. Russell, *Autobiography,* 2, 100.

94. Malcolm, *Ludwig Wittgenstein: A Memoir,* 68.

95. Russell, *My Philosophical Development,* 216.

8. *Russell and the Pragmatists*

1. Mention is made of meeting Peirce in America in Russell's letter to Louis Couturat, Feb. 11, 1899, Bertand Russell Archives. See also correspondence with Lady Victoria Welby in the same archives. See also Peirce's review of *The Principles of Mathematics, The Nation* (October 15, 1903). Russell, *Introduction to Mathematical Philosophy,* 32n. See also Russell's reference to Peirce's contribution to pragmatism in "Pragmatism," in *The Edinburgh Review* 209:428 (April, 1909)363–388.

2. Russell, *Philosophical Essays,* Preface.

3. Russell, *Autobiography,* 2, 126, 230–32.

4. Schiller to Russell, Bertrand Russell Archives, McMaster University: Russell to Schiller, the library of the University of California, Los Angeles.

5. The similarity of Schiller and Wittgenstein is noted by Reuben Abel in his "General Introduction" to his book of selections from Schiller, ed. *Humanistic Pragmatism: The Philosophy of F. C. S. Schiller* (New York: The Free Pr., 1966), 10–11. In the volume *Pragmatic Philosophy, An Anthology,* ed. Amelie Rorty (Garden City, NY: Doubleday Anchor, 1966), Amelie Rorty includes J. L. Austin's "Performative Utterances" and notes the unacknowledged similarity with the pragmatic theory of meaning, 458–59. In the same volume, Gertrude Ezorsky in "Truth in Context"

notes the similarity in the work of Strawson and Dewey. A similar comment could be made about the pragmatic criticism of a naming theory of language and a similar critique by Gilbert Ryle in "The Theory of Meaning," in *British Philosophy at Mid-Century,* ed. C. A. Mace (London: George Allen & Unwin, Ltd., 1957). Morton White finds problems of meaning central to twentieth-century philosophy as the common interest of analysts. Ernst Mach, Russell and Moore, Peirce and James are seen as the progenitors of the major schools of analytic philosophy in our time. Morton White, "New Horizons in Philosophy," in *Pragmatism and the American Mind* (Oxford: Oxford Univ. Pr. 1973), 173–74.

6. The remark about Schiller being responsible for the neglect of pragmatism was made to me several times by philosophers in Britain in the late 1940s. A. J. Ayer, *The Origins of American Pragmatism* (San Francisco: Freeman, Cooper & Co., 1968), viii. The quoted references to Dewey and Schiller are the only treatment of them in his book and occur on pp. 4–5. In his review of Ayer's book, Morton White says, "In this book he [Ayer] is bringing home a report, which may be news to some, that two Americans had begun to create an original and powerful philosophy before Russell, Moore, and Wittgenstein were born." White goes on to criticize the treatment of James from the bias of Vienna, in "Logical Positivism and the Pragmatism of James," in *Pragmatism and the American Mind,* 114.

7. F. C. S. Schiller, *Humanism: Philosophical Essays* (Oxford: Oxford Univ. Pr., 1903), xii.

8. Quoted by Reuben Abel in "General Introduction" to *Humanistic Pragmatism,* 7.

9. William James, *The Letters of William James,* 2 vols., ed. Henry James (Boston: The Atlantic Monthly Pr., 1920), 2, 270–73 (letter of April 19, 1907), 280–82 (May 18, 1907).

10. Kenneth Winetrout, *F. C. S. Schiller and the Dimensions of Pragmatism* (Columbus: Ohio State Univ. Pr., 1967), 30–31.

11. Schiller to Russell, April 17, 1919.

12. Reuben Abel, ed., *Humanistic Pragmatism,* "General Introduction."

13. Schiller to Russell, Aug. 12, 1915.

14. Bertrand Russell, "Dr. Schiller's Analysis of *The Analysis of* Mind," *Journal of Philosophy* 19, no. 24 (1922):645.

15. Schiller to Russell, Jan. 3, 1903.

16. See pp. 84–85, above.

17. Russell, "On the Nature of Truth and Falsehood," in *Philosophical Essays.*

18. Bertrand Russell, "Metaphysics for the Man of Action," *The Nation,* London (March 2, 1907):44–45. Unsigned but identified by "By Bertie Russell" written on a clipping of the article in the hand of Alys Russell, in Bertrand Russell Archives. See also the March 7, 1908 letter of Schiller in response.

19. Bertrand Russell, "On the Nature of Truth," ms. in Bertrand Russell Archives, Cat. No. 220.011250.

20. Ibid.

21. Schiller to Russell, April 7, 1907.

22. Russell, "Transatlantic 'Truth,'" *The Albany Review,* n.s. 2, no. 10 (1908): 393–410.

23. Schiller to Russell, Oct. 28, 1907.

24. Schiller to Russell, Jan. 22, 1908.

25. Schiller to Russell, March 23, 1909.

26. Ibid.

27. Russell to Morrell, #356, Feb. 23, 1912. "I am in a state of fury because Schiller has sent me a book on formal logic which he has had the impertinence to write. He neither knows nor respects the subject and of course writes offensive rot. I am already thinking of jokes I will make if I have it to review. . . . I don't really dislike Schiller; I am the only human being who doesn't." Russell to Schiller, Feb. 23, 1912. F. C. S. Schiller, *Formal Logic: A Scientific and Social Problem* (London: The Macmillan Co., 1912). Bertrand Russell, "Pragmatism and Logic," *The Nation* 11, no. 7 (May 18, 1912).

28. Schiller to Russell, April 11, 1912.

29. Russell, "Pragmatism and Logic."

30. Schiller to Russell, May 19, 1912.

31. Schiller to Russell, May 29, 1912.

32. Schiller to Russell, Dec. 13, 1912. Bertrand Russell, "The Philosophy of Bergson," *Monist* 22, no. 3 (July 1912):321–47, repr. in *Mysticism and Logic*.

33. Schiller to Russell, Feb. 27, 1913.

34. Schiller to Russell, Aug. 19, 1914, Aug. 12, 1915, Aug. 18, 1915.

35. This article in question was sent in response to a request and thus can be assumed to be Russell's review of John Dewey's *Essays in Experimental Logic* in *The Journal of Philosophy* 16 (1919):5–26. Schiller to Russell, April 17, 1919.

36. Bertrand Russell, "On Propositions: What They are and How They Mean." *Proceedings of the Aristotelian Society,* supp. vol. 2 (1919) 1–43. Repr. in *Logic and Knowledge.* F. C. S. Schiller, B. Russell, and H. H. Joachim, "The Meaning of 'Meaning,'" *Mind* 29 (1920), 385–414.

37. Ibid., 404.

38. F. C. S. Schiller, "Mr. Russell's Psychology," *The Journal of Philosophy* 19 (1922):281–92; for bibliographical data on Russell's response see n. 14, above.

39. Russell, "Dr. Schiller's Analysis," 645.

40. For William James's exchange of letters with Bertrand Russell, James's annotations on two copies of Russell's "Transatlantic 'Truth,'" and James's response to Russell in "Two English Critics," see William James, *The Meaning of Truth,* ed. Frederick B. Burkhardt, Fredson Bowers, and Ignas K. Skrupskelis (Cambridge: Harvard Univ. Pr., 1975).

41. Bertrand Russell, "The Philosophy of William James," *The Nation,* London (Sept. 3, 1910):793–94.

42. James to Russell, Oct. 4, 1908 in James, *Meaning of Truth,* 299–300. Letter in Bertrand Russell Archives.

43. Russell to James, Nov. 6, 1908, ibid., 300.

44. James to Russell, May 14, 1909, ibid., 301–2.

45. See above for the discussion of Schiller and nn. 18, 22, and 23. See also Bertrand Russell, "Logical Positivism," *Revue Internationale de Philosophie* 4, no. 11 (Jan. 1950):3–19; repr. in *Logic and Knowledge; Inquiry into Meaning and Truth,* passim, esp. chaps 21, 22, and 23.

46. William James, "Two English Critics," 48. Bertrand Russell, "Transatlantic 'Truth,'" *The Albany Review,* 400–405.

47. The same essay, reprinted in Russell's *Philosophical Essays*, 119–20.

48. Russell, "Pragmatism," in *Philosophical Essays*, 107–11.

49. William James to Bertrand Russell, undated (summer 1908), James, *Meaning of Truth*, 299. Letter in Bertrand Russell Archives.

50. James to Russell, May 14, 1909, ibid., 302.

51. James, "Two English Critics," in *Meaning of Truth*, 146–53.

52. Russell, "William James's Conception of Truth," in *Philosophical Essays*, 124.

53. James, marginal comments on "Transatlantic 'Truth,'" *Meaning of Truth*, 309.

54. James to Russell, May 14, 1909, *Meaning of Truth*, 302.

55. Russell to James, July 22, 1909, *Meaning of Truth*, 303.

56. Bertrand Russell, "Pragmatism," in *Philosophical Essays*.

57. James, "Two English Critics," in *Meaning of Truth*, 153.

58. Russell, "The Philosophy of William James," *The Nation*, London 794.

59. William James, *The Principles of Psychology*, vol. 1, chaps. 8, 9, and 15. Repr. in *The Works of William James*, ed. Frederick H. Burkhardt, Fredson Bowers, and Ignas K. Skrupskelis. Cambridge: Harvard Univ. Pr., 1981. Russell's copy of this book is liberally annotated, showing attentive appreciation of James's work. Compare Russell, "Knowledge by Acquaintance and Knowledge by Description," and *The Problems of Philosophy*. William James, "Does 'Consciousness' Exist?" *Journal of Philosophy, Psychology, and Scientific Methods* 1:18 (1904) 477–91. Repr. in *The Works of William James*, ed. Frederick H. Burckhardt, Fredson Bowers, and Ignas K. Skrupskelis. Cambridge: Harvard Univ. Pr., 1976.

60. Russell, "On the Notion of Cause," in *Mysticism and Logic*.

61. Russell, *Our Knowledge of the External World*, chap. 5; Russell, "On the Experience of Time," *Monist*, 1915.

62. Russell, *Theory of Knowledge: 1913 Manuscript*, 9.

63. William James, "The Notion of Consciousness," in *Essays in Radical Empiricism* (New York: Longmans, Green & Co., 1912). Essays originally published in 1904 and 1905 in a series of articles in *The Journal of Philosophy*. Repr. in *The Works of William James*, ed. Frederick H. Burkhardt, Fredson Bowers, and Ignas K. Skrupskelis. Cambridge: Harvard Univ. Pr., 1976.

64. Russell's comments on "neutral monism": "On the Nature of Acquaintance, Part II," chap. 2 of *Theory of Knowledge: 1913 Manuscript;* "On Propositions: What They Are and How They Mean," in *Logic and Knowledge, The Analysis of Mind*, chap. 1. For the suggested backward interpretation, I am indebted to an unpublished paper by Philip DeMatteis.

65. Robert Charles Marsh, whose comments in the editorial introduction to "On the Nature of Acquaintance" (p. 125 of *Logic and Knowledge*) are especially misleading, suggests that the essay shows Russell "engaged in philosophical debate with some of the leading American philosophers of the day, and provides us with his arguments against neutral monism, a position that he later adopted in *The Analysis of Mind* (1921) and gradually abandoned, apparently for reasons similar to those given here." It would seem *prima facie* implausible for Russell to criticize a position, then adopt it, and then abandon it because of criticisms given by himself before he adopted it; in any case Russell did not abandon neutral monism but continued to maintain it. In

addition the stress on debate with American philosophers, and Marsh's subsequent reference to the "months at Harvard put Russell in direct contact with James, Perry, Sheffer, and Demos of the 'new realist school'" suggest that the essay was part of, or an outcome of, interactions at Harvard. But James had been dead for five years when Russell came to Harvard, and the essay was published before Russell got to Harvard. In fact, as we now know, but as Russell did not see fit to inform Marsh that the critique of neutral monism was written as an early chapter in the unpublished manuscript, "Theory of Knowledge," of May 1913.

66. Russell, *Theory of Knowledge: 1913 Manuscript*, 32.

67. Victor Lenzen, notes on theory of knowledge seminar, Harvard, Spring 1914, in the Bertrand Russell Archives.

68. *Logic and Knowledge*, 218–21.

69. Ibid., 221.

70. Ibid., 222.

71. Ibid., 227.

72. Ibid., 280.

73. Russell, *Analysis of Mind*, chap. 5.

74. Ibid., 141–43.

75. Ibid., chap. 13.

76. Russell, "Pragmatism," 364.

77. Bertrand Russell, *Review of Essays, Philosophical, and Psychological in Honor of William James, Professor in Harvard University,"* The Hibbert Journal 7 (1909):204.

78. John Dewey, "The Existence of the World as a Logical Problem," *Philosophical Review* 24 (1915):357–70. Repr. in *Essays in Experimental Logic* (Chicago: Univ. of Chicago Pr., 1916). Repr. in *John Dewey: The Middle Works, 1899–1924*, vol. 8, ed. Jo Ann Boydston (Carbondale and Edwardsville: Southern Illinois Univ. Pr., 1979) 83–97. Bertrand Russell, "Professor Dewey's *Essays in Experimental Logic,"* The Journal of Philosophy 16: 1 (1919):5–26.

79. Russell, *Analysis of Mind*, 143.

80. John Dewey, *Logic: The Theory of Inquiry* (New York: Henry Holt and Co., 1938). Repr. in *John Dewey: The Later Works, 1925–53*, vol. 12, ed. Jo Ann Boydston (Carbondale and Edwardsville: Southern Illinois Univ. Pr. 1986).

81. Bertrand Russell, "Dewey's New *Logic,"* in *The Philosophy of John Dewey*, vol. 1, The Library of Living Philosophers, ed. Paul Arthur Schilpp (Evanston and Chicago: Northwestern Univ., 1939). John Dewey, "Experience, Knowledge and Value: A Rejoinder," in *The Philosophy of John Dewey.* Repr. in *John Dewey: The Later Works, 1925–53*, vol. 14, ed. Jo Ann Boydston (Carbondale and Edwardsville: Southern Illinois Univ. Pr., 1988).

82. Russell, *Inquiry into Meaning and Truth.*

83. John Dewey, "Propositions, Warranted Assertibility and Truth," *The Journal of Philosophy* 88:7 (1941):169–86. Repr. in *John Dewey, The Later Works, 1925–53*, vol. 14. See n. 81, above.

84. Bertrand Russell, *Human Knowledge: Its Scope and Limits* (New York: Simon and Schuster, Inc., 1948); Bertrand Russell, *A History of Western Philosophy* (New York: Simon and Schuster, 1944).

85. John Dewey and Arthur F. Bentley, *Knowing and the Known* (Boston: The

Beacon Pr., 1949).

86. Russell to Morrell, #1008, Mar. 22, 1914, #1022, April 24, 1914. (The other was Simon Flexner.)

87. Conversation June 1972 of Elizabeth R. Eames and S. Morris Eames with Mr. Tseng Yueh-nong, interpreter for Dewey and Russell at Chang-sha. For Russell's remembrances, see *Autobiography*, 2, 126.

88. Dewey, Russell, and Bergson as communicated by J. H. Muirhead, letter to Russell May 31, 1920, in Bertrand Russell Archives. Dewey gave lectures on the philosophies of William James, Henri Bergson, and Bertrand Russell to a Chinese audience. The lectures on Russell were intended as a preparation for Russell's lectures in China. These lectures were very brief and discussed Russell's epistemology as rationalistic, tied to mathematical logic, and as excluding the ordinary concerns of human experience. This authoritarian and scientifically oriented philosophy was contrasted with Russell's writings on social and political philosophy which emphasized freedom from the control of the state and a democratic and socialist perepective. The lectures were translated into English from the Chinese version by Robert W. Clopton and Tsuinchen Ou, first published in *Russell: Journal of the Bertrand Russell Archives*, 2 (1973) 3–10, 15–20. under the title "Russell's Philosophy and Politics." Later published in *John Dewey: The Middle Works 1899–1924*, vol. 12, ed. JoAnn Boydston (Carbondale and Edwardsville: Southern Illinois Univ. Pr., 1982) 235–50.

89. Russell to Morrell, Feb. 21, 1921. *Autobiography*, 2, 126.

90. Letter of Dewey to Richard Hocking, May 16, 1940, in Russell, *Autobiography*, II, chap. 6, 233–35. John Dewey, "The Case for Bertrand Russell," and "Russell as a Moral Case," in *The Later Works*, vol. 14, n. 81, above. *The Bertrand Russell Case*, ed. John Dewey and Horace M. Kallen (New York: Viking Pr., 1941).

91. John Dewey to Roderick Chisholm, Oct. 30, 1945, Feb. 6, 1946. Private collection of Roderick M. Chisholm, photocopies in The Center for Dewey Studies, Southern Illinois University.

92. John Dewey, "The Existence of the World as a Logical Problem," *Essays in Experimental Logic*, 298–302.

93. Russell, "Professor Dewey's Essays in Experimental Logic."

94. Russell, "The Philosophy of Logical Atomism," and "On Propositions: What They Are and How They Mean," *The Analysis of Mind*.

95. John Dewey, *Experience and Nature* (LaSalle and Chicago: Open Court Publ. Co., 1925). Repr. in *John Dewey: The Later Works, 1925–53*, vol. 1, ed. Jo Ann Boydston (Carbondale and Edwardsville: Southern Illinois Univ. Pr., 1981). John Dewey, *Art as Experience* (New York: Minton Balch & Co., 1934). Repr. in *John Dewey: The Later Works, 1925–53*, vol. 10, ed. Jo Ann Boydston (Carbondale and Edwardsville: Southern Illinois Univ. Pr., 1987).

96. Dewey, *Logic*, chap. 8 for a discussion of immediate knowledge; chap. 17, for a discussion of formal logic.

97. Russell, "Dewey's New *Logic*." See n. 99, below.

98. See above, n. 40. "Two English Critics."

99. Dewey, "Experience, Knowledge and Value: A Rejoinder," 548–49.

100. Russell, *Inquiry*, chap. 21, "Truth and Verification," and chap. 23, "Warranted Assertibility."

101. Dewey, "Propositions, Warranted Assertibility and Truth."

102. Russell, *Our Knowledge of the External World,* 2d ed., 68.

103. Russell, *My Philosophical Development,* 213.

104. Dewey and Bentley, *Knowing and the Known,* 206f, 217–20, 224f, 228f, *John Dewey and Arthur F. Bentley: A Philosophical Correspondence, 1932–1951,* eds. Sidney Ratner and Jules Altman (New Brunswick, NJ: Rutgers Univ. Pr. 1964), 41, 85. Of 65 Russell references cited in the index, many refer to different books and articles of Russell, which indicates that the authors read most of what Russell wrote in philosophy. Neither Russell's reading of Dewey nor Dewey's of Russell dispelled their reciprocal misunderstandings, however.

9. The Legacy of the Dialogue

1. Russell, *Inquiry,* chaps. 10, 19, and 22. Russell's exchanges with Ayer include a paper of Russell's, "The Limits of Empiricism," *Proceedings of the Aristotelian Society* (1935–36); and a rejoinder by Ayer "On the Scope of Empirical Knowledge: A Rejoinder to Bertrand Russell," *Erkenntnis* 7 (1938):267–74; reviews by Russell of *Language, Truth and Logic,* "Philosophy and Grammar," *London Mercury* (March 1936), and of *Philosophical Essays,* "Light versus Heat," in *The London Observer* (Aug. 8, 1954).

2. Morris Weitz, "Analysis and the Unity of Russell's Philosophy," in *The Philosophy of Bertrand Russell,* vol. 5, The Library of Living Philosophers, ed. Paul Arthur Schilpp (Evanston and Chicago: Northwestern Univ. 1944).

3. Bertrand Russell, *A History of Western Philosophy* (New York: Simon and Schuster, 1945); Bertrand Russell, *Human Knowledge: Its Scope and Limits* (New York: Simon and Schuster, 1948); *Human Society in Ethics and Politics* (London: George Allen & Unwin, Ltd., 1954).

4. Bertrand Russell, "Philosophical Analysis" (a reply to Urmson), "Logic and Ontology" (a reply to Warnock), "Mr. Strawson on Referring" (a defense of the theory of descriptions), "What Is Mind?" (a review of Ryle's *The Concept of Mind*). All are under the heading "Some Replies to Criticism" in *My Philosophical Development.*

5. Ernest Gellner, *Words and Things: A Critical Account of Linguistic Philosophy and a Study in Ideology* (London: Victor Gollanez, Ltd., 1963) Russell's "Introduction," 13–15.

6. Russell, *Autobiography.*

7. Alan Wood, "Russell's Philosophy," in *My Philosophical Development,* 273.

8. Russell, *Logic and Knowledge,* ix.

9. Kurt Gödel, "Russell's Mathematical Logic," and Bertrand Russell, "Reply to Criticisms," in *The Philosophy of Bertrand Russell,* 741.

10. Grover Maxwell, "The Later Bertrand Russell: Philosophical Revolutionary," in *Bertrand Russell's Philosophy,* ed. George Nakhnikian (London: Gerald Duckworth & Co., 1974). J. Vuillemin, *Leçons sur la première philosophie de Russell.*

11. J. L. Austin, *Sense and Sensibilia,* reconstructed from manuscript notes by G. J. Warnock (Oxford: Oxford University Pr., 1962).

12. F. P. Ramsey, "Epilogue," *The Foundations of Mathematics* (London: Routledge & Kegan Paul, Ltd., 1931).

13. Herbert Marcuse, *One-Dimensional Man* (Boston: Beacon Press, 1964).

14. Richard Rorty, *Philosophy and the Mirror of Nature* (Princeton: Princeton Univ. Pr., 1979).

15. John Rajchman and Cornel West, eds., *Post-Analytic Philosophy* (New York: Columbia Univ. Pr., 1985).

16. Roderick Chisholm, ed., *Realism and the Background of Phenonemology* (New York: The Free Press, 1960). See "Editor's Introduction."

Bibliography

Works by Bertrand Russell

The Analysis of Matter. London: George Allen & Unwin, Ltd., 1927.

The Analysis of Mind. London: George Allen & Unwin, Ltd., 1921.

"Analytic and Synthetic Philosophers." *The Nation and the Athenaeum* 31, (July 1922):538–39.

"The *A Priori* in Geometry." *Proceedings of the Aristotelian Society* 3 (1896):97–112.

The Autobiography of Bertrand Russell. Vol. 1 (1912–1914), vol. 2 (1914–1944), vol. 3 (1944–1967). London: George Allen & Unwin, Ltd., 1967, 1968, 1969, respectively.

The Collected Papers of Bertrand Russell. Vol. 1, *Cambridge Essays 1888–99,* ed. Kenneth Blackwell, Andrew Brink, Nicholas Griffin, Richard A. Rempel, and John G. Slater. Vol. 7, *Theory of Knowledge: The 1913 Manuscript,* ed. Elizabeth Ramsden Eames with Kenneth Blackwell, Vol. 8, *The Philosophy of Logical Atomism and Other Essays, 1914–19,* ed. John G. Slater. Vol. 9, *Essays on Language, Mind and Matter, 1919–26,* ed. John G. Slater with the assistance of Bernd Frohmann. Vol. 12, *Contemplation and Action, 1902–14,* ed. Richard A. Rempel, Andrew Brink, and Margaret Moran. Vol. 13, *Prophecy and Dissent 1914–16,* ed. Richard A. Rempel with Margaret Moran. London: George Allen & Unwin, Ltd., 1983, 1984, 1986, 1988, 1985, 1988, respectively.

A Critical Exposition of the Philosophy of Leibniz with an Appendix of Leading Passages. Cambridge: Cambridge Univ. Pr., 1900.

"Dewey's New *Logic.*" In *The Philosophy of Bertrand Russell.* The Library of Living Philosophers, ed. Paul Arthur Schilpp. Evanston and Chicago: Northwestern Univ., 1939.

"Dr. Schiller's Analysis of *The Analysis of Mind.*" *Journal of Philosophy* 19, no. 24 (1922):645.

"The Elements of Ethics." In *Philosophical Essays.* London: Longmans,

Green & Co., 1910.

An Essay on the Foundations of Geometry. Cambridge: Cambridge Univ. Pr., 1897.

Essays in Analysis, ed. Douglas Lackey. New York: George Braziller, 1973.

German Social Democracy. London: Longmans, Green & Company, 1896.

A History of Western Philosophy. New York: Simon & Schuster, Inc., 1945.

Human Knowledge: Its Scope and Limits. New York: Simon & Schuster, Inc., 1948.

Human Society in Ethics and Politics. London: George Allen & Unwin, Ltd., 1954.

"The Influence and Thought of G. E. Moore." *The Listener* (April 30, 1959):755–56.

An Inquiry into Meaning and Truth. London: George Allen & Unwin, Ltd., 1940.

Introduction to Mathematical Philosophy. London: George Allen & Unwin, Ltd., 1919.

"Is Position in Space Absolute or Relative?" *Mind* n.s. 10 (1901):293–317.

"Knowledge by Acquaintance and Knowledge by Description." *Proceedings of the Aristotelian Society* 11 (1910–11):108–28. Repr. in *Mysticism and Logic and Other Essays,* 1918.

"Light Versus Heat." *The London Observer.* (Aug. 8, 1954). [Review of A. J. Ayer's *Philosophical Essays.*]

"The Limits of Empiricism." *Proceedings of the Aristotelian Society* (1935–36):131–50.

Logic and Knowledge, ed. Robert Charles Marsh. London: George Allen & Unwin, Ltd., 1956.

"Logic and Ontology." In *My Philosophical Development,* 1959. [Reply to G. J. Warnock.]

"Logical Positivism." *Revue Internationale de Philosophie* 4, no. 11 (Jan. 1950):3–19. Repr. in *Logic and Knowledge,* 1956.

"Mathematical Logic as Based on the Theory of Types." *American Journal of Mathematics* 30 (May 1908):222–62. Repr. in *Logic and Knowledge,* 1956.

"Meinong's Theory of Complexes and Assumptions." Parts 1, 2, 3. *Mind* n.s. 13, nos. 50–52 (1904):(50) 204–19, (51) 336–54, (52) 509–24. Repr. in *Essays in Analysis,* 1973.

"Metaphysics for the Man of Action." *The Nation* (London) (March 2, 1907): 44–45.

"The Monistic Theory of Truth." In *Philosophical Essays,* 1910.

"Mr. Strawson on Referring." In "Some Replies to Criticism." In *My Philosophical Development,* 1959.

"My Mental Development." In *The Philosophy of Bertrand Russell.* Vol. 5, The Library of Living Philosophers, ed. Paul Arthur Schilpp. Evanston and Chicago: Northwestern Univ., 1944.

My Philosophical Development. New York: Simon & Schuster, 1959.

Mysticism and Logic and Other Essays. London: Longmans, Green & Co., 1918.

"The Nature of Truth." *Mind* 16 (1907):528–33.

"On Denoting." *Mind* n.s. 14 (1905):473–93. Repr. in *Logic and Knowledge,* 1956.

"On Finite and Infinite Cardinal Numbers." *American Journal of Mathematics* 24 (Oct. 1902):378–83.

"On the Nature of Acquaintance." *Monist* 24 (1914): 1–16, 160–87, 435–53. Repr. in *Logic and Knowledge,* 1956.

"On the Nature of Truth." *Proceedings of the Aristotelian Society* 7 (1906–7):28–49.

"On the Nature of Truth and Falsehood." In *Philosophical Essays,* 1910.

"On the Notion of Cause." *Proceedings of the Aristotelian Society* 13 (1912–13): Repr. in *Mysticism and Logic and Other Essays,* 1918.

"On the Notion of Order." *Mind* 10 (1901): 30–51.

"On Propositions: What They Are and How They Mean." *Proceedings of the Aristotelian Society* suppl. vol. 2. *Problems of Science and Philosophy* (1919):1–43. Repr. in *Logic and Knowledge,* 1956.

"On the Relation of Number and Quantity." *Mind* 6 (1896):326–41.

"On the Relation of Universals to Particulars." *Proceedings of the Aristotelian Society* n.s. 12 (1912): 1–24. Repr. in *Logic and Knowledge,* 1956.

"On Some Difficulties in the Theory of Transfinite Numbers and Order Types." *Proceedings of the London Mathematical Society* 2 (March 1906):29–53.

Our Knowledge of the External World as a Field for Scientific Method in Philosophy. Chicago: Open Court Publishing Co., 1914. Rev. ed. London: George Allen & Unwin, Ltd., 1929.

"Les Paradoxes de la logique." *Revue de Métaphysique et de Morale* 14 (Sept. 1906):627–50.

"Philosophical Analysis." In *My Philosophical Development* [Reply to J. O. Urmson.]

Philosophical Essays. London: Longmans, Green & Co., 1910.

"The Philosophical Importance of Mathematical Logic." Trans. P. E. B. Jourdain. *Monist* 23 (Oct. 1913): 484. (Originally given as a paper to a conference of L'École des Hautes Études in Paris, March 1911.) Published as "L'Importance philosophique de la logistique." *Revue de Métaphysique et de Morale* (May 1911):281–91.

"The Philosophy of Bergson." *Monist* 22, no. 3 (July 1912): 321–47. Repr. in *Mysticism and Logic and Other Essays,* 1918.

"Philosophy and Grammar." *London Mercury* (March 1936):541–43. Review of A. J. Ayer's *Language, Truth and Logic.*

"The Philosophy of Logical Atomism." *Monist* 28 (1918):495–527; 29 (1919):32–63, 190–222, 345–80. Repr. in *Logic and Knowledge,* 1956.

"The Philosophy of William James." *The Nation* (London) (Sept. 3, 1910):793–94.

Portraits from Memory. New York: Simon & Schuster, 1956.

"Pragmatism." *The Edinburgh Review* 209:428 (1909):363–88.

"Pragmatism and Logic." *The Nation* (London) 11, no. 7 (May 18, 1912):258–59.

The Principles of Mathematics. Cambridge: Cambridge Univ. Pr., 1903.

The Problems of Philosophy. London: Williams & Norgate, 1912.

"Professor Dewey's *Essays in Experimental Logic." Journal of Philosophy* 16, no. 1 (1919):5–26.

"Le Réalisme analytique." *Bulletin de la Société française de Philosophie* 11 (1911):153–82.

"Recent Work on the Principles of Mathematics." *International Monthly* 4 (July 1901):83–101.

"The Relation of Sense-Data to Physics." *Scientia* 6 (1914). Repr. in *Mysticism and Logic and Other Essays,* 1918.

"Review of *Essays in Experimental Logic* by John Dewey." *Journal of Philosophy* 16 (1919):5–26.

"Review of *Essays, Philosophical and Psychological in Honor of William James, Professor in Harvard University." The Hibbert Journal* 7 (1909):204.

"Review of Mr. G. E. Moore's *Principia Ethica." Independent Review* 7 (March 1904):328–33.

"Review of *Über die Bedeutung des Weberschen Gesetzes* by Alexius Meinong." *Mind,* 8 (1899):251–56.

"Review of *Über die Erfahrungsgrundlagen unseres Wissens* by Alexius Meinong." *Mind* 15 (1906):412–15.

"Review of *Über die Stellung der Gegenstandstheorie im System der Wissenschaften* by Alexius Meinong." *Mind* 16 (1907):436–39.

"Review of *Untersuchungen zur Gegenstandstheorie und Psychologie* by Alexius Meinong et al." *Mind* 14 (1905):530–38.

"Science, Relativity and Religion." *The Nation and Athenaeum* (London) 39 (May 29, 1926):206.

"Some Explanations in Reply to Mr. Bradley." *Mind* 19 (1910):373–78.

"Sur la Logique des relations avec des applications à la théorie des séries." *Review de Mathématique* 7 (1901):115–36, 137–48.

"Sur la Relation des mathématiques à la logistique." *Revue de Métaphysique et de Morale* 13 (Nov. 1905): 906–16.

"Théorie générale des séries bien-ordonnées." *Revue de Mathématiques* 8 (1902):12–43.

"The Theory of Implication." *American Journal of Mathematics* 28

(1906):159–202.

"Transatlantic 'Truth.'" *The Albany Review* 2, R. 10 (1908):393–410.

"The Ultimate Constituents of Matter." *Monist* 25 (1915): Repr. in *Mysticism and Logic and Other Essays*, 1918.

"What Is Mind?" In *My Philosophical Development*, 1959. [Review of G. Ryle, *The Concept of Mind*.]

"What Is Truth?" *Independent Review* (June 1906):349–53.

Works by Other Authors

Abel, Reuben. *Humanistic Pragmatism: The Philosophy of F. C. S. Schiller.* New York: The Free Press, 1966.

Austin, J. L. *The Foundations of Arithmetic.* Oxford: Basil Blackwell, 1950. Tr. of G. Frege, *Die Grundlagen der Arithmetik: Eine logisch mathematische Untersuchung über den Begriff der Zahl.* Breslau: Verlag von Wilhelm Koebner, 1884.

———. *Sense and Sensibilia,* reconstructed from manuscript notes by G. J. Warnock. Oxford: Oxford Univ. Pr., 1962.

Ayer, A. J. "On the Scope of Empirical Knowledge: A Rejoinder to Bertrand Russell." *Erkenntnis* 7 (1938):267–74.

———. *The Origins of American Pragmatism.* San Francisco: Freeman, Cooper & Co., 1968.

———. *Russell and Moore: The Analytical Heritage.* Cambridge, Mass.: Harvard Univ. Pr., 1971.

Ayer, A. J., W. C. Kneale, G. A. Paul, D. F. Pears, P. F. Strawson, G. J. Warnock, and R. A. Wollheim. *The Revolution in Philosophy.* New York: The Macmillan Co., 1965.

Bergmann, Gustav. *Logic and Reality.* Madison: The Univ. of Wisconsin Pr., 1964.

Bertrand Russell Archives. McMaster University. Hamilton, Ontario, Canada. Letters from F. H. Bradley, Harold H. Joachim, Alexius Meinong, F. C. S. Schiller, and A. N. Whitehead to Bertrand Russell. Copies of Bertrand Russell's letters to F. H. Bradley, and Harold H. Joachim from Merton College. Copies of Bertrand Russell's letters to Ottoline Morrell from Harry Ransom Humanities Research Center, University of Texas. Letters of Ottoline Morrell to Bertrand Russell. Letters to and from Alys Russell. Also Bertrand Russell's diary.

Blackburn, S., and A. Code. "The Power of Russell's Criticism of Frege, 'On Denoting,' pp. 48–50." *Analysis* 38 (1978):65–77.

Blackwell, Kenneth. "Wittgenstein's Impact on Russell's Theory of Belief." Master's thesis, McMaster Univ., 1974.

Blackwell, Kenneth, and Elizabeth Ramsden Eames. "Russell's Unpublished Book on Theory of Knowledge." *Russell: Journal of the*

Bertrand Russell Archives 19 (1975):3–18.

Bradley, F. H. *Appearance and Reality*. Oxford: Clarendon Pr., 1893.

———. *Essays on Truth and Reality*. Oxford: Clarendon Pr., 1914.

———. "On Appearance, Error, and Contradiction." *Mind*, n.s. 19 (1910):154–85.

———. "Reply to Mr. Russell's Explanations." *Mind* (1911):74–76.

———. *The Principles of Logic*. 2 vols. Oxford: Oxford Univ. Pr., 1883.

Broad, C. D. "Critical and Speculative Philosophy." In *Contemporary British Philosophy*. First Series, ed. J. H. Muirhead. London: George Allen & Unwin, Ltd., 1924.

Carnap, Rudolf. "Empiricism, Semantics, and Ontology." *Revue Internationale de Philosophie* 4, no. 11 (1950):20–40.

———. "Intellectual Biography." In *The Philosophy of Rudolf Carnap*. Vol. 10, The Library of Living Philosophers, ed. Paul Arthur Schilpp. Chicago: Open Court Publishing Co., 1963.

Cassin, Chrystin E. "Russell's Discussion of Meaning and Denotation: A Re-examination." In *Essays on Bertrand Russell*, ed. E. D. Klemke. Urbana, IL: Univ. of Illinois Pr., 1970.

The Center for Dewey Studies. Southern Illinois University. Copies of John Dewey's letters to Roderick Chisholm from the private collection of Roderick Chisholm.

Chisolm, Roderick M. "Editor's Introduction." In *Realism and the Background of Phenomenology*. New York: The Free Pr., 1960.

———. *Perceiving: A Philosophical Study*. Ithaca: Cornell Univ. Pr., 1957.

———. *Realism and the Background of Phenomenology*. New York: The Free Pr., 1960.

———. *Theory of Knowledge*. 2d ed. Englewood Cliffs, NJ: Prentice-Hall, 1977.

Clark, Ronald W. *The Life of Bertrand Russell*. New York: Alfred A. Knopf, 1976.

Davidson, Donald. "Causal Relations." *Journal of Philosophy* 64 (1967): 691–703. Repr. in *The Nature of Causation*, ed. Myles Brand. Urbana: Univ. of Illinois Pr., 1976.

Dewey, John. *Art as Experience*. New York: Minton Balch Co., 1934. Repr. in *John Dewey: The Later Works, 1925–53*. Vol. 10, ed. Jo Ann Boydston, Carbondale and Edwardsville: Southern Illinois Univ. Pr., 1987.

———. *Essays in Experimental Logic*. Chicago: Univ. of Chicago Pr., 1915. Repr. in *John Dewey: The Middle Works, 1899–1924*. Vol. 8, ed. Jo Ann Boydston. Carbondale and Edwardsville: Southern Illinois Univ. Pr., 1979.

———. "The Existence of the World as a Logical Problem." *Philosophical Review* 24 (1915): 357–70. Repr. in *Essays in Experimental Logic*. Chicago: Univ. of Chicago Pr., 1916. Repr. in *John Dewey: The Middle*

Works, 1899–1924. Vol. 8, ed. Jo Ann Boydston. Carbondale and Edwardsville: Southern Illinois Univ. Pr., 1979.

———. *Experience and Nature*. LaSalle and Chicago. Open Court Publishing Co., 1925. Repr. in *John Dewey: The Later Works, 1925–53*. Vol. 1, ed. Jo Ann Boydston. Carbondale and Edwardsville: Southern Illinois Univ. Pr., 1981.

———. "Experience, Knowledge and Value: A Rejoinder." In *The Philosophy of John Dewey*. Repr. in *John Dewey: The Later Works, 1925–53*. Vol. 14, ed. Jo Ann Boydston. Carbondale and Edwardsville: Southern Illinois Univ. Pr., 1979.

———. *Logic: The Theory of Inquiry*. New York: Henry Holt and Co., 1938. Repr. in *John Dewey: The Later Works, 1925–53*. Vol. 12, ed Jo Ann Boydston. Carbondale and Edwardsville: Southern Illinois Univ. Pr., 1986.

———. "Propositions, Warranted Assertibility and Truth." *Journal of Philosophy* 88, no. 7 (1941): 69–186. Repr. in *John Dewey: The Later Works, 1925–53*. Vol. 14, ed. Jo Ann Boydston. Carbondale and Edwardsville: Southern Illinois Univ. Pr., 1988.

———. "Russell's Philosophy and Politics." *Russell: Journal of the Bertrand Russell Archives* 2 (1973):3–10, 15–20. Repr. in *John Dewey: The Middle Works, 1899–1924*. Vol. 12, ed. Jo Ann Boydston. Carbondale and Edwardsville: Southern Illinois Univ. Pr., 1982.

———. *Studies in Logical Theory*. The Decennial Publications, Second Series, vol. xi. Chicago: The Univ. of Chicago Pr., 1903. Repr. in *John Dewey: The Middle Works, 1899–1924*. Vol. 2, ed. Jo Ann Boydston. Carbondale and Edwardsville: Southern Illinois Univ. Pr., 1976.

Dewey, John, and Arthur F. Bentley. *Knowing and the Known*. Boston: The Beacon Pr., 1949.

Dewey, John, and Horace M. Kallen, eds. *The Bertrand Russell Case*. New York: Viking Pr., 1941.

Dummett, Michael. *Frege: Philosophy of Language*. London: Gerald Duckworth & Co., Ltd., 1973.

Eames, Elizabeth R. *Bertrand Russell's Theory of Knowledge*. London: George Allen & Unwin, Ltd., 1969.

———. "Russell's Study of Meinong." *Russell: Journal of the Bertrand Russell Archives* 4 (1972):3–6.

Essays, Philosophical and Psychological, in Honor of William James, Professor in Harvard University. By his colleagues at Columbia University. London: Longmans and Co., 1908.

Finch, Peter A., Theodore Uehling, Jr., Howard K. Wettstein, eds. *The Foundation of Analytical Philosophy*. Vol. 6, Midwest Studies in Philosophy ed. Peter Finch, et al. Minneapolis: Univ. of Minnesota Pr., 1981.

Findlay, J. N. *Meinong's Theory of Objects and Values*. 2d ed. Oxford:

Clarendon Pr., 1963.

Flew, Anthony, ed. *Essays in Conceptual Analysis*. London: Macmillan & Co., Ltd., 1960.

Frege, Gottlob. "Anwendungen der Begriffsschrift." *Jenaische Zeitschrift für Naturwissenschaft* 12 (1879): suppl. 2, 29–33. English tr. "Applications of the 'Conceptual Notation.'" In *Conceptual Notation and Related Articles*, ed. T. W. Bynum. Oxford: Clarendon Pr., 1972.

———. *The Basic Laws of Arithmetic*. Vol. 1. Tr. M. Furth. Berkeley: Univ. of California Pr., 1964.

———. *Begriffsschrift, eine der arithmetischen nachgebildete Formalsprache des reinen Denkens*. Halle a.s. 1879. English tr. in *Conceptual Notation and Related Articles*, ed. T. W. Bynum. Oxford: Clarendon Pr., 1972.

———. *Conceptual Notation and Related Articles*, ed. T. W. Bynum. Oxford: Clarendon Pr., 1972.

———. "Funktion und Begriff." *der Jenaischen Gesellschaft für Medizin und Naturwissenschaft* 9:1. Jena: Verlag Hermann Pohle, 1891. English tr. "Function and Concept," tr. P. T. Geach. In *Translations from the Philosophical Writings of G. Frege*, ed. P. T. Geach and Max Black. 2d ed. Oxford: Basil Blackwell, 1960.

———. *Grundgesetze der Arithmetik*. Vol. 1. Jena: Verlag Hermann Pohle, 1893. Partial English tr. in *The Basic Laws of Arithmetic*, tr. M. Furth. Berkeley: Univ. of California Pr., 1964.

———. *Grundgesetze der Arithmetik*. Vol. 2. Jena: Verlag Hermann Pohle, 1903. Partial English tr. in *The Basic Laws of Arithmetic*, tr. M. Furth. Berkeley: Univ. of California Pr., 1964.

———. *Die Grundlagen der Arithmetik: Eine logisch mathematische Untersuchung über den Begriff der Zahl*. Breslau: Verlag von Wilhelm Koebner, 1884. English tr. in *The Foundations of Arithmetic*, tr. J. L. Austin. Oxford: Basil Blackwell, 1950.

———. "Kritische Beleuchtung einiger Punkte in E. Schröder's Vorlesungen über die Algebra der Logik." *Archiv für systematische Philosophie* 1 (1895): 433–56. English tr. "A Critical Elucidation of Some Points in E. Schröder's *Algebra der Logic*." In *Translations from the Philosophical Writings of G. Frege*, tr. and ed. P. Geach and M. Black. 2d ed. Oxford: Basil Blackwell, 1960.

———. "Lettera del Sig. G. Frege all 'Editore.'" *Revista di Matematica (Revue de Mathématiques)* 6 (1896–99):53–59.

———. *Nachgelassene Schriften und Wissenschaftlicher Briefwechsel*. 2 vols., ed. Gottfried Gabriel, Hans Hermes, Friedrich Kambartel, Christian Thiel, and Albert Veraart. Hamburg: Felix Meiner, 1976.

———. "Le nombre entier." *Revue de Métaphysique et de la Morale* 3 (1895):73–78. English tr. in "The Whole Number." *Mind* 79 (1970):481–86.

————. *On Formal Geometry and Formal Theories of Arithmetic*, tr. Eike-Henner W. Kluge. New Haven: Yale Univ. Pr., 1971.

————. "On Herr Peano's Begriffsschrift and My Own," tr. V. H. Dudman. *Australian Journal of Philosophy* 47 (1969):1–14.

————. "On the Law of Inertia," tr. H. Jackson and E. Levy. *Studies in History and Philosophy of Science* 2 (1971–72):195–212.

————. *Philosophical and Mathematical Correspondence*. Abridged from German ed. Brian McGuinness, tr. Hans Kaal. From *Nachgelassene Schriften und Wissenschaftlicher Briefwechsel*, ed. Gottfried Gabriel. Chicago: Univ. of Chicago Pr., 1980.

————. "Review of *Das Princip der Infinitesimal-Methode, und seine Geschichte* by H. Cohen." *Zeitschrift für Philosophie und philosophische Kritik* 87 (1885):324–29.

————. *Translations from the Philosophical Writings of G. Frege*, ed. and tr. P. T. Geach and Max Black. 2d ed. Oxford: Basil Blackwell, 1960.

————. "Über Begriff und Gegenstand." *Viertel jahresschrift für Wissenschaftliche Philosophie* 16 (1892):192–205. English tr. "On Concept and Object." In *Translations from the Philosophical Writings of G. Frege*, ed. and tr. P. Geach and Max Black. 2d ed. Oxford: Basil Blackwell, 1960.

————. "Über die Begriffsschrift des Herrn Peano und meine eigene." *Berichte über die Verhandlungen der Königlich Sächsischen Gesellschaft der Wissenschaften zu Leipzig*. Mathematische-Physische Klasse 48 (1897):361–78. English tr. "On Herr Peano's Begriffsschrift and My Own," V. H. Dudman. *Australian Journal of Philosophy* 47 (1969):1–14.

————. "Über formale Theorien der Arithmetik." *Jenaische Zeitschrift für Naturwissenschaft* 19 (1886): supp., 94–104. English tr. "On Formal Theories of Arithmetic." In *On Formal Geometry and Formal Theories of Arithmetic*, tr. Eike-Henner W. Kluge. New Haven: Yale Univ. Pr., 1971.

————. "Über Sinn und Bedeutung." *Zeitschrift für Philosophie und philosophische Kritik* 100 (1892):25–50. English tr. "On Sense and Reference." In *Translations from the Philosophical Writings of G. Frege*, tr. and ed. P. Geach and Max Black. 2d ed. Oxford: Basil Blackwell Pr., 1960.

————. "Über das Tragheitsgesetz." *Zeitschrift für Philosophie and philosophische Kritik* 1018 (1891):145–61. English tr. "On the Law of Inertia," tr. H. Jackson and E. Levy. *Studies in History and Philosophy of Science* 2 (1971–72):195–212.

————. *Über die Zahlen des Herrn H. Schubert*. Jena: Verlag Hermann Pohle, 1899.

————. "Über den Zweck der Begriffsschrift." *Jenaische Zeitschrift für Naturwissenschaft* 16 (1883): supp. 1–10. English tr. "On the Aim of the 'Conceptual Notation.'" In *Conceptual Notation and Related Articles*, ed. T. W. Bynum. Oxford: Clarendon Pr., 1972.

Geach, P. T., and Max Black, eds. "Preface to Frege." In *Translations from the Philosophical Writings of Frege.* Oxford: Basil Blackwell, 1952.

————. "Russell on Meaning and Denotation." *Analysis* 20 (1959):53–62.

Gellner, Ernest. *Words and Things: A Critical Account of Linguistic Philosophy and a Study in Ideology,* with an introduction by Bertrand Russell. London: Victor Gollanez Ltd., 1963.

Gödel, Kurt. "Russell's Mathematical Logic." *The Philosophy of Bertrand Russell.* Vol. 5, The Library of Living Philosophers, ed. Paul Arthur Schilpp. Evanston and Chicago: Northwestern Univ., 1944.

Goodman, Nelson. *The Structure of Appearance.* 2d ed. Indianapolis: Bobbs Merrill, Inc., 1966.

Grattan-Guiness, I. *Dear Russell-Dear Jourdain: A Commentary on Russell's Logic Based on His Correspondence with Philip Jourdain.* London: Gerald Duckworth & Co., Ltd., 1977.

Griffin, Nicholas. "Russell's 'Horrible Travesty of Meinong.'" *Russell: Journal of the Bertrand Russell Archives* 25–28 (1977):39–51.

————. "Russell's Multiple Relation Theory of Judgment." Foundations of Logic Conference. Univ. of Waterloo, April 1982.

Grossman, Reinhardt. *The Structure of Mind.* Madison: The Univ. of Wisconsin Pr., 1965.

Haller, Rudolf, ed. *Jenseits von Sein und Nichtsein.* Graz: Akademische Druck—und Verlaganstalt, 1972.

Harry Ransom Humanities Research Center, The University of Texas at Austin. Letters from Bertrand Russell to Ottoline Morrell.

Hintikka, Jaako. "Knowledge by Acquaintance—Individuation by Acquaintance." In *Jenseits von Sein und Nichtsein,* ed. Rudolf Haller, Graz: Akademische Druck—und Verlaganstalt, 1972.

Hochberg, Herbert. "Russell's Attack on Frege's Theory of Meaning." *Philosophica* 18 (1976):9–34.

Jager, Ronald. *The Development of Bertrand Russell's Philosophy.* London: George Allen & Unwin, Ltd., 1972.

James, William. "Does 'Consciousness' Exist?" *Journal of Philosophy, Psychology, and Scientific Methods* 1:18 (1904):477–91. Repr. in *Essays in Radical Empiricism.* London: Longmans, Green & Co., 1912. Repr. in *The Works of William James,* ed. Frederick H. Burkhardt, Fredson Bowers, and Ignas K. Skrupskelis. Cambridge: Harvard University Pr., 1976.

————. *The Letters of William James.* 2 vols., ed. Henry James. Boston: The Atlantic Monthly Pr., 1920.

————. *The Meaning of Truth: A Sequel to Pragmatism.* New York: Longmans, Green & Co., 1911. Repr. in *The Works of William James,* ed. Frederick H. Burkhardt, Fredson Bowers, and Ignas K. Skrupskelis. Cambridge: Harvard University Pr., 1975.

————. *The Principles of Psychology.* 2 vols. New York: Henry Holt Co., 1890. Repr. in *The Works of William James,* ed. Frederick H. Burkhardt,

Fredson Bowers, and Ignas K. Skrupskelis. Cambridge: Harvard University Pr., 1981.

Joachim, Harold H. *The Nature of Truth*. Oxford: Clarendon Pr., 1906.

———. "A Reply to Mr. Moore." *Mind* 16 (1907):410–15.

Johnson, A. H. *Whitehead's Theory of Reality*. Boston: Beacon Pr., 1952.

Keen, C. N., "The Interaction of Russell and Bradley." *Russell: Journal of the Bertrand Russell Archives* 3 (1971):7–10.

Kim, Jaegwon. "Causation, Nomic Subsumption, and the Concept of Event." *Journal of Philosophy* 70 (1973):217–36.

Klemke, E. D. *Essays on Frege*. Urbana: Univ. of Illinois Pr., 1968.

Kline, George L. *Alfred North Whitehead: Essays on His Philosophy*. Englewood Cliffs, NJ: Prentice Hall, 1963.

Lackey, Douglas. "Russell's 1913 Map of the Mind." In *The Foundation of Analytical Philosophy*. Vol. 6, Midwest Studies in Philosophy, ed. Peter Finch, et al. Minneapolis: Univ. of Minnesota Pr., 1981.

Lambert, Karel. "Being and Being So." In *Jenseits von Sein und Nichtsein,* ed. Rudolf Haller. Graz: Akademisch Druck—und Verlaganstalt, 1972.

Lehrer, Keith. *Knowledge*. Oxford: Clarendon Pr., 1974.

Lenzen, Victor. "Bertrand Russell at Harvard, 1914." *Russell: Journal of the Bertrand Russell Archives* 3 (1971):4–6.

Levy, Paul. *G. E. Moore and the Cambridge Apostles*. London: Weidenfeld and Nicholson, 1979.

The Library of The University of California, Los Angeles. Letters from Bertrand Russell to F. C. S. Schiller.

Linsky, Leonard. *Referring*. London: Routledge & Kegan Paul, 1967.

Lowe, Victor. "A. N. Whitehead on His Mathematical Goals: A Letter of 1912." *Annals of Science* 32 (1975):85–101.

———. "Whitehead's 1911 Criticism of *The Problems of Philosophy*." *Russell: Journal of the Bertrand Russell Archives* 13 (1974):3–11.

Lucas, B. J. "Moore's Influence on Russell." *Russell: Journal of the Bertrand Russell Archives* 1 (1971): 9.

Mace, C. A., ed. *British Philosophy at Mid-Century*. London: George Allen & Unwin, Ltd., 1957.

Malcolm, Norman. *Ludwig Wittgenstein: A Memoir*. Oxford: Oxford Univ. Pr., 1958.

Marcuse, Herbert. *One-Dimensional Man*. Boston: Beacon Pr., 1964.

Maxwell, Grover. "The Later Bertrand Russell: Philosophical Revolutionary." In *Bertrand Russell's Philosophy,* ed. George Nakhnikian. London: Gerald Duckworth and Co., 1974.

McGuinness, B. F. "Bertrand Russell and Ludwig Wittgenstein's 'Notes on Logic.'" *Revue Internationale de Philosophie* 26 (1972):444–60.

McMahon, M. Brian. "Russell's Denoting Relation." *The Personalist* 57:4 (1976):345–50.

Meinong, Alexius. "Abstrahieren und Vergleichen." *Zeitschrift für Psychologie und Physiologie der Sinnesorgane* 24 (1900):38–82.

―――. *Emotional Presentation,* tr. M. L. Schubert-Kalsi. Evanston, IL: Northwestern Univ. Pr., 1972.

―――. *Gesamtausgabe,* ed. R. Haller and R. Kindinger. 8 vols. Graz: Akademische Druck—und Verlagsanstalt, 1968.

―――. *Philosophenbriefe aus der Wissenschaftlichen Korrespondenz von Alexius Meinong mit Franz Brentano (et al.).* Graz: Akademische Druck—und Verlagsanstalt, 1965.

―――. *Über Annahmen.* Leipzig: Barth, 1st ed., 1902. 2d ed., 1910.

―――. *Über die Bedeutung des Weberschen Gesetzes.* Beitrage zur Psychologie des Vergleichens und Messens. Hamburg and Leipzig: Voss, 1896.

―――. *Über Emotionale Präsentation.* Vienna: Kaiserliche Akademie Wissenschaften, 1917. English tr. *Emotional Presentation,* tr. M. L. Schubert-Kalsi. Evanston, IL: Northwestern Univ. Pr., 1972.

―――. "Über die Erfahrungsgrundlagen unseres Wissens." *Abhandlungen zur Didaktik und Philosophie der Naturwissenschaft.* Band I, Heft 6. Berlin, 1906.

―――. "Über Gegestände höherer Ordnung und deren Verhältnis zur inneren Wahrnehmung." *Zeitschrift für Psychologie und Physiologie der Sinnesorgan* 21 (1899):82–272.

―――. *Über die Stellung der Gegenstandstheorie im System der Wissenschaften.* Leipzig: Voigtlander, 1907.

Meinong, Alexius, E. Mally, R. Ameseder, V. Benussi, W. Liel, W. Frankl, and R. Saxinger. *Untersuchungen zur Gegenstandstheorie and Psychologie.* Leipzig: Barth, 1904.

Merton College, Oxford. Letters from Bertrand Russell to F. H. Bradley, and Harold H. Joachim. Copies in Bertrand Russell Archives.

Moore, G. E. "An Analysis of Mind." *Times Literary Supplement.* London (Sept. 29, 1921):622.

―――. "An Autobiography." In *The Philosophy of G. E. Moore.* Vol. 4, The Library of Living Philosophers, ed. Paul Arthur Schilpp. Evanston and Chicago: Northwestern Univ., 1942.

―――. "Cause and Effect." In *Dictionary of Philosophy and Psychology,* ed. James Mark Baldwin. First published 1901. New ed. with corrections, 1925. Repr., New York: Peter Smith, 1940.

―――. "The Conception of Reality." *Proceedings of the Aristotelian Society* n.s. 18 (1917–18):101–20.

―――. "Critical Notes: *An Essay on the Foundations of Geometry.*" *Mind* n.s. 8 (1899):397–405.

―――. *Ethics.* London: Williams & Norgate, 1912.

―――. "External and Internal Relations." *Proceedings of the Aristotelian Society* (1919–20):40–62. Repr. in *Philosophical Studies,* 1922. London:

Routledge & Kegan Paul Ltd., 1922.

———. "Freedom." *Mind* n.s. 6 (1898):179–203.

———. "Identity." *Proceedings of the Aristotelian Society* n.s. 1 (1900–1901):103–27.

———. "Is Existence a Predicate?" *Proceedings of the Aristotelian Society* supp. vol. 15 (1936). Repr. in *Philosophical Papers*.

———. "Mr. Joachim's *Nature of Truth*." *Mind* 16 (1907):229–35.

———. "The Nature of Judgment." *Mind* n.s. 8 (1899):176–93.

———. "The Nature and Reality of Objects of Perception." *Proceedings of the Aristotelian Society* n.s. 6 (1905–6):68–127. Repr. in *Philosophical Studies*, 1922.

———. "Necessity." *Mind* n.s. 9 (July 1900):289–304.

———. *Philosophical Papers*. London: George Allen & Unwin, Ltd., 1959.

———. *Philosophical Studies*. London: Routledge & Kegan Paul, Ltd., 1922.

———. *Principia Ethica*. Cambridge: Cambridge Univ. Pr., 1903.

———. "Professor James' 'Pragmatism.'" *Proceedings of the Aristotelian Society* n.s. 8 (1907–8):33–77. Repr. in *Philosophical Studies*, 1922.

———. "The Refutation of Idealism." *Mind* n.s. 12 (1903):433–53. Repr. in *Philosophical Studies*, 1922.

———. "Russell's 'Theory of Descriptions.'" In *The Philosophy of Bertrand Russell*. Vol. 5, The Library of Living Philosophers, ed. Paul Arthur Schilpp. Evanston and Chicago: Northwestern Univ., 1944. Repr. in *Philosophical Papers*, 1959.

———. "Some Judgments of Perception." *Proceedings of the Aristotelian Society* (1918–19):1–29. Repr. in *Philosophical Studies*, 1922.

———. *Some Main Problems of Philosophy*. London: George Allen & Unwin, Ltd., 1953.

Moore, G. E., and G. F. Stout. "Symposium: The Status of Sense-Data." *Proceedings of the Aristotelian Society* n.s. 14 (1913–14):355–80.

Morscher, Edgar. "Von Bolzano zu Meinong: zur Geschicte des Logischen Realismus." In *Jenseits von sein und Nichtsein*, ed. Rudolf Haller. Graz: Akademische Druck—und Verlaganstalt, 1972.

Najjar, Ibrahim, and Heather Kirkconnell. "Russell's Foreword to the First German Translation of *The Problems of Philosophy*." *Russell: Journal of the Bertrand Russell Archives* 17 (1975):27–29.

Nakhnikian, George, ed. *Bertrand Russell's Philosophy*. London: Gerald Duckworth & Co., 1974.

Parsons, Terence. "A Meinongian Analysis of Fictional Objects." *Grazer Philosophische Studien* 1 (1973):73–86.

———. *Nonexistent Objects*. New Haven: Yale Univ. Pr., 1980.

Peano, Guiseppe. *Formulaire de Mathématiques*. 4 vols. Vol. 1, Turin: Bocca Frères, 1895. Vol. 2, Turin: Boca Frères, 1897-99. Vol. 3, Paris: Georges carré et C. Naud, 1901. Vol. 4, Turin: Bocca Frères, 1903.

Pears, D. F. "The Relation Between Wittgenstein's Picture Theory of Propositions and Russell's Theories of Judgment." *Philosophical Review* 86 (April 1977):177–96.

Peirce, C. S. "Review of *The Principles of Mathematics* by Bertrand Russell." *The Nation* (New York) 77, no. 1998 (Oct. 15, 1903):308.

Quine, W. V. O. *From a Logical Point of View: Logico-Philosophical Essays.* Cambridge: Harvard Univ. Pr., 1953.

———. *The Roots of Reference.* Lasalle, IL: Open Court Publ. Co., 1973.

Rajchman, John, and Cornel West, eds. *Post-Analytic Philosophy.* New York: Columbia Univ. Pr., 1985.

Ramsey, F. P. *The Foundations of Mathematics.* London: Routledge & Kegan Paul, Ltd., 1931.

Ratner, Sidney, and Jules Altman, eds. *John Dewey and Arthur F. Bentley: A Philosophical Correspondence, 1932–1951.* New Brunswick, NJ: Rutgers Univ. Pr., 1964.

Rorty, Amelie, ed. *Pragmatic Philosophy: An Anthology.* Garden City, NY: Doubleday Anchor, 1966.

Rorty, Richard M. *Philosophy and the Mirror of Nature.* Princeton: Princeton Univ. Pr., 1979.

———. "The Subjectivist Principle and the Linguistic Turn." In *Alfred North Whitehead: Essays on His Philosophy,* ed. George L. Kline. Englewood Cliffs, NJ: Prentice Hall, 1963.

Rosenbaum, S. P. "G. E. Moore's *The Elements of Ethics.*" *The University of Toronto Quarterly* 38 (April 1969):214–32.

Routley, Richard. *Exploring Meinong's Jungle and Beyond.* Canberra: Australian National Univ., 1980.

Routley, R., and V. Routley. "The (Logical) Importance of Not Existing." *Dialogue* (Canada) 18 (1979):129–65.

Ruja, Harry. "Principles of Polemics in Russell." *Inquiry* 11 (Fall 1968):282–94.

Russell, Bertrand, and A. N. Whitehead. *Principia Mathematica.* Cambridge: Cambridge Univ. Pr., vol. 1, 1910, vol. 2, 1912, vol. 3, 1913.

Ryle, Gilbert. "Intentionality-Theory and the Nature of Thinking." In *Jenseits von Sein und Nichtsein,* ed. Rudolf Haller. Graz: Adademische Druck—und Verlaganstalt, 1972.

———. "The Theory of Meaning." In *British Philosophy at Mid-Century,* ed. C. A. Mace. London: George Allen & Unwin, Ltd., 1957.

Santayana, George. "Russell's Philosophical Essays." *The Journal of Philosophy, Psychology and Scientific Methods.* I, "The Study of Essence" 8, no. 3 (Feb. 3, 1911):57–63; II, "The Critique of Pragmatism" 8, no. 5 (March 2, 1911):113–24; III, "Hypostatic Ethics" 8, no. 16 (Aug. 3, 1911):421–32. Repr. with new section, "A New Scholasticism," as chap. 4 in *Winds of*

Doctrine: Studies in Contemporary Opinion. New York: Charles Scribner's Sons, 1913.

Schermann, Hans. "Husserl II. *Logische Untersuchung* und Meinong's *Hume-studien.*" In *Jenseits von sein und Nichtsein,* ed. Rudolf Haller. Graz: Akademische Druck—und Verlaganstalt, 1972.

Schiller, F. C. S. *Formal Logic: A Scientific and Social Problem.* London: The Macmillan Co., 1912.

———. *Humanism: Philosophical Essays.* Oxford: Oxford Univ. Pr., 1903.

———. *Humanistic Pragmatism: The Philosophy of F. C. S. Schiller,* ed. Reuben Abel. New York: The Free Pr., 1966.

———. "Mr. Russell's Psychology." *The Journal of Philosophy* 19 (1922):281–92.

Schiller, F. C. S., Bertrand Russell, and H. H. Joachim. "The Meaning of 'Meaning.'" Symposium, *Mind* 29 (1920):385–414.

Schilpp, Paul Arthur, ed. "Intellectual Biography." *The Philosophy of Rudolf Carnap.* Vol. 10, The Library of Living Philosophers. Chicago: Open Court Publ. Co., 1963.

———. *The Philosophy of Alfred North Whitehead.* Vol. 3, The Library of Living Philosophers. Evanston and Chicago: Northwestern Univ., 1941.

———. *The Philosophy of Bertrand Russell.* Vol. 5, The Library of Living Philosophers. Evanston and Chicago: Northwestern Univ., 1944.

———. *The Philosophy of G. E. Moore.* Vol. 4, The Library of Living Philosophers. Evanston and Chicago: Northwestern Univ., 1942.

———. *The Philosophy of John Dewey.* Vol. 1, The Library of Living Philosophers. Evanston and Chicago: Northwestern Univ., 1939.

Searle, John R. "Russell's Objections to Frege's Theory of Sense and Reference." *Analysis* 18 (1957–58):137–43. Repr. in *Essays on Frege,* ed. E. D. Klemke. 337–45. Urbana: Univ. of Illinois Pr., 1968.

Sluga, Hans D. "Frege's Alleged Realism." *Inquiry* 20 (1977):227–42.

Smith, Janet Farrell. "Theory of Reference and Existential Presuppositions in Russell and Meinong." Ph.D. diss., Columbia Univ., 1975.

Sommerville, S. I. "Types, Categories, and Significance." Ph.D. diss., McMaster Univ., 1979.

Spadoni, Carl. "Russell's Rebellion Against Neo-Hegelianism." Ph.D. diss., Univ. of Waterloo, Ontario, 1977.

Stebbing, L. Susan. "Moore's Influence." In *The Philosophy of G. E. Moore.* Vol. 4, The Library of Living Philosophers, ed. Paul Arthur Schilpp. Evanston and Chicago: Northwestern Univ., 1942.

Sternfeld, Robert. *Frege's Logical Theory.* Carbondale and Edwardsville: Southern Illinois Univ. Pr., 1966.

Strawson, P. F. "On Referring." *Mind* 59 (1950):320–44. Repr. in *Essays in Conceptual Analysis,* ed. Anthony Flew. London: Macmillan & Co., Ltd., 1960.

Suter, Ronald. "Russell's 'Refutation' of Meinong in 'On Denoting.'" *Philosophy and Phenomenological Research* 217 (1967):511–16.

Urmson, J. O. *Philosophical Analysis.* Oxford: Clarendon Pr., 1956.

Vuillemin, Jules. *Leçons sur la première philosphie de Russell.* Paris: Librairie Armand Colin, 1968.

Warnock, G. J. "Metaphysics in Logic." In *Essays in Conceptual Analysis,* ed. Antony Flew. London: Macmillan & Co., Ltd., 1960.

Weitz, Morris. "Analysis and the Unity of Russell's Philosophy." In *The Philosophy of Bertrand Russell.* Vol. 5, The Library of Living Philosophers, ed. Paul Arthur Schilpp.

Wells, Rulon S. "Frege's Ontology." *Review of Metaphysics* 4 (1951):537–73. Repr. in *Essays on Frege,* ed. E. D. Klemke. Urbana: Univ. of Illinois Pr.

White, Morton. "New Horizons in Philosophy." In *Pragmatism and the American Mind.* Oxford: Oxford Univ. Pr., 1973.

———. *Pragmatism and the American Mind.* Oxford: Oxford Univ. Pr., 1973.

Whitehead, Alfred North. *The Aims of Education and Other Essays.* New York: The Macmillan Co., 1929.

———. "The Anatomy of Some Scientific Ideas." In *The Organisation of Thought,* 1917.

———. "Autobiographical Notes." In *The Philosophy of Alfred North Whitehead.* Vol. 3, The Library of Living Philosophers, ed. Paul Arthur Schilpp. Evanston and Chicago: Northwestern Univ., 1941.

———. "The Axioms of Projective Geometry." *Cambridge Tracts in Mathematics and Mathematical Physics,* no. 4, Cambridge: Cambridge Univ. Pr., 1906.

———. *The Concept of Nature.* Cambridge: Cambridge Univ. Pr., 1920.

———. *An Enquiry Concerning the Principles of Natural Knowledge.* Cambridge: Cambridge Univ. Pr., 1919.

———. *An Introduction to Mathematics.* Home University Library of Modern Knowledge. London: Williams and Norgate, Ltd., 1911.

———. "The Logic of Relations, Logical Substitution Groups, and Cardinal Numbers." *American Journal of Mathematics* 25, no. 2 (1903):157–78.

———. "Memoir on the Algebra of Symbolic Logic." *American Journal of Mathematics* 23, no. 2 (1901):139–65 and no. 4: 297–316.

———. "Note." *Mind* 35 (1926): 130.

———. "On Cardinal Numbers." *American Journal of Mathematics* 24, no. 4 (1902):367–94.

———. "On Mathematical Concepts of the Material World." *Philosophical Transactions of the Royal Society (1906).* Repr. in *Alfred North Whitehead: An Anthology,* ed. F. S. C. Northrop and Mason W. Gross. New York: The Macmillan Co., 1953.

———. *The Organisation of Thought.* London: Williams and Norgate, 1917.

———. "The Organisation of Thought." *Report of the 86th Meeting of the British Association for the Advancement of Science* (1916):355–64. Repr. in *The Organisation of Thought* 1917, and in *The Aims of Education and Other Essays,* 1929.

———. *Science and the Modern World.* Lowell Institute Lectures, 1925. New York: The Macmillan Co., 1925.

———. "Sets of Operations in Relation to Groups of Finite Order." Abstract. *Proceedings of the Royal Society of London* 64 (1898–99):319–20.

———. "Space, Time, and Relativity." *Proceedings of the Aristotelian Society* n.s. 16 (1915–16):104–29. Repr. in *The Organisation of Thought,* 1917, and in *The Aims of Education and Other Essays,* 1929.

———. "Theorems on Cardinal Numbers." *American Journal of Mathematics* 26, no. 1 (1904):31–32.

———. "La Théorie relationniste de l'espace." *Revue de Métaphysique et de Morale* 23 (May 1916):423–54.

———. *A Treatise on Universal Algebra.* Vol. 1. Cambridge: Cambridge Univ. Pr., 1898.

Whitehead, Alfred North, and Bertrand Russell. *Principia Mathematica.* 3 vols. Cambridge: University Pr. Vol. 1, 1910; Vol. 2, 1912, Vol. 3, 1913.

Winetrout, Kenneth. *F. C. S. Schiller and the Dimensions of Pragmatism.* Columbus: Ohio State Univ. Pr., 1967.

Wittgenstein, Ludwig. *Letters to C. K. Ogden with Comments on the English Translation of the Tractatus-Logico Philosophicus.* Ed. with intro. by G. H. von Wright. Oxford: Basil Blackwell, 1973.

———. *Letters to Russell, Keynes and Moore,* ed. G. H. von Wright. Oxford: Basil Blackwell, 1974.

———. *Notebooks 1914–1916,* ed. G. H. Von Wright and G. E. M. Anscombe. Oxford: Basil Blackwell, 1969.

———. *Philosophical Investigations,* ed. G. E. M. Anscombe and R. Rhees. Tr. G. E. M. Anscombe. Oxford: Basil Blackwell, 1953. 2d ed., 1958.

———. *Prototractatus,* ed. B. F. McGuinness, T. Nyberg, and G. H. von Wright. Tr. D. F. Pears and B. F. McGuinness. Ithaca, NY: Cornell Univ. Pr., 1971.

———. *Tractatus Logico-Philosophicus.* London: Routledge & Kegan Paul, 1922.

Wood, Alan. "Russell's Philosophy." In Bertrand Russell, *My Philosophical Development.* New York: Simon & Schuster, 1959.

Wright, George Henrik von. "Biographical Sketch." In *Ludwig Wittgenstein: A Memoir.* Norman Malcolm. Oxford: Oxford Univ. Pr., 1958.

Index

In order to achieve compression, this index makes use of abbreviations for the names of the protagonists of the dialogue and for the titles of Russell's works referred to in the text.

The following are the abbreviations for the names of the philosophers: F. H. Bradley, FHB; John Dewey, JD; Gottlob Frege, GF; William James, WJ; H. H. Joachim, HHJ; Alexius Meinong, AM; G. E. Moore, GEM; Bertrand Russell, BR; F. C. S. Schiller, FCSS; A. N. Whitehead, ANW; Ludwig Wittgenstein, LW.

The following abbreviations are used for Russell's works: *The Analysis of Matter, AMa; The Analysis of Mind, AMi; Autobiography, Au; A Critical Exposition of the Philosophy of Leibniz, CPL; The Collected Papers of Bertrand Russell, CPBR;* "The Elements of Ethics," *EE; An Essay on the Foundations of Geometry, EFG;* "A Free Man's Worship," *FMW; A History of Western Philosophy, HWP; Human Knowledge, HK; Human Society in Ethics and Politics, HSEP; An Introduction to Mathematical Philosophy, IMP; An Inquiry into Meaning and Truth, IMT;* "Knowledge by Acquaintance and Knowledge by Description," *KAKD; Logic and Knowledge, LK;* "The Monistic Theory of Truth," *MTT;* "Meinong's Theory of Complexes and Assumptions," *MTCA; My Philosophical Development, MPD;* "On Denoting," *OD;* "On the Experience of Time," *OET;* "On the Nature of Acquaintance," *ONA;* "On the Nature of Truth and Falsehood," *ONTF;* "On the Notion of Cause," *ONC;* "On the Notion of Cause with Application to the Free Will Problem," *ONCFW;* "On Propositions: What They Are and How They Mean," *OP;* "On the Relations of Number and Quantity," *ORNQ; Our Knowledge of the External World, OKEW; Philosophical Essays, PE;* "The Philosophical Importance of Mathematical Logic," *PIML;* "The Philosophy of Logical Atomism," *PLA;* "Pragmatism," *P; The Principles of Mathematics, PofM; Principia Mathematica, PM; The Problems of Philosophy, PofP;* "The Relation of Sense-Data to Physics," *RSDP;* "Sensation and Imagination," *SI;* "Some Explanations in Reply to Mr. Bradley," *SRB; Theory of Knowledge: The 1913 Manuscript, TK;* "Transatlantic Truth," *TT;* "The Ultimate Constituents of Matter," *UCM;* "What Is Logic?", *WL;* "William James' Conception of Truth," *WJCT.*

In cases where reference is made to Bertrand Russell's interaction with other philosophers, such as "collaboration with," "correspondence with," "exchanges with," and so forth, these entries are indexed under the names of the other philosophers, not under Russell's name. Because of the complexity of the index, *see also* entries have been eliminated, and the user is advised to look under other related topics or names of other related individuals.

Names

Ameseder, R., 86

Aristotle, 214, 223

Austin, J. L., 215, 224

Ayer, A. J.: and BR, 5, 160, 215, 234; on experience, 224; on GEM and BR, 34; on pragmatism, 171; on truth, 213

Balzano, B., 63

Barnes, Alfred, 206

Bentley, Arthur F., 214

Bergmann, Gustav, 62

Bergson, Henri, 182

Berkeley, George, 42

Black, Max, 220

Boole, George, 66, 181

Bosanquet, B., 8

Bradley, F. H.: and FCSS, 172; *Appearance and Reality,* 8, 10–18, 20–21; as critic of realism, 85; *Ethical Studies,* 20; "On Appearance, Error, and Contradiction" and BR, 20; on monistic relations, 9; on *PofM,* 8, 22–25; on propositions, 9; on subject and predicate, 9–10; *The Principles of Logic* and BR, 9, 19; "Reply to Mr. Russell's Explanations," 20–21; BR and, issues with, 30–34; BR's agreement with, 31–32; BR's criticism of, 21, 217; BR's interactions with, 4, 5, 8, 19–30; BR's misinterpretation of, 13

Brentano, F., 63, 78, 93

Cantor, G., 66

Carnap, Rudolf: and ontology, 62, 221; and BR, 2, 134, 168, 211, 215, 223; method of construction of, 222

Chisholm, R., 228

Clark, Ronald, 4, 101

Couturat, L., 4, 5

Dedekind, R., 66

Descartes, R., 1, 134

Dewey, John: and belief, 202; and experience, 214; and BR, parallel careers of, 209; and sensation, 213; answer to BR's criticisms, 210–13; *Art as Experience,* 209; *Essays in Experimental Logic,* 205; "The Existence of the World as a Logical Problem," 205; *Experience and Nature,* 209; in *HWP,* 205; interactions with BR, 5, 204–6; *Knowing*

and the Known, and BR, 205; *Logic: the Theory of Inquiry,* 205, 209, 213; on BR, 205, 208, 210–11, 217; "Propositions, Warranted Assertibility and Truth," response to BR, 205; BR on, 208, 210, 211–12; BR's answer to criticism, 207–8; *Studies in Logical Theory,* mentioned, 204–5

Donagan, A., 227

Einstein, A., 121, 129

Frege, Gottlob: and Balzano, 63; and classes, 68, 74–77; and Husserl, 63; and indirect contexts, 71, 90–91; and Kant, 63; and logicism, 95; and nonscientific propositions, 93; and BR, 5, 61, 66–67, 94; and LW, 139, 155; as idealist, 63; *Begriffschrift,* 68; "Begriff und Gegenstand," 73–74; correspondence with Jourdain, 94–95; correspondence with BR, 68, 70–71, 74; criticized by BR, 88–89; defended against BR, 61–62; function and variable, 71–73; *Grundgetsetzes der Arithmetik,* 68; meaning and naming, 93; mentioned, 64, 66–67, 83; on *PM,* 95; on propositions, 94; sense, 95; "Sinn und Bedeutung," 69–70

Geach, P. T., 77, 222

Gellner, E., 215

Gödel, Kurt, 165, 219

Goodman, N., 62, 221

Grassmann, Hermann, 105

Grattan-Guinness, I., 4

Grossman, Reinhardt, 62

Hamilton, Sir William, 105

Hegel, G. W. F., 13

Hintikka, Jaako, 62

Hochberg, H., 90

Holt, E. B., 199

Hume, David: and empiricism, 1, 185, 199; and skepticism, 208

Husserl, E., 63

James, William: A. J. Ayer on, 171; and FCSS, 172; critized by BR, 44, 179, 187–90; "Does 'Consciousness' Exist?," 195;

neutral monism of, 44, 198–202; on experience, 200; on realism, 191–92; on BR's criticism, 187, 190–92; on specious present, 196–97; on subject/object, 98; on time, 196–97; *A Pluralistic Universe,* 193; *Pragmatism,* 179; *Pragmatism* rev. by GEM, 44; *The Principles of Psychology,* 196; pure experience in, 203; relations with BR, 5, 170, 186–87; BR influenced by, 127, 187, 203–4; "Two English Critics," 191–92, 194; *The Varieties of Religious Experience,* 194; "The Will to Believe," 193; "The Will to Believe" rev. by BR, 179

Jeffrey, R., 227

Joachim, H.H.: agreed with BR, 31–32; and BR, issues between, 30–31; interactions with BR, 5, 8; *The Nature of Truth,* 13–16; *The Nature of Truth* rev. by BR, 13; on GEM, 13–18; on propositions, 15; on relations, 16; on BR, 12–18; on sensation, 15; BR on, 15–18

Johnson, A. H., 104

Jones, E. E. C., 3

Jourdain, P. E. B., 74, 94–95

Kant, I.: and GF, 63; mentioned, 64, 78; GEM on, 13, 35–37; BR on, 113

Katz, J. J., 227

Kripke, S., 222

Lambert, K., 62

Leibniz, G.: on relations, 9–10, 18; on sufficient reason, 8; perspectives of, 1; BR on, 8–9, 36, 39

Linsky, L., 61, 222

Lotze, H., 10

Lowe, V., 104, 114

Mach, E., 199

McTaggart, Ellis, 7, 19, 34

Mally, E., 86

Marcuse, H., 227

Marsh, R. C., 198

Maxwell, G., 220

Meinong, Alexius: "Abstrahieren und Vergleichen," 78; and Brentano, F., 63, 78; and Graz school, 86; and Hume, 78; and Husserl, 63; and Kant, 78; defended against BR's criticism, 62–63; exchanges with BR, 4, 5, 61, 95–96; influence on

BR, 93–94; on assumptions, 74, 81, 97; on belief, 29; on logic, 93–94; on objects, 79–80; on *objektiv,* 79–80, 138; on realism, 52, 80; on theory of objects, 83, 86; on truth, 97; BR on, 5, 38, 78–79, 82–86, 96–98, 148; BR's changes on, 181, 216; *Uber Annahmen,* 78; "Uber die Bedeutung des Weberschen Gestzes," 78; "Uber Gegenstände Höhore Ordnung und deren Verhältnis zur inneren Wahrnehmung," 78

Mill, John Stuart, 1, 7, 214

Montague, W. P., 199

Moore, G. E.: and idealism, 40–42; and WJ, 44; and HHJ, 14, 16; and Kant, 13, 35–36; and AM, 82; and BR, 34–59; and LW, 44, 57–58, 140; "Autobiography" LLP, 33; "The Conception of Reality," 51–52; criticized by BR, 59; dissertations of, 35–36; *Ethics,* 44; evaluation of, 54–57; "External and Internal Relations," 45; "Freedom," 36; influence of, 114; influence of, on BR, 7–8, 33–36; influenced by BR, 2; interactions with BR, 2, 5, 12, 33–36; lectures, 1910, 42; life and character, 33–43; "The Nature and Reality of Objects of Perception," 40, 42; "The Nature of Judgment," 36, 64; "Necessity," 37; on common sense, 56; on experience, 52; on pluralism, 38; on truth, 54–55; *Philosophical Papers,* 57; *Philosophical Studies,* 56; *Philosophical Studies* rev. by BR, 56; *Principia Ethica,* 40–41, 43; *Principia Ethica* rev. by BR, 40; "The Refutation of Idealism," 9, 40, 42; reply to critics, LLP, 44; revs. of BR, 40, 46, 56, 59; BR's revs. of, 40, 46, 55–56; "Some Judgments of Perception," 45; *Some Main Problems of Philosophy,* 42; "The Status of Sense-Data," 45

Morrell, Lady Ottoline: and BR, 137; BR's correspondence with, 102, 115, 139–42, 144–53

Nagel, Thomas, 227

Neurath, Otto, 211, 215

New Realists, 127

Parsons, T., 62, 222

Peano, Giuseppe: and BR, 9, 39, 66–68, 106; on numbers, 65; BR's criticism of,

67; symbolism of, 66, 100, 108
Peirce, C. S.: and BR, 170; Ayer on, 171; on truth, 210
Perry, R. B., 199
Putnam, H., 227

Quine, W. V.: and ontology, 62, 222; and *PM,* 134; influence of BR on, 168; on denial of being, 90; on Frege, 77; on ANW, 105

Ramsey, F. P.: on philosophy, 226; on BR's philosophy, 219; on the 2nd ed. *PM,* 164–65, 219; on theory of descriptions, 57
Reichenbach, Hans, 211, 215
Reid, Thomas, 42
Rorty, R., 227
Routley, R. and V., 62
Russell, Alys (BR's first wife): and BR, 7, 39, 46, 101–2
Russell, Bertrand: *AMa,* 121, 127, 129, 164, 167, 209; *AMi,* 46, 127, 129, 195, 199; and analysis, 29, 137–38, 214; and analytic realism, 137–38; and City College, 170, 206; and contradiction of classes, 76–78; and extensional logic, 63; and the five-term complex, 147–51; and new realists, 199; and other philosophers, 2–5, 215–19; and psychology, 199–204; and religion, 193–94; and return to philosophy, 1917, 120–21; and unsettlable arguments, 218; and World War I, 102–4; archives of, 41; as behaviorist, 183–84; as respondent, 216–19; as student, 99; autobiographical introduction, LLP, 33, 99, 136; *Au,* 46, 99, 136, 215–16; *CPBR,* 4, 220; *CPL,* 3, 57; construction in, 221–22; *EE,* 41; *EFG,* 8, 36–38; *FMW,* 193; historical study of, 220; *HWP,* 206, 215; *HK,* 215; *HSEP,* 215; *IMP,* 126, 159–60; *IMT,* 104, 164, 209; *KAKD,* 3, 43, 160, 195; *LK,* 198, 216; *MTT,* 13, 20, 30, 45, 55, 76; *MTCA,* 79–86; *MPD,* 99, 136, 160, 164–66, 215; on acquaintance, 196–200; on assertion, 74; on attention, 197; *OD,* 40, 60, 86, 87–94; *OD,* critics of, 61–63; *OET,* 143; on facts, 180; *ONA,* 143–45, 198–99; *ONTF,* 29–30, 176, 181; *ONC,* 50–51; *ONCFW,* 50; *OP,* 183–84, 199, 203; *ORNQ,* 8; on specious present, 196–97; on time, 197; on universals, 55–

56, 137; *OKEW,* 45, 110, 117–21, 159, 201; *PE,* 144, 178; *PIML,* 160–62, 199; *PLA,* 121, 201; *P,* 44, 178–79, 193; *PofM,* 20–22, 36, 38, 64–69, 74–75, 100, 105–7, 166, 176; *PM,* 9, 39, 66, 77, 133, 135, 136, 159, 164–65, 169; *PofP,* 9, 42–43, 98, 110, 137, 196; *RSDP,* 119; *SI,* 143; *SRB,* 20; *TK,* 121, 143–53; theory of reference, 222; theory of truth, 97, 174–79; theory of types, 76–78; *TT,* 114–15, 178–79, 190–92; *UCM,* 117–19; *WL,* 142; *WJCT,* 178
Ryle, Gilbert, 171, 215, 220

Santayana, G., 4, 44, 48
Schiller, F.C.S.: and Dewey, 173; and James, 173; and Oxford, 172; and Peirce, 173; *Formal Logic,* 172, 181; *Humanism: Philosophical Essays,* 172; interactions with BR, 4, 5, 170–86; "The Meaning of Meaning," 183–86; on induction and pragmatism, 188–89; on logic, 181; on psychology, 183–84, 214; on BR, 180–81, 185; on truth, 176–77; BR on, 174–76, 179–80; BR's rev. of *Formal Logic,* 181; BR's rev. of *Studies in Humanism,* 177
Searle, John R., 222
Sommerville, S. I., 142, 147, 157, 159
Spadoni, C., 7
Spinoza, Benedict, 10
Sternfeld, R., 77
Stevenson, Charles, 49
Stout, G. F., 34, 87
Strawson, P.F., 93, 215, 220, 222

Tarski, A., 223

Urmson, J. O., 2, 215, 220

Vuillemin, Jules, 220

Ward, J., 34
Warnock, G. F., 215
Watson, J. B., 98, 203
Weitz, M., 215
Welby, Lady Victoria, 170
Whitehead, A. N.: "The Anatomy of Some Scientific Ideas," 116; and *PM,* 9, 66, 100–101, 105–17; and BR, reciprocal influence, 2, 3, 5, 135; collaboration, 39, 100–117; collaboration ended, 118–21,

126; *The Concept of Nature*, 110, 117, 122; correspondence with BR, 100–102, 108–11; *An Enquiry into the Principles of Natural Knowledge*, 110, 117, 120–21; *An Introduction to Mathematics*, 109; on extensive abstraction, 111; *On Mathematical Concepts of the Material World*, 108; on matter, 110–11; on propositions, 107; on BR, 113–14; on science and philosophy, 225–26; on space, 109–10; on time, 109–10, 113–14; *The Organisation of Thought*, 116, 120; *The Principle of Relativity*, 126; *Process and Reality*, 104; BR on, 103–4, 135, 213, 218; BR's influence on, 2, 5; *Science and the Modern World*, 132; "Space, Time, and Relativity," 116; "La Théorie relationniste de l'espace," 115; *A Treatise on Universal Algebra*, 100, 105

Whitehead, Eric (son of ANW), 103
Whitehead, Evelyn (wife of ANW), 10
Whitehead, North (son of ANW), 103
Wiener, Norbert, 2
Wilson, John Cook, 172
Wittgenstein, Ludwig: and extensional logic, 165; and Frege, 139, 155; and logical atomism, 160–61; and ordinary language, 169; and *PM*, 155, 164–66, 219, 222; and BR, differences with, 161–62, 168; as critic of judgment; 145–46, 152, 153, 157–59; as critic on proposition, 153, 156–57, 208; as critic of *TK*, 121, 149–51, 153–59, 201; followers of, 169, 215, 219–20, 229; influence on BR, 21, 56, 147, 160–67, 209; interactions with BR, 2, 5, 61, 136, 139–43, 144–53, 161–62, 163–64; judgment on BR, 168; *Letters to Russell, Keynes and Moore*, 4; *Logisch-philosophische Abhandlung*, 162–63; "Notes on Logic," 152, 154–59, 164; on complexes, 143–45; on ethics and morals, 140; on formal analysis, 213; on meaning, 171; on philosophy, 140; BR's response to, 139, 151, 153, 160, 164, 168; *Tractatus Logico-philosophicus*, 139, 155, 159, 165, 167; *Tractatus Logico-philosophicus* and logical positivists, 219; *Tractacus Logico-philosophicus* and BR, 163

Wood, Alan, 216

Subjects

Acquaintance: and content, 96–97; and description, 43, 94, 98, 114, 119, 195–96; and imagination, 96; and theory of knowledge, 143–44; and understanding, 148–49; as abandoned, 197–98; nature of, 143–45, 196–99; propositions, 146–47; sensation, 96; subject and object in, 51–52; with form of a relation, 146; with logical data, 137–38, 146; with relations, 145–67

Analysis: and phenomenology, 228; and BR, 221–22; and synthesis, 151–52, 167; and ANW, 134–35; method of, 29, 138–39, 160–61, 221–22; of meaning, 93–94

Analytic philosophy, 227–28
Analytic realism, 137
Argument: methods of, 217–19
Artificial language, 223–24
Assertion, 74, 82, 84
Assumptions, 82, 84, 97
Atomic proposition, 148–49, 161
Attention, 196–97, 200
Aussersein, 80

Axiom of reducibility, 107, 164–65

Behaviorism, 127, 183–86, 203
Being, 79–80, 84, 90
Belief: analysis of, 43, 148, 157–59, 199, 202; and action, 194; and consequences of, 189–90; and disbelief, 85; and fact, 29–30, 177–78; and multiple relation, 30, 146, 151; and pragmatism, 202; and "propositional verb," 208; and value, 175; and working, 177–79; content of, 212; history of, 188–89; in existence, 195, 208; in AM and BR, 97; in neutral monism, 202; in religion, 193–94

Bifurcation of nature, 123
Body-mind, 198–99, 203

Calculus, 105–6
Cause, 50–51, 123, 128, 130–31
Class: and class calculus, 66, 106; and class concept, 73, 75; and classes of classes, 75–77; and incomplete symbols, 87–94, 107; and individual, 65; FHB on, 25;

contradiction of, 24–25, 68, 75–77;
difficulties with, 25, 75; infinite, 75; in
GF, 75–76; in *PofM,* 24–25; nature of, 75;
null, 65, 75; relation to its members, 75;
unit, 65, 75; views of, 77
Cognitive and noncognitive, 196
Coherence, 211–12
Common sense, 55, 57
Complex: analysis of, 80–82; and judgment,
82; and names, 152; and proposition, 142;
as object, 53; as universal, 79; being and
nonbeing of, 84; five-term, 147–51; form
of, 149–50; problem of, 142, 149–50;
relations of, 81, 146–48
Concept: as referent, 22–24; as subject, 73–
74; in GEM, 8, 36–37; orders of, 74;
realism of, 37–38, 64
Consciousness, 12, 127, 143, 198
Construction: method of, 52–53, 87–94,
110–21, 159, 201
Content, 52, 79, 96
Contradiction: in philosophy, 26, 89, 217–18
Copulae, 142
Correspondence, BR's volume of, 216

Data, 185, 207, 211–12
Deductive structure of physics, 128
Definition, 189, 191, 229
Denoting concept, 69–70, 107
Denoting phrase, 88, 89–92
Descriptions: of the world, 225–26; theory
of, 87–94, 107, 137–38, 195–96, 222
Disjunction, 22
Dualism, 52, 64, 127
Duration, in ANW, 122

Emphatic particulars, 202
Empiricism and realism, 228–29
Epistemology, 128, 141, 155
Error, 17, 82, 188
Ethics, 44, 47–48, 126, 140
Event, 119, 124, 130–31
Event-description, 62
Existence, 57–58
Existentialism, 173
Existents, 128
Experience: analysis of, 5, 196–97, 223–24;
and common sense, 115–16; and events,
98; and memory, 197; and nature in JD,
214; and overlapping presents, 197; and
BR, 213; and the subject, 200; as

cognitive, 204; as stream in ANW, 117;
description of, 143–44, 197–98;
immediate, 200; in ANW and BR, 119–
20, 130–33; pure, 203
Extensive abstraction, 111–12, 119
External world, 117–21, 128, 131, 207–8

Fact, 150–51, 180, 200–201
Fallacy of simple location, 132–33
Fallibilism, 229
False propositions, 85–86
Form: of a complex, 149–50; of a
proposition, 150; of a relation, 145–47
Formal analysis, 66, 223
Formal logic and philosophy, 212–13, 227–
28
Foundationalism, 224–25
Freedom of the will, 36, 40–50
Function, 66–67, 71–73
Function-correlates, 74

Gedanke, 70–71
Geometry, 8, 28, 37, 110, 129
Good, 47

Historical study of BR, 4, 220
History of philosophy, 63
Holism, 210
Humanism, 172–73, 180
Human survival, 228

Idealism: and internal relations, 17–18; and
logic, 10–12, 20–21; and monism, 22; and
GEM, 36–37, 42, 56–57, 64; and
philosophy of mathematics, 65–66; and
BR, 7–12, 64, 174; and FCSS, 174; and
sufficient reason, 18; and truth, 15–18;
and whole, 24; influence of, 7; issues
with realism, 30–32; necessity in 26–27
Identity: FHB on, 23–24; GF on, 70; in *PM,*
107, 165–66; GEM on, 38
Illusory object, 53
Imagination, 143, 204
Immanence, 83–85
Immediate knowledge, 196, 205, 209
Implication, FHB on, 22
Incomplete symbol, 138
Indirect context, 71, 88, 90
Induction, 179, 188, 225
Inference, 143, 207

Inquiry, 209–10
Instants, 110, 118
Intentional inexistence, 78
Intentionality, 98
Internal relations, 9

Judgment: and content, 79; and
presentation, 97; and truth, 82; as
relation, 145–51; criticisms of, 144–46;
five-term complex of, 147, 151; in theory
of knowledge, 143–53; AM on, 81; GEM
on, 36–37; multiple relation theory of,
144–46; BR's early theory of, 144

Knowledge: by acquaintance, 94; by
description, 94, 196; object of, 12

Language, 161, 169, 223
Law of Excluded Middle, 63, 212
Leading on, of ideas, 191
Linguistic turn, 223
Logic: and complexes, 142; and inquiry,
196, 209, 213–14; and philosophy, 9–11,
137–38, 156, 219, 221–22; as extensional,
63, 164–65; FCSS on, 176, 181–82;
subject-predicate, 9; LW on, 154–56
Logical atomism: and behaviorism, 183–84;
and neutral monism, 199; and BR, 126–
28, 138–39, 159–61; as method, 126–28;
criticized, 220
Logical constants, 156
Logical empiricism, 61–62, 219–20, 223
Logical entities, 138
Logical form, 149–50, 160
Logical objects, 5–6, 146, 156–57
Logical positivism. *See* Logical empiricism
Logical possibility, 27, 151–52
Logical propositions, 147, 160, 165
Logical terms, 22
Logical truths, 5–6, 43, 53, 137–38, 209
Logic of relations, 106

Mathematical logic and philosophy, 2, 40,
166, 221–22
Matter, 115, 137, 142
Meaning: and behavior, 184–85, 222–23;
early BR theory of, 61–62, 71, 91–92, 93–
94, 220; pragmatic, 183; theory of,
criticized, 220; verificationist theory of,
221
Metaphysical issues, 221

Methodology, 104, 137–38
Modal concepts, 27, 62–63, 83–84
Molecular propositions. *See* Atomic
proposition
Monism. *See* Neutral monism
Multiple relation theory of judgment, 155,
202–3
Mysticism, 132–33, 162–63

Names: and acquaintance, 155; and
descriptions, 92; and meaning, 93–94;
and propositions, 156–57; fictitious, 70;
proper, 70
Naturalistic fallacy, 44, 47–48
Nature, description of, ANW and BR, 134
Necessity, 27, 37, 50, 83–84
Negation, 23, 84–85, 158, 160–61
Neutral monism, 44, 84–85, 127, 143, 198–
204
New realists, 199
Noncognitivism, 48–49
Non-Euclidean geometry, 96, 129
Nonexistent referents, 62–63, 92–93
Null class. *See* Class: null
Number, definition of, 41, 66

Object: constructed, 113; of acquaintance,
45, 52; of common sense, 51–53, 117; of
judgment, 28; of perception and belief,
30, 124–25; scientific, 117, 124–25;
theory of, in GF, 73; theory of, in AM,
79–81, 83, 86, 96
Objektiv in AM, 79, 83
Ontology, problem of, 62, 222
Organism, philosophy of, in ANW, 133
Other persons, belief in, 42, 58, 131
Overlapping presents, 131–32, 197
Oxford philosophy, and BR, 215, 220, 224–25

Passage, in ANW, 122–24, 132
Past, knowledge of, 43, 58
Perception: and data, 211; and immediacy,
209, 211, 224; causal theory of, 123, 127–
28, 130–31
Perceptual premises, 211–12, 224
Permutation-groups, 151–52, 157
Personalism, 172–73
Perspectives, 124, 185
Phenomenology, 221, 228
Philosophical exchanges, 3–4, 185, 208,
215–19

Philosophy: and language, 168–69; and science, 1, 56, 155, 168, 224–26, 228–29; as nonanalytic, 226–27; as technical, 227; methods of, 32; nature of, 31–32; of nature, 125–26; of science, 228–29; scope of, 1, 5, 155, 219, 225–26; value of, 137, 140

Pluralism, 11, 18, 38, 174, 221

Points, 110–12, 131–32

Postanalytic philosophy, 227

Pragmatism: and neutral monism, 201–4; and religion, 192–214; BR on, 114–15, 179–80, 195, 210–11, 213, 218; theory of meaning of, 171; theory of truth of, 171, 174, 187–90, 210–11

Predicate term, 64, 69–70, 72–74

Presentation, 80–81, 83, 96–98

Principia Mathematica: and later philosophy, 219; and LW, 155, 165; GF on, 94–95; propositions in, 138–39; questions on, 182; second edition of, 133, 164–66, 219; theory of descriptions in, 87; topics in, 87, 100–101, 105–17

Problematic situation, 21, 211

Proposition: acquaintance with form of, 150; and belief, 97, 210; and complex, 142, 149–50; and fact, 165–67, 201; and meaning, 70–71, 93–94; and propositional function, 67, 88, 106, 182; and referent, 148; and subject of, 150, 157–58; as entity, 54, 64–65, 149–50; as incomplete symbol, 97, 148; as non-truth-functional, 161–65; as object, 148; as tool, 210; as true or false, 14, 65, 70–71, 85–86, 165, 202–3; atomic and molecular, 111; criticism of BR on, 22–23, 74, 156–58, 192; definition of, 142, 148; denoting and nondenoting, 87; difficulties with, 138–39, 148; fictitious, 65; in *PM,* 164–65; negative, 65, 85–86; of logic, 65, 155; primitive, 66, 106, 155; syntactical, 166–67; unasserted, 74, 82, 97; understanding the form of, 150; LW on, 142, 157–58, 165, 205, 209

Psychology, 127, 183–85, 199

Qualitative series, 128

Quasisein, 80

Realism: analytic, 204; and empiricism, 228; causal, 48; early, 9, 51–52, 64; in

ethics, 44, 46–49; metaphysical, 9; of classes, 74–75; of concepts, 1, 9, 37; of logical truths, 54, 137–38, 167; of object of knowledge, 12, 38, 42, 64, 79, 80, 218; of propositions, 12, 21, 81, 107, 138; of terms, 81, 107; of universals, 54, 64

Realists, and BR, 98, 199, 204

Reference: and GF, 69–70, 88–89; indefinite, 65; of proposition and terms, 88; theory of, 61–62, 222; to nonexistents, 80, 95–96

Relational complexes, 157

Relations: analysis of, 9–10, 22; and complexes, 148, 151; and identity, 24; and substance, 11; external and internal, 12–15, 30–31, 45, 52–53, 221; form of, 144–45; in idealism, 11, 25–26; of space-time, 128; sense of, 10–11, 144–47; symbolism for, 149

Relativity, theory of, 121, 129

Religion, 137, 140–42, 174, 192–95

Science and philosophy. *See* Philosophy: and science

Self, 53, 185

Self-evidence, 97, 188

Semantics, 223

Sensation, 78, 96, 122, 143, 198–99

Sense and reference, 64–72, 88–89, 94–95

Sense-Data: and construction, 119, 137, 142; and experience, 42–53; epistemological role of, 161, 197, 206–8, 224

Sensibilia, 119

Sign, 71, 94, 184

Simples, 185

Situations, 210–11

Skepticism, 58, 141, 208

Solipsism, 113

Space: and objects, 113; relational theory of, 116–17; visual and tactual, 130; ANW on, 110–12, 115, 130

Space-Time, 128

Specious presence, 196–99

Subject: and act, 51–52; and content, 51, 96; and object, 7, 12, 96–97; and proposition, 161; as individual, 165; as unobservable, 184, 199–200; term and existence, 68, 89

Subject-predicate logic, 9–17, 82–83, 181

Substance, 11, 122

Symbolism: and ontology, 222; and relational complexes, 151; as arbitrary,

142, 157; in *PM,* 106
Syntactics, 223

Terms and philosophical vocabulary, 22, 64
Testimony of others, 131
Tests of theory of meaning, 89–90
Theory of knowledge: and logic, 155; and
   philosophy of science, 228; and science,
   155; in *AMi,* 127–28; problems of, 143;
   seminar on, 96, 143; LW's effect on, 153,
   166–67
Theory of types, 69, 74–77, 107, 110, 142,
   156–57, 165
Time, 110–11, 123–25, 143, 196–97
Truth: and belief, 177; and coherence, 17,
   28, 211–12; and error, 18; and fact, 161,
   201, 208, 214; and propositions, 29–30,
   95–96; as ultimate, 214; changes in, 176–
   77; correspondence theory of, 85, 138–
   39, 155–56, 204; definition of, 54–55,
   97, 225; logical and empirical, 155, 209;
   logical empiricists on, 225; theory of,

alternative, 176–77; theory of, in
   idealism, 17–18; theory of, pragmatic,
   177–94, 204, 210, 212, 225; theory of,
   pragmatic defense of, 190, 191, 210, 212;
   theory of, problems in, 85–86, 176–78;
   whole and part of, 17
Truth-functions, 164

Understanding: and acquaintance, 148; and
   other relations, 152; in *TK,* 145; relation
   of subject and object in, 148; symbolism
   for, 150; verbs of, as psychological, 158
Universals: acquaintance with, 144; and
   particulars, 143; as real; 43, 56
Use and mention, 90, 94

Variable: real and apparent, 66–67, 156, 164
Verification, 187, 191, 210, 225, 229
Voluntarism, 172–78

Warranted assertibility, 210, 212–13
World War I, 102–3

ELIZABETH RAMSDEN EAMES holds a Ph.D. from Bryn Mawr College, has taught at Smith College, the University of Missouri, and Washington University in St. Louis, and is presently professor of philosophy at Southern Illinois University-Carbondale. She has traveled and lectured widely in the Far East and has participated in international conferences in Europe and America. She is the author of *Bertrand Russell's Theory of Knowledge* (1969), the editor of Bertrand Russell, *Theory of Knowledge: The 1913 Manuscript* (1984), Vol. 7 in *The Collected Papers of Bertrand Russell,* and a contributor to many journals and volumes of papers here and abroad. She and her late husband, S. Morris Eames, wrote *Lectures in the Far East* and *Logical Methods.*